WOMEN IN GERMAN HISTORY
From bourgeois emancipation to sexual liberation

UTE FREVERT

WOMEN IN GERMAN HISTORY

From Bourgeois Emancipation
To Sexual Liberation

Translated by
Stuart McKinnon-Evans (*Material Word*)
in association with
Terry Bond and Barbara Norden

BERG
New York / Oxford / Munich
Distributed exclusively in the US and Canada by
St Martin's Press, New York

First English edition published in 1989 by
Berg Publishers Limited
Editorial offices:
165 Taber Avenue, Providence R.I. 02906, USA
150 Cowley Road, Oxford OX4 1JJ, UK
Westermühlstraße 26, 8000 München 5, FRG

English Paperback edition first published in 1990

Originally published as *Frauen-Geschichte zwischen Bürgerlicher Verbesserung und
Neuer Weiblichkeit*. Suhrkamp Verlag 1986. © Suhrkamp 1986.
English translation © Berg Publishers 1988 1990

British Library Cataloguing in Publication data
Frevert, Ute.
Women in German history: from bourgeois emancipation to sexual liberation.
  1. Germany. Society. Role of women, 1750–1988
  I. Title   II. Frauen-Geschichte Zwischen Bürgerlicher Verbesserung und
neuer Weiblichkeit. *English*
305.4'2'0943
ISBN 0–85496–685–4

Library of Congress Cataloging-in-Publication data
Frevert, Ute.
  [Frauen-Geschichte zwischen bürgerlicher Verbesserung und neuer
Weiblichkeit. English]
  Women in German history : from bourgeois emancipation to sexual
liberation / Ute Frevert; translated by Stuart McKinnon-Evans.
    p. cm.
  Translation of: Frauen-Geschichte zwischen bürgerlicher
Verbesserung und neuer Weiblichkeit.
  Bibliography: p.
  Includes index.
  ISBN 0–85496–685–4: $14.50 (est.)
  1. Feminism–Germany–History. 2. Feminism–Germany (West)–
–History. 3. Women's rights–Germany–History. 4. Women's rights–
–Germany (West)–History. 5. Women–Germany–Social conditions.
6. Women–Germany (West)–Social conditions. I. Title.
HQ1627.F69713 1988
305.4'2'0943–dc19   88–13123
                                                    CIP

Printed in Great Britain by Short Run Press Ltd., Exeter

Contents

Tables

Introduction

Over the last few years it has become fashionable, not only in politics, but gradually in the academic disciplines too – and particularly in history – to discuss the costs and limits of social 'modernisation': to weigh up the pros and cons of industrialisation and urbanisation, and to compare the benefits of social rationality and calculability with the stricter norms and regulations to which the individual is subjected. The more apparent it becomes that there are limits to industrial growth, and that the political course taken by the state is no longer wholly rational, the more tempting it is to turn to the past in search of patterns and evidence of alternative, less costly ways for German society to develop. In addition to ecology, the labour market, mass media and the welfare state – to name only a few themes – the 'woman question' is also one of those sensitive areas which places 'progress' in an ambivalent light. At a time when women have by no means achieved legal, social and material equality, economy and society are already setting off in a curious change of direction. As the waves of economic rationalisation make themselves felt, more and more women (many more than men) are disappearing from the official labour market, and are becoming full-time workers in hidden areas of the economy. Fewer and fewer women are going on to higher education. Fewer and fewer girls can find apprenticeships or jobs after training. The statistical picture is accompanied by the German state's policy of passively watching the exodus of women from the labour market, and of assigning a higher ideological value to their return to the hearth and cradle. At the same time political parties of every hue are trying to woo women by making grand statements and formulating ambitious programmes. In March 1985, for example, the Christian Democratic Union (CDU) devoted a Party Conference to the new partnership between the sexes, and in the campaign for elections to Land assemblies, the Social Democratic Party (SPD) declared itself in favour of universities researching into women's issues.

This paradoxical situation – in which the inequality of men and women on the labour market is increasing, while politics is devoting more and more attention to the question of equality – has provided me with the impetus to undertake a critical study of women's lives in Germany over the last two hundred years, and to attempt to measure their condition on a theoretical scale of equality. Ever since 1792, at the very latest, ideas about the emancipation of women and equality between men and women have provided food for public thought in Germany. The principle of equality has been enshrined in the constitution since 1919, and since 1945 this has had consequences for legislation on pay and the family. No one would deny that German women have been moving towards their declared aims of equal rights and sexual equality. All the same there is still a long way to go. Yet recently a lively debate has started over whether it is even desirable to try and make women and men 'equal' and to ensure that they have equal opportunities and choices of action. What is surprising, moreover, is the fact that the debate is not being conducted only by conservatives, as one would expect, but also by feminists and their (not always welcome) supporters.

Many women doubt that in a society based on male norms of achievement, equality can ever lead to anything other than the unsatisfactory situation in which women adapt to standards defined by men. They object to adhering to rules and expectations which, while declared to be universally valid, are in actual fact biased towards male needs and abilities. Instead, they have begun creating their own space for action, places where they set the standards themselves and where they are able to develop feminine individuality, interests and talents unfettered by male competition and dominance. The utopia envisaged by this group, which for all intents and purposes comprises the autonomous women's movement of the 1980s, is a society free of the hegemonial influence of men, in which men and women have equal power to define and shape their lives, and can choose freely from a variety of options to act as they see fit. In this scheme, it remains to be seen whether such a society would see the sexes reserving for themselves different 'spheres' and 'space', as has hitherto been the case.

The new sense of unease about equality has been accompanied by a not so novel tendency to regard social conditions far removed in both time and space from our own as idyllic, a tendency engendered by the disappointments and critical attitudes that result from unfavourable historical developments and society's current shortcomings. Here, women, the 'second sex' as Simone de Beauvoir calls them, are seen predominantly as victims of modern, bourgeois industrial society. In a controversial essay, Ivan Illich has written that while a small elite may have benefited from economic, cultural and legal innovation, the majority of women are 'worse off than before'.[1] This is also the conclusion of recent works on women's history, which portray the nineteenth century in Germany as a period in which the oppression of women became more severe: 'For Prussian women in the nineteenth century, the characteristic feature of social reality was a relative deterioration of their position. The pressures appear to have become more intense, and the disparities between the sexes more marked, particularly where access to power, money and social wealth was concerned.' Moreover, salvation has not been found in the twentieth century. On the contrary, women in all social strata have seen how a new kind of double burden has taken root, forcing them to be both 'married domestics' and 'extra-domestic income earners'.[2]

Writers less critical of modernisation maintain, by contrast, that women have without doubt benefited from the social changes that have occurred over the last two hundred years. Despite continuing 'underprivilege', disparities between the sexes have narrowed: women have conquered for themselves a greater slice of public terrain, improved their employment opportunities, profited from the expansion of school education, and even risen to ministerial positions. Optimistic views of this kind regard women as not-yet-entirely-modernised, the semantic loading of 'not-yet' suggesting that they will be in the future.[3] Criticism can be levelled at both the optimistic and the pessimistic views for not declaring the criteria upon which their respective judgements are based. Which premises make it possible to welcome as progress a situation in which

1. I. Illich, *Gender*, London/New York 1983, p. 17.
2. B. Duden and E. Meyer-Renschhausen, 'Landarbeiterinnen, Näherinnen, Dienstmädchen, Hausfrauen: Frauenarbeit in Preußen', in *Preußen: Zur Sozialgeschichte eines Staates*, ed. P. Brandt, Reinbek 1981, pp. 265–85, quoted from pp. 267, 285.
3. I searched in vain in textbooks and works of general history for any comments on the changing situation and role of women in Germany. In most cases, women do not even feature (see, for example, H.-U. Wehler, *The German Empire 1871–1918*, trans. K. Traynor, Leamington Spa 1985; G. Mann, *The History of Germany Since 1789*, trans. M. Jackson, Harmondsworth 1985). The few works which do mention women avoid interpretations which offer any long-term historical perspective based on clearly presented premises (see, for example, T. Nipperdey, *Deutsche Geschichte 1800–1866*, Munich 1983; G. Craig, *Germany 1866–1945*, Oxford 1978). The remarks included here are taken from the social historical essays by W. Conze and W. Zorn in *Handbuch der deutschen Wirtschafts- und Sozialgeschichte*, vol. II, Stuttgart 1976, esp. pp. 452–53, 633ff., 894ff.

differences in the social, economic, legal, cultural and political status of men and women have merely become smaller? How can we determine whether formal sexual equality does not merely camouflage real inequality? Is it not the case that the imperative of equality forces women to 'reach out' to be what men have been even though the conditions from which they start are not the same? Has there ever been any mention of men adapting to women (except in a few circles of youth and student movement sub-culture)? The 'pessimists' should also be asked to state which yardstick they use to measure the apparent worsening of the feminine condition. A historical gender that has yet to be investigated and conceived of? Or the ideal image of bourgeois society as a society of equals? Or the utopia of balanced gender relations?

No one who is attempting to write a history of women in Germany, of their material conditions and social movements over the last two centuries, can avoid these questions. Neither the rosy scenario of the slow, but nonetheless unabated realisation of women's demands for equality, nor the search for patterns of social harmony in pre-modern times, should be accepted uncritically. Although the former thesis is weakened by copious evidence that the obstacles against women's progress stubbornly persist, and that women may now be at an even greater disadvantage, the latter cannot be verified because of our lack of empirical knowledge. A scientific basis for attempts to portray earlier forms of society as more favourable to women will continue to evade us for as long as we know so much more about gender relations in the nineteenth and twentieth centuries than in the sixteenth, seventeenth and eighteenth.

Ever since Max Weber (if not before him) historians have been aware of how important it is both to be clear themselves and to make clear to readers what it is they are trying to establish, and on which premises they are basing their assessment. This also puts them in a position to identify, scrutinise and criticise the selective criteria and the value judgements that enter into their scientific analysis. The underlying assumption in this book is as follows. The goal of equal legal and material participation by men and women in social life, in the exercise of power and in decision-making in the economic, social, cultural and political system, is a desirable one. This requires equal access to the resources of action, and an end to the gender-specific ascription of spheres of action. Any society which had realised this goal would look quite different from the present one, which tends to pursue such aims on a programmatic basis. The consistent and comprehensive establishment of sexual equality at all levels would almost automatically presuppose, and result in, fundamental changes in the sexual division of labour, and occasion radical re-orientation in male and therefore (still) general social norms of behaviour.

In almost all societies and cultures known to us – including Germany – power, influence, political rights and opportunities to pursue economic profit are distributed unequally between men and women: men literally are the *masters*. The forms and dimensions of inequality vary greatly, depending upon the particular society's level of economic and cultural development. Women in different strata in different ages have equally varying scope for experience and limits to their expectations.

A whole range of reasons have been offered at different times to explain women's inferior position. With the advent of the rationalistic, 'demystified' society of the modern age, evocation of the divinity of the world order became less and less convincing. Its place was filled by medical and biological theories of the 'predetermined nature of woman' (and indeed, these are far from exhausted when women 'have to be put in their place'). However, the bourgeois concept of civil society marked the limits of attempts to justify sexual inequality as 'natural'. Drawn up in the eighteenth century, the bourgeois scheme envisaged a society of free, rational, self-determining individuals striving to liberate themselves from the fetters of incomprehensible traditions and the rigid stratification of the feudal order. It could not easily reconcile the lofty political ideals with the strategies by which members of society who were held to be *a priori* equals tried to impose barriers and hierarchies on each other. In conjunction with the radical shifts that were taking place in customary forms of life and work, these ideological tensions provided fertile ground for social movements which took up arms against inequality, and fought to transform the positive guiding thoughts of bourgeois change into tangible policies of equality. Among those who believed they were disadvantaged by progress, by 'modernism', were the women, bourgeois and proletarian alike, who, from the middle of the previous century, had been making public their concrete demands for change. As the 1898 edition of the *Brockhaus* dictionary put it, the women's movement made 'the principle of the relation of the sexes one to another' into an issue, and the movement drew attention to what the dictionary entry described as the 'woman question': 'the totality of problems and demands that have most recently been called forth by the transformation of society and of its ways of life, with respect to the position of the female sex among modern peoples'.

The 'woman question' has still not been solved today. In fact, it is perhaps an even more burning political issue than ever. Of course the position of women has changed over the last two hundred years. Their legal status, their employment and educational opportunities, as well as their participation in political and public life, have improved, and over the last few decades in particular the scope many women have for decision-making and action has expanded considerably. At the same time, it would be nonsense to say that the sexual hierarchy of normal, everyday life has been eliminated, for in almost every sphere of social life male privileges are just as much in evidence as they were before, even though in some cases they have acquired a different form.

This book investigates this deficit of equality: why it exists, to what it is connected, how it manifests itself. My central question is how bourgeois society, while claiming to be a society of free and 'emancipated' individuals, has treated women, and how women in Germany have come to grips with the 'conditions and restrictions'[4] they have experienced. What scope for action were they allowed? Were they content with this, or did they endeavour to increase it? What obstacles were put in their way? Were there any developments which helped them? Which of their aims did they achieve? Where did they fail? Finally, what was the cost of progress?

Limited space is only one reason why this study must necessarily be selective. I have also had to contend with the problem of the unequal spread of research into the subject. A study which asks only general questions cannot entirely remove many of the gaps in our knowledge. In the Federal Republic of Germany books on women's history are still very rare, even if research has covered the surface of some periods much more than others. Women's history has been researched, taught and published in and outside German universities for only a decade or so. It usually lacks support, and often even comes up against the resistance of established historiography.[5] To some people the putting together of a synoptic account of two hundred years of women's history in Germany may

4. Taken from the title of U. Gerhard's pioneering work of women's history, *Verhältnisse und Verhinderungen: Frauenarbeit, Familie und Rechte der Frauen im 19. Jahrhundert*, Frankfurt 1978.
5. G. Bock, 'Historische Frauenforschung: Fragenstellungen und Perspektiven', in K. Hausen (ed.), *Frauen suchen ihre Geschichte*, Munich 1983, pp. 22–60; U. Frevert and T. Schuler, 'Frauen in der Geschichte und in der Geschichtswissenschaft', *Geschichtsdidaktik*, 7, 1982, pp. 331–7; U. Frevert, 'Bewegung und Disziplin

thus seem to be a hasty and premature undertaking. They may be confirmed in their view by the shortcomings of this work. Apart from the great pleasure I have derived from writing it, however, there is another, more serious, justification for it. For the 'woman question', which has been burning for a long time in political debate and will presumably continue to do so, the historical dimension is hugely important. In order to assess the chances and missed opportunities of the 1970s and 1980s we need the historical depth of focus and comparative basis that has been lacking in almost all recent analyses by social and political science. Since, in addition, existing historical studies cover only short periods of time and limited aspects of problems, an attempt at synthesis cannot but be welcome.

The current relevance of women's issues also explains why some themes have been omitted entirely and why others are only touched on. In Chapter 5, for example, which looks at the post-1945 period, the situation of women in the German Democratic Republic is only mentioned in passing. Agricultural and rural life is mentioned only in Chapter 1, to provide a backdrop for the world of the urban middle classes. The processes of political, economic and cultural change which have in the long term been crucial for women have not occurred in the countryside, but in the bourgeois milieu of the towns and cities. What is more, industrialisation and urbanisation exposed ever greater numbers of women to this environment. Consequently, I have concentrated throughout on towns and the women who lived in them.

The book is ordered chronologically into five parts, which take us from the late 1700s right up to the present day. The nineteenth century is dealt with as a whole, while the twentieth is divided into three periods, the key dates relating to political events (the First World War, Nazi seizure of power, Nazi defeat). In the twentieth century, the lives of women have been influenced by a succession of political systems and currents to a far greater degree than they were in the nineteenth.[6] This is not to suggest by any means, however, that changes before 1900 had any less impact. But since they did not occur in stages that accompanied distinct political developments it seemed more appropriate to examine the nineteenth century as a whole made up of a number of sub-periods. Part V proved the most

---

in der Frauengeschichte', *Geschichte und Gesellschaft*, 14, 1988, p. 240–62.

6. This is brought out in autobiographical writings by women who were born early in the twentieth century: I. Weyrather, *'Ich bin noch aus dem vorigen Jahrhundert': Frauenleben zwischen Kaiserreich und Wirtschaftswunder*, Frankfurt, 1985, esp. pp. 15ff.

difficult to write since I had to select, analyse and ponder on events more from the perspective of a witness of my own age, of someone affected by what I had studied, than from that of a detached historian. It is anything but easy to have actively experienced the advent of the new women's movement, to have been personally influenced by its aims and values, and nevertheless to have to maintain academic distance and use impartial historical judgement. I leave it to the reader to decide whether my experiment is a success.

Ute Frevert

I
Human Rights and Women's Duties in the Late Eighteenth Century: Bourgeois Society and Gender

1
The Terms of the Debate
Emancipation, the Family and Relations between the Sexes

In 1792 Theodor von Hippel, a civil servant from Königsberg, published a polemical work entitled *Über die bürgerliche Verbesserung der Weiber* (The Civil Advancement of Women), in which he declared that those human and civil rights that men were claiming for themselves should be granted to women also. With zeal characteristic of the Enlightenment he appealed to the good sense and humanity of men, and challenged them to pass the same critical judgement on their own despotic rule over the female sex as they would on the rule of an absolutist sovereign over his oppressed subjects. In an age 'when human rights are preached loudly from the rooftops', women had to be accepted as citizens in their own right, and be allowed to 'think and act in their own interests and by their own efforts'.[1]

Hippel, one of the more enlightened men of his age, who wanted to replace the absolutist system with a constitutional, civil society of free citizens, touched a raw nerve in the still nascent middle-class public with his anonymously published plea for the emancipation of women. The self-same concepts and ideas with which the bourgeoisie criticised the system of estates and feudalism surfaced in Hippel's philippic against the 'slave-owning' role of men, and he deliberately pointed out the analogy between the state and the home. If the citizen, insisting on his natural rights, wished to be freed from state control, then he, for his part, had to release his wife from domestic custody and recognise her as a responsible person, vested with the same inalienable human rights, the same right to freedom and justice as himself.

The previous year a Frenchwoman, Olympe Marie de Gouges,

---

1. Reprint of 1828 edition, Berlin 1981, pp. 120, 114; intro. by J. Dittrich-Jacobi, who explains the origin of the book. See also T. G. von Hippel, *On Improving the Status of Women*, ed. T. F. Sellner, Detroit 1979.

had presented to the Paris National Assembly a 'Declaration of the Rights of the Woman and Citizeness',[2] and had argued in exactly the same manner. In her view, the 1789 Declaration of Human Rights was incomplete unless women also derived real, practical benefits from it. The Laws of Nature and Reason did, after all, demand that women, as citizens of a nation, be allowed to participate equally in economic, social and political life. If this participation were denied them, then 'public misery and the corruption of the government' would be unavoidable. In 1793 Olympe de Gouges was executed, the women's organisations were disbanded, and the female right of assembly suspended.

Hippel was spared such a fate, though his ideas met with just as little approval east of the Rhine. The new middle classes, comprising university professors and grammar school teachers, doctors and clergymen, civil servants, merchants and industrialists, had in fact shared, with varying degrees of commitment, the Enlightenment criticisms of the absolutist order of estates; but they adhered to tradition when it came to the role and rights of women. They were up in arms against the nobility's inherited privileges, demanded the abolition of class barriers, and rebelled against repression by an authoritarian state. Freedom and equality, achievement and competition were to govern relations between people, while the state, kept in check by law and justice, had merely to ensure that these principles were not violated. The liberation of the individual from the fetters of birth, tradition and the despotism of sovereigns would release vast productive forces and induce unstoppable advances in economics, culture and social harmony.[3] Of this there was no doubt.

The fact that women were excluded from this universal vision of progress and freedom struck very few people at the time as a contradiction in bourgeois thought. The Enlightenment ideal of autonomous, self-determining beings who would freely develop their talents and interests applied, of course, only to men. As the representatives of reason, they played the dominant role in economy, society and politics. The civil rights and freedoms they hoped to wrest from the state were theirs alone. They formed the bour-

2. The Declaration is reproduced in H. Schröder (ed.), *Die Frau ist frei geboren: Texte zur Frauenemanzipation*, vol. I: *1789–1870*, Munich 1979, pp. 32ff.
3. M. Riedel, 'Gesellschaft, bürgerliche', in O. Brunner et al. (eds.), *Geschichtliche Grundbegriffe*, vol. II, Stuttgart 1975, pp. 719–800; W. Ruppert, *Bürgerlicher Wandel: Studien zur Herausbildung einer nationalen deutschen Kultur im 18. Jahrhundert*, Frankfurt 1984.

geois public which worked, conducted debate, grumbled about human fortune, and devised political alternatives. By contrast, woman should 'not actually be considered a person at all in civil society': such was the conclusion of the civil servant Adolf von Knigge, also a supporter of the Enlightenment, in 1788.[4] The female sex was to remain as much excluded from involvement in the bourgeois public sphere as they were from the world of employment; and politics was certainly out of bounds.[5] Women's exclusive domain was the household or, as it had been known since the late eighteenth century, the 'family'.

As late as the first half of the eighteenth century, the word 'family' (*Familie*) was virtually unknown in the German-speaking world. In 1735, Zedler's *Universallexikon* (Universal Dictionary) mentioned only the term 'familia', which referred to the social and generational unit of ancient Rome. The German equivalent was the 'household' (*Haus*), run jointly by the *Hausvater* and *Hausmutter*, though each had different ambits of authority. Along with the heads of the house lived not only their children and possibly other relatives, but also those outside the family. This meant farmhands in the farming world, apprentices and journeymen in craftsmen's households, and clerks in the case of merchants. Whether related or not, they all lived under one roof, ate together, worked and relaxed together. This social unit had a strictly hierarchical internal structure. At the top there was the 'housefather', who was responsible for the general organisation of the household, commanding over wife, children and employees. The 'housemother', who owed her husband obedience, generally had control of the household's internal economy. Children were integrated into the normal process of work according to age, and their education consisted of the imitation of maternal or paternal skills and behaviour. The household was organised around the idea that each member had a different job to do, although the purpose of the domestic unit lay in the 'attain-

---

4. A. von Knigge, *Über den Umgang mit Menschen*, ed. G. Ueding, Frankfurt 1982, p. 165. On the efforts of philosophers and literary men at the time to design civil society exclusively in male terms, see U. Frevert, 'Bürgerliche Meisterdenker und das Geschlechterverhältnis: Konzepte, Erfahrungen, Visionen an der Wende vom 18. zum 19. Jh., in Frevert (ed.), *Bürgerinnen und Bürger – Geschlechterverhältnisse im 19. Jahrhundert*, Göttingen 1988, pp. 17–48.
5. On the 'bourgeois public' see Ruppert, *Wandel*, pp. 96ff.; J. Habermas, *Strukturwandel der Öffentlichkeit*, Neuwied 1971. On the 'work of sociability' in bourgeois associations see T. Nipperdey, 'Verein als soziale Struktur in Deutschland im späten 18. und frühen 19. Jahrhundert', in Nipperdey, *Gesellschaft, Kultur, Theorie*, Göttingen 1976, pp. 174–205.

ment of common good'.[6]

Half a century later Krünitz's *Oeconomische Encyklopädie* (Economic Encyclopaedia) included the Germanised term *Familie*, which by now referred almost exclusively to 'married couples and their children'. Only 'occasionally', Krünitz noted, 'does this expression also include farmhands and domestics'.[7] Here, too, emphasis on the family's economic and productive functions was little in evidence. This was no accident: in the latter half of the century the bourgeois literature of the Age of Enlightenment clearly specified 'the family' as a sphere of social interaction and reproduction outside work, and one reserved exclusively for marriage partners and their children. Servants were excluded from the intimate circle: although their labour remained indispensable to the household, their influence over the children was to be nonetheless curtailed. Nursemaids and nannies were to be banished completely from the middle-class household, for they infected the rising generation with vices and diseases endemic to the lower orders, against which the bourgeoisie sought with the utmost care to protect itself. The tasks of these women now fell to the natural mother, who was expected to devote herself primarily to bringing up children in a way that was affectionate, well-regulated and character-strengthening. Now that the middle-class wife was to a large extent freed from productive work, which was henceforth to be defined as a purely masculine domain, her task was to create within the family a refuge for private and intimate life, a refuge that would harmoniously complement the outside world of work, the world of competition for power and money.[8]

Since the early years of the eighteenth century, many writings of an educational and popular-scientific nature had been published under the influence of the Enlightenment, and these included advice on how to create such a refuge. Newspapers, novels, pamphlets and periodicals proclaimed the principles of enlightened bourgeois mor-

6. See the entry on 'familia' in *Großes Universallexikon aller Wissenschaften und Künste*, vol. 9, published by J. H. Zedler, Halle 1735, esp. pp. 205–6; and most importantly O. Brunner, 'Das "Ganze Haus" und die alteuropäische "Ökonomik"', in Brunner, *Neue Wege der Verfassungs- und Sozialgeschichte*, Göttingen 1968, pp. 103ff.

7. J. G. Krünitz, *Oeconomische Encyklopädie oder allgemeines System der Staats-Stadt- Haus- und Landwirthschaft*, vol. 12, Brünn 1788, p. 170, entry on 'Familie'.

8. On the concept of the bourgeois family see H. Rosenbaum, *Formen der Familie*, Frankfurt 1982, pp. 261ff.; D. Schwab, 'Familie', in *Grundbegriffe*, vol. II, pp. 253–301. On the bourgeois debate on domestic servants see J. Donzelot, *The Policing of Families*, London 1980, pp. 10ff., and D. Müller-Staats, *Klagen über Dienstboten*, Frankfurt 1987.

ality, education and upbringing, between them providing the basis for a detailed rule-book of male and female duties and responsibilities. This literature addressed a social stratum whose patterns of life and work were beginning to distance it markedly from society's traditional ways. By this time, university professors and schoolteachers, civil servants and professional persons were only partly members of the integrated society of the 'whole household'. Increasingly, their work was performed outside the home and organised as a 'profession', in such a way that wives and children no longer had any direct part in it. It was recompensed with a salary meant to support the whole family. The separation of occupation and family went hand in hand with a redefinition of the sexual division of labour: the close co-operation of the 'housemother' and 'housefather' in running the economy of the 'whole household' gave way to a general differentiation between male and female spheres of activity, now clearly separate both in location and in content.

The social stratum exposed to this radically changing state of affairs was rapidly increasing in numbers, and was in need of new models of behaviour to help it reinterpret and transform the structure and foundation of the male–female relations that had existed in traditional society. The alternative model popularised by Enlightenment literature – the bourgeois family – was attempting to fill the vacuum left by the changing pattern of life, while at the same time taking account of the wishes of the educated middle class to make its own innovations and differentiate itself clearly from other classes. The barriers that were deliberately erected against both the nobility and the lower orders were especially important to the political and social consciousness of the bourgeoisie, and should not be underestimated. By the same token, the new family norm was not only of ideological significance. Thus, for example, the enormous attention lavished by middle-class families on the education of children, and particularly on the education of sons, was primarily the result of perceived changes in the way individuals were located in society, changes that came about because the society was itself leaving behind the rules and traditions germane to the old social structure. Unlike the sons of farmers, noblemen or craftsmen, the son of a government official or a schoolteacher had no self-evident claim to his father's employment and social status, but had to earn both by his own achievements. Investment in education and training was therefore an important pre-condition for such achievements and for their reward in the form of an official position, and a professional and social niche in life.

This investment included not only careful attention to school and vocational education, but also to childhood socialisation as it took place within the family itself. With the differentiation of a mother-role came the evolution of a child-role, based on intimate, loving and protracted contact between mother and child.[9] Such a close emotional relationship was not only a response to the infant's need for care and protection; it also had a positive effect on the long-term stability and continuity of bourgeois society. Rearing and caring for children in an orderly fashion,[10] and without interference from outside, appeared to be a rational way of controlling behaviour, and a means of guaranteeing that the distractions of temperament and passion would be indulged sparingly in adult life. It was thus an important condition for successfully instilling the bourgeois values of work, industry, ambition, thrift and self-control. But the family could not be reduced simply to a means of inculcating these pur-posive, conformist patterns of behaviour. Emotion, love and trust could also be experienced, so long as they remained strictly con-fined to the intimate sphere. With this dual function, the middle-class family ideal fitted neatly into the social environment of the time. One could display a rather guarded openness to the outside world, while maintaining loyalty and intense family feeling within the inner sanctum, and this arrangement permitted the male family members the necessary flexibility and self-confidence to assert themselves in their public and professional lives. Equipped with all the virtues of a meritocratic bourgeois society – virtues learnt in the bosom of the family – they could brave the tough, competitive world of business and then return to the contemplative peace and seclusion of the familial preserve, there to renew their energies for forthcoming tasks and confrontations.

In their triple role as wives, mothers and housekeepers women were the generators and guarantors of family cohesion. They were expected to conduct their lives exclusively within their own four walls and to concentrate on their married lives, organising the household and bringing up the children. Outwardly this only reproduced the traditional sexual division of labour, which had already assigned to the *Hausmutter* primary responsibility for the domestic economy and the care of children and female employees.

9. See the classic study by P. Aries, *Centuries of Childhood*, Harmondsworth 1979; I. Peikert, 'Zur Geschichte der Kindheit im 18. und 19. Jahrhundert', in H. Reif (ed.), *Die Familie in der Geschichte*, Göttingen 1982, pp. 114–36.

10. See the analysis of advisory medical literature in U. Öttmüller, 'Mutterpflich-ten: Die Wandlungen ihrer inhaltlichen Ausformung durch die akademische Medi-zin', *Gesellschaft: Beiträge zur Marxschen Theorie* 14, Frankfurt 1981, pp. 97–138.

Certain responsibilities and powers were untouched. Indeed it was expected even of the middle-class housewife that she should 'ensure the well-being, honour, domestic peace and happiness of her husband with thoughtfulness, neatness, cleanliness, diligence, thrift and economic wisdom'.[11] What was new, however, was the emphasis on the emotional support that women, as wives and mothers, were expected to give their husbands and children. A woman's first priority was to make her husband happy by 'sweetening his life with affectionate co-operation, love, care and assistance' and to distract him from his everyday worries (Campe). Her next responsibility lay towards her children, whom she had to bring up to be decent men and women. Only then did her economic talents come into play. Although these constituted 'one of the most fundamental aspects of marital bliss',[12] they were unequivocally subordinated to the wife's caring role. This ordering of priorities was also reflected in the traditional economic literature of the eighteenth century. From the middle of the century, books aimed at 'housemothers' had increasingly been taking up themes which went beyond the management of household affairs and which addressed the 'interested woman'.[13] The fact that the *Moralische Wochenschriften*, the 'moral weeklies', established comprehensive standards for female education which no longer regarded housekeeping skills as paramount, was even more significant.[14] Now, women were to acquire suitable general knowledge and a basic knowledge of history, literature, languages and biology, so that they would be understanding wives to their husbands and intelligent mothers to their children.

Any attempt to justify education beyond these limits – as an end in itself – was, however, considered reprehensible. It was no accident that the 'learned woman' was one of the most frequent and spiteful caricatures of the late eighteenth and nineteenth centuries. Whereas the early Enlightenment, in its enthusiasm for rational and educated thought, had conceded to women the right to 'learnedness', it had, at the latest since the publication in 1762 of Rousseau's widely-read educational novel, *Émile*, been a commonly held belief that it was best for a learned woman to 'die an old maid' since 'a

11. J. H. Campe, *Väterlicher Rath für meine Tochter*, Brunswick 1789, partly reproduced in Gerhard, *Verhältnisse*, pp. 369–81, quote at p. 372.

12. von Knigge, *Umgang*, p. 168.

13. G. Frühsorge, 'Die Einheit aller Geschäfte: Tradition und Veränderung des 'Hausmutter'-Bildes in der deutschen Ökonomieliteratur des 18. Jahrhunderts', in *Wolfenbütteler Studien zur Aufklärung*, vol. 3, Wolfenbüttel 1976, pp. 137–57.

14. W. Martens, *Die Botschaft der Tugend*, Stuttgart 1968, esp. pp. 520ff.; P. Nasse, *Die Frauenzimmer-Bibliothek des Hamburger «Patrioten» von 1724: Zur weiblichen Bildung der Frühaufklärung*, 2 vols, Stuttgart 1976.

female wit is a scourge to her husband, her children, her friends, her servants, to everybody'.[15] A woman who read too many novels, or worse still academic literature, would neglect her female duties and develop needs which could not be satisfied in everyday life.

The model of the modern bourgeois family was based accordingly on a new form of sexual division of labour, which assigned to men and women neatly divided spheres of influence and allowed neither to step outside the prescribed limits. The justification for such a division was also new. Attempts to legitimate it on social and religious grounds were replaced by principles which ascribed the difference between the sexes to intrinsic, innate, natural and therefore universal characteristics. 'By nature' women were inclined to be passive and emotional, men active and rational. Sexual characteristics predestined women to work with people, as within the family, and men to engage in suitable productive activities in the realms of economy, politics, culture and science. Whilst he had to, and wanted to prove himself 'in the hostile world', she, the 'modest housewife' (Schiller), who developed and perfected her feminine characteristics by caring lovingly for husband and children, stayed at home.[16]

On a theoretical level, this concept of polarized gender characteristics did not yet entail the attribution to the sexes of varying degrees of social value and authority. Man and woman, with their respective qualities, together formed a harmonious whole; positions of authority were not defined. In practical terms, however, it quickly became clear that the model obligingly fitted in with the claims of the male sex to authority. This has never been articulated more clearly than by the Enlightened educationalist Joachim Heinrich Campe when, in his influential pamphlet *Väterlicher Rath für meine Tochter* (Fatherly Advice for my Daughter) (1789), he spoke openly of the 'natural destiny' of women 'to live in a state of dependence, no less real for being masked in outward signs of respect, and perhaps even rather oppressive'. For it was the 'combined will of nature and human society that man should be woman's protector and leader, and woman, by contrast, his true, grateful and obedient companion and helper, clinging to him, turning to him and leaning on him'.

By resorting to the 'eternal laws of nature' and the universal

---

15. J.-J. Rousseau, *Émile*, trans. B. Foxley, London 1972, pp. 371–2.
16. On the origin and justification of the concept see K. Hausen, 'Family and Role Divisions', in W. R. Lee and R. J. Evans (eds.), *The German Family*, London 1981, pp. 51–83.

history of mankind an image of woman was constructed which possessed traditional and modern traits in equal proportions. On the one hand there was a desire to carry forward the model of the old European *Hausmutter*; but this became detached from its historical and social context, leaving only the torso of the perpetually caring housewife, busily providing for husband and children. On the other hand the requirements of the new age had to be taken into account: the woman, moving increasingly to the fringes of economic and political activity, was defined primarily as a wife and mother, whose work within the family would make possible, and safeguard, her husband's success outside the home. Linked to the revaluation of the family as a place of purely human values, in direct contrast to the public, competition-orientated sphere, was the veneration of a new type of feminity, which had nothing in common either with the nobility's ideals of courtly culture and gallant literature or with the farmer's and craftsman's household leitmotif of the *Hausmutter*, toiling incessantly on the farm or in the workshop.

The concepts of equality which the Enlightenment occasionally proposed stood no chance in the face of this partly modern, partly historicised model. Equal rights, decision-making power and freedom of action for women would certainly have satisfied the bourgeois notion that human rights belonged to all. The price of this theoretical harmony would, however, have been – or so it seemed – a fundamental destabilisation of the structure of society. Potentially, women would compete directly against men, and relations between the sexes would be founded on a new basis. Amid all the joy of innovation and the readiness for advancement it was felt that at least a degree of certainty and dependability should remain, for without it the ideas of political, economic and social emancipation could not ultimately be put into practice, even for men. The rapid change in economic structures, the cultural and intellectual revolution and the political upheaval could only be shaped and integrated by the middle classes if the emotional side of family life was left intact. Women, as 'natural beings', represented this stability and continuity and enabled men, as 'social beings', to expose themselves to the dynamic flux in their environment. The emancipation of women would have rocked the foundations of a system based on polarity and complementarity, eroded the differences between family and society, and endangered the socio-psychological reproduction of the bourgeois social character. It was distinctly more simple, less dangerous and less binding to argue for 'public enlightenment', to advocate education and self-determination for the 'poor peasant' or to champion the 'civil advancement of the Jews'[17] than to cut the ground from under one's own feet with the 'civil advancement of women'. So, whereas during the course of the Prussian land reform even peasant *Hausväter* were gradually released by the lords of the manor and landed aristocracy from their personal dependence, and in the years after the Prussian Edict of 1812 the humiliating *Sonderstatus* of Jewish men was replaced by something approaching cultural, economic and social equality, women waited for emancipation in vain. Instead, educationalists, philosophers, doctors, lawyers and men of letters had developed and popularized the bourgeois model of the family, a model which would henceforth provide the guiding principles for women's actions and a measure of their worth.

Before we turn to the nineteenth century, the 'bourgeois age' itself, and try to assess the real nature of women's lives, let us look at the historical context in which the debate on the family, sexual characteristics and bourgeois society in the second half of the eighteenth century was conducted. On what experiences and knowledge were the new images, models and concepts based? By which section of society were they influenced and shaped? Which social milieu were they aimed at? There was no doubt as to the intended audience of writings which formulated models and standardised norms: they were meant to 'enlighten' and 'educate' the literate middle classes, who were among the most avid subscribers to the types of contemporary journals and pamphlets which set out to moralise, instruct and inform. Thus Campe's educational pamphlet, which was aimed 'primarily at young women from the fortunate middle classes', was bought mainly by clergymen, civil servants, merchants, doctors, bookkeepers, lawyers and pharmacists, and in many cases by literary societies too. The following discussion concentrates precisely on this new, 'restive' bourgeoisie.[18] Although numerically it represented only a small section

---

17. W. Ruppert, 'Volksaufklärung im späten 18. Jahrhundert', in *Deutsche Aufklärung bis zur Französischen Revolution 1680–1789*, Munich 1980, pp. 341–61; J. Voss,'Der Gemeine Mann und die Volksaufklärung im späten 18. Jahrhundert', in H. Mommsen and W. Schulze (eds), *Vom Elend der Handarbeit*, Stuttgart 1981, pp. 208–33; R. Rürup, *Emanzipation und Antisemitismus*, Göttingen 1975, esp. pp. 11–36. *Über die bürgerliche Verbesserung der Juden* was the title of a pamphlet of 1781 by the Berlin representative of the Enlightenment Christian Wilhelm Dohm. His manifesto provoked a lively discussion on the emancipation of Jews.
18. P. Michelsen, 'Der unruhige Bürger', in R. Vierhaus (ed.), *Bürger und Bürgerlichkeit im Zeitalter der Aufklärung*, Heidelberg 1981, pp. 101–30.

of the total population – estimates for the turn of the century suggest less than 10 per cent[19] – it fostered innovative forces and a desire for action, and developed new social forms which were gradually emulated by other classes and strata. In the nineteenth century 'bourgeois' family structures and gender roles were to be found not only among academics, civil servants and industrialists; they gradually won favour also with clerks and manual workers, and finally even in peasant communities.

The long-term success of the bourgeois model and its enormous attraction even for those sections of the population outside the middle classes justify concentration, even in this section dealing with the eighteenth century, on the social stratum in which it was developed and tested. Of course, it is essential constantly to bear in mind the insular position occupied by the new, mostly urban bourgeoisie, surrounded as it was by a rural, agrarian society still shaped by feudalist ideas. A brief overview of the social and economic background to middle-class innovation might perhaps make it easier to understand these complex perspectives. The following is necessarily brief because literature on the position and function of the wives and families of farmers and agricultural labourers is extremely rare, and the rural population therefore eludes historical scrutiny even more than does the urban bourgeoisie. Towards the end of the eighteenth century, middle-class women had already begun to write more frequently in order to relieve their feelings[20] and we have to thank, more than anything, their posthumously-published letters for the fact that we can reconstruct, at least in part, their wishes and yearnings as well as a picture of their everyday lives and behaviour. By contrast, the wives of independent peasants and tenant farmers neither revealed their innermost thoughts in diaries, nor exchanged letters with each other. As a result, indirect information taken from contemporary accounts is virtually all that exists about them.

---

19. D. Saalfeld, 'Die ständische Gliederung der Gesellschaft Deutschlands im Zeitalter des Absolutismus', *Vierteljahrschrift für Sozial- und Wirtschaftsgeschichte*, 67, 1980, pp. 457–83, quote at p. 478.

20. R. M. G. Nickisch, 'Die Frau als Briefschreiberin im Zeitalter der deutschen Aufklärung', *Wolfenbütteler Studien zur Aufklärung*, vol. 3, Wolfenbüttel 1976, pp. 29–65.

2
Rural Society

Whereas the rising bourgeoisie was concentrated in fairly large university towns and centres of government, the bulk of the population in late-eighteenth-century Germany lived in the country, in farming communities, villages and small market towns. As late as 1818 three-quarters of the approximately 30 million inhabitants of the German Confederation lived in rural settlements and only a quarter lived in the 2500 towns, of which only 70 had more than 10,000 inhabitants.[1] This does not mean, however, that either urban or rural society was marked by any degree of social homogeneity. Just as in the towns rich merchants, prosperous Guild Masters and poor day-labourers lived side by side, so there were many levels of land ownership in the country. Around the year 1800 25–30 per cent of the rural population were farmers, just under a third owned no more than a smallholding, a further third no land at all, and 10 per cent practised a non-guild craft.[2] Although yeoman farmers (*Vollbauer*) were now in the minority everywhere, rural society retained its farming structure well into the nineteenth century and even into the twentieth. Farming traditions, values and patterns of behaviour were passed on via family relationships and godparenthood even to those social strata in which the type of work done was already quite alien to people in the rural economy.[3]

The 'whole household' was very well defined in rural society. The sort of family relations described in Enlightenment literature were not be found here. Women did not resemble in the slightest the notion of the demure wife, housewife and mother, caring first and foremost for husband and children, with work coming last and even then undertaken in a covert way. In fact, the rural housemother worked incessantly, as was plain for all to see. Admittedly the tasks which devolved to her were, in the main, those carried out in

1. R. Rürup, *Deutschland im 19. Jahrhundert 1815–1871*, Göttingen 1984, p. 87.
2. Calculated from Saalfeld, 'Gliederung', p. 478, table 3.
3. J. Mooser, *Ländliche Klassengesellschaft 1770–1848: Bauern und Unterschichten, Landwirtschaft und Gewerbe im östlichen Westfalen*, Göttingen 1984, p. 197.

and around the house: according to Krünitz's *Encyklopädie* (1788), 'supervision and work in the kitchen and cellar, the rearing of cattle, pigs and poultry, the maintenance, cleaning and production of clothing and linen, bedmaking, brewing, baking, washing, sewing, spinning, weaving and other work with wool and flax, and indeed anything concerning the cleanliness of the house and the maintenance of household equipment'. In addition, she had to see to the education of her daughters and the supervision of female servants. Her husband, along with his sons and farmhands, was responsible for work in the fields and woods.[4] This gender-specific division of the various areas of work could, however, be temporarily suspended by seasonal requirements. If, for instance, more hands were needed at harvest time, the women would go out into the fields as well. Likewise, boys learned how to spin and knit, though spinning, weaving and sewing remained, in general, women's work.[5]

The central thrust of female 'industry within the farming classes' focused on 'the preservation, care, maintenance and finally on the productive, profitable, well-budgeted, thrifty and intelligent use of resources'. Inasmuch as farmers' wives were also responsible for the cultivation of flax, from which they produced linen, for their fruit orchards and vegetable gardens and for the dairy cattle and poultry, they too participated 'in productive agriculture'.[6] Despite distinct labour functions, there was in the farming household no gender-specific differentiation or division between production and consumption. Men and women worked side by side, albeit with different responsibilities. The household was their joint domain and every task carried out – whether by the *Hausvater* or the *Hausmutter* – was important and indispensable for the farm's prosperity.[7] Nevertheless, just because a man's and a woman's work was recognised as having equal value, this did not mean that they had equal standing within the family hierarchy. On the contrary, the

4. Krünitz, *Encyklopädie*, vol. 14, 1788, entry on 'Frau', pp. 787–97, and vol. 22, 1789, entry on 'Haus-Vater', pp. 411–30.
5. On sexual demarcation as regards tools and work processes see B. Duden and K. Hausen, 'Gesellschaftliche Arbeit — geschlechtsspezifische Arbeitsteilung', in A. Kuhn and G. Schneider (eds), *Frauen in der Geschichte*, Düsseldorf 1979, pp. 11–33; M. Mitterauer, 'Geschlechtsspezifische Arbeitsteilung in vorindustrieller Zeit', *Beiträge zur historischen Sozialkunde*, no. 11, 1981, pp. 77–87; Illich, *Gender*.
6. Krünitz, *Encyklopädie*, vol. 14, 1788, p. 790; vol. 60, 1793, pp. 453ff. See also Duden and Hausen, 'Gesellschaftliche Arbeit'.
7. See the study by M. Segalen, *Love and Power in the Peasant Family*, Oxford 1982, on relations between the sexes in France around the middle of the nineteenth century, and J. Weber-Kellermann, *Landleben im 19. Jahrhundert*, Munich 1987, esp. pp. 132ff.

Hausmutter was clearly subordinate to the *Hausväter*, the 'head of domestic society' (Krünitz). 'The authority of the *Hausväter* over his wife' was, Krünitz argued in the 1789 edition of his *Encyklopädie*, based on his role as 'protector and breadwinner'. The wife was, as a rule, weaker and needed special protection, since nature, 'through pregnancy, childbearing and other female contingencies', had left her far less able to manage the most important activities than was her husband. Consequently it was not feasible for 'two completely equal powers to exist in a single government'. By virtue of tradition and the laws of nature 'the internal government of the family', which encompassed both the right to punish wife, children and employees and the selection of future sons- and daughters-in-law, fell to the man.[8]

Despite the unequivocal authority enjoyed by the man, whose duty it was, as head, to represent the household to the outside world the wife of a farmer was anything but his slave. In 1735 Zedler's *Universallexikon* stated that 'because the wife, as housemother, has also to help her husband administer and supervise the household, some authority can be ascribed to her'. Assisted by maids, who were under her control and subject to her 'education', she managed matters relating to the household's internal economy more or less autonomously. She trained her daughters and they grew into their future roles as farmers' wives by imitating their elders and taking on tasks from an early age. Conscious upbringing, such as was being called for by Enlightenment educationalists, was unknown in peasant society. 'The education of children was "incidental"'.[9] Mothers had neither the time, nor did they see the need, to treat their children in any particular manner or pay them special attention, to encourage their talents or awaken particular interests. From an early age children were integrated into the working life of the farm so that they could replace hired labourers as soon as possible. Daughters helped their mothers, sons their fathers. If a farm did not yield enough to keep the whole family, the children were sent to work for more prosperous farmers.[10]

But it was the ambition of every farmer's daughter 'to become a

8. Krünitz, *Encyklopädie*, vol. 22, 1789, pp. 411–12.

9. J. Schlumbohm (ed.), *Kinderstuben: Wie Kinder zu Bauern, Bürgern, Aristokraten wurden 1700–1850*, Munich 1983, p. 68.

10. See the accounts of the childhood of peasants and farmers in Schlumbohm (ed.), *Kinderstuben*, pp. 76ff., and the autobiographical texts in I. Hardach-Pinke and G. Hardach (eds.), *Kinderalltag: Deutsche Kindheiten in Selbstzeugnissen 1700–1900*, Reinbek 1981, pp. 80ff., and Rosenbaum, *Formen*, pp. 89ff.

farmer's wife on a good farm'.[11] How quickly she achieved this depended on the size of her dowry. Marriage was, however, only possible if the couple had a chance of making a living, that is, when a farm was inherited or parcelled out. As a consequence the age of marriage for women, as well as for men, was relatively high, generally in the late twenties. Late marriages, as well as long periods of breast-feeding ranging from one to two or even three years, had the effect of keeping down the number of children in a marriage. Only occasionally did a farmer's wife bear more than six or seven children and only around 50 per cent of all children born survived their critical first years of life.[12]

Farmers' daughters who would otherwise have had to wait some time for a good match, above all in regions where the right of succession was to an undivided estate, could, by lowering their sights as to social status and economic wealth, establish their own household at an earlier age. Smallholders willingly took as wives the daughters of farmers with medium-sized or large holdings.[13] After all, such marriages secured not only a handsome dowry, but also good relations with the rich and powerful of the village. For the woman marriage to a smallholder meant, admittedly, a loss of social status, but was always preferable to being unmarried. As an unmarried sister in the household of a married brother she would almost certainly have been kept busy but had little standing or say in decisions. As the wife of a smallholder she was also a *Hausmutter*, even if under different social and economic conditions. A smallholding only very occasionally yielded enough to keep the family, which was thus usually dependent on supplementary commercial activity, mostly in the form of spinning or weaving for the market. It was predominantly the women who took on this kind of work, while the farming was left to the men. A similar division of labour was to be found among tenant farmers (*Heuerlinge*), a section of the rural population which grew enormously in the eighteenth century. They owned no land of their own, but were the tenants of a farmer or leased a small plot of land from him. They depended, even more than the smallholder, on extra-agricultural sources of income which

11. A priest from Ravensberg quoted from the year 1786, in Schlumbohm (ed.), *Kinderstuben*, p. 79.
12. Ibid., pp. 31–2; M. Mitterauer, 'Der Mythos von der vorindustriellen Großfamilie', in M. Mitterauer and R. Sieder, *Vom Patriarchat zur Partnerschaft: Zum Strukturwandel der Familie*, Munich 1984, p. 60.
13. On marriage in peasant and farming circles see Mooser, *Klassengesellschaft*, pp. 194ff., and Mooser, 'Familien, Heirat und Berufswahl: Zur Verfassung der ländlichen Gesellschaft im 19. Jahrhundert', in Reif (ed.), *Familie*, pp. 137–62.

enabled them to pay for their lodgings or ground rent. The whole family, though chiefly wife and children, spun and wove, earning around 80 per cent of the family's income.[14]

Dependence on market demand and economic cycles made those who are now termed proto-industrial producers[15] more susceptible to crises, but at the same time made them more independent of the unwritten laws and customs of rural society. Whereas marriage in the families of yeoman farmers was subject to many restrictions relating to ownership and power, the smallholder and labouring classes were now free of traditional norms which expected prospective spouses to be able materially to sustain the marriage from the land they worked. As demand for commercial products grew, some 'surplus' farmers' offspring, not set to inherit, preferred to settle down and make a living from cottage industry rather than be confined to the celibacy of a servant's life. As the bulk of the household's income was earned by producing or processing saleable goods, the workers could, in principle, marry at a younger age. Yet relatively few seem to have taken this opportunity. Recent studies have, in fact, pointed out that compared to smallholders or even yeoman farmers, male tenant farmers were more likely to marry before they were twenty-four; but the majority adhered to traditional farming marriage patterns.[16] Women of the tenant farmer class married at a later age even than those whose fathers owned their land.[17] For both sexes, marriage apparently followed several years' service on a farm, with savings from this period being used to help raise a family.

The structure of these proto-industrial families was also based on the 'whole household', though they did not include anyone from outside the family. They worked at home, and consumption took place at home. The sexual division of labour was less strict than in the household of yeoman farmers. Women were involved in the

14. Mooser, *Klassengesellschaft*, p. 49.

15. See P. Kriedte et al., *Industrialisierung vor der Industrialisierung*, Göttingen 1978, esp. chapters 2 and 3, by H. Medick, on proto-industrial family-based economic activity and demographic development.

16. Mooser, *Klassengesellschaft*, pp. 88–9. The theory that the age of marriage was lower in the families of homeworkers due to economic factors is, on the other hand, supported by Medick in Kriedte et al., *Industrialisierung*, esp. pp. 166ff., and R. Braun, *Industrialisierung und Volksleben: Veränderungen der Lebensformen unter Einwirkung des verlagsindustriellen Heimarbeit in einem ländlichen Industriegebiet [Zürcher Oberland] vor 1800*, Göttingen 1979, pp. 59ff.

17. See the tables on the age of marriage of men and women in the agrarian lower classes and of peasants and farmers in J. Kocka et al., *Familie und soziale Plazierung: Studien zum Verhältnis von Familie, sozialer Mobilität und Heiratsverhalten an westfälischen Beispielen im späten 18. und 19. Jahrhundert*, Opladen 1980, p. 190 (Mooser) and p. 268 (Schüren).

production of commercial goods at least to the same degree as men; men cultivated small plots of land and performed some tasks in the home.[18] Bourgeois observers always appeared irritated at the similarity between men and women of the 'common people'. According to Krünitz: 'to look at, the wives of the common man, who very often have to do the heaviest of work, are more like men than women. They can be seen mingling with their menfolk in the market places, in the fields, everywhere. They buckle under just the same loads and when they go home more work awaits them. The woman seems to belong to both sexes and does not just have to do her own work, but also very often has to take on the work of the man.'[19]

In these classes the modification of economic roles resulted in a weakening of the man's position of authority, something demonstrated primarily by the convergence of patterns of social behaviour. Women started to visit public houses, took part in hunger and bread riots, and adopted freer sexual mores. Middle-class contemporaries who, as priests, schoolteachers or rural doctors, came into closer contact with these sections of the population, found such behaviour 'shameless', 'unladylike' and scandalous, and bemoaned the decline in the moral standards of the female sex. By comparison, the farming family was considered positively virtuous, although measured against the strict standards of the bourgeois family model it was still felt to be deficient in some respects. Repeated criticism was levelled above all against the unsatisfactory nature of children's education, and mothers were strongly urged to take greater care in such matters.

The bourgeoisie was even more critical of family life among the nobility, however. Noble ladies, it was said, showed not the slightest interest in their offspring. Instead of caring for and bringing up their children, they preferred to dance the night away at sumptuous parties and to sleep or idle away the days with trivial visits to friends and acquaintances. Their husbands, meanwhile, pursued their business interests and squandered feudal rents on their mistresses. Servants – firstly wet nurses, then nursemaids, governesses and tutors – were engaged for the children. Numerous Enlightenment

18. On proto-industrial, family-based economic activity see Mooser, *Klassengesellschaft*, pp. 71ff.; H. Medick, 'Zur strukturellen Funktion von Haushalt und Familie im Übergang von der traditionellen Agrargesellschaft zum industriellen Kapitalismus: Die protoindustrielle Familienwirtschaft', in W. Conze (ed.), *Sozialgeschichte der Familie in der Neuzeit Europas*, Stuttgart 1976, pp. 254–82; Rosenbaum, *Formen*, pp. 189ff.

19. Krünitz, *Encyklopädie*, vol. 14, 1788, p. 807, entry on 'Frauenzimmer'.

pamphlets found fault with the egoistic behaviour of aristocratic mothers. In an epistolary novel of 1784 by the educationalist Christian Gotthilf Salzmann, the hero meets a noble lady who has entrusted her child to a female attendant who dreadfully neglects it. To his question as to why she does not take care of her infant herself, the noble lady replies, 'Do you think I am a farmer's daughter, that I should bother myself with little children? That a woman of my age and standing should allow her very strength to be sucked dry by children?'[20]

Such accounts were certainly exaggerted: aristocratic society served predominantly as a negative foil against which idealised portraits of middle-class life stood out in a more favourable and shining light. Yet the image was not completely false. Particularly in the circles of the higher nobility, children lived, to a large degree, isolated from their parents and had, instead, their own 'royal households', staffed by servants, governesses, private teachers and tutors. Immediately after birth the infant was handed over to a wet nurse. It was almost unheard of for a natural mother to breast-feed a child. The education and care of children lay in the hands of others, although parents furnished governesses and private tutors with detailed instructions on how to go about their tasks. From their mostly French governesses the daughters of the nobility learned everything considered fitting for their status, in particular drawing, piano-playing, dancing and French conversation. The less wealthy and select, however, set great store by teaching girls the basics of housekeeping, so that later in life they would be capable of managing the finances of a large household. Fontane, for example, described Adelheid von Stechlin, of the Brandenburg March, an unmarried woman living on an endowment, as 'a good hostess', who 'hailed from the old days, when women learned and could do everything from "slaughtering" to "skinning eels"'.[21]

Even though the daughters of the nobility were brought up for the role of the 'lady of the house', many of them were denied this desirable existence. Marriage opportunities were extremely limited, especially since the strictly defined family structure took care to safeguard the continuity and stability of its hierarchy. In Westphalia, for example, where the eldest son, as the future head of the

---

20. C. G. Salzmann, *Carl v. Carlsberg oder über das menschliche Elend*, vol. I, Leipzig 1784, p. 84.

21. T. Fontane, *Der Stechlin* (first published 1898), Munich 1979, p. 259. See also M. Bacherler, *Deutsche Familienerziehung im Zeitalter der Aufklärung und der Romantik*, dissertation, Stuttgart 1914, esp. p. 74.

family, was generally the only male child to marry, little more than a third of upper-class women married. The rest had to make do with endowments. Their lives were, admittedly, in keeping with their rank, but also frugal and uneventful; and their social standing bore no comparison to that of their married sisters and cousins. Married women shared the social status enjoyed by their husbands, who took over their 'guardianship' as soon as they left the parental home. Their standard of living lay way above that of women dependent on an endowment, and as the mothers of future heirs and heads of family they enjoyed personal standing. As a hedge against family crisis – the death or sterility of the eldest son, or his marrying outside his rank – and in order to guarantee the survival of the family line, it was considered important to have a large number of children. Thus the wives of the Westphalian nobility in the eighteenth century brought, on average, ten children into the world, of whom perhaps six reached the age of twenty. Wet nurses, nurse-maids, private tutors and governesses were on hand to educate the children, which meant that noblewomen, when not involved in childbirth, could devote themselves to their organisational, supervisory and social duties.[22]

Relations between marriage partners were often distant and lacked emotional intensity. In a marriage the issue was not personal preference but family strategy. The choice of a partner lay with the parents and relatives, although the child did have a right of veto. It was not, however, fitting for a woman to turn down a suitor. Only an heiress could afford the privilege of making up her own mind. Although the age difference between marriage partners was not very great – women generally married at the age of 20 or 21, men at 26 – there was a pronounced difference between the authority of each, which was underpinned by both legal and economic factors. Traditional, patriarchal right adjudged the man to be indisputable head of the household, the guardian of his children and of his wife. He was the sole owner of the family's assets, including his wife's dowry. He decided how the family would live, and administered the property.

Nevertheless, noblewomen were able to eschew their husbands' control to a considerable degree, largely because these couples lived relatively separate lives. The spaciousness of the nobility's ancestral seats, palaces and manor houses allowed the partners their own private chambers; separate bedrooms were the norm. The frequent

22. H. Reif, 'Zum Zusammenhang von Sozialstruktur, Familien- und Lebenszyklus im westfälischen Adel in der Mitte des 18. Jahrhunderts', in M. Mitterauer and R. Sieder (eds), *Historische Familienforschung*, Frankfurt 1982, pp. 123–55.

absence of the husband, and the wife's visits and spa trips, enabled both to lead lives of their own, and their diverging social circles were often held together only by their joint social duties. This kind of 'open' relationship offered women, relieved as they were of the burden of work and bringing up children, real opportunities to pursue their own interests and predilections; in this atmosphere it was possible for what has been described in numerous novels and letters as 'galante Kultur' and the semantics of love to flourish outside marriage and alongside women's duty to reproduce. But only married women were free to engage in the art of *amour passion* without loss of honour, to practise it with finesse and to cultivate an erotic, seductive femininity.[23]

23. N. Luhmann, *Love as Passion: The Codification of Intimacy*, trans. J. Gaines and D. Jones, Cambridge 1986, esp. pp. 118ff.

3
The New Bourgeoisie and New Femininity

The bourgeoisie of the late eighteenth century dissociated itself as much from the femininity of aristocratic culture, which it regarded as immoral and dishonourable, as from the 'unfeminine' woman it had detected in the farming and lower classes. Even women from the old urban middle classes – the wives and daughters of guilded craftsmen, innkeepers and retailers – did not find favour with the new bourgeoisie. As was the case in farming society, women in the traditional artisan classes were fully integrated into the production process. As a matter of course it was expected of a master crafts-man's wife 'that she should be able to help her husband in his business and with his craft, and either work with him a little, or learn how to sell his wares skilfully and at a profit'.[1] In addition she ran a large household, which comprised not only the immediate family (parents and children) but also a wider circle including, for example, domestic servants, journeymen and apprentices.[2] Until well into the nineteenth century, and in some crafts even late in the century, it was usual for journeymen and apprentices to receive board and lodging in their master's house. Similarly, a merchant's 'family' contained not only the domestic servants, but also the clerks. For example, at the beginning of the nineteenth century, the home of the Königsberg merchant David Lewald housed, in addition to his wife and children, a nanny, a cook, a housemaid, two office deputies, three clerks and an apprentice.[3]

Although similar in terms of size and composition to the concept of the 'whole household', the Lewald family was more closely allied to the norms of the new bourgeoisie than to those found among the traditional urban middle classes. Indeed, in the eighteenth century

---

1. Krünitz, *Encyklopädie*, vol. 14, 1788, p. 791.
2. H. Möller, *Die kleinbürgerliche Familie im 18. Jahrhundert*, Berlin 1969; Rosenbaum, *Formen*, pp. 121ff.
3. F. Lewald, *Meine Lebensgeschichte*, ed. G. Brinker-Gabler, Frankfurt 1980, pp. 39, 86.

export-oriented merchants, whose business further afield brought them into contact with other attitudes and modes of behaviour deliberately distanced themselves more and more from the craftsmen and small retailers who clung to their vested rights and 'respectable' way of life. Nor did those financially powerful people who, by putting work out to homeworkers, had benefited from the boom in proto-industrial commerce, or the manufacturers who, though fewer in number, between them employed several thousand workers in decentralised or centralised production units, count themselves any longer as members of the urban middle-class 'estate'. They emphasised their superior social and economic position, which offered a new alternative within the usual system of estates (nobility, 'burghers' and farming classes).[4] Since 1794 this special status had been legally recognised in Prussia. The Prussian Civil Code (the *Allgemeines Landrecht*) created for rich merchants, industrialists, civil servants and academics the status of 'exempts' (*Eximierte*). These 'exempts' enjoyed privileged legal status, their sons were excused from military service and their daughters were permitted to marry into the nobility.[5] Until the second half of the nineteenth century, however, the industrial bourgeoisie was only poorly represented in this explicitly state-approved upper-middle class. Economic development in Germany lagged way behind that in France, not to mention Britain, and not until the middle of the nineteenth century did it become possible to talk in terms of a broader industrial bourgeoisie. Around the end of the eighteenth century it was the educated middle classes, the *Bildungsbürger*, who clearly predominated among the 'exempts'. The expansion and consolidation of absolutist government and the resulting development of the state had given rise to a huge demand for well-qualified civil servants, which could and should not be satisfied by the nobility. More and more members of the middle classes had entered the service of the sovereign and occasionally been promoted to the highest positions. University-educated experts on administrative law, judges, priests, professors and teachers, along with doctors and lawyers, formed the core of the 'new bourgeoisie', which in the larger towns developed into a specific social group differentiated from the other inhabitants by its housing, dress, cultural norms and

4. R. Vierhaus, *Deutschland im Zeitalter des Absolutismus 1648–1763*, Göttingen 1978, pp. 36ff., 51.
5. For this and the other special privileges (e.g. legal penalties graded according to rank) see R. Koselleck, *Preußen zwischen Reform und Revolution: Allgemeines Landrecht, Verwaltung und soziale Bewegung von 1791–1848*, Stuttgart 1982, pp. 89ff.

professional practices.[6]

The commercial and educated middle classes met in the new institutions of the bourgeois public: in coffee houses, masonic lodges, clubs and at dinner parties. They came together in associations which 'served the community', setting themselves the task of debating and tackling the political, educational, social, economic, scientific and technical problems of the age.[7] They bought educational journals and books and joined literary societies, not only for the reading material, but also in order to cultivate social links with each other.[8] These modern, multi-professional organisations, in which the new bourgeoisie created a forum for the discovery of its own social, cultural and political identity, were almost exclusively male preserves. Not only did the philanthropic societies working on specific reform projects admit only men; even social and educational associations excluded women. There were, of course, individual literary societies open to women, and some music societies admitted women as their husbands' companions, indeed considered it an honour if 'ladies' were sitting in the audience at a public concert. But they were not welcomed as paying and participatory members of the society. For example, the Stuttgart Museum Association, founded in 1807, regarded itself exclusively as a union of 'educated men' and its Frankfurt counterpart, founded in 1808, sought eleven expert opinions as to 'whether women should be granted admission to the museum'.[9]

At the very time when bourgeois men were becoming increasingly oriented towards the world outside the home both in their professional capacities and in their leisure time, they clung to the belief that it was not fitting for a woman to appear alone in public. Whereas they themselves gradually bade farewell to the old order, its conventions, restrictions, traditions and customs were to remain

6. On the new bourgeois classes see Vierhaus, *Deutschland*, pp. 77ff.; H. H. Gerth, *Bürgerliche Intelligenz um 1800*, Göttingen 1976.
7. R. Vierhaus (ed.), *Deutsche patriotische und gemeinnützige Gesellschaften*, Munich 1980; U. Im Hof, *Das gesellige Jahrhundert: Gesellschaft und Gesellschaften im Zeitalter der Aufklärung*, Munich 1982; W. Hardtwig, 'Strukturmerkmale und Entwicklungstendenzen des Vereinswesens in Deutschland 1789–1848', in O. Dann (ed.), *Vereinswesen und bürgerliche Gesellschaft in Deutschland*, Munich 1984, pp. 11–50.
8. O. Dann, 'Die Lesegesellschaften des 18. Jahrhunderts und der gesellschaftliche Aufbruch des deutschen Bürgertums', in U. Herrmann (ed.), *'Die Bildung des Bürgers': Die Formierung der bürgerlichen Gesellschaft und die Gebildeten im 18. Jahrhundert*, Weinheim 1982, pp. 100–18.
9. On the Stuttgart Museum Society see Nipperdey, 'Verein', p. 440, n. 21; on the Frankfurt Museum Society and middle-class music societies see P. Schleuning, *Das 18. Jahrhundert: Der Bürger erhebt sich (Geschichte der Musik in Deutschland)*, Reinbek 1984, pp. 216ff.

in force for their wives. All those areas, such as education and individual achievement, which endowed the bourgeoisie with self-confidence and conviction, shut women out. They worked quietly and unobtrusively in the home and family, and only now and then, on their husbands' arms, did they decorate a ball or concert with their pleasing appearance.

Born in 1790, the wife of the merchant David Lewald was the model of a virtuous bourgeois woman. She took great care of her eight children, read to them, taught them their alphabet and poetry, and trained her daughters in the art of housekeeping. She 'worshipped' her husband, obeyed his every command and strove 'untiringly' to tend to his needs. With him at her side she fulfilled the social duties pertaining to her rank, arranged social gatherings and dinner parties, attended balls and accepted private invitations. In addition to bringing up the children, her main job was to direct the labour-intensive work required to run the household, which in those days was largely based on the principle of making in the home most of what was needed. In her spare time she knitted, spun or embroidered, skills to which she introduced her young daughters. The eldest daughter Fanny complained that intellectual stimulation was something she had never received from her mother. Having grown up herself without any formal education, Frau Lewald subdued her daughter's thirst for knowledge with the argument 'that there is nothing more objectionable and useless than an educated and impractical woman'.[10]

This view was shared by the overwhelming majority of her contemporaries, men and women alike. A woman such as Dorothea von Schlözer, who was brought up as a child prodigy by her father, professor of history August Ludwig von Schlözer, and who in 1787, at the age of seventeen, was awarded a doctorate from the University of Göttingen, was a most exceptional case, and the object of astonishment and ridicule. In 1781 Caroline Michaelis, likewise the daughter of a Göttingen professor, wrote of her: 'It is true that Dortchen is incredibly talented and intelligent, but to her misfortune, since she cannot expect these abilities or her father's eccentric plans [for her], which will arouse in her the greatest conceit, to bring her either happiness or respect. Women are judged only according to what they are as women.'[11]

---

10. Lewald, *Lebensgeschichte*, p. 69.
11. *'Lieber Freund, ich komme weit her schon an diesem frühen Morgen': Caroline Schlegel-Schelling in ihren Briefen*, ed. S. Damm, Darmstadt 1981, p. 75.

But in the age of Enlightenment more was demanded of a bourgeois woman than that she possess simply the qualities of a good,
thrifty and economically-able *Hausmutter*. A certain amount of
general knowledge and aesthetic reading was essential in order that
her husband should not find home life tiresome and that her
children should be properly brought up. All the same, autobiographical accounts suggest that there was no uniform pattern to
female education in bourgeois society. Between the ages of three
and six Johanna Schopenhauer, born in 1766 into the family of a
Danzig merchant, attended an elementary school. As was 'the general
custom at the time', her parents then engaged a private tutor who
gave her an hour-long lesson every morning for seven years. Afterwards a friend of the family taught her English and a dancing
instructor came daily, as did a 'kind old woman who came to teach
me to darn and make fine clothes'. Every afternoon Johanna spent
five hours with a French governess, who taught her pupils French,
handwriting, a little geography and 'conventional decorum and
social mores'. Of her mother's education Johanna once wrote, 'a
couple of polonaises, the odd jig on the piano, a couple of songs to
which she could provide her own accompaniment, reading and
writing for the purposes of housekeeping. That was virtually all she
was taught.'[12]

Not all parents spent their money on private tutors or governesses, but as a rule those who did considered it more important to
invest in the education of sons, whose future social and professional
positions were quite definitely dependent on formal educational
qualifications. In families of the educated middle classes the father
often taught his sons himself, and if the daughters were interested
they could listen too. Johann Ludwig Huber, who was born in 1723
and whose father, a minister, prepared him for law studies, wrote in
his memoirs of his sister, one year his elder: 'Of her own accord
and, when he noticed her wishes, not without my father's encouragement, she kept me company in all my lessons, from the alphabets
of the scholarly languages onwards. . . . My dear mother required
part of her time so that she could be taught the art of housekeeping.
Otherwise, by dint of her greater attentiveness, she would certainly
have surpassed me in everything.'[13]

Yet even in this case identical educations for both sexes did not
mean the same thing. Whereas the road to university and a career as

12. Reproduced in Hardach-Pinke and Hardach, eds. *Kinderalltag*, p. 168.
13. Reproduced in ibid., p. 154.

a civil servant was marked out for the son, the daughter's only possible career was that of a mother. Greek, Hebrew and Latin were of no use to her. They were therefore not taught to the majority of middle-class girls.

The joint education of sons and daughters, as was practised in the Hubers' rectory, disappeared when it became customary to send boys, at as young an age as possible, to municipal grammar schools. Of course even after 1763, when compulsory general education for all was introduced in Prussia, affluent families still had the right to have their children taught at home by private tutors. But as the state increasingly standardised both the expectations of academic performance and the entitlements that education conferred, public educational establishments became continuously more important, with the result that in nineteenth-century towns the old system of teaching children at home became largely a thing of the past. Grammar schools, however, remained closed to the daughters of the bourgeoisie, and other state educational establishments above elementary level were also exclusively for boys. Whereas their brothers left home to take ever more comprehensive and detailed courses of study in preparation for their future educational and professional careers, the education and training of middle-class girls continued to take place predominantly in the home. Even if they attended an educational establishment for several years, as had been more common since the beginning of the nineteenth century, they were not qualified for a profession. Fanny Lewald from the age of six attended a private school, to which 'the most respectable families in Königsberg' sent their daughters. There she learned reading, writing, arithmetic, religion, geography, history, French, singing and drawing. After she left school at the age of thirteen, her days lacked all variety and, as she bitterly writes, she spent her time 'pointlessly':

For five hours every day I sat in the living room, on a particular seat in the window, and learned how to darn stockings, mend clothes and lend a hand with tailoring and other work. I spent two hours at the piano, bored myself for an hour with the contents of my old schoolbooks, which at that time I knew off by heart from start to finish, and another hour writing out poetry to practise my handwriting. In between I ran errands from the kitchen to the pantry and from the living room to the nursery, looked after the three youngest children now and again, and in the evening had the terrible feeling that I had done nothing worthwhile all day.[14]

14. Lewald, *Lebensgeschichte*, p. 78.

*education was useless for ♀,
but at they got some knowledge*

Only by marrying could women do anything worthwhile, have responsibility or make decisions. They therefore spent their youth waiting for their husbands-to-be, for marriage and for a home of their own. Bridegrooms were chosen by the bride's parents, who started to look around early on for a good match: a man with a suitable social position, with a secure income and promising promotion prospects. Marriage between people of different 'rank' contradicted the 'bourgeois order' and 'paved the way for discord between the two families'.[15] It disrupted the most important networks of human relations in a society which assigned status not, as bourgeois criticism of absolutism demanded, on the grounds of achievement and talent, but according to criteria of class and birth. Standing apart as it did from traditional class hierarchy, the new bourgeois class more than any other saw relatives and the family as an indispensable part of social and economic influence and personal security. They functioned as the security and regulatory mechanisms that this social group otherwise lacked, and acted as a crucial source of personal support and advancement, without which individuals would have been fully exposed to the hazards and adversity of their social surroundings. Marriage was therefore always a means of forging links between families who could be of mutual benefit. It was, in bourgeois society as in aristocratic and farming circles, part of a strategy to expand, consolidate and protect property and power. The choice of suitable marriage partners was a matter not only of the happiness of the young couple, but also explicitly of the interests of the family organisation.

15. Rousseau, *Émile*, p. 370.

4

The Bourgeois Marriage

When the parents of Maximiliane La Roche, with the help of their friends and acquaintances, started in 1770 to look around for a suitable husband for their then fourteen-year-old daughter, their choice fell at first on a successful and high-ranking civil servant 'with a great deal of wealth', who, however, withdrew for career reasons. Thoroughly disconcerted and infuriated by this 'disgrace', Maximiliane, then seventeen, was married off to a 'much richer' Frankfurt merchant by the name of Brentano who was twenty-two years her senior. For the La Roche family his wealth was the decisive factor – they wanted to see their daughter well provided for. 'All the business wives in Frankfurt are happy.' Besides his bride's not inconsiderable dowry Brentano, on the other hand, valued more than anything the political and commercial benefits which he drew from his father-in-law's connections as a minister at the court of the Electorate of Trier. It did not matter that the couple were quite different in their temperaments, interests and needs. The young, witty and multi-talented Maximiliane had, of course, to fit in with the habits of her husband, who out of jealousy forbade her contact with intellectual friends and always wanted her to 'stay at home'. In twenty years of marriage she brought twelve children into the world and died in 1793 at the age of thirty-seven. Certainly she had no financial problems and did not need to worry about her children's material future; but the marriage had thwarted the expression of her own self. Predestined by nature and upbringing for a glorious existence 'in high social circles', wrote her mother, she spent her life bearing and bringing up children and running her influential husband's household.[1]

Although her convent education, and the teaching given to her by her highly educated mother, were not typical for bourgeois society at that time, her life still comprised a string of elements from which

1. All quotations from '*Ich bin mehr Herz als Kopf*'. *Sophie von La Roche: Ein Lebensbild in Briefen*, ed. M. Maurer, Munich 1983, pp. 338, 256.

we can draw general conclusions. Marriages were generally arranged by parents, who looked around for suitable husbands within the wider circle of their acquaintances. They wanted a 'good family', a solid education and favourable career prospects, and, if possible, wealth. These things, after all, seemed to offer their daughters and grandchildren a life free of care and in keeping with their rank. A handsome dowry, determined by her family's financial position and the number of brothers and sisters she had, bought the bride into her husband's family. The fact that bridegrooms were expected to have a certain economic and professional status meant that only older men were able to marry, since the training of a civil servant, merchant or industrialist lasted several years. Family records from Lower Saxony show that between 1750 and 1849 the average age of marriage for important merchants and businessmen was thirty-three. Men from the educated middle classes were also invariably over thirty by the time they entered into their first marriage.[2]

Whether a girl was ready and suitable for marriage was assessed on the basis of different criteria, which were more easily met. Besides a modest elementary education, the most important thing was a knowledge of housekeeping. The accounts from Lower Saxony give the average age of marriage between the years 1750 and 1849 as twenty-one to twenty-two. According to the saying, the younger the bride, the better the marriage. Men valued their wives above all for their ability to adapt, an ability which was greater in girls with no preconceptions than in mature women. The judgement given by poet, professor of philosophy and private tutor Christoph Martin Wieland of his own wife's qualities is most illuminating in this context. After first criticising her 'lack of etiquette, confused appearance and finally that lack of intellect, which is naturally the result of ignorance', he continued: 'But in her attitudes to my person she is, in every sense, what I desire. Without moods, even-tempered, calm, agreeable, easy to amuse, used to an almost monastic way of life, content with everything as long as she can see an expression of contentment and affection in my face. She fits in effortlessly, and without being forced, with my taste, my mood, and my way of life.'

The same man who fifteen years earlier, at the age of seventeen, had expected of his future wife above all imagination, acumen,

---

2. A. von Nell, *Die Entwicklung der generativen Strukturen bürgerlicher und bäuerlicher Familien von 1750 bis zur Gegenwart*, dissertation, Bochum 1973, tables pp. 74–5.

interest, seriousness and critical reflection, and in addition breeding, experience and a knowledge of the world, wrote in 1765 of his 'little woman': 'I do not require a grain of intellect from my wife. I have plenty of that in my books.'[3]

The Wieland family, which within twenty-four years grew to sixteen people, can be regarded as a model example of bourgeois harmony and intimacy in the late eighteenth century. Frau Dorothea Wieland, daughter of an Augsburg merchant, was its source of tranquility whose 'very happiness is invested in and drawn from simply living for me and our family'. She respected her husband so much that she could never bring herself to use the familiar form of address with him and used the distanced, reverential polite form throughout her life. Wieland too regarded his wife with deep affection, foregoing long trips for her sake, and in 1805, after forty years of marriage, wrote that he had been 'happy' with her 'without having been held back in my course'. At the same time it had not been great passion which had brought about their marriage, but so-called rational love. Twenty-two days after his wedding Wieland argued that 'there is nothing more foolish than that scorching passion, which one generally leaves behind at the beginning of a marriage', and called for well-balanced sensuality which safeguarded the difference in authority between the marriage partners and did not allow the man to become his wife's sexual slave.

Sexual attraction was not a prerequisite for matrimony; indeed it even appeared to be a disadvantage. In 1784, three weeks after her marriage to a doctor by the name of Böhmer, who was ten years her senior, Caroline Michaelis, the daughter of a Göttingen professor, predicted, 'It will last because it is not excessive.' She felt 'respect and affection' for her husband, not burning passion. 'My fondness for him does not bear the mark of blazing emotions.'[4] If autobiographical writings and letters can be believed, most marriages arranged by third parties knew little of amorousness, the beating of hearts and sweaty palms. A marriage was not a lovematch, but an operation planned with military precision and with clearly defined goals and tasks. For the man it meant, according to his socio-economic position, the opportunity to continue the family line and pass on his property, social status, cultural traditions and qualities to legitimate heirs. At the same time he added to his own status by establishing a

---

3. These and the following statements of Wieland's are to be found in his letters to Sophie La Roche, reproduced in *'Ich bin mehr Herz als Kopf'*, pp. 78ff., 38ff., 387.
4. Reprinted in *Frauenbriefe der Romantik*, ed. K. Behrens, Frankfurt 1982, p. 258.

family, freed himself from paternal authority and, as head of a household, became a complete person with all the rights and duties of his rank. Moreover, his professional career was set to gain if he had a household of his own, held social gatherings and received visitors. For all this he needed a wife who knew how to do the honours and whose afternoon teas with the wives of his business associates and colleagues did not have too little influence on his professional advancement. Of course, she did not have to cook or serve the meals herself: paid servants did that. Most bourgeois households contained kitchen staff and housemaids. It was, however, the job of the wife, relieved as she was of the burden of physical activity, to organise the work. She supervised the shopping, managed the various stages of domestic production and processing, saw to the purchase of goods which could not be homemade, and kept accounts of the expenditure.

At this point it should be remembered that a bourgeois household in the eighteenth and early nineteenth centuries was a centre of extremely complex economic activity. It was not based, as was the farming household, on the principle of self-sufficiency, since many foodstuffs and requisites had to be bought, but even then they had to be processed before use. Only very few finished items could be bought from the retailer; among them expensive, exotic luxury goods such as tea, coffee, sugar, oil and spices. Meat, on the other hand, was to be had by the slaughter of the household's own animals; it was the job of the housewife and her servants to preserve it by smoking or curing. Likewise butter was made in the home, and fruit and vegetables were preserved. Bread was baked at least every other week, and candles and soap were also produced at home.[5]

The lady of the house was expected to keep a firm grip on her housekeeping. The keys which she wore on her belt were symbolic of this. The linen cupboards and pantries were under her supervision and control, and it was considered a sign of the most shocking wastefulness and disorganisation if she delegated these rights and duties to the staff. In 1791, thirteen months after their marriage, the first criticism levelled by Professor Bürger of Göttingen at his wife related to her sloppy household management. The 'government of the house' was run not by her, but by 'slovenly maids' who had free access to all the resources. They worked 'just as they liked', whilst Elise was hardly ever to be seen in the kitchen

5. M. Freudenthal, 'Bürgerlicher Haushalt und bürgerliche Familie vom Ende des 18. bis zum Ende des 19. Jahrhunderts', in H. Rosenbaum (ed.), *Seminar: Familie und Gesellschaftsstruktur*, Frankfurt 1978, pp. 375ff.

or pantry. There was not a single trace of saving, planning or thrift as the husband's wealth and income were rapidly eaten away. Bürger, expressing the heartfelt opinions of his contemporaries, made very exacting demands when it came to his wife's economic abilities. After all, the prosperity of the family depended on them at least as much as on his earnings. 'It is incumbent on the housewife not so much to earn money, but rather to be as sparing as possible with even small amounts of her husband's earnings.' For this reason she should, for example, wash up the good china herself, so that it was not damaged by 'the paws of rough maids'. In fact, she must 'not allow the servants to manage things for themselves and without supervision at all, but rather follow them everywhere and watch every move they make'. She should inspect the kitchen, pantries and stillrooms daily, in order to 'keep an eye on everything in the house, so that perishables are kept in the recommended manner and other items will last as long as possible'.[6] A man whose wife adhered to these principles was free of all domestic cares. If, in addition, she also strove for his personal well-being, complied with his wishes and needs, and listened to his admonition and criticism, then he could be more than content with this 'easing of my wearisome life' (Bürger).

Contrary to first impressions, not only the husband profited from such an arrangement but also the wife. After all, marriage was the only acceptable thing for the daughters of the bourgeoisie. Even a woman who 'faced a limited destiny with a husband with whom she was not compatible' still had 'an enviable fate compared to that of an unmarried woman'.[7] Indeed the alternative – eking out a bleak and empty existence as an 'old maid' merely tolerated by the parents or unmarried siblings with whom she was forced to live – was not alluring. Very few opportunities existed for a woman 'from the better classes' to earn her own living. At best she could seek employment as a governess, although aristocratic applicants from good families and with social polish had a far better chance. In any case, an ancillary serving position in someone else's household offered not more but less freedom and scope than a position as a married woman, who shared her husband's social status, belonged to his 'rank' and enjoyed the same privileges as he did. In return for her running the house for him, he was obliged to provide for her in

---

6. All quotations from *Bürgers Liebe: Dokumente zu Elise Hahns und G. A. Bürgers unglücklichem Versuch, eine Ehe zu führen*, ed. H. Kinder, Frankfurt 1981, pp. 82–3.
7. Lewald, *Lebensgeschichte*, pp. 110–11.

keeping with her social standing'. Furthermore, he gave her protection and support against third parties who attacked her person, her honour or her property.

All the same, marriage was not a relationship of exchange between equals; partners did not give and take equally. This can be seen well enough from a glance at the legal provisions which governed relations between husband and wife. The Prussian Civil Code made it patently clear that 'the man is the head of the conjugal community and his decision is final in matters affecting that community.'[8] Accordingly, the wife required her husband's formal consent if she wished to 'pursue a particular career', i.e. earn money within or outside the home. Her property, her dowry, her claim to an inheritance were, as a rule, under her husband's control, although these rights could also be reserved for the wife by contract. The patriarchal structure of this marriage and family law became totally clear in the paragraphs which governed the relationship between parents and children. Although they owed both parents 'respect and obedience', children born in wedlock were subject 'primarily' to the authority of the father. He made the decisions affecting their education and training. It was only during the first four years of the child's life that the mother was responsible for its supervision and care, and she could not be deprived of this against her will. Having taken their preferences into account, the father determined his sons' future professions, and none of his children were permitted to marry without his consent. Naturally, the children and his wife bore his name; only illegitimate children bore the mother's name and in such cases the father had none of the usual rights whatsoever and also none of the duties.

The rulings of the Civil Code are not the only indications we have of the unequal position of men and women within marriage. Autobiographical reports handed down from that period also make it clear that, although marriage was important to both sexes, they occupied different positions and enjoyed different rights. For a man of the bourgeois classes, marriage represented only a part of his life. His professional life and the social contacts derived from it were at

---

8. §184 of the *'Allgemeines Landrecht für die preußischen Staaten' 1794*, quoted from the text of the law, ed. H. Hattenhauer, Frankfurt 1970. The most important provisions of family law in the *Allgemeines Landrecht* mentioned in the text are also specified in W. Hubbard, *Familiengeschichte: Materialien zur deutschen Familie seit dem Ende des 18. Jahrhunderts*, Munich 1983, pp. 45ff. See also H. Dörner, *Industrialisierung und Familienrecht: Die Auswirkungen des sozialen Wandels dargestellt an den Familienmodellen des ALR, BGB und des französischen Code civil*, Berlin 1974, pp. 31ff., and Gerhard, *Verhältnisse*.

before

least as important. The wife, on the other hand, saw marriage as the only sphere in which she had scope to act, and to which all other activities within the framework of society were linked. For her the domestic sphere, her relationship with husband and children, had to be infinitely more important and all-consuming. There may have been a positive side to this: in as much as women did not go 'out into the hostile world', there to enter the eternal contest to 'hunt down happiness' and fill the storehouse, as Schiller put it in his poem *Die Glocke* of 1799, nor were they exposed to the pressures and conflicts which governed the world where people earned a living and competed against each other. On the other hand, they had no share in the compensations and advantages of life outside the home, of its challenges and rewards in the form of successful professional careers or greater personal standing. Women possessed no money of their own, were not able to dispose of their property themselves and were therefore dependent on their husbands for everything they wanted or needed. Yet it was not only material barriers which were responsible for the fact that so few of the women of this period laid claim to a freer, more independent life; what was fitting for a woman and what was not was defined above all by social custom. Household and family duties were but an additional factor keeping a housewife and mother within her own four walls.

In this respect, a great deal can be gleaned from the letters of Sophie La Roche (1730–1807), daughter of a doctor, mother of the aforementioned Maximiliane and the wife of a high-ranking civil servant. Whilst her husband was off on extensive business and private trips, she stayed at home and looked after the five children. She had never personally met many of the friends with whom she corresponded. Her own plans to travel failed because of money or family obligations. 'To travel would have been my all-consuming passion' if 'duty' had not intervened. After her children had left home, she took care of her ailing husband and only after his death in 1788 did she gain the 'freedom to live according to my nature, something that has hitherto only been possible through my writing'. As a widow living primarily on her husband's pension, she was economically and socially independent. Remarriage was no longer fitting at her age and so for the first time she could devote herself completely to her own interests and wishes.[9]

Middle-class women spent the 'best part' of their lives bearing

9. '*Ich bin mehr Herz als Kopf*', esp. pp. 209–10, 230, 262, 311, 314–15.

and bringing up children. Statistical and biographical sources testify to the large size of bourgeois families. In Lower Saxony between 1750 and 1824, for example, educated middle-class families contained on average 6.8 children.[10] Often more than a decade passed between the first and last births. Bettina von Arnim, daughter of Maximiliane Brentano, had her first child in 1812 and her seventh in 1827; in other words she spent thirty to forty years looking after dependent children.[11] Motherhood was a lifelong duty, which became all the more important and character-moulding as the bourgeois family and sexual ideology of the late eighteenth century turned it into a profession with a high socio-cultural status. The biologically and socially defined role of the mother was virtually tailored to her body: tight-fitting and impossible to cast off.

Motherhood did not, however, mean simply work and social recognition; it also entailed substantial health risks which women accepted with fatalistic stoicism. When Sophie Mereau told Clemens Brentano of her pregnancy she did so with the words: 'To think that pain, pleasure, life and death rest entwined in one being.'[12] Childbirth without analgesics was painful, but that was not all: it could also prove fatal. A faulty foetal presentation inevitably resulted in the death of mother and child, since the techniques applied in such cases by midwives or male accoucheurs (forceps delivery and caesarian sections) were very rarely successful. Out of sixty-one births which the Augsburg obstetrician Deisch attended in the mid-eighteenth century, forty-three children and twenty-two mothers lost their lives. Of course, difficult births were relatively unusual and most women gave birth naturally, at home with the help of a neighbour, relative or midwife. The few maternity homes which existed were reserved for unmarried mothers, with whom students of obstetrics and budding midwives could gain their first practical experience.[13]

Even if she survived the birth, the mother could not yet breathe easily. Childbed held other and much greater dangers. Septic infections, and the notorious puerperal fever still not fully under-

10. von Nell, *Entwicklung*, table p. 48.
11. See the biography by I. Drewitz, *B. von Arnim*, Düsseldorf 1984, and G. Dischner, *B. von Arnim: Eine weibliche Sozialbiographie aus dem 19. Jahrhundert*, Berlin 1977.
12. *Lebe der Liebe und liebe das Leben: Der Briefwechsel von C. Brentano und S. Mereau*, ed. D. von Gersdorff, Frankfurt 1981, p. 285.
13. U. Frevert, 'Frauen und Ärzte im späten 18. und frühen 19. Jahrhundert', in A. Kuhn and J. Rüsen (eds), *Frauen in der Geschichte*, vol. II, Düsseldorf 1982, pp. 177–210.

stood), led to high mortality rates. Towards the end of the eighteenth century roughly one in twelve women in Germany died of the after-effects of childbirth.[14] A tolerant and passive outlook on all questions relating to the 'nature' of the female underlay the stoicism and resignation to their fate with which women faced the potentially fatal risks that pregnancy entailed. It was quite natural for a woman to have her first child within one or two years of her wedding and for this pattern to continue in the following years of marriage. It would certainly have been technically possible to control artificially the number of children born. Methods of contraception such as condoms and coitus interruptus were already known in the late eighteenth century, but were used mainly in extra-marital affairs. No such precautions were generally taken for 'marital embraces', where children were planned and wanted. What is more, 'nature' itself limited population growth. Nutritional problems, inadequate hygiene and medical incompetence caused high infant mortality rates, and to the people of that time it was, as Justus Möser wrote in 1786, 'an unfailing law of nature that 50 per cent of children must perish before their tenth year'.[15]

More recent demographic studies confirm this overall view, but at the same time point out that children from middle-class families were more likely to survive. 'Only' 22.4 per cent of children born to the Lower Saxon bourgeoisie in the second half of the eighteenth century died before their sixteenth birthday, just under half of them in their first year.[16] Better material conditions, and possibly more attentive care and education, kept mortality rates lower among the offspring of the bourgeois classes. Nevertheless, in the second half of the eighteenth century medical science had begun to undermine the seemingly certain laws of nature and to question their divine and natural legitimacy. Enlightenment pamphlets, home doctors and specialised guides for women outlined a complex system of rules, which would help reduce the infant mortality rate in the long term. They contained precise instructions on what to do during pregnancy, forbade the bottle-feeding of new-born babies and propagated breastfeeding as a 'most sacred maternal duty'. If a mother lavished a great deal of time and all her energy on her young

---

14. This figure is based on a study by A. E. Imhof in four provincial and rural communities in Germany between 1780 and 1899; *Die gewonnenen Jahre*, Munich 1981, p. 155. Although not without some problems, his findings can serve as a rough guide.

15. J. Möser, *Anwalt des Vaterlands* (1786), Leipzig 1978, p. 327.

16. von Nell, *Entwicklung*, table p. 63.

children, at the same time following medical instructions most meticulously, she would not, or so she was promised, lose them. Many women from the educated strata of the population heeded such advice and the pro-breastfeeding propaganda in particular seems to have had a great impact on the public. Bürger noted that his wife, a vigorous woman, 'wanted to acquire a good reputation by feeding her child herself'.[17] The subject of 'nursing mothers' comes up again and again in letters written at the time. But despite all maternal care and sacrifice, the lives of small children continued to be exposed to great risks, for medical science had nothing with which to combat serious illnesses such as smallpox, dysentery, diphtheria, measles and whooping cough.

If women had devoted themselves to the care of their infants, as up-to-date educational and medical writings demanded of them, then the death of a child must have hit them very hard indeed. The more doctors emphasised that a child's progress was dependent on the love and active care of its mother, the greater were the feelings of guilt and failure mixed with grief if the child died. So long as a woman could believe that her child had been summoned by 'the unfathomable will of God', then, lamentable though the death might be, she was not to blame. The new, secular interpretation of the world, on the other hand, charged mankind itself with the responsibility for its destiny and granted it the freedom to bring about changes. If nothing changed, then it was the fault of the incompetent, foolish and immoral individual. Sophie Mereau-Brentano was wracked with self-reproach for having entrusted her first child to a paid nurse, and felt responsible for its untimely death. During her second pregnancy she prepared herself thoroughly for the event: 'My greatest duty of all now is to take care of the new, fragile life within me. I am determined that at no time during the early stages of its life, by night or by day, will I entrust it to a stranger.' Yet even the daughter whom she tended in accordance with all the medical advice died of scarlet fever after a few weeks. Sophie Brentano imputed even this death to herself and suffered in the belief that she could not grant her husband the joys of fatherhood, which were so apparent in his brothers and brothers-in-law.[18]

'Without children', wrote Clemens Brentano to his wife in 1805, 'marriage is inconceivable.'[19] To Sophie's mind, things were the

17. Kinder (ed.), *Bürgers Liebe*, p. 76.
18. von Gersdorff (ed.), *Lebe der Liebe*, pp. 324–5 and 354.
19. Ibid., p. 352.

other way round. She accepted Clemens Brentano's proposal of marriage only when she was expecting his child; 'Nature commands it.' Although it would thwart her wishes for a free and self-determined life, the marriage seemed to her unavoidable: to give birth to and bring up an illegitimate child was unthinkable in bourgeois society at the time. Though the ban on pre- and extra-marital sex was no longer observed in certain literary and intellectual circles, the taboo on illegitimacy remained unchallenged. Mother and child would have been stigmatised, and exiled from 'genteel society' for ever. When in 1793 the widowed Caroline Böhmer discovered, after a brief romance with an officer of the French Revolution, that she was pregnant, she was gripped with panic, for 'the shame, indeed the scandal' would have meant a major 'turn for the worse' in her life and that of her eight-year-old daughter. With the help of some good friends she hid herself away in a small, remote country town for months before the birth, and found foster parents for the new-born baby so that the 'child of ardour and night' would remain hidden from the world.[20]

In contrast to farming and rural communities, in which pre-marital sex was not taboo and illegitimate children were in many cases only legitimised years later when their parents married,[21] in the bourgeois classes great care was taken to ensure that daughters were 'untouched' when they married. While it was acceptable for the much older bridegroom to have had experience of women from lower down the social order, the virginity of the bride was guarded like treasure. Her husband took her 'pure and innocent' into his possession and could be perfectly sure that she enjoyed his amorous skills without preconceptions or any possibility of comparison.

That pre- and extra-marital sex did occasionally take place, however, despite all bans and controls, is clear from the existence of so-called maternity hospitals for those who were secretly pregnant. In Cologne, for example, there was an establishment sponsored by the Prussian government and run by the director of the local school of midwifery, where 'respectable' women paid a high daily residential charge and awaited their confinement without fear of 'unwarranted investigation'. They lived in comfort and luxury and could take their own female attendants with them. Silk gowns and veils esured that they were not recognised. Immediately after birth the

20. Behrens (ed.), *Frauenbriefe der Romantik*, pp. 282ff.
21. M. Mitterauer, *Ledige Mütter: Zur Geschichte unehelicher Geburten in Europa*, Munich 1983. In Prussia between 1816 and 1820 7.1 per cent of all children were born out of wedlock: Hubbard, *Familiengeschichte*, p. 109.

infants were sent to orphanages or to wet nurses, where they usually died after a few months from defective diet and inadequate care.[22] We do not know how well patronised these establishments were. The fact that their business flourished suggests that there was a lively market for their services. We also know nothing about the age and origin of the mothers-to-be, but the high cost of the more or less voluntary internment limited the clientele to a small, wealthy circle. So although it was not usual, it is obvious that even bourgeois women indulged in pre- and extra-marital sex, the 'outcomes' of which had to be hidden.

22. L. von Rönne and H. Simon, *Das Medicinal-Wesen des Preußischen Staates*, vol. II, Breslau 1846, pp. 486ff.

5
The Scope for Freedom

Violation of the rules governing bourgeois family ethics and sexual morality was not exactly commonplace in the late eighteenth century, but it was not unknown. The new norms regulating relations between the sexes and the new notions of male and female behaviour met with resistance from time to time, and in some cases this 'non-conformism' is even recorded first hand. In letters written by Sophie La Roche, Rahel Varnhagen and Sophie Mereau, to name but a few, we have documents which sketch out the lives of women who did not blindly accept prescribed ways.

Sophie La Roche was one of the first middle-class women to publish her literary writing. Her books and reviews made her a celebrity and her Coblenz salon was a meeting place for writers, artists and courtiers. The life she led was far from isolated and introspective, and yet she saw herself first and foremost as a wife to her husband and mother of her children. She enjoyed earning her own money to pay for her clothes, books and travels, but at the same time had to ask her husband's permission to spend this money on her private needs. She harboured resentment against her father for denying her an education under a well-known scholar, and continually bemoaned the fact 'that I have a heart instead of a brain'. On the other hand, she was proud to be a good housewife, who herself understood the art of cookery, delegated work to the servants and supervised them, kept the accounts accurately and conscientiously, sewed or embroidered while her husband read aloud from the newspaper. Although with her literary career she had clearly and visibly stepped outside the female sphere, her novels, aimed at bourgeois women and girls, her letters and educational articles extolled self-contentment and the virtuous fulfilment of duty.

Similar contradictions can be found in the biographies of other middle-class women who were able to boast 'public careers' in the eighteenth century. Disregarding social conventions, their aim in life was personal happiness; they were not trying to blaze the trail for other women. One of the most famous is Caroline (1763–1809), born Michaelis, widowed by Böhmer, divorced from Schlegel and married to Schelling. She lost her first husband in 1788 after four years of marriage, and their three children died in 1788, 1789 and 1800. Her widow's pension allowed her considerable freedom. She travelled, lived through the Jacobin Republic in Mainz in 1792, was taken prisoner by Prussian troops and shunned by society because of her republican views, inspired Friedrich Schlegel and in 1796 married his brother August Wilhelm. Together they translated Shakespeare and took part in the social life of the Romantic circle at Jena. Soon, however, she fell in love with a professor of philosophy by the name of Schelling, who was twelve years her junior and whom she married in 1803 after her divorce from Schlegel. Despite the turbulent and unconventional course of her life, she upheld the principles of female duty and utterly condemned those who violated them. In 1791 she wrote of Elise Bürger, who was in the habit of deceiving a husband nearly twice her age with younger men, 'I feel very sorry for Bürger. A sensible woman, more suited to his years, would have made a respectable man of him, but now his household is threatened with total collapse because she concerns herself with nothing, not even her child. Women should not have lovers because they so easily neglect their children and their household duties.'[1]

She remained silent, however, about Bürger's numerous affairs (he publicly vaunted his libertinage). The different standards of behaviour permitted to men and women were evidently accepted even by Caroline with her 'penalty of independence'. Furthermore, she felt that other women should not necessarily be obliged or allowed to demand individual happiness, as she did herself. The famous Romanticist was a long way from seeing herself as a pioneer of women's emancipation.

Her friend and rival Dorothea, née Mendelssohn, likewise ventured to take only limited steps beyond the bounds of social convention, though they were steps which required great personal courage. Born in 1764, she was the daughter of the famous Jewish representative of the Enlightenment, Moses Mendelssohn. He gave her an exhaustive education and then married her off at the age of nineteen to a banker named Veit. After sixteen years of marriage she left her husband, by whom she had two children, got divorced and went to live with Friedrich Schlegel in Jena. At that time such

1. Quoted in E. Kleßmann, *Caroline*, Munich 1979, p. 85. See also the biography by G. Dischner, *Caroline und der Jenaer Kreis*, Berlin 1979, the volume of her letters *'Lieber Freund'*, and the selection in *Frauenbriefe der Romantik*, pp. 247–328.

behaviour was revolutionary, a scandal. She and Schlegel lived together unmarried for several years. His income was insufficient to support her, so she herself wrote, and used the money she earned from these writings (which were mostly published either anonymous, or under Schlegel's name) for housekeeping. Eventually in 1804 she became converted to Christianity and married Schlegel. What set her apart from her fellow women was the consistent and thorough-going nature of the course of action she followed. Whereas other women resigned themselves to the fate of a less than happy marriage, she followed her convictions and gave up a materially secure, socially respected life for a love affair that was libertarian and without ties – or so it must have appeared to the outside world. Naturally public opinion was against her, and gossip thrived. Looking back, she was almost shocked herself that 'when already middle-aged I turned my back on everything I disliked, seizing everything that my passionate heart desired'. Despite this courageous step which, as she wrote three weeks after her divorce, 'freed me from a long period of slavery', Dorothea Mendelssohn was not a woman to cast all bourgeois conventions to the winds. In her relationship with Friedrich Schlegel she showed an unmistakeable propensity to self-sacrifice, and complete devotion to and accommodation of the man and his needs. Although she herself worked as a writer and supported him with her royalties, in her eyes he was a master whom she idolised; she also sanctioned the supremacy of the man in marriage in general. 'Women can be made unhappy by the unreasonable rule of men', she wrote, 'but without this rule they are, without exception, lost for ever.'[2]

Formally, at least, a woman was entitled to revolt against her husband's 'unreasonable rule' and to separate from him. But marriage was understood at the time to be insoluble in principle, and more than anything the fact that it was rooted in religious ritual confirmed the non-temporal nature of this 'most holy relationship, on which, and on the continuation of which, civil society as a moral society is founded'.[3] In the eighteenth century, however, philosophy and jurisprudence developed other interpretations inspired by natural law, the most famous of which originated with the Königsberg scholar Immanuel Kant. He defined marriage as a contract concluded between two people of opposite sex which

---

2. A selection of her letters is reprinted in *Frauenbriefe der Romantik*, pp. 329–69.
3. E. Brandes, *Betrachtungen über den Zeitgeist in Deutschland in den letzten Decennien des vorigen Jahrhunderts* (first pub. Hanover 1808), Kronberg 1977, p. 197.

regulated the use of sexual characteristics.[4] The Prussian Civil Code defined the main purpose of marriage a little less drastically as being 'the procreation and raising of children' for the 'mutual benefit' of the marriage partners. As early as in the reign of Frederick II (1740–86) marriage laws in Prussia were increasingly oriented towards the principles of the contract theory of marriage based on natural law, and formally made separation easier by codifying numerous grounds for divorce. Furthermore, as sovereign, the king took the liberty of granting divorce over the head of the courts whenever he was obviously justified in so doing. Not least in the interests of population policy, he endorsed the dissolution of marriages in which the marriage partners lived 'in permanent bitterness against each other' and 'therefore procreated no children together'.[5] The Civil Code regarded the dissolution of childless marriages as unproblematic and established the grounds for divorce in such cases as 'insurmountable antipathy'. It only became complicated when there were children. By no means every case of bad behaviour entitled someone to a divorce. It was up to the courts to decide how restrictively or liberally they interpreted the statutory provisions and decrees issued by sovereigns. Adultery, wilful desertion, attempted murder, insanity, impotence, and 'persistent' and 'obdurate denial of conjugal duties' were all 'substantial' grounds for divorce. 'Less serious behaviour' and verbal abuse were inadequate grounds, as were 'drunkenness, wastefulness and improper housekeeping'. Paragraph 703 of the Civil Code was a kind of blanket clause which accepted 'incompatibility and quarrelsomeness' as grounds for divorce if 'as a result of it the life or health of the innocent party is endangered'.[6]

In terms of formal law, then, a marriage in the late eighteenth century was not necessarily a lifelong union, ended only by death, as the young wife Caroline Böhmer had supposed: 'I no longer look forward to a rosy future. My lot is cast.' Courts could grant divorce, and did, though only rarely. Professor Bürger of Göttingen caused a great sensation when he filed for divorce in 1792 and accused his wife, Elise, of several cases of adultery. The judges found Elise, who

4. See B. Duden, 'Das schöne Eigentum: Zur Herausbildung des bürgerlichen Frauenbildes an der Wende vom 18. zum 19. Jahrhundert', *Kursbuch*, 48, 1977, pp. 125–40.
5. Order of council of Frederick II of 22 May 1783, quoted in E. Hubrich, *Das Recht der Ehescheidung in Deutschland*, Berlin 1891, p. 186.
6. See the complete text of the law in Hattenhauer (ed.), *Allgemeines Landrecht*, pp. 367ff., and excerpts in Hubbard, *Familiengeschichte*, pp. 50–1; Hubrich, *Recht*, pp. 186–204.

admitted her affairs, to be the guilty party and granted the separation. Whereas Bürger was then entitled to remarry, his ex-wife was denied this right. She was also unable to reclaim the dowry which she had brought into the marriage since, as she testified under pressure from Bürger, 'my neglectful housekeeping and excessive expenditure have also been very injurious to my former husband'.[7] However, the ban on marriage pronounced by the Göttingen judges on guilty parties in a divorce was no longer in keeping with the spirit of the times. Other states, such as Prussia, Württemburg and the Electorate of Saxony, were more liberal in this respect.[8]

Although the relevant sections of the law were worded in a neutral manner as regards gender, in practice the right to file for divorce meant very different things for men and for women. Whereas a divorced man retained his position as a citizen (job, income, house and home), the woman shed a relationship which had afforded her protection, maintenance and social respect. With no husband and, in addition, the stigma of divorce, she was virtually an outcast from a society which did not accept women as people with rights of their own, but only as wards of their fathers or husbands. Her economic and social position was, as a rule, extremely precarious. Even if her ex-husband paid her an allowance, this was unlikely to be enough to maintain her previous standard of living. Austerity followed social isolation. Friends 'of the family' retreated; even if the wife was not the guilty party in the divorce people kept their distance. Unless a divorced woman had money of her own or part of her dowry remained, she had no alternative but either to return to live with her parents or relatives, or to look around for an income for herself – an unpromising prospect, given the lack of employment and career opportunities.

Only very few women managed to pursue an independent career in those days. After her divorce Elise Bürger joined a theatre company and led a thoroughly non-bourgeois and disreputable demi-monde life as a travelling actress. Sophie Mereau, divorced in 1801 from Jena professor of law Friedrich Mereau after eight years of marriage, earned her living by writing. In addition to the annuity of 200 Taler which her husband settled on her and their daughter, her poems, translations and short stories brought in enough money for her to be able to live 'in style'. Unlike Caroline Schlegel, who remarried immediately after her divorce, Sophie Mereau enjoyed

7. Kinder (ed.), *Bürgers Liebe*, p. 150.
8. D. Schwab, *Grundlagen und Gestalt der staatlichen Ehegesetzgebung in der Neuzeit bis zum Beginn des 19. Jahrhunderts*, Bielefeld 1967, p. 244.

her new-found freedom and held out long and hard against a second marriage. After she had married Clemens Brentano her literary work came to a standstill. Only when her husband was away did she find time for it.

As an eighteen-year-old Caroline Michaelis too had dreamed of a life without marriage: 'If I were quite my own boss and could also live in decent and pleasant circumstances, I would far rather not marry at all, but seek to be of use to the world in some other way.'[9] The above-average education which she had received as the daughter of a professor had awoken in her the need to 'play a greater role' and not to waste away like 'Cinderella' between kitchen and nursery. Like her, a handful of other middle-class women managed at least for a while to step outside the narrow field of their domesticity. Unusually well educated and ambitious, they secured for themselves a place in that grey area, the world that was no longer private and yet was not quite public, represented by the salon. Despite its aristocratic image, the salon was a genuinely *bürgerliche* institution to the extent that it did not select its members according to rank resulting from birth or office, but acknowledged only 'educated figures' who had individual merits. The normal social barriers between the aristocracy and the bourgeoisie, Jews and Christians, men of letters and merchants, officers and civilians, were blurred in the salon; women too had the chance to be accepted as individuals and to win respect. As hostesses they gathered a public around themselves which not only paid homage to female beauty but also honoured intelligence, spontaneity and great imaginativeness.[10]

The most famous contemporary salon was that of the Jewess and merchant's daughter from Berlin, Rahel Levin, who between 1790 and 1806 received her guests in an attic in her father's house. Rahel was an autodidact and free-thinker, receptive to anything new and original, interested in art and literature, philosophy, aesthetics and politics. Neither rich nor beautiful, her keen intellect sparkled and she captivated her visitors with her ability to listen closely and speak her mind plainly. Financially secure after her father's death, she lived a free and independent life with many intellectual friends, but longed nevertheless for that which she did not have: a husband and children. Her Jewish origins and her great intelligence and edu-

---

9. Damm (ed.), *'Lieber Freund'*, pp. 77, 92.
10. I. Drewitz, *Berliner Salons: Gesellschaft und Literatur zwischen Aufklärung und Industriezeitalter*, Berlin 1965; D. Hertz, 'Salonières and Literary Women in Late Eighteenth-Century Berlin', *New German Critique*, 5, 1978, pp. 97–108.

cation, however, frightened off many potential suitors. Eventually, in 1814 at the age of forty-three, she married August Varnhagen von Ense, a diplomat fourteen years her junior, in order that she might finally enjoy a bourgeois lifestyle. Her second Berlin salon (1819–33) took place not in a garret but in an imposing villa, and although she occasionally bemoaned the procession of visitors, she kept open house because 'it makes me think and inspires me'.[11]

The fact that women were inspired and could be inspired, that they were trying out 'thinking for themselves' (Rahel Levin) and disregarding preconceived ideas and tradition, was closely linked to the spirit of the Enlightenment, which prevailed upon the educated middle classes more than anyone. 'There are three things', wrote the Hanoverian civil servant Ernst Brandes in 1808, 'which, particularly in the final decade of the last century, had an effect on the spirit of the age in Germany; (1) the French Revolution; (2) the notion of the constant progress of man; (3) the rapid spread of news and ideas through newspapers, journals and leaflets.'[12] Optimistic notions of progress, new forms of information and communication, the experience of rapid political change – all these brought turbulence and unrest in their wake. To some contemporaries everything seemed to be disintegrating, and nothing seemed capable of withstanding rational criticism. The dethronement of the patriarchal *Hausvater* corresponded to the loss of loyalty experienced by the absolutist sovereigns, the enthusiasm for republican forms of state accompanied the repudiation of the female vocation and the rebellion against marriage and family. Though such fears were extremely exaggerated, there were a few women who sought 'room to take their own steps' (Rahel Varnhagen) in the lee of the spirit of the time. Ambition, inspiration, improvement – these were the leitmotifs of bourgeois awakening which inspired them to rebel against the constraints of their domestic 'vocation' and, not without compromise, strive for individually more satisfying lives. This has rarely been expressed so clearly and coherently as by Rahel Varnhagen when she wrote to her sister in 1819:

Whereas for men employment is, at least in their own eyes, not only to be regarded as important, but is also something which flatters their ambition and gives them a chance to get on, whilst being inspired by social contact;

11. Reproduced in *Frauenbriefe der Romantik*, p. 243. On Rahel Varnhagen see the biography by H. Arendt, *Rahel Varnhagen: The Life of a Jewish Woman*, New York 1974, and R. Varnhagen, *Gesammelte Werke*, ed. K. Feilchenfeldt, 10 vols, Munich 1983.
12. Brandes, *Betrachtungen*, p. 180.

we only ever have before us the fragments which pull us down, the small tasks and services which must relate to our husbands' standing and needs. It contradicts the principles of anthropology for people to imagine that our minds are different and made up of different needs or that we could, for example, derive lasting pleasure from the lives of our husbands and sons alone. Such ideas arise only from the assumption that a woman has nothing more important in her mind than the wants and needs of her husband in the outside world, or the talents and wishes of her children. If that were the case then *every* marriage would be, *simply* as such, the highest human condition. But it is *not* so. Of course, one loves, shares and cherishes the wishes of one's own family, submits to them, makes them one's greatest worry and most pressing preoccupation. But they cannot fulfil us, rally us, rest us in readiness to further activity and suffering. Nor can they strengthen and invigorate us throughout our lives.'[13]

Yet even women who cast such a critical eye on the world around them could not imagine a life without marriage. What they had in mind was less a marriage 'as such' than a formally legitimized relationship based on love, with all the particular meaning which Romantic writers bestowed on that word: passionate devotion to the other person, fusion into a homogeneous whole and at the same time respect for both identities. That was the scheme of Romantic love formulated primarily in works such as Goethe's *Werther* (1774) and Friedrich Schlegel's *Lucinde* (1799). Clemens Brentano also longed for a 'Romantic woman' with whom he could lead a free, poetic life 'quite secretly'.[14] Friendship, sensuousness, passion and harmony merged together in what Romanticism called love, and the marriage which embraced such a love was a union of independent, individual people responsible for themselves. This daring blueprint envisaged free people who distanced themselves from preconceived ideas and shunned regulation by others. A Romantic marriage could not function with men and women who accepted their 'sexual characteristics' as given and adhered to existing ways. These characteristics would have to be kept in proportion; the man would have to control any 'unbridled hunger for mastery' and the women avoid 'selfless devotion'; people would have to make every effort to resist natural temperaments. 'Only independent femininity, only gentle masculinity are good and noble,' wrote Schlegel. In particular women bound by 'nature' and 'circumstance' to a very restrictive domesticity had to struggle, with the help of privileged men, against being entangled in this way, and rise to their 'true' vocation: namely to become human beings capable of independent thought, action

13. Behrens (ed.), *Frauenbriefe der Romantik*, p. 239.
14. Gersdorff (ed.), *Lebe der Liebe*, pp. 188–9, 192–3.

and desire.[15]

The Romantic notion of femininity, which sought to moderate, if not completely neutralise, the polarity of sexual characteristics and press for the 'perfeçtion of masculinity and feminity into humanity as a whole' (Schlegel), was linked to the historical background in two ways. On the one hand, the notion was inconceivable without the example of those women seeking 'room to take their own steps'. The young writers who rebelled at the turn of the century against a bourgeois 'machine-made' mentality, against rationally calculating 'cold emotion' (Schlegel) and the 'miserable, enlightened times' (Brentano), enthused about the courageous and obstreperous women who, according to *Lucinde*, 'abandoned all deference and severed all ties' and lived 'freely and independently'.[16] They saw them as the embodiment of that 'inclination towards the Romantic' which they regarded as the antithesis and critique of a world ossified by convention and rational utilitarianism. Taking these women as their model, they devised the concept of combined sexual characteristics, which draped female striving for independence and identity in a cloak of philosophical legitimation and evolutionary historicism. However, it was precisely this philosophical model which made it difficult to enshrine as general principles the individual endeavours which women were making to bring about change. For the Romanticists, change took place in the spiritual and idealistic realms, so the spiritual structure of mankind, above all that of women, had to be reshaped. Demands such as those made by von Hippel were ignored and no one gave any thought to the actual conditions responsible for this spiritual structure. The legal, social, economic and political inequality between men and women was not important. The crucial factor was the fusion of characteristics within the symbiotic relationship which partners had to make every effort to create.

The Romantic concept failed to meet acclaim and its impact was minimal. For one thing, contemporary debate did not take up the idea of the unification of femininity and masculinity into humanity; for another, the model of Romantic life and love did not become fashionable. The extreme nature of the 'pair' ideal, the couple who directed their energies inwards on the nurturing of a relationship which could be harmoniously enhanced by children born of love: this must have seemed incredibly alien to the people of the eight-

15. See F. Schlegel, *Theorie der Weiblichkeit*, ed. W. Menninghaus, Frankfurt 1983, pp. 61, 88ff.
16. F. Schlegel, *Lucinde*, Stuttgart 1973, p. 70.

eenth century. Even the essentially moderate Enlightenment notion of the family was at loggerheads with prevailing social custom; the bourgeois marriage of the time was bound to be impervious to 'rational love', since the normal age difference between husband and wife was at least ten years, and completely separate areas of experience did not help to promote closeness, understanding and the 'inner union of souls' between marriage partners. So what chance had Romantic love? It was even further removed from reality. Young girls may well have dreamed of it, but their parents did not choose sons-in-law for their good looks, charm or sensuousness. They valued more useful virtues.

Compared with the traditional type of male–female relations, which still held good in bourgeois circles, the Enlightenment model represented for women a more attractive proposition. Their role as 'companion' qualified them as educable individuals and broke with their restricted position as keeper of a household. Perceptibly greater value was placed on their achievements in educating their children. The importance placed on emotionality and intimacy, and the emphasis on (more rational) love in match-making, granted women too, as of right, a greater freedom of choice, relaxed social convention and left more scope for individuality and personal development. All this was theoretically on offer, but theory seldom corresponded to reality. Only a few men and women succeeded even partially in constructing their lives on the model and in having a 'marriage of companions', the focus of which was, despite the separate spheres in which they moved, an emotionally and intellectually satisfying marital relationship for both partners. Even in the early Romantic circles of the literary and scientific intelligentsia the experiment of 'gentle masculinity' and 'independent femininity' was short-lived; Novalis claimed still to understand only nursery, kitchen, garden, cellar, dining room, bedroom, guestroom, attic and storeroom as the 'female sphere'.[17] The Romantic idea of community tried out in Jena and Heidelberg, in which both sexes had a share, was replaced in 1811 by the Christian German Dining Society (*Christlich-deutsche Tischgesellschaft*), which strictly excluded women and where Johann Gottlieb Fichte was able to lecture on his theories on the 'almost unlimited subjugation of the wife to the will of the husband' in marriage.[18]

17. Novalis (Friedrich von Hardenberg), 'Über Frauen und Weiblichkeit', in Schlegel, *Theorie*, p. 159.
18. On Fichte's concept of marriage and feminity see H. Schröder, *Die Rechtlosigkeit der Frau im Rechtsstaat, dargestellt am Allgemeinen Preußischen Landrecht,*

The late eighteenth century, then, was a period in which various conceptions of bourgeois femininity competed with each other. Most bourgeois families were like that of Christoph Martin Wieland. Frau Dorothea concerned herself with the large household and her many children, and anticipated her husband's every wish. She took no active part in his professional and social life, restricting herself exclusively to the domestic sphere. Henriette Schleiermacher represented another type of woman. She regarded herself not primarily as a housewife and mother, but as an intellectual companion to her husband. For her, marriage was not a productive relationship based on the division of labour, but a means through which both partners could together develop into more fully-rounded human beings.[19] Those women who took seriously the semantics of love as defined by bourgeois discourse on the family and marriage set themselves similar targets, and ended relationships which did not comply with the new code. Viewing it from the perspective of the late twentieth century, these women's quest for individual happiness and fulfilment seems to have been incomplete, obstructed, and artificially brought to a standstill. In the German middle classes of the late eighteenth century, women such as Elise Bürger, Sophie Mereau, Caroline Michaelis or Dorothea Mendelssohn were regarded as revolutionaries who opposed convention and custom, and claimed the 'right to say *I*' (von Hippel) to which, in fact, only men were entitled. They were outsiders, lone warriors, and yet also products of a society barely able to conceal the systematic contradiction between its programme of universal human rights and its insistence on a specific 'female estate' unaffected by this programme. It was precisely this ambivalence which enabled a few women from the rising middle classes to deviate from that strict moral code which Sophie La Roche had continued to honour and used as a defence against her deviatory dreams and desires: 'The most worthy souls of all are those who faithfully carry out the duties set before them by God.'[20]

---

am Bürgerlichen Gesetzbuch und an J. G. Fichtes Grundlage des Naturrechts, Frankfurt 1979, and Duden, 'Eigentum'.

19. G. E. Jensen, 'H. Schleiermacher: A Woman in a Traditional Role', in J. C. Fout (ed.), *German Women in the Nineteenth Century: A Social History*, New York 1984, pp. 88–103.

20. *'Ich bin mehr Herz als Kopf'*, p. 249. E. Walter, in *Schrieb oft, von Mägde Arbeit müde*, Düsseldorf 1985, recounts the lives of eleven female authors born between 1760 and 1770.

II
The Nineteenth Century

6
The Biedermeier Period

The enthusiasm for innovation in male–female relations waned just as quickly as the intellectual excitement of the Romantics – and with them of large sections of the bourgeoisie – for the French revolution had been stilled by Jacobin terror. After Napoleon's army had occupied German territory, thoughts turned to the search for national identity. There was no place for the Romantic ideal of harmonious, fully developed personalities in the new hierarchical values of loyalty to the crown, Christianity, and 'true Germanness'. Divisions between male and female preserves were drawn more and more sharply, and the catalogue of womanly duties regulated down to the finest detail. The philosophical and political debates following the 'wars of Liberation' are near-perfect examples of this process. The model of the family and marriage that emerged fitted neatly into the new political climate of Restoration, and drew on the strict gender-specific differentiation of roles and characters of the pre-Romantic age without, however, incorporating the products of the Enlightenment and doctrine of natural laws. Thus in 1820, the philosopher Georg Wilhelm Friedrich Hegel polemicised against Kant's 'crude' notion of degrading marriage 'to the level of a contract for reciprocal use.' To his mind, it was equally reprehensible to equate love and marriage, as the Romantics did: 'Passionate love and marriage are two different things.' Marriage was essentially an 'ethical relationship', which placed it on a plane above the 'transient, fickle and purely subjective'. As the foundation and germ cell of the state, what marriage needed was long-term stability immune to the vicissitudes of emotions and sensibilities. Its moral purpose was, moreover, obvious: it should be 'regarded as in principle indissoluble'. Since, however, feelings were always present, every marriage could potentially end in divorce. Thus state legislation 'must make its dissolution as difficult as possible and uphold the right of the ethical order against caprice'.[1]

1. G. W. F. Hegel, *Philosophy of Right*, trans. T. Knox, Oxford 1967, §§161–9

It was not only among philosophers that the ethical, organic concept of marriage and family took firm root. Theologians, too, defended it. In the years before 1848, antipathy towards the liberal divorce law of the Prussian Civil Code (*Allgemeines Landrecht*) turned into practical action as both the Catholic and Protestant clergy increasingly refused to marry divorcees.[2] From the 1840s onwards the Prussian Ministry of Justice was drawing up plans to make divorce far more difficult. There was to be a drastic cut in the number of legitimate grounds for divorce, and adultery by the woman was to be more severely punished than if the man was the guilty party. After all, argued von Savigny, the Minister of Justice, in 1845, it was 'in the nature of the sexes that the woman is generally far more culpable. The value of a woman lies primarily in her moral and sexual purity, and if she loses this, she forsakes her dignity and the harmony of marriage and home, and sacrifices the upbringing of her children.'[3] In 1808 a councillor of the Royal Prussian Supreme Court opined, on the other hand, that if a man, a being by nature 'created to take the world by storm and endowed with unbridled passions', indulged in an affair or two, he should not be judged fundamentally to have damaged his marriage.[4] However, the existence of two sets of rules for appraising male and female behaviour was not only justified by nature: the state, too, had a supreme interest in maintaining and protecting the family as one of its 'basic props' (von Savigny). Since, as Hegel claimed, the woman's 'substantive destiny' was found through the family, her infidelity shook the very foundations of this set of relationships. The unfaithful man, on the other hand, who according to von Savigny 'belongs to the world through many more different channels', may well shock his wife, but not the social order.[5]

In the debate before 1848 over reform of the marriage law, arguments of both an ideological and a pragmatic political nature

---

(see also Hegel's additions and marginal notes in *Werke*, vol. 7: *Grundlinien der Philosophie des Rechts oder Naturrecht und Staatswissenschaft im Grundrisse*, Frankfurt, 1970).

2. Hubrich, *Recht der Ehescheidung*, pp. 221–31.

3. Quoted in Gerhard, *Verhältnisse*, pp. 451–2.

4. F. A. F. von Greveniz, *Unterricht zur Kenntniß der vorzüglichsten und wichtigsten Abweichungen der gesetzlichen Vorschriften des Code Napoléon von den in den neuerlich abgetretenen preußischen Provinzen sowohl den deutschen, als polnischen, bisher gültig gewesenen*, Leipzig 1808, p. 66.

5. A draft divorce law proposed by von Savigny and von Gerlach ran up against resistance from both the public and the administration, but law on divorce procedure was made more stringent during the 1840s. See D. Blasius, *Ehescheidung in Deutschland 1794–1945*, Göttingen 1987, esp. pp. 58ff.

were combined in a most revealing way. As far as the male of the species was concerned, predestined as he was to 'take the world by storm', it was natural that he should shake off the bonds of the complex social net of the 'whole household', and through his role as a citizen and professional enter into contact with numerous individuals and institutions. The woman's place in the family was, meanwhile, justified by the claim that she had 'always' been responsible for the kitchen, the children and the garden; indeed nature had selected her for this. Her sexual characteristics determined her for a life limited to constant care and sacrifice for the good of her husband and their children. Her happiness was as intimately bound up with the family as her identity was consumed by it. Thus, as politicians of social and legal affairs before 1848 never ceased to maintain, for women at least, marriage represented far more than a mere contractual relationship. For men too it was no doubt important, but not as necessary and dominant. Marriage and the family provided him with emotional support and ensured the continued existence of his 'household'. But his personal identity and social position were located in the 'actual substantive life of the state, in learning and so forth, as well as in labour and struggle with the external world and with himself'.[6]

According to the ideology of the Restoration period, the family was first and foremost a moral, organic natural unit into which individuals were woven,[7] and as such it was addressed mainly to women. It is obvious that in order to find a counterbalance to the dynamic trends attendant upon the male sphere – trends which were increasingly becoming part of women's experiences – the intact, indestructible family bond was evoked as the 'truly complete and fully-rounded entity' (*wahre Gesamtpersönlichkeit*),[8] and raised to the status of the foundation stone of both the liberal and the conservative state. As the external world changed more rapidly and radically (one only has to think of the revolutionary innovation of the railway after 1835, or progress in industry and technology), in other words, as men's professional and public activities grew more and more animated, so the disparities between the family life of women and the vocational orientation of men became more distinct. While the role of the middle-class man, armed with ambition and the prospect of success, was to step out into the world, discovering

6. Hegel, *Philosophy of Right*, §166.
7. Schwab, 'Familie', pp. 290–1.
8. *Das Staats-Lexikon: Encyklopädie der sämtlichen Staatswissenschaften für alle Stände*, vol. IV, Altona 1846, p. 592.

and changing it, his wife was faced with maintaining equilibrium in the family, seeing to repetitive daily chores, and ensuring that she herself functioned like clockwork. Upheaval, movement, 'progress': all these were to be found in the world beyond the front door; the family was expected to stick by its old ways.

In the light of this gender-specific segmentation of life worlds in bourgeois society, the picture that historiography has painted of the Biedermeier period suddenly becomes distorted and blurred. The term 'Biedermeier' derives from the 1850s, and is a derogatory and mocking word used to describe the lifestyle and culture of the bourgeoisie in the Restoration era. It holds that the bourgeoisie, seeing that policies hostile to liberal ideas and supportive of the old order had succeeded in staving off middle-class aspirations for political representation and participation, retreated in a mood of resignation into the inner sanctum of the family, there to follow the way of simple domesticity. The devotion and loving care that the bourgeois patriarch lavished upon his wife and children is presumed to have offset the disappointment he felt as a result of political immobility. However, a closer look gives us some grounds for doubting the validity of such a theory. The stolid figure of the archetypal bourgeois male, surrounded by his family, wrapped in a comfy gown, enjoying his middle-class wealth with an air of self-satisfaction, is much more a blurred image of ideology. It is, admittedly, the case that the middle classes were excluded from political power (in Prussia at least, although between 1818 and 1820 constitutions had been adopted in the southern German states). They could bring their influence to bear on affairs of state only through their positions in the civil service. However, although the press was censored, and 'demagogues' persecuted, even the Age of Restoration had its bourgeois public sphere, one which was particularly colourful and varied for the very reason that political abstinence was the order of the day. In other words, the average Herr Biedermeier did not only sit around in the warmth of his living room, flanked on one side by his wife busily doing her needlework, and on the other by his respectably attired children. His prime preoccupation was his business, and when his working day was over, he was involved in organisations which pursued the most varied aims. Besides bodies whose concerns were education and welfare, or the promotion of trade and business, the period saw the formation of cultural, religious, scientific, military and athletic associations, as well as professional and economic organisations. Merchants, doctors and master craftsmen acted as honorary functionaries in local welfare schemes for the poor, raised money for the civic museum, and improved their fitness on the parallel bars.[9]

If the image of Biedermeier domesticity and idyllic family life applied to anyone at all, then it was to the females. Middle-class wives and daughters really were almost exclusively immersed in the household, making the family into what it was supposed to be: a site of well-ordered intimacy, where one could sit in contemplative peace and relax in complete comfort. The face the family showed to the outside world was one of sensibility, love and tenderness. The impression was that work – measured in time and money – was performed only by the man in his job. In order to keep familial and vocational spheres quite separate, 'work' was not permitted in the home. Be that as it may, if any man wanted to find out how important his wife's economic qualities were for the family's wealth, he only had to look at the household accounts. This ambivalence – work was necessary but forbidden to appear as such – reinforced the widely accepted notion that a woman sought her identity only through love of her husband, a love which inspired her to carry out all her tasks with ease, charm and a happy song. Accordingly, men praised the 'delightful virtues' of their wives, the 'grace and effortlessness' (Rousseau) with which they went about their domestic duties, and women boasted the fact that 'everything always had to proceed in its calm and silent way; the noise of industry should never be heard, and others were not to notice that there was too much to do.'[10] They subtly transformed domestic chores into 'pleasant business spiced with the cheerfulness and lively chatter of girls' (Otto-Peters). A classic description of the aesthetic sight of a woman working is to be found in Goethe's *Wilhelm Meister's Travels*, published in 1821:

With the right hand she turns the wheel and stretches out as far and as high as she can reach, whereby beautiful movements come into play, and a slim figure, by graceful turns of the body and the rounded fulness of the arms, shows itself to a very great advantage; the position ... gives a very picturesque contrast, so that our finest ladies would have no need to fear a loss of real attractiveness and grace, if they would for once take to the spinning-wheel instead of the guitar.[11]

Converting work into something charming and loving was made

9. Nipperdey, 'Verein'; Hardtwig, 'Strukturmerkmale'.

10. L. Otto-Peters, *Frauenleben im Deutschen Reich*, Leipzig 1876, quoted in Gerhard, *Verhältnisse*, p. 284.

11. J. W. von Goethe, *Wilhelm Meister's Travels*, trans. E. Bell, London 1892, pp. 316–17.

all the easier because the more arduous housework, such as washing, scrubbing, cleaning ovens and ironing, was entrusted to servants and charwomen. In the first half of the nineteenth century, the middle-class household did not actually produce its own consumer goods, but purchased and stored raw or semi-finished products which it would then spend a great deal of time processing. Most families of the bourgeoisie kept one or two kitchen or parlour maids who were responsible for dirty and heavy work. Herr Fontane, for example, was a chemist and his household had seven members, including four children, and an apprentice chemist; in the early 1830s they employed one housekeeper, one cook, two housemaids and a coachman. On special occasions, such as when geese or pigs were being slaughtered, they were joined by 'a contingent of old women, perhaps four of five of them, who the rest of the time would eke out their existence by taking in washing or even weeding gardens'.[12] Apart from purely economic exigencies, delegating more menial jobs to subordinates was part of bourgeois lifestyle. A bourgeois family could not possibly dispense with servants and hope to retain social status. Even poorly-paid primary school teachers laid claim to middle-class respectability by having a maid. As late as 1871, 17.3 per cent of all households in Berlin had servants, while in Hamburg the figure was 21.6 per cent and in Bremen as high as 24 per cent.[13] Nannies, too, had no reason to fear unemployment, despite the spread of Enlightenment views on education, which from the eighteenth century had decried their presence in the middle-class home. In particular it was the better-off, larger families, where the wife's duties were increasingly oriented to appearances, who kept a nanny to take the children for walks, supervise them in the nursery and look after their physical weal and woe. Even in the case of the petty-bourgeois milieu of artisans and small traders, it cannot be said that mothers devoted a great deal of time to their children, or that there was an exclusive emotional relationship between mother and child. Although there was no expensive nanny to take the natural mother's place, the fact that until well after 1848 wives of artisans were involved in the day-to-day running of their husbands' businesses meant that they

12. T. Fontane, *Meine Kinderjahre* (first published 1893), Frankfurt 1983, pp. 110–11. Descriptions of bourgeois households can be found in Lewald, *Lebensgeschichte*, pp. 87–8, and in Otto-Peters, *Frauenleben*, reprinted in Gerhard, *Verhältnisse*, pp. 282–94.
13. R. Engelsing, 'Das häusliche Personal in der Epoche der Industrialisierung', in Engelsing, *Zur Sozialgeschichte deutscher Mittel- und Unterschichten*, Göttingen 1978, pp. 225–61, quote at pp. 239–40.

generally had little time for raising their children in a planned and meticulous manner. The much-cited Biedermeier ideal of the bourgeois woman caring unremittingly and single-handedly for her home and children is one which rarely matched reality.

In another respect too there is a discrepancy between reality and the picture that has traditionally been painted. For despite the strict separation of functional spheres, women participated in public life as well, albeit to a limited degree. They flocked to the Hambach Festival of 1832, which marked the zenith of the liberal national movement before 1848. Indeed, they had been invited: 'German women, young and old, whom the European political order ignores to its shame and loss – adorn and enliven the gathering with your presence!'[14] Most middle-class associations, however, were not particularly bothered about this presence, and men kept athletics, singing, museums and professional matters to themselves. Even in those voluntary bodies which hoped to help overcome the division of people into different estates and professions, there was never any mention of mixing the sexes. They merely retraced the sharp line between male and female domains that had been drawn since the break-up of the 'whole household' and the separation of work and family.

But women did have their own institutions and gatherings where they were active in society outside the family. During the Wars of Liberation, the royal and princely houses had encouraged the formation in many towns of the first patriotic women's associations, which tended to wounded soldiers and looked after war widows and orphans. While some were disbanded when peace came, others broadened their scope to include general care for the poor, and backed up public community welfare schemes with personal services. Their work centred on caring for the poor and the sick, supporting destitute women with infants, and setting up soup kitchens. In addition, they helped establish and run schools for the poor, taught needlework to the daughters of poor families, and made clothes for the needy.[15] More often than not these activities took place under the aegis of the church. Charitable, religious lay organisations known as Associations of Elisabeth (*Elisabethvereine*) were formed, usually on the initiative of women themselves,

14. Reprinted in M. Twellmann, *Die Deutsche Frauenbewegung: Ihre Anfänge und erste Entwicklung, Quellen 1843–1889*, Meisenheim 1972, p. 1.
15. A. Salomon, 'Die Frau in der sozialen Hilfsthätigkeit', in *Handbuch der Frauenbewegung*, ed. H. Lange and G. Bäumer, vol. II, Berlin 1901, pp. 1–122, quote at pp. 19ff.

particularly in the Rhineland, a Catholic area, from the 1840s onwards; they incorporated existing Catholic women's organisations.[16] Protestant women also came together to do charitable work: some looked after female ex-convicts, others taught poor girls how to knit, still others provided families who had fallen on hard times with food, bedlinen and clothing. In 1832 in Hamburg, Amalie Sieveking, the thirty-eight-year-old unmarried daughter of a senator, founded the Women's Association for the Care of the Poor and the Sick (*Weiblicher Verein für Armen- und Krankenpflege*). Within a short time, similar groups followed in other towns. On the recommendation of government welfare organisations, members of these associations, all of whom were middle-class women from the locality, would go out visiting poverty-stricken families, offering material and moral support.[17] By committing themselves to philanthropic and religious causes of this kind and actively helping to solve the social problems of the day, women such as Amalie Sieveking, and those who joined her struggle, found they could upgrade their marginal social position, and compensate in a meaningful way for the fact that they were single and had no children.

Since 1836 the Rhenish-Westfalian Association of Deaconesses (*Rheinisch-Westfälischer Diakonissenverein*) in Kaiserswerth had been training Protestant nurses, who were then sent by the mother house to serve in social institutions. The result was the emergence of a new, often life-long, feminine vocation for the daughters of the Protestant middle classes. As the nineteenth century progressed, demand for them grew and grew: in 1898 there were 13,309 deaconesses working in Germany's hospitals, poorhouses, infirmaries, orphanages, infant schools, creches and in communal welfare.[18]

Although the energies women devoted to matters outside the home were alien to the Biedermeier family model, they did not in principle run counter to customary notions about the nature and place of women. If middle-class women visited the homes of women who were destitute and sick or who had young infants, prayed with them, encouraged them to be clean, thrifty and sober-minded, and made some nourishing soup, or if they taught the

16. A. Kall, *Katholische Frauenbewegung in Deutschland: Eine Untersuchung zur Gründung katholischer Frauenvereine im 19. Jahrhundert*, Paderborn 1983, pp. 23ff.
17. C. M. Prelinger, 'Prelude to Consciousness: A. Sieveking and the Female Association for the Care of the Poor and the Sick', in Fout (ed.), *German Women*, pp. 118–32.
18. Salomon, 'Hilfsthätigkeit', pp. 16, 58ff. See also C. M. Prelinger, 'The 19th-Century Deaconessate in Germany', in R.-E. B. Joeres and M. J. Maynes (eds), *German Women in the 18th and 19th Centuries*, Bloomington 1986, pp. 215–29.

daughters of the poor how to sew and knit, they were merely carrying on in other people's families the work they normally did for their own. They were not breaking down the female domain they knew in their own homes – one of selfless and compassionate human-oriented activity – but simply reproducing it in other households. Of course, men were also involved in practical social work, and communal welfare systems, which at the start of the 1800s had been reformed, survived largely because civic dignitaries fulfilled honorary functions. For men, public activity of this kind was a kind of passport to positions of responsibility in local administration: they earned their qualification by serving an apprenticeship in care for the poor. By contrast women, who helped administer such care through private, and usually religiously motivated, good works, could lay no claims to associated political rights. Their commitment was described as a 'labour of love'; it was commensurate with their feminine nature and did not require remuneration. Nevertheless, in the medium term female philanthropy was significant. From the 1840s onwards women began collectively to press for changes in their conditions, particularly where educational and employment opportunities were concerned. They focused on professions where they had already been able to gain experience and which seemed to be in tune with their 'feminine' characteristics: teaching, medicine, pharmacy and welfare. The life of the bourgeois woman who tended to her family and engaged in voluntary social work was embodied in the activities of upbringing, caring, helping, and curing the sick. It was obvious that if the need arose, specifically feminine job descriptions could be tailored to suit her skills.

The need did arise, particularly for those women who, by choice or otherwise, did not marry, who abandoned unsatisfactory relationships, or who from the outset rejected the arrangements that had been made for them. Personal experience had led them to believe that their own fates were not unique to them, and in both word and deed they became the vanguard of the organised women's movement. Fanny Lewald (1811–89) and Malvida von Meysenbug (1816–1903) refused to accept the marriage plans their parents had in store for them, and set out to make their own living. Johanna Kinkel (1810–58), Louise Aston (1814–71) and Mathilda Franziska Anneke (1817–84) all divorced husbands they did not love, and entered into new relationships which both gave them emotional fulfilment and allowed them to pursue independent literary or educational activities. Likewise Louise Otto (1819–95), the most active and important figure in the early women's movement, did not share the fate of most of her contemporaries. After her parents died at an early age, she ran a manless household together with her sisters, and did not marry until she chose to, at the age of thirtynine. She was widowed soon after. In contrast to the famous women of the age of Romanticism, who had likewise managed to assert their claims to happiness against social convention, their successors saw 'the general fate of many thousands in their own experiences', as Louise Aston once wrote.[19] The rebellious women of the Biedermeier period did not only draw personal conclusions from their 'conflict with social conditions',[20] but raised a cry for collective resistance.

19. L. Aston, *Meine Emancipation, Verweisung und Rechtfertigung*, Brussels 1846, reprinted in R. Möhrmann (ed.), *Frauenemanzipation im deutschen Vormärz*, Stuttgart 1978, pp. 68–82, quote at p. 70. On Aston see the documentation in G. Goetzinger, *Für die Selbstverwirklichung der Frau: L. Aston*, Frankfurt 1983.
20. M. F. Anneke, *Das Weib im Conflict mit den socialen Verhältnissen*, n.p. 1847 (extracts reprinted in Möhrmann, *Frauenemanzipation*, pp. 82–7). See also M. Wagner, *M. F. Anneke in Selbstzeugnissen und Dokumenten*, Frankfurt 1980. For material on Louise Otto see R.-E. Boetcher Joeres (ed.), *Die Anfänge der deutschen Frauenbewegung: L. Otto-Peters*, Frankfurt 1983. Fine biographical insights are provided in F. Böttger (ed.), *Frauen im Aufbruch: Frauenbriefe aus dem Vormärz und der Revolution von 1848*, Darmstadt 1979.

7
The Women's Movement of 1848

It is impossible to discuss and explain the emergence in 1848 of the first women's movement in Germany, organised in local branches and brought together by a publication which covered all regions, without referring to general political events.[1] In the 1840s turbulence reigned throughout the country: social tensions went hand in hand with growing liberal opposition to a corporate, feudalist social structure, police censorship and an authoritarian state. The bourgeoisie, now the leading force in economy and society, pressed harder and harder for the right to political participation, for freedom of the press and of association, the introduction of parliamentary government, democratisation of the judicial system, and for a constitution. The lower social strata, above all factory workers and the rising generation of urban skilled workers, were also becoming politicised, and through their educational associations and support funds developed their own ideas on how to change their social, economic and political position for the better.[2] When news of the Paris February Revolution of 1848 reached Germany, crowds poured out onto the streets to hand petitions to the local authorities. Berlin witnessed street battles between demonstrators and the military in March, until the king eventually surrendered to the revolution. The following months were a period of hectic political toing and froing. Since press censorship and the ban on parties had been temporarily suspended, political associations, gatherings, clubs and election committees sprang up everywhere, and congresses convened to draw up lists of demands.

Under these circumstances, the voice of women rang out for all to hear. Already in the years directly preceding the revolution, books – both political statements and works of fiction – by female authors

---

1. U. Gerhard, 'Über die Anfänge der deutschen Frauenbewegung um 1848', in Hausen (ed.), *Frauen suchen ihre Geschichte*, pp. 196–200.
2. On the causes, approach and course of the revolution of 1848 see the standard work by V. Valentin, *1848: Chapters in German History*, London 1940; W. Siemann, *Die deutsche Revolution von 1848/49*, Frankfurt 1985.

had appeared drawing attention to the 'unequal relations' between the sexes. Journals and newspapers published articles by women who demanded better education for girls or even 'the participation by women in the life of the state' (Louise Otto).[3] Women were also actively involved in church lay movements, for example the German Catholics (*Deutsch-Katholiken*) who campaigned against papism, or the 'Friends of Lights' (*Lichtfreunde*) and Free Communities (*Freie Gemeinde*) who subscribed to liberal, rational Protestantism. Institutions such as these granted women the same rights to speak and hold office as men, at least formally. At the time, the principle of joint organisation was something entirely novel and unconventional. Religious lay movements seemed to have left behind the 'unholy dualism' between the sexes; they regarded the existence of separate bodies for women as 'antiquated'. On the other hand, separate women's organisations were often formed within these lay movements, to allow women to overcome the disadvantages of their starting positions, and gain 'a clear sense of themselves, the ability to think independently and act in a strong-minded way'.[4] In Hamburg for example, a Women's Educational Association (*Frauenbildungsverein*) was founded on the initiative of the local German Catholic community, which opened a University for the Female Sex (*Hochschule für das weibliche Geschlecht*) in 1850. Under the aegis of its chancellor Carl Fröbel, a nephew of Friedrich Fröbel, the father of the kindergarten, it offered young girls the chance to broaden their knowledge of academic, pedagogic and domestic affairs, so that later on they could work as governesses or in nursery schools, or even 'just' deal with the demands that 'practical, social and spiritual life at its highest levels' placed on 'women of cultivation'.[5]

The traditional pattern of distinct male and female organisations

3. A selection of texts is to be found in Möhrmann, *Frauenemanzipation*.
4. *Frauen-Zeitung*, no. 27, 6 July 1850: 'Sind Frauen-Vereine zweckmäßig oder nicht?', reprinted in U. Gerhard et al. (eds), '*Dem Reich der Freiheit werb*' *ich Bürgerinnen*': *Die Frauen-Zeitung von L. Otto*, Frankfurt 1979, pp. 280–1. On the German Catholic movement see F. W. Graf, *Die Politisierung des religiösen Bewußtseins. Die bürgerlichen Religionsparteien im deutschen Vormärz: Das Beispiel des Deutschkatholizismus*, Stuttgart 1978. Approximately half of the 100,000 or so members of German Catholic communities in the 1840s were Protestants. On these 'dissidents' see J. Brederlow, '*Lichtfreunde*' *und* '*Freie Gemeinde*': *Religiöser Protest und Freiheitsbewegung im Vormärz und in der Revolution von 1848/49*, Munich 1976.
5. *Frauen-Zeitung*, no. 10, 9 March 1850: 'Plan der Hochschule für das weibliche Geschlecht in Hamburg', reprinted in Gerhard (ed.), '*Dem Reich*', pp. 226ff.; C. M. Prelinger, 'Religious Dissent, Women's Rights and the Hamburger Hochschule für das weibliche Geschlecht in Mid-nineteenth Century Germany', *Church History*, 45, 1976, pp. 42–55.

proved to be firmly embedded in other areas too. For instance, membership of the political associations, and of the democratic or liberal clubs and committees which burgeoned during the revolution, was restricted to men. Women were allowed, however, to come and observe meetings, which they apparently did in large numbers. In the Frankfurt Paulskirche, where the first German parliament elected by men assembled in April and May of 1848, two hundred seats were reserved on the platform for 'ladies', and tickets sold fast.

Women organised themselves autonomously as well. In many towns they formed democratic women's associations, raising money for freedom fighters and victims of political persecution, supporting their dependants and submitting pleas for amnesty to the authorities. For instance, the Mainz women's association Humania, presided over by Kathinka Zitz-Halein, daughter of a merchant family and wife of a lawyer, had almost 1,700 members in 1849.[6] A small number of women were not satisfied with listening to speeches, raising money and signing petitions: they helped build barricades and fought alongside the democratic volunteer corps against the military.[7] Such 'unfeminine' conduct, which contemporaries railed against, was very much the exception, however. On the whole women confined themselves to indirect political action. But even that caused quite a stir. They were no longer content to embroider pennants for male gymnastic associations: instead they formed their own female gymnastic clubs, in order 'to do physical exercises twice weekly, free of the inconvenience of tight linen gymnastics clothing', as well as 'outside the gymnasium to reject and cast off each and every restriction to the body which hinders movement and thus damages health', as the statutes of one Frankfurt club put it.[8] Freedom meant liberation, not only from political restrictions, but also from the aesthetic instruments of torture which fashion foisted upon women in the form of lace-up and whale-bone corsets.

Political catchwords such as 'freedom' and 'liberation' were highly malleable. The slogan which headed Louise Otto's *Frauen-*

6. See B. S. Zucker, 'German Women and the Revolution of 1848: K. Zitz-Halein and the Humania Association', *Central European History*, 13, 1980, pp. 237–54. Hardly anything is known about the membership or structure of other women's associations; indeed, little research has been conducted in general into the very localised first women's movement. An exception is C. Lipp (ed.), *Schimpfende Weiber und patriotische Jungfrauen: Frauen im Vormärz und in der Revolution 1848/49*, Bühl-Moos 1986.
7. G. Hummel-Haasis (ed.), *Schwestern, zerreißt eure Ketten: Zeugnisse zur Geschichte der Frauen in der Revolution von 1848/49*, Munich 1982.
8. Reprinted in Twellmann, *Quellen*, pp. 80–1.

Zeitung, first published in April 1849, ran 'Recruiting Women Citizens for the Realm of Freedom' (*Dem Reich der Freiheit werb' ich Bürgerinnen*), which meant primarily 'the right to use all our powers freely to develop that in us which is purely human, and the right to be responsible and self-determining citizens of the state'.[9] Otto criticised those men who had only the masculine half of humanity in mind when they demanded freedom, and accused them of being half-hearted. Yet for women too, the 'realm of freedom' was not to be infinite. Its boundaries were marked by the rules of general conduct and feminine morality. Even the strident women of the 1848 revolution had clear ideas about 'a woman's station', and it never entered their heads that they might want to be 'emancipated' from it. They did not challenge the pride of place that the family held in the female experience. But a woman could not fulfil her duty as a mother, run the household and raise a family properly if she was kept shut away in her home; if she was to bring up her children to be responsible members of society, she would need to understand the world outside, see how the events of public life were inter-related, and be in a position to influence them. This explains why one of the major demands presented by the women's movement of 1848 to society at large was an insistence that higher schooling for girls should include more than the usual female subjects such as languages, needlework, drawing and music.

Thought was also given to unmarried women, for whom a sound education was particularly important. Only by acquiring vocational qualifications could they lead any sort of independent lives at all, and avoid either becoming a burden on their families, or selling themselves more or less unwillingly to a man who would provide for them. In 1847 Louise Otto proposed that more women be allowed to work in commerce and in teaching, so that 'marriage in Germany might rediscover its natural rights, and not merely be reduced to a "welfare institution" for the female sex, as is so frequently the case today'.[10] For the time being, however, such ideas had to remain visions of the future. Although retail assistants in Berlin were complaining to the Prussian Ministry of State as early as 1848 about growing competition from 'young madams in our shops', it was not until the last third of the nineteenth century that offices and shops became normal places of employment for women. After 1860

9. 'Programm', in *Frauen-Zeitung*, no. 1, 21 April 1849, reprinted in Gerhard (ed.), *Die Frauen-Zeitung*, p. 37.
10. Reprinted in Twellmann, *Quellen*, p. 14.

private commercial schools for girls were being established in many towns, offering one-year courses for women who wished to prepare for a career in business. By 1895 there were as many as 13,044 female office employees in Germany, the majority of them daughters of middle-class public servants, doctors, or businessmen.[11]

Teaching was felt to be more fitting for respectable 'young ladies', for it seemed to allow them to continue their familial role of upbringing outside the home. From the early nineteenth century, primary and girls' schools were employing female teaching staff, and by 1822 there were 620 women teachers (compared with 21,886 male teachers) in Prussian state primary and secondary schools.[12] The majority of them had finished school, and proceeded to spend a few years as assistants to their former teachers, mainly at private higher girls' schools, which qualified them to take up teaching posts of their own.

The first steps towards the creation of more systematic training schemes were taken in the 1830s. A few girls' schools set up teacher training classes for suitable pupils, and the state also began to organise training for women teachers and establish pre-training institutes. But the women who graduated were permitted to teach in elementary schools only, or in the lower grades in girls' schools; male teachers attended to academic subjects and the whole of senior school teaching. There were no women teachers at all in boys' schools, and the staff at private and state girls' schools was predominantly male. Nevertheless, the proportion of women among teachers in Prussia's girls' schools did rise from 35 per cent in 1833 to 57 per cent by the turn of the century, with the total number of women teachers increasing by a factor of twenty over this period.[13]

As a result of the expansion of the education system for girls,[14] middle-class women now had more chance of making independent

11. For a history of women clerical workers in the nineteenth century see U. Nienhaus, *Berufsstand Weiblich: Die ersten weiblichen Angestellten*, Berlin 1982.

12. W. Fischer et al., *Sozialgeschichtliches Arbeitsbuch I*, Munich 1982, table pp. 224–5. There are no figures either for the number of women teachers in private girls' schools, or for private education in general in the nineteenth century.

13. On the history and development of women in teaching and its relation to the course of higher education for girls, see G. Bäumer, 'Geschichte und Stand der Frauenbildung in Deutschland', in *Handbuch*, vol. III, 1902, pp. 1–128, esp. pp. 90ff; J. Zinnecker, *Sozialgeschichte der Mädchenbildung*, Weinheim 1973, pp. 29–60 (quoted details on p. 46).

14. In 1850 there were 60 state higher girls' schools, and as many as 213 by 1901. If we include private schools, there were in total 342 girls' schools in 1833, and 869 in 1901 (from Zinnecker, *Sozialgeschichte der Mädchenbildung*, pp. 31, 37). In 1901, 53,409 girls attended state higher girls' schools in Prussia, and 72,932 private schools: Bäumer, 'Geschichte und Stand', table V, p. 128.

careers for themselves. The adamant call by the women's movement after 1840 for improved and extended schooling for girls was, in other words, also a plank in a strategy of what may be termed 'active professionalisation': women set about creating their own professional fields. For a long time, however, it remained difficult to break into the closed educational network. If schools for young ladies prepared their pupils for anything at all, then it was for school-teaching, and such teachers found employment exclusively in primary and girls' schools. Other kinds of learned professions were not open to women at that time. Since they were not allowed to go on to study, they could not become doctors, lawyers, priests, or scientists. It was not until the turn of the century, when women were admitted to universities, that the monocultural nature of women's professions gradually began to be eroded.

The demand of the early women's movement that socially acceptable positions of employment should be open to women did not, however, go very far. It was only single women who were to seek through their occupation 'a substitute for the happiness' that married women found in matrimony and motherhood.[15] On the one hand, then, the women's movement subscribed to the contemporary view that the sexes had distinct roles, their own specific characteristics, and particular needs for activity. On the other, they demanded that women who did not become wives and mothers should be allowed access to the male world of employment in a way that suited their innate feminine nature. Though this sounds like an extremely timorous proposition today, it was downright revolutionary at the time. For what it seemed to invite was a general realignment of male–female relations. At root, the bi-polar model of gender-specific natures was based on a universally valid allocation of immutable innate characteristics and types of 'vocation' to each sex, regardless of individuals, groups and social strata. In the long term, any exceptions to this rule would have the effect of undermining the whole system. The storm of indignation that the women's movement stirred up among educated men of the nineteenth-century bourgeoisie, and the colossal resistance that educated men offered their female peers, had less to do with any threat of competition than with the fear that if partial, politically motivated concessions were made to women, the traditional and socially desirable difference between the paid work which men did in their jobs and the unpaid work that women did at home would be

15. Quoted in Twellmann, *Textband*, Kronberg 1976, pp. 98–9.

fundamentally open to attack.

Despite the accusations often levelled against them, under no circumstances did middle-class women and their organisations wish to see the principle of a sexual division of labour abolished, nor 'to blur the differences between the sexes in each and every facet of life as we perceive it'.[16] In 1849 Louise Otto had firmly rejected the idea that she was advocating women's 'emancipation', which in the language of the day meant an end to sexual differences and the negation of all innate and hence inalterable sexual characteristics. The contemporary idea of emancipated women, imported from France and glorified by the young German *literati*,[17] conjured up figures such as George Sand or Louise Aston, 'hermaphrodites' who dressed like men, smoked cigars, wore their hair short, and paid homage to free love and the 'emancipation of the flesh'. It was not only respectable men who distanced themselves from such 'he-women'; the early women's movement did too: they had little time for 'unbridled passions' and the emulation of masculine behaviour but, following the 'eternal laws of true femininity', insisted upon women's right to self-development in family and society. In return, they offered society their services in education and social welfare, not only in their own families, but particularly to those 'who languish forgotten and neglected in poverty, misery and ignorance'.[18]

The bourgeois women's movement did not create the projects of social welfare and care for poor families in which it became involved. But in contrast to traditional, charitable women's associations, the new organisations were not contented with merely doing good works. As the *Frauen-Zeitung* put it in 1850, they wanted to penetrate deeper, 'beyond the immediate necessities of life, to the more fundamental issue of root causes', and remedy matters at this level.[19] Like democratic men's associations, the women's movement was also sensitive to the new 'social question' that had been thrown up by the pauperism of the late eighteenth and early nineteenth centuries. In the *Vormärz* period what had been worrying people was not poverty itself, the fates of the old and the sick who simply did not have the strength to make a living and had to rely on public and private help. There seemed to be a much more pressing political

16. *Brockhaus' Konversations-Lexikon*, vol. 7, Leipzig 1898, p. 235.
17. R. Koselleck and K. M. Grass, 'Emanzipation', in Brunner et al. (eds), *Grundbegriffe*, vol. II, 1975, pp. 153–97, esp. pp. 186ff. Louise Otto's attitude is described in Twellmann, *Die Deutsche Frauenbewegung*, pp. 85–6, and in Gerhard, *Die Frauen-Zeitung*, pp. 39–40, 42ff.
18. *Programm der Frauen-Zeitung*, no. 1, 1849, reprinted in ibid., p. 37.
19. Ibid., p. 258.

and 'moral' danger emanating from the artisans and factory proletariat who were never far from the poorhouse door. These families
had no savings with which to stave off the vagaries of economic
cycles or personal crises such as ill-health and invalidity, which led
to unemployment or temporary loss of income. Such events often
sent the family down the slippery slope to poverty from which they
found it difficult to escape. From the 1840s onwards – and particularly after 1848 – bourgeois associations began to emerge which
aimed to interrupt this cycle with social measures, and to integrate
the 'labouring classes' into the moral, economic and cultural fabric
of society.[20] Some women's associations also played a part in these
kinds of initiatives. In Berlin, for example, the Women's Association for the Relief of Need among Small-Scale Manufacturers and
Artisans (*Frauenverein zur Abhilfe der Not unter den kleinen
Fabrikanten und Handwerkern*), an organisation for the wives of
prominent industrialists, businessmen and public officials, raised
money for a fund which could provide the needy with cash
advances.[21]

For the most part, though, democratic women's groups focused
their energies on helping women: seamstresses, lace-makers, need-
lewomen, tailoresses, knitters, women factory workers, and servant
girls. The *Frauen-Zeitung* published a striking number of articles
about these women, on how badly they were paid, the long hours
they worked, and how their health suffered. The articles complained
that the surplus supply of female labour was dragging wages down,
and that the situation was not helped by competition from middle-
class women who sold their handicrafts secretly and well below the
going rate. The only way out seemed to be through 'association':
Assoziation, the magic word of 1848, was understood as the coming
together of workers in common defence of their interests against
their employers – factory owners, retailers or master craftsmen.
Political and trade union associations of workers and journeymen
had been formed throughout Germany in 1848, which set out to
realise their demands for higher wages, shorter working hours, etc.,
by means of collective and if necessary strike, action. When a
national umbrella organisation, the German Working Men's Brotherhood (*Deutsche Arbeiterverbrüderung*), was constituted in Berlin,

20. U. Frevert, *Krankheit als politisches Problem 1770–1880: Soziale Unterschichten in Preußen zwischen medizinischer Polizei und staatlicher Sozialversicherung*,
Göttingen 1984, esp. pp. 116–25, 151ff.; F. Tennstedt, *Sozialgeschichte der Sozialpolitik in Deutschland*, Göttingen 1981, pp. 69ff.
21. Hummel-Haasis (ed.), *Schwestern*, pp. 82–3.

Louise Otto reminded the men not to forget women workers, and to help defend their interests through organisation. Bourgeois women's associations were also encouraged to make the cause of their proletarian 'sisters' their own, to play their part in the organisation of male *and* female workers, and to help 'put an end to . . . all the most terrible consequences of social inequality'.[22]

In 1849, the Democratic Women's Association (*Demokratischer Frauenverein*) in Berlin presented a petition to the National Assembly on behalf of 'poor women workers who are enslaved by their bosses'. Moreover, it encouraged its members 'kindly to pledge themselves to wear only clothes made from indigenous materials'.[23] The *Frauen-Zeitung* pondered what practical measures might be taken. The suggestion was made that women should purchase certain products only if they had been made and sold exclusively by women; women should be given greater opportunity to do a range of jobs wider than just the handicrafts and domestic service to which they had hitherto been confined. Such thoughts expressed more than a merely general interest in concepts of social organisation and reform, an interest which men shared. They also conveyed a feeling which was not in evidence among men: a sense of 'sisterhood' which ignored class divisions, the idea that women shared the same basic experiences. A cursory glance would show a great disparity between the socio-economic conditions of bourgeois and working-class women – while the former were not allowed to go out to work, the latter had to earn money if they were not to starve. But by digging deeper, common ground could be found: all women lacked political rights, and were subjugated by law to their husbands, irrespective of social stratum. In planning their personal lives, bourgeois and proletarian women had similar matters to consider. While 'young ladies', faced with the impossibility of finding employment, were obliged to seek a marriage that would provide for their material wants, girls from the 'lower orders', suffering from the oppressive conditions of work, longed for a husband who, they hoped, would go out to earn on their behalf.[24] None of them were in a position to decide freely whether to marry or not. In the view of the early women's movement, higher wages

22. See the two articles by Louise Otto in *Verbrüderung*, the journal of the German Working Men's Brotherhood, no. 8, 1848, and no. 39, 1849, reprinted in Gerhard (ed.), *Die Frauen-Zeitung*, pp. 57–61. See also her articles entitled 'Für die Arbeiterinnen' in *Frauen-Zeitung*, no. 20, 1 September 1849, and no. 21, 8 September 1849, reprinted in ibid., pp. 134–8, 141–4 (quote at p. 144).

23. *Frauen-Zeitung*, no. 2, 28 April 1849, in ibid., p. 55.

24. Ibid., p. 144.

and shorter working hours for women of the working class, and better education and vocational qualifications for their sisters in the bourgeoisie, meant that in the future *all* women would be better placed to seize the opportunity to 'develop freely'.

8
Working Women and Workers' Wives

It is unlikely that in the mid-nineteenth century working-class women recognised that they had anything in common with women of the bourgeoisie, or that they took the offer of 'getting together in sisterhood' very seriously. As housemaids, seamstresses, tailoresses, washerwomen and launderers in middle-class households, they regarded their mistresses not as sex comrades, as women who were oppressed like themselves, but as their employers and 'masters' who seemed little inclined to pay them higher wages for less work. Tenant farmers' daughters could expect a life quite unlike that of girls raised in the families of public officials and entrepreneurs. What awaited daughters of the lower classes was hard, tedious and badly paid work which had to be done for the family to survive. Girls – along with their brothers – were set to work when they were only four or five. In the small and poor peasantry, they would help their mothers with daily chores in the house and garden, and tend small animals; in families of spinners and weavers they would wind yarn onto bobbins or deliver finished goods; in families of factory workers they would gather herbs, run errands, scour harvested fields for left-over potatoes and vegetables, or even work in the factory with their parents. In addition they would help keep an eye on younger brothers and sisters.[1] For the family to 'get by' everyone had to lend a hand, and even then they only just about managed to bring in enough between them to cover basic needs such as food, shelter, lighting and heating. Children soon learned that the family was primarily a community of labour and production, which could consume only what had been created. Extra mouths to feed, and the old and the sick, were heavy burdens for such economies of scarcity to bear; and school, which was compulsory in Prussia after 1763

---

1. On child labour in the nineteenth century see R. Alt, *Kinderausbeutung und Fabrikschulen in der Frühzeit des industriellen Kapitalismus*, Berlin 1958; W. Feldenkirchen, 'Kinderarbeit im 19. Jahrhundert', *Zeitschrift für Unternehmensgeschichte*, 26, 1981, pp. 1–41; and autobiographical reports in Schlumbohm (ed.), *Kinderstuben*, ch. 3, and Hardach-Pinke and Hardach (eds), *Kinderalltag*, pp. 197ff.

and attended by 60 per cent of children by 1816,[2] took child labour and earnings away from the family.

When girls finished their statutory education at the age of thirteen or fourteen, they looked for a job or a position which would provide the family with a steady income. Even if they no longer lived at home, they would regularly send their family money. Only a few had the chance to learn a trade, for example as tailoress, seamstress or shop assistant, because they would earn nothing during training; on the contrary, they had to pay for their apprenticeship. Moreover training opportunities were limited, since girls could not become bakers, butchers, bricklayers or metalworkers – no master would ever have offered them an apprenticeship.

In rural areas, employment was almost always limited to agriculture. A girl would enter service with a fairly well-off farmer, and receive a fixed annual wage, and food and shelter in addition to payments in kind such as flax, yarn or cloth. The cloth was made into articles for her bottom drawer, and part of the money was put into a savings bank towards a dowry which would help her start her own family. Life as a maid-cum-farmhand was generally regarded as a limited period of transition lasting ten to fifteen years and ending in marriage.[3] But the wife of a poorer peasant, tenant farmer or day labourer could not expect to live a life of leisure – her workload was more likely to double. In addition to her domestic and family duties, she was also an agricultural labourer, or she helped run the farm or small-holding if some land was either acquired or leased.[4] 'Assisting relatives' (*mithelfende Familienangehörige*) was the title used in employment statistics to describe these women, as well as the wives of master craftsmen, small traders and innkeepers. In 1882 they numbered more than three million in the German Reich as a whole, most of them in agriculture.[5]

It was by no means every servant girl who took marriage vows. The fewer possessions she had, the worse her chances were of so doing. In most German states marriage law was restricted by being tied, for example, to local residence laws, which ruled that proof had

2. By the 1880s all children were attending compulsory schooling in Prussia. See P. Lundgreen, *Sozialgeschichte der deutschen Schule im Überblick*, vol. I: *1770–1918*, Göttingen 1980, p. 93.
3. On the position of female farmhands see R. Schulte, 'Bauernmägde in Bayern am Ende des 19. Jahrhunderts', in Hausen (ed.), *Frauen suchen ihre Geschichte*, pp. 110–27; Weber-Kellermann, *Landleben*, pp. 160ff.
4. See a contemporary investigation by E. zu Pulitz, *Arbeits- und Lebensverhältnisse der Frauen in der Landwirtschaft in Brandenburg*, Jena 1914.
5. The restrictive counting methods used in the employment statistics for the years 1882, 1895 and 1907 mean that the numbers of 'assisting relatives' were

to be given of sufficient means of subsistence. These restrictions were not lifted until 1868 in the states of the North German Confederation, with southern Germany following a little later.[6] The relatively high number of single people in many areas in the first half of the nineteenth century was due not least to the fact that local communities feared not being able to afford to care for the poor. After the middle of the century, however, when industrialisation began to take off, creating an unforeseen demand for labour, stemming the poverty that town and country had witnessed between 1815 and 1848, and giving rise to enormous demographic shifts (in 1910 only 40 per cent of Germans lived in the country, i.e. in communities of fewer than 2,000 people, compared with 63.9 per cent in 1871), the chances of obtaining official permission to marry, and thus of starting a family, became greater.

Industrialisation destroyed some jobs, as faster and cheaper manufacturing processes made the techniques of cottage industry uneconomic. At the same time thousands of new jobs were created, since more goods were produced and new markets established at home and abroad. Employment opportunities for women existed primarily in the textile, clothing, food, paper and tobacco industries, then later on in the chemical and electrical industries (see Tables 1–2, p. 328.)

The daughter of a tenant farmer, a spinner or a weaver became a factory worker who stood at her machine for eleven to fourteen hours every day, Monday to Saturday. Female labour was particularly widespread in industries which did not require highly qualified personnel. The metallurgical industries needed a high degree of precision craftsmanship, with the result that the sector almost never took anyone on except trained metalworkers, smiths and so on; but textile manufacturing could function using semi-skilled labour that

---

recorded very incompletely. Thus the figure for 1882 was given as 1.9 million, while for 1925, when the definition of the term was broadened, the figure was 5.4 million. But whereas the population had grown by 38 per cent in the period, the number of 'assisting relatives' had risen by 181 per cent. In order to compensate for the misleading nature of the data, which derives from the various survey methods used, I have used estimates, as does A. Willms in 'Grundzüge der Entwicklung der Frauenarbeit 1880–1980', in W. Müller et al. (eds), *Strukturwandel der Frauenarbeit 1880–1980*, Frankfurt 1983, pp. 25–54. It is assumed that for each married self-employed person in agriculture there was one member of the family who helped. In the discussion of female employment below, these estimates will be used. See also R. Stockmann, 'Gewerbliche Frauenarbeit in Deutschland 1875–1980', *Geschichte und Gesellschaft*, 11, 1985, pp. 447–75.

6. K.-J. Matz, *Pauperismus und Bevölkerung: Die gesetzlichen Ehebeschränkungen in den süddeutschen Staaten während des 19. Jahrhunderts*, Stuttgart 1980.

could be trained inside a few weeks. Thus, spinning and weaving mills, laundries and clothing manufacturers employed mainly women. For example, the proportion of women workers in the Bielefeld linen industry was as high as 55 per cent in the early 1860s, and by 1900 it was 70 per cent.[7] Most of the women who sought employment in factories were young (see Table 3, p. 329): girls who had just left school, and in the early days even children who preferred working in factories to going into domestic service. After all, in factories people worked regular, if long hours, had Saturday afternoons and Sundays free, and a fixed wage: all such advantages went to offset the poor reputation factory work had. By comparison, the material situation of servant girls was hardly enviable. Their labour was ruthlessly exploited, as the 'master and mistress' did with them as they pleased. Unlike factory laws, the body of rules governing relations between servants and masters, the *Gesindeordnung*, which was in force from the early 1800s right up until 1918, did not recognise fixed working times, the contractual right to time off at night and on Sundays, or legally enforceable wage rates. Since a servant girl usually lived in her master's house – at best in an unheated attic room, at worst in a hanging floor in the hallway or in a corner in the kitchen – she was the subject of constant scrutiny and could be called on any time of the day. As the maid-of-all-work she was responsible for all the housework – cleaning the rooms, cooking, washing up, laundering, and ironing. In addition, she had to serve the people of the household – she was a nanny, lady's maid and valet all rolled into one. Since only a few wealthy families could afford several servants each with a separate function, the typical family had a single servant girl, an *Alleinmädchen*, who was paid the least for working hardest. At the end of the nineteenth century in Berlin, the city with the highest wage rates in the German Empire, an *Alleinmädchen* earned between 150 and 200 Reichsmark a year.[8] Factory wages were more generous. A woman could earn more than 600 Reichsmark a year in 1890 in the Bielefeld linen industry; spinning and weaving mills paid about 500 Reichsmark for female labour.[9] It is true that factory workers had to live entirely from their

---

7. K. Ditt, *Industrialisierung, Arbeiterschaft und Arbeiterbewegung in Bielefeld 1850–1914*, Dortmund 1982, p. 207.
8. D. Wierling, "'Ich hab meine Arbeit gemacht – was wollte sie mehr?' Dienstmädchen im städtischen Haushalt der Jahrhundertwende', in Hausen (ed.), *Frauen suchen*, pp. 144–71; Wierling, *Mädchen für alles: Arbeitsalltag und Lebensgeschichte städtischer Dienstmädchen um die Jahrhundertwende*, Berlin 1987.
9. Ditt, *Industrialisierung*, table p. 212.

earnings, while servant girls were given accommodation and food by their masters. But even so, wages in domestic service lagged behind factory rates.

It was not normal for either servant or factory girls to receive a fixed and adequate yearly income. Since average wages only rarely exceeded the minimum necessary for existence – and more often they did not – ill-health or unemployment meant drastic cuts in wages and a dramatic deterioration in women's living standards. Many middle-class families dismissed their servants during the summer or just before Christmas so as to save on Christmas presents.[10] Cyclical slumps also occasioned massive redundancy, a problem which was particularly acute for waitresses and women employed in domestic trades and seasonal occupations, who were able to find paid work for only a few months each year. Faced with this situation, many young women saw no alternative but to earn their living by prostitution. They had plenty of opportunity to do so in the rapidly growing industrial and administrative metropolises, where the culture of entertainment and leisure was blossoming.

In the second half of the nineteenth century, prostitution became rife in the cities. Contemporary estimates suggest that Berlin accommodated some 16,000 prostitutes in 1870, and 40,000 by 1909.[11] Only a fraction worked in closed establishments and brothels licensed by the state. The majority preferred to walk the streets, since they could enjoy greater anonymity, flexibility and independence. This new phenomenon of mass, open prostitution on streets, squares, elegant avenues and in business quarters caused concern among polite society, particularly its female half who, in appearance at least, could hardly be distinguished from the 'false ladies'. From the 1880s onwards fears of medical and moral contamination prompted the state to be more vigilant. Prostitutes underwent regular medical examinations, and vice squads maintained surveillance. The women were obliged always to carry an identity card with them, and their conduct, dress and behaviour had to conform to strict regulations. The authorities' actions were intended to make clear once again the dividing line between respectable bourgeois society and these 'impure' women, which had become hazy, and to

---

10. R. Schulte, *Sperrbezirke: Tugendhaftigkeit und Prostitution in der bürgerlichen Welt*, Frankfurt 1979, p. 87.
11. K. Walser, 'Prostitutionsverdacht und Geschlechterforschung: Das Beispiel der Dienstmädchen um 1900', *Geschichte und Gesellschaft*, 11, 1985, pp. 99–111, quote at p. 104; Schulte, *Sperrbezirke*, p. 20; on prostitution in Zurich see A. Ulrich, *Bordelle, Straßendirnen und bürgerliche Sittlichkeit in der Belle Epoque*, Zürich 1985.

show prostitutes that their place was 'marginal'. The clarity with which this line was drawn had a disastrous impact on the servant girls, factory workers, shop assistants and waitresses for whom prostitution was a second or part-time job. Once they had been registered as *Kontrollmädchen* ('registered girls') they could expect society to humiliate and stigmatise them, which would permanently damage their chances of returning to a 'normal life'.

The fact that in the late nineteenth century about one third of all prostitutes had previously been servant girls, fuelled speculation that these women were particularly susceptible to a life of immorality, and reinforced the distrust the middle classes showed towards their domestic staff. In fact, however, servant girls were not over-represented among prostitutes, since they also topped statistics on overall employment in cities: in Berlin in 1885, 32 per cent of all females in work were servant girls.[12] In the German Empire as a whole, the average in 1882 was 17.9 per cent compared with the 8.6 per cent who worked in trade and industry.[13] Although industrialisation forged ahead, employment statistics for 1907 still showed more women in domestic service than in factories and craft industries.

Because some highly industrialised regions, like the Ruhr, were dominated by mining and heavy industries employing only men, there too women were unable to find work other than service in middle-class families. For young girls drawn to the towns from the country, domestic service was more acceptable than the much-maligned existence as a factory worker for the simple reason that it allowed them to join a family. It was said of women factory workers – at least of those no longer living at home – that their very lack of attachment endangered their morality and made them hopelessly prey to the temptations of urban life. Work conditions – the dirt and the smell – were still more effective deterrents, and they even functioned as criteria of social differentiation among factory girls themselves. For example, by the turn of the century the Ravensberg spinning mill in Bielefeld, which in the 1850s had been recruiting almost exclusively indigenous labour, was having to recruit women workers from East Prussia, Bohemia and Silesia, since girls from Bielefeld and the locality preferred the cleaner (and better paid) work they could find in weaving mills. In 1905, a journalist in Bielefeld wrote of how in dance halls, 'weavers look down on

12. Walser, 'Prostitutionsverdacht', p. 102.
13. Willms, 'Grundzüge', p. 54.

spinners with such condescension. A weaver would never allow a spinner to sit down at the same table.' In turn, weavers played second fiddle to 'the maidens from the linen factory' whose work was more delicate, cleaner and better paid.[14]

In the nineteenth century positions in both domestic service and manufacturing were, with very rare exceptions, occupied by young, single women who left the official world of employment when they married, or at the latest when they had their first child. This is not to say, however, that they disappeared from the labour market altogether. Hardly any working-class family was able to live on the father's income alone – after all, he was paid according to his labours, not the size of his family. Only a few highly skilled workers earned enough to cover all of the family expenditure: they comprised the 'labour aristocracy'. Here, a wife engaged in employment outside the home was something to be ashamed of: a man's social status – and his domestic comfort – would be enhanced much more by his wife dedicating herself exclusively to housework and bringing up the children, à la bourgeoisie. But while this may have been an ideal state of affairs, at the time only a small number of families could afford it. At the end of the last century in Vienna, for example, a mere 10–20 percent of working-class women belonged to this privileged group, 40 per cent were in full-time employment, and as many had a series of part-time occupations.[15] The chief sources of casual earnings were working at home for an outside employer, sub-letting accommodation, tending a small garden, or offering service such as cleaning, washing or ironing to middle-class families.[16] From the numerous records of working-class family budgets which history has bequeathed to us, we can see that most working-class families boosted their income with the wife's earnings. Indeed, large families with young children depended for their existence on them.

In the nineteenth and twentieth centuries, homeworking became particularly common for married working-class women.[17] The linen

14. Quoted in Ditt, *Industrialisierung*, p. 205.

15. J. Ehmer, 'Frauenarbeit und Arbeiterfamilie in Wien: Vom Vormärz bis 1934', *Geschichte und Gesellschaft*, 7, 1981, pp. 438–73, quote at p. 451.

16. Rosenbaum, *Formen*, pp. 402ff.

17. R. Beier, *Frauenarbeit und Frauenalltag im Deutschen Kaiserreich: Heimarbeiterinnen in der Berliner Bekleidungsindustrie 1880–1914*, Frankfurt 1983; K. Hausen, 'Technical Progress and Women's Labour in the Nineteenth Century: The Social History of the Sewing Machine', in G. Iggers (ed.), *The Social History of Politics: Critical Perspectives in West German Historical Writing Since 1945*, Leamington Spa 1985, pp. 259–81; B. Franzoi, 'Domestic Industry: Work Options and Women's Choices', in Fout (ed.), *German Women*, pp. 256–69.

and clothing industries did not start to switch to factory-based production until around 1900, and even then many of the more unprofitable tasks and individual operations were contracted out for seamstresses working from home. Outwork offered these women the chance of tying paid employment, housework and childcare all to the same place, though the price they paid was self-exploitation. In order to earn enough money, only a minimum amount of time was to be spent cooking, cleaning and washing clothes, and the children had to be largely left to their own devices. The kind of harmonious family life that the bourgeoisie made so much noise about was unthinkable in such circumstances. In contrast to the family economy of proto-industrial cottage industries, where the husband, wife and children had taken on all the necessary work together, without strict role differentiation, the household engaged in industrial home-work revolved around a strict division of labour. The husband worked in the factory, and the wife saw to food, clothing, children and the house itself, in addition to her remunerated activity. This gave rise to a hierarchy from the very outset. Since the husband earned the most income, his work was regarded as the more important, and his needs were given priority. The work performed by the wife – in and for the house – was more intangible and less easily measured in monetary units. Even if she was gainfully employed outside the home, she would earn less than her husband. The situation within the family was but an extension of the market undervaluation of female labour. This was justified by reference both to the fewer qualifications and skills women had, and to their being tied to the family, which, so the argument ran, gave female wage-labour the status of supplementary employment.[18] A 1908 official publication of the Union of Construction Workers read as follows:

It is like this in working-class families. The man, the one who after all has to work (*sic*), consumes the largest share of the available food. The children too have as much as possible. In most cases, the mother is left out – she has to be satisfied with one or two mouthfuls if there is not enough to go round, and lives on bread, coffee and potatoes. A working man's wife makes daily sacrifice for her family. She is happy if nobody shouts for more, even is she is still hungry herself.[19]

18. A good example of this was the argument that a 'family wage' existed, which justified lower wage rates for women workers. If men then pointed to their family commitments and demanded a higher wage which took family size into account, they were answered with the argument that work was rewarded according to achievement.
19. *Lebenshaltung und Arbeitsverhältnisse der Deutschen Bauhülfsarbeiter*, Ham-

The sacrificial role of working-class women, which is also documented in autobiographical writings, was reflected not least in their lower life expectancy compared with men. Demographic studies have shown that in the nineteenth century, married, middle-aged women were more likely to die than men. Their health suffered primarily from the 'multifarious and simultaneous burdens they had to carry as women, mothers, nursemaids, nurses, gardeners, cooks . . . factory workers, good neighbours and washerwomen'.[20] Their strength was whittled down further by frequent pregnancy, abortion and childbirth. Unlike peasants and the bourgeoisie, who for economic reasons were forced to postpone marriage, workers, whose earnings were highest when they were young, married at a fairly early age, with the result that they were also blessed with a large number of children. Nine pregnancies per marriage was no rare occurrence, although abortions and a high infant mortality rate meant that not all pregnancies resulted in surviving children. Nevertheless, working-class families in the nineteenth and early twentieth centuries tended to be large. One survey carried out in the Berlin workers' district of Wedding showed that in 1885 over 25 per cent of households had more than five offspring.[21] According to a representative investigation, working-class couples who had married before 1905 and were still together in 1939 had, on average, 4.67 children. Of the working population in the industrial and service sectors, workers had the most children. Only farmers and agricultural workers showed higher figures (see Table 4, p. 329).

Yet there was a marked stratification within the industrial working class. Wives of unskilled workers had more children than wives of skilled workers, since from the early 1900s the latter, believing their consumption needs were increasing, and benefiting from an ever more efficient social security system, tended to raise smaller families, and provide their children with better schooling and vocational training.[22] Women in these families began to concentrate more on household duties and bringing up children, and to create for their dear ones that 'home sweet home' that middle-class observers so

burg 1908, p. 48. See also M. T. W. Bromme, *Lebensgeschichte eines modernen Fabrikarbeiters* (first published 1905), Frankfurt 1971, p. 25, and H. Mehner, 'Der Haushalt und die Lebenshaltung einer Leipziger Arbeiterfamilie (1887)', in Rosenbaum (ed.), *Seminar: Familie*, pp. 309–33, esp. p. 318.

20. Imhof, *Gewonnene Jahre*, p. 151.
21. Rosenbaum, *Formen*, p. 435.
22. See U. Linse, 'Arbeiterschaft und Geburtenentwicklung im Deutschen Kaiserreich von 1871', *Archiv für Sozialgeschichte*, 12, 1972, pp. 205–71, esp, pp. 218ff; R. Spree, *Health and Social Class in Imperial Germany*, Oxford, 1988, pp. 84ff.

seldom came across among the leisureless and impoverished working population. The best prepared women were those who had spent their single days in domestic service, and had become used to living in comfort, eating healthy food and maintaining a decent standard of hygiene. As a result, servant girls were often preferred as potential marriage partners, and it was common knowledge that many workers 'will only take a factory girl as a wife if she has also spent some time in service and learned something of housekeeping and farming'.[23]

The vast majority of women, however, were still far from becoming housewives and mothers and nothing more. Rather, the opposite was the case: towards the end of the nineteenth century there was a marked rise in the number of married women working in factories. Whereas in 1875 only about 20 per cent of female factory workers were married, by 1907 the figure had risen to 27 per cent, and this at a time when the absolute size of the total female factory workforce had also increased. It is debatable whether this rise can be attributed to more working-class women turning to, or having to turn to, waged work, since real wages went up during the same period. It was more probably the case that married women increasingly gave up working from home for little return in favour of better-paid factory work, a trend which will have been reinforced by the fact that sectors employing most outworkers (linen, clothing) were gradually turning to factory systems. Some enterprises took account of the special circumstances of married factory women, allowing them to start their dinner break half-an-hour earlier and to extend it over an hour and a half, so that they could quickly put together a meal for the family. The remaining domestic chores had to be done in the evenings, after a working day which lasted between ten and fourteen hours, in the mornings before work, and on Sundays. If they did not yet go to school, children were supervised by relatives – by grandparents in particular – or were left to fend for themselves.

The bourgeoisie, clergy, doctors, teachers and factory inspectors constantly inveighed against these conditions, and demanded a radical reform of the conditions in which the proletarian family lived. In the interests of healthy offspring and an ordered family life, they called for a ban on married women working in factories or, when in more reserved mood, for the government to impose re-

---

23. *Ergebnisse der über die Frauen- und Kinder-Arbeit in den Fabriken auf Beschluß des Bundesraths angestellten Erhebungen*, Berlin 1877, p. 62.

strictions and provide support through social programmes. The German government's reaction, however, was cautious. In most cases, employment protection legislation merely reiterated conditions which already existed. After 1878 women were prohibited by law from working underground or within three weeks of giving birth, and after 1891 from working at night. 1910 saw the introduction of the ten-hour maximum working day for women, and of a compulsory eight-week break between childbirth and resumption of employment. But insurance funds did not start paying money to women in childbed until 1883. Even then, it amounted to one half of the local average day wages, and was so low that the financial problems of many women who had just given birth forced them to go straight back to the factory, ducking the regulations by changing jobs. Protective legislation, which in any case applied only to women factory workers, not to those in domestic industry, agriculture and domestic service, had little effect on the dual burden which sapped the strength of married women. On the contrary, their burden was made even heavier during the last third of the nineteenth century, when various associations, institutions and campaigns interested in social issues began to encourage the working classes to emulate bourgeois home life, with an eye to improving health standards. Not least, bourgeois women and their organisations joined in this project of 'civilisation', in the hope that they could help solve the great social problem of the day 'woman to woman'.

9

Proletarian Women and their Allies
Men of the Proletariat or Women of the Bourgeoisie?

Middle-class women had shown an interest in the living and working conditions of proletarian women as early as 1848, when for the first time they had appeared as an organised group, and debated ways of alleviating the oppressive social and economic situation facing their counterparts lower down the social scale. From the 1840s, a spirit of 'self-help through association' had been taken up in bourgeois and proletarian circles alike; it seemed commendable and practical for lower-class women too. Unlike men, however, who as journeymen had over a century's experience of organising themselves, women would require reinforcements from outside as the idea of the collective representation of interests was quite foreign to them.

The working men's associations founded during the revolution proved disinclined to afford women the help they needed. Their members were predominantly journeymen, who maintained their existing structures – in particular relief funds – and sought to add nothing more than trade union functions to their activities. The associations of book printers and cigar makers were alone in developing new and national forms of organisation and in spelling out their political aims. Membership of both these bodies, along with allied journeymen's associations, was open exclusively to men. This is not surprising on the whole, since most craft industries formally employed no women at all. But it was in those sectors in which women did work for a wage – for example in tailoring and cigar manufacturing – that opposition to female labour was most vociferous. A year after its formation in 1848, the second congress of the Association of German Cigar Makers (*Association der Zigarrenarbeiter Deutschlands*) passed a resolution calling for a ban on female factory labour. In this case 'factories' were deemed to be sites not only of centralised production but also of decentralised, home-based production. Cotton printers and tailors also objected to female colleagues, and sent petition after petition to the government demanding the prohibition of, or at least wide-ranging restrictions on, female labour. They reasoned that the severe wage competition – women earned less – was not only harming their own situation, but would also ultimately bring about the collapse of the entire trade. Tailors more than any others felt their economic existence to be seriously threatened; admittedly, they were powerless in the face of non-guild member tailoresses, who made women's and children's clothing in the homes of their bourgeois employers. This kind of work was not deemed to be the practice of an independent trade, and thus did not require an official licence. In the case of tailoresses, however, who worked from home and in addition employed assistants and apprentices, the government was called upon to step in and shut the business down. Local police authorities only rarely pursued this since in reality it was extremely difficult to distinguish between women who were independent traders and those who were engaged in waged labor. Many women who sewed and tailored for middle-class families took some of their work home with them, and enlisted the help of their colleagues. 'Forced to consider the employment conditions of women and girls who are reliant on their earnings from needlework', the Prussian Trade Ministry likewise felt it expedient not to yield to the fear of competition and the monopolistic demands of male craftsmen and labourers.[1]

While working men protested against the 'dirty tricks of competition' from their female colleagues, a combination of relatively liberal trade policies, which put paid to most outmoded guild practices, and a rapidly rising demand for labour in the expanding industrial economy, saw to it that such complaints fell largely on deaf ears. There was a jump in women's employment in the textile and tobacco industries. In tobacco and cigar factories in Baden, there were three women for every two men in 1861, and when domestic industry grew in the 1860s the ratio moved further in women's favour.[2] After the retail system for drapery expanded in the 1840s, women were also rapidly making inroads into the tailoring trade. In 1867 Berlin's tailors and clothiers had twice as many women as men on their pay-roll, and in 1870 in Hamburg the ratio

1. Petitions, and ministerial responses, are reprinted in J. Kuczynski, *Studien zur Geschichte der Lage der Arbeiterin in Deutschland von 1700 bis zur Gegenwart*, Berlin 1964, pp. 333ff. On tailoresses see Hausen, 'Technical Progress', p. 159.

2. Calculated from U. Engelhardt, *'Nur vereinigt sind wir stark': Die Anfänge der deutschen Gewerkschaftsbewegung 1862/63 bis 1869/70*, vol. I, Stuttgart 1977, pp. 307, 267.

of male to female tailors' assistants was 1:3.6.[3] The trade unions for cigar makers and tailors, which had re-emerged in the mid-1860s, nevertheless battled on to keep their ranks free of women. Point 10 on the agenda for the First General Congress of Cigar Makers, held in Leipzig, in 1865, concerned 'the removal of women and children from the workplace in the interests of morale and standards of behaviour'. The General German Tailors' Association (*Allgemeiner Deutscher Schneiderverein*), formed in 1867, explicitly excluded women from membership.

Both these unions were politically allied to Ferdinand Lassalle's General German Workers' Association (*Allgemeiner Deutscher Arbeiterverein*) of 1863, which had adopted a resolute stance against any further growth in the number of industrial jobs. In the eyes of the Lassalleans, whose hopes were pinned more on a future socialist state than on improvements in the existing order, female industrial labour was undesirable, as it undermined the economic and social strength of the workers to fight capitalism. The leaders of workers' educational associations (*Arbeiterbildungsvereine*) took a more pragmatic approach, and following the failure of the revolution in Saxony and South Germany in particular, they launched into a period of intense political activity. Founded and headed by members of the progressive and liberal bourgeoisie, the majority of these associations adopted the position that 'women are entitled to perform the labour of which they are capable', as a resolution of the Third Congress of Workers' Associations put it in 1865.

The Pforzheim manufacturer, Moritz Müller, who was especially active on this issue, encouraged delegates to go even further and implement specific educational measures to improve women's employment skill, thereby opening to them (almost) all trades and activities. But Müller's radical proposal failed to win unanimous approval. Some local associations were prepared to accept it only on certain conditions, and argued for restricting women's employment to specifically feminine occupations and domestic industries, in order not to endanger men's jobs and wage levels. Others followed the Lassalleans, demanding that women should be barred completely from factory work; much better to send them into domestic service and turn them into good housewives. They also insisted that men should receive higher wages (for the whole family), and thus free their wives and daughters from the shackles of 'mechanical

---

3. Ibid., p. 343; J. J. Breuilly, *Joachim Friedrich Martens (1806–1877) and the German Labour Movement*, Ph.D., York 1978, p. 118–19. See also Breuilly and W. Sachse, *J. F. Martens und die deutsche Arbeiterbewegung*, Göttingen 1984.

labour'.[4]

To classify these attitudes under the crude heading of 'proletarian anti-feminism'[5] is to distort the historical perspective and fail to recognise the motives which led men to argue as they did. The workers' associations of the 1850s and 1860s were organisations mainly of journeymen, whose jobs were still in many cases based on craft practices, and who perceived the industrial system as a threat to their traditional working methods and life patterns. But even those among them already employed in factories took a sceptical and guarded view of the new order, which was making redundant the rules and rhythms of work and life they had been used to. It was, of course, an unquestioned feature of the 'good old days' that a woman worked at home, ran the household, tended the garden, looked after the children and animals, and gave her husband a hand in his trade when the need arose. But women in a factory? This was nothing short of a blatant transgression of customs and morality. It was enough for men to have to become accustomed to working outside the home; women at least ought to stick to the old ways and salvage some parts of the 'perfect world' from the ravages of the new regime. If financial considerations made this impossible, women ought to enter trades which could be classified without question as feminine occupations. One indignant cigar maker wrote the following in a letter to a journal: 'If all women socialists promise to keep well away from our businesses, then we also shall solemnly avow not to become cooks, cleaners, lacemakers, needleworkers, flower girls, knitters, seamstresses etc. etc.'[6] In line with customs in agriculture, male and female workers were where possible kept strictly apart. What lay behind protests and resistance to female labour in trade and industry outside the home were archaic ideals, not a positive commitment to the bourgeois model of the modern family which, in any case, was not part of working-class experience. Moreover, the fact that the debate on women became so heated cannot be explained simply by referring to fear of competition and the closed-shop mentality of existing occupational groups, because

4. The debate over female labour described here can be read in the *Allgemeine deutsche Arbeiter-Zeitung*, Coburg 1865–6, esp. the following editions: 130–2, 139–40, 143–4, 148–9, 151–3, 155, 161, 167.
5. W. Thönnessen, *The Emancipation of Women: The Rise and Decline of the Women's Movement in German Social Democracy 1863–1933*, trans. J. de Bres, London 1970, pp. 15ff. See also H.-U. Bussemer, 'Bürgerliche und proletarische Frauenbewegung (1865–1914)', in A. Kuhn and G. Schneider (eds), *Frauen in der Geschichte*, Düsseldorf 1979, pp. 34–55, quote at p. 38.
6. *Concordia: Organ der Association der Cigarrenarbeiter*, Berlin, no. 34, 7 December 1849, p. 141.

such arguments were also part of the armoury used to ward off unskilled male labour.

The bourgeois mentors of the workers' educational associations, those progressive and liberal-minded lawyers, professors, entrepreneurs and teachers who campaigned for the right of women to paid and factory employment, espoused socio-cultural values and orientations that were quite different to those of the organised proletariat. To their minds, industrialisation meant primarily progress: the releasing of human energies and labour from the bonds of artificial restriction and stagnation. They welcomed the new possibilities for cheaper consumption, faster travel and communication, and the opportunities for earning higher incomes. 'Considerations of the national economy' alone led them to believe that the 'setting free of women's labour' was called for, and they searched for ways of 'enabling its utilisation'.[7] The underlying motor of economic development was, in their view, personal work and the achievement ethic, and it was consequently 'a duty and an honour for the female sex' to be available to the industrial labour market.[8] But there were also political and ideological reasons for promoting female employment outside the home. First, it was high time that bourgeois society's promise of freedom and equality for women be realised, and for women to be raised to the status of 'respected assistants (*Gehilfinnen*) of men and members of humanity enjoying their full rights'. Second, women had to be liberated from personal 'slavery', and rendered capable of a self-determined existence free of enforced economic dependence on their husbands. There was no reason why, if necessary, employment could not be fitted in with family duties, although it would be inadmissable for family life to become anything but 'the crown of a woman's entire life, as it is at the moment and always should be'.[9]

When bourgeois politicians sympathetic to the working class argued for the use of female labour in trade and industry, they did

7. Motion proposed by Moritz Müller at the Third Congress of Workers' Associations in 1865, reprinted in *Allgemeine deutsche Arbeiter-Zeitung*, no. 140, 3 September 1865, p. 766. Further evidence that female labour was viewed positively by the liberal bourgeoisie is provided by the activities of the trade unions founded in 1868–9 by the liberal politicians Hirsch and Duncker. They not only organised women, but also called for 'complete freedom of labour' for women. See Engelhardt, *'Nur vereinigt sind wir stark'*, p. 307.

8. Motion proposed by Professor Eckardt at the German Women's Conference in 1865, reprinted in *Allgemeine deutsche Arbeiter-Zeitung*, no. 147, 22 October 1865, pp. 815–16.

9. M. Müller, 'Vortrag über die Frauenfrage', a speech given at the third workers' conference in Stuttgart, reprinted in *Allgemeine deutsche Arbeiter-Zeitung*, no. 143, 24 September 1865, pp. 790–2.

so in terms of social justice, individual freedom, and gains for the economy as a whole. Though major political conferences were able to reach majority decisions, debate over fundamental issues continued to be animated. Over the ensuing years, great minds were divided over the issue of whether the labour movement should welcome industrial female labour as a vehicle which would further the cause of economic and social emancipation, or fight against it as one which depressed wages and destroyed families. When the Social Democratic Party (SPD), which emerged from the movement of workers' associations, was created in 1869, motions presented to the founding congress in Eisenach calling for the abolition of female labour were accompanied by an objection demanding equal wages for men and women. In the end, delegates reached a compromise, and adopted the demand for 'a restriction on female labour' for their programme. The Gotha Congress of 1875, where Lassallean and Eisenach Social Democrats were united into one party, came to a decision that was both more rigid and more differentiated: it wanted to see a ban on 'female labour where it might be deleterious to health and morality'.

The dispute over women's labour and organisation was also carried on in the new trade unions that emerged under the impetus of the formation of a socialist party. After fierce debates, in 1869 the General German Association of Cigar Makers decided to open its membership to women in the future, in an effort to put an end to wage competition. Many local branches drew the line at this, however, and managed to exempt themselves from the new statute. Above all, the trade bodies whose structure reflected their artisan roots (lithography, book binding, glove making, millinery, etc.) adhered firmly to closed-shop principles of organisation, admitting neither women nor unskilled workers as members. Evidence clearly suggests that workers in spinning and weaving mills had fewer reservations about joint organisation for both sexes. For instance, the Trade Association of Manufacturing, Factory and Manual Workers (*Gewerksgenossenschaft der Manufaktur-, Fabrik- und Handarbeiter*), formed in 1869, recruited men and women, and by 1870 numbered more than 1,000 women as well as 6,000 men. [10] This was, however, a conspicuous exception among the socialist trade unions of the 1870s and 1880s. In 1892 only 4,355 women – a mere 1.8 per cent of total membership – were organised in the Free

10. W. Albrecht, *Fachverein-Berufsgewerkschaft-Zentralverband: Organisationsprobleme der deutschen Gewerkschaften 1870–1890*, Bonn 1982, pp. 46–7, 60–1.

Trade Unions, though they accounted for more than 20 per cent of the whole trade and industrial workforce. In the same year, the first general union congress called upon all affiliated organisations to accept women, and to regard the recruitment of women members as 'requisite for maintaining strength'. Most took note of the recommendation, with the result that four years later 15,265, or 4.6 per cent, of all unionised workers were female. The rise was due mainly to the new industrial unions (textiles, metallurgy, wood) which placed less emphasis on the difference between skilled and unskilled labour and took a less suspicious view of women.[11]

The opposition which male workers' organisations for a long time showed towards the co-organisation of women, and to having their own unions represent women's interests too, was one reason why middle-class women took up the cause themselves. As early as 1848, Louise Otto had defended the view that working-class men should not be alone in supporting working-class women in their collective 'association'; there was, she claimed, a role also for bourgeois women's associations. It was probably due to her influence too that women's right to membership was laid down in the statutes of the German Working Men's Brotherhood, formed in 1848 as the first labour organisation covering all trades, and dissolved in 1850. However, the pledge to pay adequate attention to the interests of working women was no more than a formal promise. The Brotherhood was at root a federation of journeymen and factory workers with craftsmen's qualifications, who were not prepared to accept female labour either in employment outside the home or in 'masculine' jobs. By contrast, the fact that an increasing number of women from the lower classes were engaging in paid employment, whether in factories or at home, was less of a problem of principle for bourgeois women's associations and the middle-class founders and leaders of workers' educational associations and trade associations. They were more concerned to criticise the tangible outcomes of female wage labour: inadequate earnings, long working hours, sexual exploitation at work, and the temptation to turn to prostitution.

Much in the same way that progressive liberals such as Hermann Schulze-Delitzsch, Max Hirsch or Moritz Müller – 'friends of the working class' – approached working men with a message of 'help-

---

11. G. Ritter and K. Tenfelde, 'Der Durchbruch der Freien Gewerkschaften Deutschlands zur Massenbewegung im letzten Viertel des 19. Jahrhunderts', in H. O. Vetter (ed.), *Vom Sozialistengesetz zur Mitbestimmung*, Cologne 1975, pp. 61–120.

ing you to help yourselves', middle-class women attempted to lend organised support to working women. In Berlin in 1869, an Association for the Further Education and Intellectual Exercise of Working Women (*Verein zur Fortbildung und geistigen Anregung der Arbeiterfrauen*) was formed. Its aim was to establish a school of vocational training and hall of residence for women, and to set up a relief fund for women workers.[12] Similar associations were created elsewhere, defining their prime activities in terms of education and the provision of welfare assistance, to the exclusion of wage struggles and trade union functions in the narrower sense. Organisations such as the Association for the Defence of Working Women's Interests (*Verein zur Wahrung der Interessen der Arbeiterinnen*), formed in Berlin in 1885 and concerned to 'regulate pay conditions' and 'lend mutual support in wage disputes', had to dispense with the financial and personal co-operation of the middle-class, who found such aims too radical and political. Though it did encourage proletarian women to learn new skills, manage their money more economically and adopt stricter moral standards, in order that they improve their situation themselves, the bourgeois women's movement saw itself primarily as a campaign of education and petitioning, not as an offensive, militant organisation fighting 'issues of daily bread and basic needs'.[13]

With these aims in mind, from the 1850s onwards middle-class women established Sunday schools for working-class girls, taught them to knit, sew and master other needlework skills. They read them stories suitable for their 'intellectual, religious and moral training', which would impress upon them the necessity of virtues such as 'a passion for cleanliness, hard work and tidiness'. They helped firms organise schools and courses on home economics for women workers, and founded cookery schools where, having finished general education, young girls from poor families could learn the art of 'simple cooking'. They set up milk kitchens which dispensed, and taught women how to prepare, germ-free milk, and instructed working-class women on how correctly to look after and feed infants.[14] They launched 'People's Kitchens' for working-class

12. On the creation of these early associations, see Twellmann, *Textband*, pp. 155ff; also H.-U. Bussemer, *Frauenemanzipation und Bildungsbürgertum: Sozialgeschichte der Frauenbewegung in der Reichsgründungszeit*, Weinheim 1985, pp. 191ff.
13. On the self-image of the movement see the article entitled 'An die Leserinnen' in *Neue Bahnen: Organ des allgemeinen deutschen Frauenvereins*, vol. 10, no. 1, 1875, reprinted in E. Frederiksen (ed.), *Die Frauenfrage in Deutschland 1865–1915*, Stuttgart 1981, pp. 46–8.
14. U. Frevert, 'The Civilising Tendency of Hygiene: Working-class Women

families, as well as day-nurseries to which married women factory workers could entrust their young children while they went to work. They played a part in creating schools of further industrial and vocational training, some of which they controlled directly and to their own personal advantage: in 1876, for instance, the Association of Berlin Housewives (*Berliner Hausfrauenverein*) set up such a school for domestic servants.

Through involvement in these projects, bourgeois women's associations joined the ranks of a social movement embracing many occupational groups and bearers of social forces, which in the second half of the nineteenth century sought to integrate and 'civilise' the working-class population – and working-class women in particular. What underlay these well-meant endeavours were not merely a philanthropic bent and a sense of shock at the depressing conditions in which proletarian women and families existed. A further motivating factor was the interest of these women in making the norms and 'virtues' of bourgeois society, which they regarded as right and proper, more widely accepted. Not infrequently did the objects of this interest blatantly reject it. Working-class women did not like using the crèches and day nurseries, perhaps because 'the demands made of mothers to keep their children clean, punctual and well-groomed [were] too strict'.[15] The educational efficacy of welfare initiatives and institutions depended on working-class women having to accept an even greater burden of housework. But lack of time was bound to keep chores to a minimum. Working-class women were now expected to bring this minimum into line with bourgeois standards, without, however, the aid of either servants or domestic appliances.

If, as far as proletarian women were concerned, this kind of social assistance was ambivalent both in intention and in effect, for middle-class women it provided the opportunity to engage in new spheres of activity and to pursue a vocation which was deemed socially useful and politically worthy. Towards the end of the century, the traditional, honorary commitment that bourgeois women's associations had made to private welfare schemes was superseded by publicly accepted and institutionally guaranteed forms of involvement in communal welfare projects which no longer merely addressed the clients of the poor house, but which were now

---

under Medical Control in Imperial Germany', in Fout (ed.), *German Women*, pp. 320–44.
15. *Ergebnisse*, p. 64.

concerned with the worse-off population in the wider sense. From the 1880s onwards, more and more local authorities began to enlist women in caring for the poor. In some towns – for example in Kassel, Königsberg and the Silesian town of Ratibor – women as well as men were entitled to become honorary welfare workers with all the rights and duties this office conferred. Elsewhere men raised objections. In Berlin in 1896 three thousand employees of the welfare service threatened to stage a mass protest and resign their posts if the Civic Assembly went ahead with its decision to take on women too.[16] In most cases women and their associations did not enjoy equality with their male colleagues in communal welfare, but were seen as auxilliaries responsible for particular, specialised tasks. This did not always occur simply as a result of pressure from the associations, who offered their services to the civic administration, but sometimes because local authorities themselves came to appreciate that female assistance was inexpensive. For example, in 1880 the welfare authorities in Elberfeld called upon middle-class women to 'make themselves available to provide additional and auxilliary services for the public care of the poor'. In emergency cases, which fell outside the remit of public welfare administration, associations were to offer support and 'take suitable measures to prevent poverty'. Three months later, 200 women gathered together and formed the organisation which had been called for; within only a few months, there were 1600 female members and 100 male 'friends'. Its work focused on running crèches for the children of mothers who '*are forced* to obtain employment outside the home whether this is because they are responsible for supporting the family, or because the husband's income is so insufficient as to need supplementing'. The association's own children's recreation centre was likewise intended for working-class children, as was the day nursery that was meant to protect girls from 'waywardness and the dangers of the streets'. In addition, the association attended to the needs of orphans and fatherless or motherless children placed with foster parents, and of destitute women in childbed. The latter were provided with a picnic basket full of everything 'requisite in such cases for personal hygiene and care, bedlinen and clothing, and printed teachings'.[17]

The majority of women involved in this association were married,

16. Salomon, 'Die Frau in der sozialen Hilfsthätigkeit', p. 41.
17. Wuppertal Civic Archives, S III 31b: 'Elberfelder Frauen-Verein. Kurze Darstellung seiner Gründung und seiner Tätigkeit. Festschrift zur Feier des 25jährigen Bestehens des Vereins. 1880–1905'.

and they all came came from the middle and upper ranks of the town bourgeoisie. The board of directors comprised the wives of men of various professions: of a superintendent, a pastor, a tax collector, a district judge and a district court councillor, of three chemists, a civic architect, a police inspector, a rabbi, and a head teacher. Their work for the association was a source of added prestige and public acknowledgement. Although for the purposes of membership registration they used the names and titles of their husbands, the women's personal status benefited from official involvement in socially important, communal activities. The recognition did not take a monetary form, however. Since husbands saw to financial affairs, it was taken for granted that wives would volunteer their services.

Neither did local authorities initially perceive any need to pay their 'auxilliary female troops'. Of the 488 women caring for orphans under the auspices of the Berlin city administration in 1901, only very few received an official salary.[18] The situation changed as the system of care for the urban poor gradually assumed the character of comprehensively planned and regulated welfare policy. The expansion after the turn of the century in local authority housing and health care services gave rise to new types of qualified occupations which in almost every case provided positions for women. In cities such as Leipzig and Breslau an increasing number of paid posts for women welfare workers were created, not least so that the authorities could exercise efficient control and legitimately issue instructions. From the beginning of the twentieth century Berlin also began to pay women to work in infant care and poor relief alongside volunteers. A survey conducted in 1910 in German towns with more than 10,000 inhabitants found that a total of some 400 women held salaried posts in local authority welfare systems. Five years later a similar investigation conducted in forty-five large towns concluded that, besides almost 10,000 female volunteers, 761 women were being paid for looking after infants, orphans and the poor, for working in housing and educational welfare, and for staffing employment exchanges.[19]

In the 1860s and after, the middle-class women so keen to be part of poor relief schemes fully expected to be asked to carry out this kind of social work on a voluntary basis. There were two main reasons: first, poor relief at that time was wholly in the hands of

18. Salomon, 'Die Frau in der sozialen Hilfsthätigkeit', pp. 48ff.
19. C. Sachße, *Mütterlichkeit als Beruf: Sozialarbeit, Sozialreform und Frauenbewegung 1871–1929*, Frankfurt 1986, pp. 286, 353–4.

teachers, businessmen, master craftsmen and so on, who, in addition to their paid occupations, did such work on an honorary basis; second, women's associations initially did not set their sights on broadening the range of job opportunities open to middle-class women. Women's work in welfare was regarded much more as a 'labour of love', and as a conscious contribution to the maintenance of social peace. Bourgeois women felt both suited for, and obliged to undertake, the task. Their suitability was grounded above all in the fact that they led 'lives of unmistakable sympathy for others' on account of which they could not but be destined to work with those who had 'lost courage', 'the desperate' and those who had 'sunk to the lowest depths'. 'Motherliness', an apparently innate feminine characteristic, particularly qualified women for social work, for this requires 'a transfer of a mother's love from her home to the community'.[20] Women were to lavish upon families of the lower classes the same motherly attention that they devoted to educating their own children, keeping floors clean and tidy, cooking healthy food, and managing the housekeeping without undue expenditure. The conviction was widespread amongst the bourgeoisie that the 'social question' – class conflict between the propertyless workers and the wealthy classes – could at least be alleviated, if not solved once and for all, by educational measures on a grand scale. Relying on their own experiences, middle-class women would set the working classes a positive example of how to run a household sensibly and look after children, irrespective of the scarcity of economic resources. They would thereby play a part in relieving working-class families of their social and moral predicament, and transform their political dissatisfaction into energies which would serve useful social purposes and encourage commitment to the existing order.

In this way, the women of the 'property-owning classes' contributed to the pacification of the 'dangerous classes'. If they were nevertheless affected 'frequently by a strong sense of being partly to blame' for the tangible bitterness and discontent exhibited by the working-class population, it was true that their 'lack of interest for, and understanding of, the views and expectations of the poor classes, along with complete inexperience of personal contact with these circles, heightened that bitterness'.[21] Such was the self-

20. Salomon, 'Hilfsthätigkeit', p. 5. See also D. Peters, *Mütterlichkeit im Kaiserreich: Die bürgerliche Frauenbewegung und der soziale Beruf der Frau*, Bielefeld 1984.

21. Quoted in M. Simmel, 'A. Salomon: Vom Dienst der bürgerlichen Tochter am Volksganzen', in C. Sachße and F. Tennstedt (eds), *Jahrbuch der Sozialarbeit 4: Geschichte und Geschichten*, Reinbek 1981, p. 372.

criticism expressed in a statement issued when the Berlin Girls' and Women's Social Relief Work Groups (*Mädchen- und Frauengruppen für soziale Hilfsarbeit*) were founded in 1893. The body acted as an agency for middle-class women who worked as voluntary assistants in social institutions, primarily in child and youth welfare. From 1899 onwards, it set up courses to train interested women for their activities, and this led in 1908 to the first non-denominational Social School for Women in Berlin, initiated and run by Alice Salomon, a doctor of the social sciences and member of the executive of the Federation of German Women's Associations (*Bund Deutscher Frauenvereine* – BDF).

10
Middle-Class Women and Their Campaign in Imperial Germany

Alice Salomon, the daughter of a wealthy Jewish business family, was born in Berlin in 1872. She belonged to a generation deeply influenced by the class structures and conflicts of Imperial Germany. After the German national state had come into being, the industrial working class had been radicalised and mobilised against capitalist domination and state authority by trade unions and the Social Democratic Party (SPD). Despite harsh repression by the state between 1878 and 1890, the SPD had managed to build mass support and increase its number of parliamentary representatives to 110 out of a total of 397 seats contested at the Reichstag elections in 1912. More than four million men had voted for the SPD, and shortly before the First World War more than one million men and women carried party cards. In the second half of the century the amorphous sense of unease that before 1848 had gripped the bourgeois classes in the face of pauperism and the proletariat, now became a more intense and genuine fear of revolution. Every strike, every Social Democratic Party congress, every demonstration, was evidence of the omnipresence of the 'red threat' endangering the wealth of the bourgeoisie and the stability of the social order. At the time, only a handful of people put their faith in the ability of a consistent policy of social reform to ward off the peril. The vast majority of the German bourgeoisie opposed the Social Democratic 'enemies of the Reich', sought the embrace of the nationalist movement, and opted for solutions to the crisis which avoided any need for domestic political concessions. By the 1870s, a spirit of imperialistic enthusiasm was bubbling through interest groups, the press, parliament and the state bureaucracy: clearly, for Germany to pursue a powerful *Weltpolitik*, centring ultimately on the acquisition of colonies, would not only accommodate the economic and status interests of the bourgeoisie, but also divert to abroad the reformist and revolutionary energies of left-wing liberal and social-democratic forces.[1]

The pattern of political mobilisation and the formation of political camps corresponded to a socio-economic division of society into classes, of which the contemporary public mind was becoming increasingly aware. The expansion of the industrial economy since the 1850s may have been generating a rapid growth in national income, but the gap between high and low incomes continued to widen. Although real annual incomes rose for all manual workers by almost 80 per cent between 1871 and 1914, they lagged a long way behind levels of income and wealth among the middle classes, for these were rising even faster.[2] But everything paled in relation to the profits accruing to industrialists and entrepreneurs. From the *Gründerjahre* at the latest – the period of rapid industrial expansion after German unification in 1871 – when investment in the industrial economy was boosted by a combination of French war reparations and expectations of a growth of domestic markets, and when even the occasional business-minded civil servant acquired a few shares in the hope of laying the foundations for a fortune, the divisions between rich and poor became increasingly marked. As cities grew – in 1871 only less than 5 per cent of Germans lived in towns with over 100,000 inhabitants, by 1910 the figure had risen to over 20 per cent – working-class housing districts appeared, well apart from the bourgeois quarters with which they now shared no more than a common water supply. While entrepreneurs had luxurious villas built, situated in park-like settings reflecting their owners' commercial standing, their workers had to make do with badly-lit tenement blocks or, at best, cramped housing estates. In 1842, the Essen industrialist Alfred Krupp had had the family home built in the factory grounds; but in 1873 he moved to the 'hill' just outside the town and, just like in feudal times, created a residence which testified to the family's wealth and to the firm's success.[3] The rather modest lifestyle of the bourgeoisie before 1848 was replaced after 1850 by an ostentatiously luxurious way of life, which was also reflected in forms of interior decoration. While furnishings in the Biedermeier period had been down-to-earth and somewhat spartan, although solid and reliable too, in the *Gründerjahre* interiors became overcrowded, intricate and excessively adorned. Reception

1. Wehler, *German Empire*, pp. 102ff., 176ff.
2. Ibid., pp. 144–5.
3. T. Buddensieg (ed.), *Villa Hügel: Das Wohnhaus Krupp in Essen*, Berlin 1984; see in particular the contribution by K. Borchardt, 'Der Unternehmerhaushalt als Wirtschaftsbetrieb', pp. 10–31.

rooms were packed with ornaments and upholstered furniture of different styles.[4] These fittings looked impressive and expensive, and they signalled to the visitor that he was in the presence of a respectable and well-off family.

The entrepreneur, successful independent professional or senior public official had more than simply a house to demonstrate and embody his wealth: there was also his family. Marriages within the nineteenth-century bourgeoisie were affairs less of the heart than of the purse-strings. A match at the right time and place could write off debts, win over loyal members of a firm, create business relationships and cement political coalitions. Not surprisingly, the sons of entrepreneurs usually married the daughters of entrepreneurs. Families of senior public officials and academics also belonged to the bourgeois economic marriage circuit.[5] In this setting, eligible daughters came to serve as investment funds used with the explicit aim of helping business to prosper. As wives, they headed a large household, co-ordinated and supervised several servants, and ensured the family maintained the appearances expected by its peers. A great deal of time and money was spent arranging balls, ladies' tea parties, gentlemen's dinner parties and children's birthdays: the family's public face was a decisive factor in whether the outside world had faith in the firm's creditworthiness. A manufacturer's wife was highly personal proof of the prosperity and stability of her husband's business; her demonstrable idleness, ever-changing and fashionable wardrobe and collection of tasteful jewellery, and her dilettantish interest in public cultural life were all standard trappings of bourgeois affluence. She was the living projection of the aristocratic leanings nurtured by large sections of the wealthy bourgeoisie. Far removed from the world of toil and the compulsion to make a profit, she was there to exude a lifestyle of luxury and display the refinements of social graces; free of the necessity to pursue any particular end, she was to devote herself to the fine arts, and to develop her hospitality in such a way that guests felt they were with cultivated and educated beings.[6]

Even if this ideal was reality for only a narrow stratum of the wealthy upper class, it was one which fired the imagination of a

4. E. J. Hobsbawm, *The Age of Capital 1848–1875*, London 1975, pp. 230ff.
5. J. Kocka, 'Familie, Unternehmer und Kapitalismus: An Beispielen aus der frühen deutschen Industrialisierung', in Reif (ed.), *Die Familie in der Geschichte*, pp. 162–86, esp. p. 178.
6. For a discussion of how aristocratic lifestyles and modes of behaviour were transferred to bourgeois women, see Rosenbaum, *Formen*, p. 325, and U. Blosser and F. Gerster, *Töchter der Guten Gesellschaft*, Zurich 1985, esp. pp. 103, 114ff.

broad section of the bourgeoisie. For families of public officials too life revolved around the motif of the bourgeois 'lady', but economic stringencies enforced compromises, and these always weighed more heavily on the women. In order to maintain the appearance of a respectable lifestyle, they had no choice but to be extremely thrifty and undertake an enormous amount of work – which, however, was to remain hidden from the outside world. The following, for example, was said of Frau O., the wife of a middle-ranking Prussian public official in the 1860s:

Since but one servant was there to help keep in order a five-room residence with five, and later seven, beds, with every single drop of water for drinking, cooking and cleaning having to be carried up and down the stairs; since all the laundry, including the children's clothes, was washed at home, although in the end a washerwoman was called in to help; since all the children's clothes, except boots and hats, were sewn and knitted at home, and since, in addition, several children demanded constant attention; and since two births came within three years without any extra domestic help: the life of the housewife comprised little more than toil and effort.[7]

Over the next few years, her husband's speedy rise up the career ladder did not, however, mean that she had much extra work to do in the home, despite the fact that they were able to move to a large house and were expected to maintain even higher standards of appearance. Two maids and infrastructural improvements in the form of direct gas and water supplies removed the burden of housework from her shoulders, and the family was now in a position to purchase finished articles of clothing for the children.[8] On the other hand, there was no let-up as far as her duties as a mother were concerned. Between 1853 and 1872 she gave birth to seven children, two of whom died. The eldest son had completed his fourth term as a student when the youngest daughter first saw the light of day. Frau O. spent almost forty years bringing up her

7. G. Hermes, 'Ein preußischer Beamtenhaushalt 1859–1890', *Zeitschrift für die gesamte Staatswissenschaft*, 76, 1921, pp. 43–92, 268–95, 478–86.
8. S. Meyer, in *Das Theater mit der Hausarbeit: Bürgerliche Repräsentation in der Familie der wilhelminischen Zeit*, Frankfurt 1982, attempts to salvage the honour of the bourgeois housewife by arguing that, like their counterparts in the working class, bourgeois women also constantly toiled away at home in a manner very much unlike the image of a life of idleness and cultivation of the intellect would suggest. This may well be an attempt to revise outdated prejudices, but its effect is to create new myths. More exact differentiation between bourgeois strata and attention to various phases of the family cycle may have helped to avoid excessive generalisations about the enormous burden of work on 'the' middle-class woman. Similar tendencies can be found in Meyer, 'The Tiresome Work of Conspicuous Leisure: On the Domestic Duties of the Wives of Civil Servants in the German Empire (1871–1918)', in M. J. Boxer and J. H. Quataert (eds), *Connecting Spheres*, New York 1987, pp. 156–65.

children, which considerably restricted her scope for social activities.

With five children, the family of Herr O., public official, was slightly larger than the average academic's family.[9] The following generation produced considerably fewer children. Of the couples who married before 1905 and who were still together in 1939, the average number of children born to those in the liberal professions was 3.21, while the figure was 3.04 for teachers and 2.98 for commercial white-collar workers, compared with an average for the whole population of 4.67.[10] The 'new middle classes' of white-collar workers and public officials were the first to use birth control as a deliberate method to restrict family size and thereby enhance children's as well as mothers' chances of surviving. Voluntary reduction in the number of children was accompanied by a tangible decline in infant mortality. Whereas in 1877–9, 17.5 of every 100 children born to public officials died before they were one year old, in 1912–13 only 8.3 suffered the same fate. While it is true that during this period the infant mortality rate went down in other social groups as well, the decline among public officials and white-collar workers was relatively higher.[11] A possible explanation of this might be that reducing the number of births encouraged mothers to pay more careful attention to their children they planned, and be better prepared – and more willing – to look after them; this found direct expression in the child's greater chances of survival. In these circumstances, fewer children did not necessarily cut down the amount of work, but it usually did mean that middle-class women spent a shorter period of their lives being tied to the home and family through pregnancy, lying-in and rearing young children.

The pattern of a declining birth rate was particularly distinct in families of the assimilated Jewish bourgeoisie. As early as the turn of the century, only a minority in this group had more than two children,[12] and even then nursemaids were often employed to look after offspring. Relieved of the burdens of childcare and domestic duties, the wives of Jewish businessmen, entrepreneurs, bankers and

9. von Nell, *Entwicklung*, p. 48.
10. Spree, *Health and Social Class*, table 14, p. 204.
11. In the population as a whole, the infant mortality rate went down from 20.1 per cent to 14.8 per cent, i.e. by 26.4 per cent, while the decline among public officials was 52.6 per cent and among white-collar workers 50 per cent. Calculated from ibid., table 4, p. 194.
12. M. A. Kaplan, *The Jewish Feminist Movement in Germany: The Campaign of the Jüdischer Frauenbund 1904–1938*, London 1974, p. 70; M. Richarz (ed.), *Jüdisches Leben in Deutschland: Selbsterzeugnisse zur Sozialgeschichte im Kaiserreich*, Stuttgart 1979, p. 14.

professionals were able to devote themselves to public affairs and the demands of the social world to a greater degree than Gentile women of the same social group. Before 1850 it had been taken for granted that wives helped in their husbands' businesses; now growing affluence led them to retreat more and more into family life. Education and culture were high on the agenda in the Jewish middle classes, and from the beginning of the nineteenth century, women started to play a crucial mediating role. Excluded from traditional Jewish educational canons, from an early age they familiarised themselves with the languages, literature and culture of the world beyond the ghetto, and maintained this cultural dominance even when emancipation and assimilation attentuated the divisions between Jewish and non-Jewish society. On the whole, the school education given to daughters of the Jewish bourgeoisie was superior to that enjoyed by their non-Jewish friends, and they were clearly overrepresented in higher girls' schools and universities.[13] When they were married, they played an active part in the local Jewish community, and performed charitable works for impoverished and sick people in the locality. The duty to become involved in social welfare was much more firmly rooted in Judaism than in Protestantism, and welfare institutions in Jewish communities were exemplary in terms of both their number and the range of their provision. It should therefore come as no surprise that Jewish women played such an important role in female social work and gave such decisive impetus to 'social feminism' (Kaplan). Moreover, Jewish women were generally far more willing to join organisations than their Gentile counterparts. Approximately 20–25 per cent of all Jewish women over thirty belonged to the Jewish Women's Federation (*Jüdischer Frauenbund (JFB)*) formed in 1904.[14]

As a result of anti-semitism in Imperial Germany – which was not always merely latent – social contact between Jewish and Christian families was not very common, and relations between the two groups were normally restricted to business connections between men. Despite this, the Jewish Women's Federation showed no hesitation in joining the Federation of German Women's Associa-

---

13. Richarz, *Jüdisches Leben in Deutschland*, pp. 51–2; Richarz, 'Vom Kramladen an die Universität: Jüdische Bürgerfamilien des späten 19. Jahrhunderts', *Journal für Geschichte*, 2, 1985, pp. 42–9; M. Kaplan, 'Tradition and Transition: The Acculturation, Assimilation and Integration of Jews in Imperial Germany: A Gender Analysis', *Leo Baeck Institute Yearbook*, 27, 1982, pp. 3–35; J. Carlebach, 'Family Structure and the Position of Jewish Women', in W. E. Mosse et al. (eds), *Revolution and Evolution: 1848 in German-Jewish History*, Tübingen 1981, pp. 157–87, and the comment by M. Kaplan in ibid., pp. 189–203.

14. Kaplan, *The Jewish Feminist Movement*, p. 11.

tions, the umbrella organisation for all women's associations. Although they pursued specifically Jewish aims, such as establishing female suffrage in their own communities, and were interested in maintaining their Jewish identity, the Jewish Women's Federation proved to be sensitive to the fact that they shared experiences with middle-class women who had no particular religious commitments, and that these women's husbands also enjoyed legal, political and economic advantages. Consequently, Jewish women felt able to lend unreserved support to the programme of the larger body, whose aim was to 'improve the situation of the female sex in economic, legal, intellectual and physical matters, and thus to further the common good'.

When the Federation of German Women's Associations was created in 1894, following the example set by the Americans, thirty-four groups joined. Twenty years later, membership had already risen to forty-six associations catering for 500,000 women. In addition to national bodies, whose responsibility lay with particular issues (reforming fashions and encouraging practical, simple clothing; teetotalism; pre-school care for children; female suffrage; higher education for women, etc.) and regional associations and religious organisations (German-Evangelical Women's Federation, Jewish Women's Federation), other types of female associations existed, for example for teachers, clerical staff, post office and telegraph employees, and midwives. One of their important functions was to act as the women's movement's 'fountain of youth' (see Table 5, pp. 329–31).[15]

The widely-held notion that everyday life for middle-class women centred exclusively on the triad of kitchen, children and church has to be revised in view of the very multiplicity and variety of women's associations that existed, particularly since this variety was even more pronounced at local levels. It is clear that women too were part and parcel of the emergence of social associations, a process which had begun in the late eighteenth century and made a decisive impact on the political structure of Imperial Germany.[16]

15. A. Bensheimer, 'Die Organisation des Bundes Deutscher Frauenvereine', in *Jahrbuch der Frauenbewegung 1913*, Leipzig 1913, pp. 83–7.
16. Wehler, *German Empire*, pp. 83ff.; H.-J. Puhle, 'Parlament, Parteien und Interessenverbände', in M. Stürmer (ed.), *Das kaiserliche Deutschland*, Düsseldorf 1977, pp. 340–77; T. Nipperdey, 'Interessenverbände und Parteien in Deutschland vor dem Ersten Weltkrieg', in H.-U. Wehler (ed.), *Moderne deutsche Sozialgeschichte*, Königstein 1981, pp. 369–88; G. A. Ritter (ed.), *Die deutschen Parteien vor 1918*, Cologne 1973; H. J. Varain (ed.), *Interessenverbände in Deutschland*, Cologne 1973. None of these articles or books mentions women's associations or the women's movement.

Parties and pressure groups of all social classes were organised on a national scale and began to influence political decision-makers and the legislative process through parliamentary means or direct channels of power. Farmers, workers manual and non-manual alike, entrepreneurs, engineers and doctors all joined bodies representing their trade or profession; religious groups and trade unions were established; artisans and small traders as well as professors and others in the educated middle classes enrolled in national organisations. Most of these associations, akin to modern-day pressure groups, were solely male: women, who were not credited with the ability to engage in a trade, let alone in politics, were excluded. But even in those branches of industry which did employ women, men set up separate organisations. The statutes of the various associations of (male) shop assistants barred women from joining, for while female shopworkers were regarded as a 'serious social and moral danger threatening the entire life of our nation', the real danger for men was the possibility of female labour exerting a downward pressure on wages and undermining male prestige. Women clerical workers thus had no choice but to create their own organisations of interest representation – which indeed they did in 1889, with the support of a few men and the bourgeois women's movement.[17]

A cursory inspection of the multitude of women's associations in Imperial Germany shows that organisations were also set up to represent interests other than those related purely to occupation and trade. Let us take as an example a typical medium-sized German town such as Wuppertal-Elberfeld. Just before the outbreak of war in 1914, there were some thirty women's associations, of which six were trade-related. Four were concerned with strictly welfare issues; two were of a general religious character; and the energies of the great majority were devoted to quite specific matters such as the reform of women's clothing, or campaigns against the consumption of alcohol or for the right of women to vote. There were associations for legal protection and for career advice, clubs for ladies' athletics, female *Wandervogel* groups, old school associations[18] – in short, a highly developed, local culture of women's associations and

17. Nienhaus, *Berufsstand Weiblich*; U. Frevert, 'Vom Klavier zur Schreibmaschine: Weiblicher Arbeitsmarkt und Rollenzuweisungen am Beispiel der weiblichen Angestellten in der Weimarer Republik', in Frevert, *Frauen in der Geschichte*, pp. 82–112, esp. p. 87; Kuhn and Schneider, 'Traditionale Weiblichkeit und moderne Interessenorganisation: Frauen im Angestelltenberuf 1918–1933', *Geschichte und Gesellschaft*, 7, 1981, pp. 507–33, esp. 525ff.
18. Wuppertal Civic Archives, S XIII 25.

organisations. Most though not all of them felt themselves to be part of the bourgeois women's movement, and they were linked to the Federation of German Women's Associations either directly or as branches of national organisations.

The oldest member of the Federation, and the one richest in tradition, was the General German Women's Association (*Allgemeiner Deutscher Frauenverein* – ADF), founded in 1865 in Leipzig and chaired by Louise Otto. After the first women's movement had been silenced by a wave of political repression in 1849–50, it was a decade and a half before the original cause – the right of middle-class women to education and employment – was taken up and defended by new organisations. In contrast to the associations of 1848, which had been closely allied to the democratic-liberal movement, the bodies of the 1860s carefully maintained their distance from political parties and groupings. Even during their own meetings, the women avoided making overtly political statements, for the sword of Damocles hung over their heads – in the form of state legislation on associations, which made it a punishable offence for women to take part in political organisations and gatherings. Nevertheless their near-identification with liberal positions was unmistakable. This was shown by the close organisational contact between the Leipzig Women's Educational Association, founded in 1865 by Louise Otto, and the middle-class liberal members and sponsors of the (male) workers' educational associations who from 1863 held annual congresses. What the two organisations had in common was an intention to 'better' through education and self-help the women on whose behalf they were working, and to improve the conditions of their economic and social lives by exerting collective pressure on legislative and administrative agencies. The major goal of the Leipzig Association in 1865 was to raise women's intellectual qualifications and win for them the right to paid work. The targets of such endeavours were the relatively unfortunate 'sisters' of the proletariat. Evenings of entertainment were arranged, dealing with cultural topics as well as practical matters related to health and child care. A Sunday school for girls was also set up, with middle-class women giving lessons in the club-house of the Leipzig Workers' Educational Association, whose chairman, August Bebel, was acquainted with Louise Otto.

In a similar vein, the first women's conference to be held in Germany, in Leipzig in October 1865, focused on the problems faced by female wage-earners. The presence of a number of leading figures from working men's associations may have been instrumental in setting the agenda. The conference, attended by about 150 women, discussed production associations, vocational schools for women, trade exhibitions, and hostels for working women. Less attention was paid to demands that higher education for women should be expanded, and that women should have easier access to university and to the academic professions. This was a reflection of a pattern of political argumentation which had been distinguishable in the 1848 movements, and which proceeded to become ever more pronounced. Middle-class women tended to combine their interest in improving educational and occupational opportunities with their charitable commitment to the welfare of women from the lower classes, when necessary justifying one in terms of the other. Pointing to the contribution they made to mitigating class antagonisms and propagating middle-class norms of morality and behaviour, they hoped that equal access to institutions of higher education, academic professions and offices in state and local government administration would be the reward for their trouble.

The General German Women's Association, formed at the Leipzig Women's Conference, also followed a 'dual strategy' of this kind. Working-class women were hardly an issue at leadership level. While the Association did petition for better occupational training for young proletarian women, and for their employment in the post and telegraph office, its energies were primarily directed towards ensuring that the 'young ladies' higher up the social scale could enjoy sound educational and employment opportunities. The Association's communiqués to national and local government bodies insisted that schooling for girls be improved, and demanded that a greater number of qualified women hold office in education authorities and in local government.[19] In contrast to the activities co-ordinated by the centre, local groups and affiliated associations concentrated on providing on-the-spot support, care and education for proletarian women and children. They set up crèches and day nurseries for children whose mothers went out to work, offered servants further education, ran cultural events, and organised lectures. In 1913 there were fifteen local groups in the general organisation, with a total of 1,200 members. In addition, a further forty-nine member associations brought together 12,000–13,000

19. G. Bäumer, 'Die Geschichte der Frauenbewegung in Deutschland', in *Handbuch*, vol. I, 1901, pp. 1–166, esp. pp. 48ff. See Bussemer, *Frauenemanzipation*, pp. 94ff., for a meticulous analysis of local and national women's associations involved in the General German Women's Association and the Lette Association between 1865 and 1875.

women.[20]

The General German Women's Association was not the only nationwide body. In 1869 seventeen women's associations from Berlin, Brunswick, Bremen, Breslau, Kassel, Karlsruhe, Darmstadt, Hamburg, Mainz and Rostock joined together to form a Union of German Women's Educational and Employment Associations (*Verband deutscher Frauenbildungs- und Erwerbsvereine*). This happened largely on the initiative of the Association for the Advancement of the Employment Skills of the Female Sex (*Verein zur Förderung der Erwerbsfähigkeit des weiblichen Geschlechts*), established in Berlin in 1866 and called the 'Lette Association' after its founder and chairperson. Lette was president of the Prussian Central Association for the Well-Being of the Working Classes (*Zentralverein für das Wohl der arbeitenden Klassen*); created in 1844, this was an assembly of public officials and entrepreneurs who subscribed to bourgeois notions of social reform. In a memorandum of 1865, Lette addressed the issue of why new employment opportunities needed to be found for middle-class women. In order to put his ideas into practice he formed the association under the patronage of the Princess Regent of Prussia. Three hundred women and men from 'Berlin's most intelligent social classes' joined without hesitation.[21] The first thing they did was to set up an employment agency exclusively for middle-class women looking for posts as governesses, nursery nurses, book-keepers, fine embroiderers, and so forth. The association also ran a market selling merchandise hand-made by women. Just like the General German Women's Association, whose articles of association described its task as 'removing all obstacles hindering the expansion of female labour', the Lette Association set out to eradicate 'the prejudices and obstacles hindering the employment of women'. Unlike the General Association, however, it closed its ears to the voices calling for wider emancipation. The first report in 1866 stated that nothing could be further from the aims of the Association than 'so-called emancipation for women in the social, not to mention the political, sphere'.[22] While the General Association, wary of the public's

20. *Jahrbuch der Frauenbewegung, 1913*, p. 12. See Twellmann, Quellen, pp. 455ff., on the activities of local associations.
21. Ibid., p. 143.
22. Quoted in L. Hauff, *Der Lette-Verein in der Geschichte der Frauenbewegung*, Berlin 1928, pp. 101. See also A. Kaiser, '"Frauenemanzipation" wider Willen: Die pragmatische Politik des Lette-Vereins 1866–1876', in A. Kuhn and J. Rüsen (eds), *Frauen in der Geschichte*, vol. III, Düsseldorf 1983, pp. 167–94, and Bussemer, *Frauenemanzipation*, pp. 101ff.

prejudices, did not write an explicit demand for political sexual equality into its programme, its leading women made no secret of the fact that political emancipation was their fundamental long-term aim: women would first have to prove that they deserved the rights and duties of citizens. After Lette died in 1868, the two organisations adopted more similar positions. In 1876, Jenny Hirsch, who sat on the executive, made it clear that the Lette Association did not reject female suffrage out of hand, but felt that such moves were premature; instead she advocated 'gradually preparing the ground by making it more common for women to work and receive a more thorough education, such that an edifice may be erected for which the right of women to vote will be, so to speak, the crowning glory'.[23] In the same year, the General German Women's Association and the Lette Association signed a joint agreement underlining their similar views and aims.

It may well be that this organisational link was in part what led the Lette Association to abandon in 1877 its guarded attitude towards the 'wives and daughters of working people' and to lend them a 'helping hand'. Hitherto its sole concern had been 'young ladies', the 'girls of the middle and upper classes', who had been keen to take advantage of the training the association offered. Between 1866 and 1878, the number of young women attending Lette schools for trade, commerce and drawing had risen from 28 to 1,043.[24] They were largely the daughters of public officials, teachers, pastors, businessmen and master craftsmen, and were preparing for employment. As Lette had written in his memorandum, these women were undergoing training because of 'pressing need', not because they felt it was an enjoyable pastime, nor because they were consciously using it as a stepping stone to personal emancipation and liberation from family ties and social conventions. As early as the 1840s the problems faced by single women from the urban middle classes had become an issue. By the second half of the century the 'woman question' was on everyone's lips; even the editors of the 1898 *Brockhaus* encyclopaedia felt obliged to include an entry on it: with middle-class men increasingly disinclined to marry, and in any case tending to marry at a later age, it was argued, the number of single women was rising; appropriate employment had to be found for young women between school and marriage; consequently more jobs for women were needed in order to break down the 'manifest contradictions' between 'life's exigencies' and

23. Quoted in Twellmann, Textband, p. 207.
24. Ibid., p. 131.

traditional ideas about womanhood.[25]

In the attempt to explain the 'woman question', it was frequently argued that there was a surplus of women, or a lack of marital enthusiasm on the part of men. Demographical facts did not, however, support these assertions: not only was the statistical excess of women enormously exaggerated, but the number of marriages did not decline as much as was claimed.[26] The statement that men were marrying late in life was equally misleading, for in the eighteenth century, also, academics and businessmen had tended to marry later, but the 'woman question' had never been raised. An increase in their number was not the reason for single middle-class women becoming a political issue; the new factor was, rather, a *combination* of women's social conditions and their willingness to take their fate into their own hands.

Women of the nineteenth-century bourgeoisie in general waited longer than their predecessors had done before marrying, settling down when they were twenty-five or twenty-six.[27] As a result, the transition from childhood to married life stretched over some ten years; but this period of late youth lacked binding orientations and modes of behaviour controls. Simultaneously, the structure of the bourgeois family was undergoing changes in the second half of the century. Private households were relieved of some of their burdens because basic needs were being commercialised, and consumer industries and retail trade were expanding. Many articles which in 1800 had been home-made, or purchased in the form of raw products requiring laborious processing, could now be acquired ready-made in shops. While there were families whose meagre income necessitated thrifty housekeeping and in which the wife and servant girl were rarely idle, the productive energies of entire bevvies of daughters – let alone unmarried sisters, cousins and sisters-in-law – were now superfluous. Working at home for money was most common at the level of poorly-paid junior and middle-ranking public officials: daughters, and sometimes mothers too, sewed and embroidered 'behind closed doors', then sold their products to shops for next to nothing. Perhaps because of the very impossibility of gaining an accurate, objective picture of the extent of this 'disgraceful' phenomenon, it became a more and more frequent, and controversial, subject in contemporary literature. Working from home could conceal the fact that women were

25. *Brockhaus' Konversations-Lexikon*, vol. 7, 1898, pp. 235–8.
26. Bussemer, *Frauenemanzipation*, p. 23ff.
27. von Nell, *Entwicklung*, p. 74.

gainfully employed – a taboo in bourgeois society – and maintained the appearance that they lived a life of leisure. For ultimately it was a mark of status if middle-class women clearly *did not* work – proof of the absence of financial stringencies, and an illustration of the wealth and respectability of the family and husband.

To middle-class young women the prospect of spending the long years between school and marriage embroidering, sewing and crocheting, either secretly for the market or privately for their own dowries, seemed even less appealing when they compared their lot to their brothers', who could go on to university after school, and were tied to the parental home only by the need to collect their monthly allowance. Even though 'the prejudice of social class', as the 1898 *Brockhaus* maintained, continued to prevail against middle-class women going out to work, heads of families could no longer easily refute the economic prudence of their daughters undergoing vocational training. This applied even to a senior public official, whose family circumstances between 1859 and 1889 we can trace in exact detail from meticulous house-keeping records. This father, who was on a high income, not only paid for his three sons to study but also made provision for the future of his two daughters. They attended a higher girls' school (*höhere Mädchenschule*), and had private piano and singing lessons. Moreover, they were expected to train for a profession, for their 'prospects of being provided for by a husband were not favourable owing to a lack of money'. Although 'the vast majority of his peers felt his actions to be unworthy of his status', and even scorned them as a sign of his pandering to emancipation', the father demanded obedience, and ensured his daughters did not forget the following 'serious considerations': 'You are not pretty, you have no money, so marriage is out of the question'. The elder daughter refused to comply with his plans, preferring balls, afternoon tea parties and cultural events to vocational training, but the seventeen-year-old opted to train as a teacher. Family friends 'castigated her for being a blue-stocking', and regarded her decision as 'unladylike'.[28]

Of all the careers deemed fit for middle-class women, from the early nineteenth century onwards teaching was one of the most popular. In 1896 Prussia had 14,600 full-time women teachers; 10,000 worked in elementary schools and the rest in private and state higher girls' schools.[29] Most of them had themselves com-

28. Hermes, 'Ein preußischer Beamtenhaushalt', pp. 281–2.
29. R. and L. Wilbrandt, 'Die deutsche Frau im Beruf', in *Handbuch der Frauenbewegung*, vol. IV, 1902, table p. 320.

pleted higher girls' schooling, which at maximum lasted ten years, and then trained in special teaching seminaries. Until 1908, however, there were no standardised guidelines in Prussia either for girls' education or for the training of women teachers. Instead there was a series of individual ministerial decrees which were meant to give some structure to the almost incomprehensible myriad of school types, curricula and training courses.

Since 1895, girls had been able to take externally the *Abitur*, the highest school examination, after completing five years at a grammar school (*Gymnasium*) which followed the higher girls' school,[30] but this was not the normal course to take until 1908. After that date, three possible routes were open to the pupils of higher girls' schools (which in the meantime had been provided with standard curricula). If they had completed ten years' schooling (i.e., at the age of fifteen or sixteen), they could transfer to another kind of girls' secondary school, a *Lyzeum* or *Oberlyzeum*. There they chose either 'women's education' (*Frauenbildung*) in what were known as 'women's school classes' (*Frauenschulklassen*), or teacher training, which entailed three preparatory academic years plus one year on the practice and methods of teaching. The former route did not lead to a useful qualification, but the latter culminated in the official teaching examination which qualified women to teach in middle and higher girls' schools. The third choice – a scholarly profession – was available if they had spent seven years at a higher girls' school and six years in a grammar school or similar institution preparing for the *Abitur*.

For years education ministries, professional academic bodies and the bourgeois women's movement had been engaged in a bitter tug-of-war over grammar schools for girls and university courses for women. It was not until 1908 that the Prussian Minister of Education officially acknowledged that women could become 'proper' (*ordentlich*) students, though in some southern German states they had been allowed to study since the turn of the century. But even in states less intent on preserving the pomp and ceremony of militaristic student fraternities (*Burschenschaften*) there had been tenacious resistance from conservative public officials and professional groups. In 1871 the Senate of Heidelberg University described 'the attendance of ladies at academic lectures' as 'an unsavoury and disturbing phenomenon', and instructed lecturers not

---

30. There were only six grammar school courses, attended by 262 girls, in Prussia in 1902.

to tolerate it.[31] Until 1896 Prussian women required ministerial permission to attend lectures; after that, they needed the consent of the university rector. In 1896–7, 223 women were admitted as guest students to lectures in Prussian universities. They were largely unmarried Protestants, from families of academics and entrepreneurs, and most were interested in learning languages, art, history and literature.[32] The summer term of 1900 marked the first time that women in Germany were allowed to become fully registered students entitled to sit examinations: the medical faculty of Heidelberg University lifted its ban on female enrolment. A year later, Heidelberg was admitting women to all faculties. By contrast, it took another seven years before the pragmatists, who argued that Prussia should make up the ground lost to the other states and countries,[33] and institute general, standardised tertiary education for women, were able to breach conservative resistance in the Prussian cabinet.[34] At the beginning of the winter term of 1913–14 3,649 women – 6.3 per cent of all students – were studying at German universities.[35]

The women's movement chalked this up as a great success, for it had been campaigning for almost half a century for women to go to university. While, as in the case of female suffrage, the General German Women's Association initially argued rather unambitiously, and in 1888 petitioned education ministries to allow women to study medicine, the Women's Association for Reform (*Frauenverein Reform*), founded that year, demanded that women be entitled to enrol generally at university, not just for selected courses. Demands like this at first fell on deaf ears in ministries, but they did cause a stir in the press, parliaments, and among the general public. The women's vociferous opponents gained the upper hand during the 1870s, proffering physiological, social, moral and economic reasons why they were not cut out for academic study. A woman's 'nature', which placed her at the mercy of her physical make-up and cyclical fluctuations, was itself sufficient to make academic life impossible; but more than anything it was the wo-

31. Quoted in E. Beckmann (ed.), *Die Entwicklung der höheren Mädchenbildung in Deutschland 1870–1914*, Berlin 1936, p. 85.
32. K. H. Jarausch, *Students, Society, and Politics in Imperial Germany: The Rise of Academic Illiberalism*, Princeton, NJ, 1982, table p. 111.
33. Women had been admitted to universities since 1853 in the USA, 1861 in France and 1878 in Great Britain.
34. See Jarausch, *Students*, p. 109–13, on the motives behind and resistance to this decision. The explanation offered by R. J. Evans in *The Feminist Movement in Germany 1894–1933*, London 1976, pp. 17ff., is too vague.
35. Calculated from R. Riese, *Die Hochschule auf dem Wege zum wissenschaftlichen Großbetrieb*, Stuttgart 1977, pp. 340, 349.

man's 'natural role' – also a consequence of her physical attributes – which had the last word in the matter.[36] University professors from all faculties spoke out, warning against the moral and social effects the presence of female students would have. The most that could be conceded to young women was a provision for higher school education, which would offer them a challenging form of 'preparatory training to housewifery', as the national-liberal historian Heinrich von Sybel put it in 1870.[37]

Almost thirty years later opinion had shifted considerably. According to a survey conducted among 122 German professors, writers, and teachers in girls' schools, most basically agreed that women were suited to academic study. However, only a tiny minority was unreservedly in favour of admitting women to universities; even men who had said yes in principle detailed a whole number of restrictions and conditions. It was generally felt that the achievements of even the most gifted women 'can only be run-of-the-mill in matters of creativity and thus in science in general . . . if [they] are not to relinquish some of their feminine characteristics', as Georg Runze, a theology professor in Berlin, opined.[38] Many experts expressed a fear that mixed scholarly activity would blur natural sexual differences by rendering women unfeminine and men unmasculine. As Otto Gierke, a professor of law from Berlin, said: 'Our main concern must be that our men remain men. It always was a sign that things were going downhill when masculinity began to desert men and seek refuge among women!' Max Planck, who was Director of the Institute of Theoretical Physics at the University of Berlin and a member of the Academy of Sciences, also warned against meddling in nature's affairs. Even if individual women were indeed talented and gifted and showed an aptitude for academic

36. Twellmann, *Textband*, pp. 57ff.; Bäumer, 'Geschichte' in *Handbuch*, vol. I, pp. 88ff.

37. Quoted in Twellmann, *Textband*, p. 71. The teachers in girls' schools took this view too at their conference in Weimar in 1872, when, motivated by their corporate interests, they wrote to the German governments calling for standard girls' education throughout the Reich. The letter claimed that women ought be offered an education that was, not identical, but equal in value to men's, 'so that the German man should not be bored at home by the intellectual myopia and pettiness of his wife, and that his interest in higher things not be paralysed' (quoted by Bäumer in *Handbuch*, vol. III, p. 111).

38. This and the following quotations from A. Kirchhoff (ed.), *Die akademische Frau: Gutachten hervorragender Universitätsprofessoren, Frauenlehrer und Schriftsteller über die Befähigung der Frau zum wissenschaftlichen Studium und Berufe,* Berlin 1897. It proved impossible to compare the ayes with the noes in the survey, since only very few had unequivocal opinions. The majority, in typically professorial deliberation, were careful not to be pinned down and qualified their answers in several ways.

study, it could 'not be stressed enough that Nature herself assigned to women the role of mother and housewife, and that to ignore natural laws is to invite great damage which will in this case be inflicted upon coming generations'.

There were many men in medicine and law who, while having no objection to women studying *per se*, were not prepared to see female doctors, judges and lawyers practising their profession, whatever the circumstances. They did accept the notion, however, that women could be medical and legal *assistants*. While it was quite clear that these men feared professional competition, there were many academics who were at least as anxious about the effect female involvement would have on the reputation of their field. The Breslau historian Jacob Caro felt that the very foundations of historical sciences were at risk: 'Giving a say to women – who are generally interested in little more than the fortuitousness of a given situation – would be tantamount to declaring a state of permanent revolution'. Apart from very few exceptions, the general tenor of the debate was that women did not need to go to university; indeed it would be disadvantageous to all concerned. However, since it was impossible to deny that women had any abilities and aptitudes, it was difficult to close lecture theatres to them as a matter of principle. But they would have to produce the necessary qualification – the *Abitur*.

This was, however, an equally difficult condition for women to fulfill, since the various grammar and senior schools (*Gymnasium, Realgymnasium, Oberrealschule*) where pupils took university entrance examinations were open to boys only. Thus the women's movement regarded university education for women and the establishment of grammar schools for girls as two sides of the same coin. In 1887, following a host of unproductive submissions and initiatives, Berlin women sent yet another petition to the Prussian Ministry of Education and to the Parliamentary Assembly. This time they set out their aims in an accompanying document known as the Yellow Pamphlet. The author, a teacher named Helene Lange, was sharply critical of the limited educational aims and unacceptable pedagogical principles pursued by existing girls' schools. She complained above all that contemporary schooling led girls into a cul-de-sac; girls' schools should be reformed and offer, she insisted, school-leavers qualifications which would allow them a greater choice of vocational training. While on the one hand the Yellow Pamphlet called for equality with higher boys' schools, it also went to great lengths to state that female education was of a particular type, and that women had different interests and learning abilities. Consequently it favoured keeping boys' and girls' schools institutionally separate, and demanded, furthermore, that women teachers – who were clearly underrepresented in state girls' schools and taught the lower grades, if they taught at all – should be given considerable influence over schooling policy. 'The kind of women we wish to see cannot possibly be educated solely by men'. Accordingly, straightforward training in a teaching seminary would no longer suffice for women teachers; like their male colleagues they would need to undergo the academic education which hitherto had been denied them.[39]

The Parliamentary Assembly ignored the documents; the Ministry consigned them to the files. The press reacted sympathetically and encouraged the women, whereas male teaching associations were indignant. Helene Lange's Yellow Pamphlet found favour with many women teachers. In the 1870s individual, locally-based professional associations had been springing up, campaigning in particular for female staff to teach at senior level in girls' schools. In 1890 Helene Lange and some of her friends and colleagues from Berlin founded the 'General German Association of Women Teachers' (*Allgemeiner Deutscher Lehrerinnenverein*): it had 3,000 members after only a few months, and by the turn of the century 16,000 had joined, making it the largest professional association for women in the whole of Germany. Both its leaders and its political programme became influential in the bourgeois women's movement. Many of the movement's more famous and respected leaders were trained teachers: Auguste Schmidt, Gertrud Bäumer, Hedwig Dohm, Minna Cauer, Anita Augspurg and, of course, Helene Lange. Many of them had not married (they were explicitly forbidden to do so if they taught in state schools).[40] As a result they put all their energy into their work, and the obstacles they came up against made their political commitment seem all the more justified. In view of their personal experiences, it is hardly surprising that they were particularly active on education issues, and that they perceived the 'woman question' as first and foremost one of education and employment.

What is less obvious is why these women, most of them single

39. Lange's argument can be found in Bäumer, 'Geschichte und Stand der Frauenbildung', in *Handbuch*, vol. III, pp. 116ff.
40. M. Joest and M. Nieswandt, 'Das Lehrerinnen-Zölibat im Deutschen Kaiserreich: Die rechtliche Situation der unverheirateten Lehrerinnen in Preußen und die Stellungnahmen der Frauenbewegung zur Zölibatsklausel', in *Die Ungeschriebene Geschichte*. Dokumentation Wien 1984, Vienna n.d., pp. 251–8.

and gainfully employed, provided the women's movement with an ideological concept that is usually described in terms of 'intellectual', 'organised' or 'extended motherliness' (*Mütterlichkeit*). What moved middle-class women to formulate precisely the quality of motherliness as an ideological maxim and indispensable fulcrum of political action for the women's movement, when they themselves had overcome all family and social pressure, taken a courageous step into the male-dominated world of work and public life, and relinquished – if not betrayed – their 'natural vocation' as wives, mothers and homemakers? Why, furthermore, was this theory taken up so enthusiastically by the movement's supporters? Why did so few protest against a political ideology founded essentially on the very pre-conceptions and assumptions, now regarded as stultifying and outdated, that for a century had restricted their options and kept them in the home?

Given that the demand for skilled work for women met with such fierce resistance in Imperial Germany, it might be tempting to believe that tactical requirements explain why the women's movement argued tentatively and timidly, leaving women with a role in life which was slightly broader in scope than before but still essentially 'feminine'. However, such an interpretation would be inconsistent with the wealth of official and unofficial statements testifying to the deeply-held conviction that men and women were different beings with naturally diverse functions. Aside from recalcitrants such as Hedwig Dohm or the young Lily von Gizycki (later Lily Braun), even in the late nineteenth century women who subscribed to the bourgeois movement firmly believed that the female sex was without exception 'destined for motherhood', as Helene Lange put it, and that this destiny determined women's 'physical and psychic constitution'.[41] The women's movement should seek to preserve this natural constitution and ensure its free development wherever advantageous. It went without saying that the family represented the best environment for motherhood; a woman's most important job had always been looking after her children, husband and home.

Nevertheless, society as a whole needed feminine 'cultural influence' as well, in order to avoid, or at least mitigate, the effects of various deleterious phenomena such as, first and foremost, social

41. Quoted in B. Clemens, 'Der Staat als Familie' – oder 'Menschenrechte haben kein Geschlecht': Zwei politische Konzeptionen der deutschen bürgerlichen Frauenbewegung vor der Jahrhundertwende', in *Die Ungeschriebene Geschichte*, p. 54. See also I. Stoehr, 'Organisierte Mütterlichkeit': Zur Politik der deutschen Frauenbewegung um 1900', in Hausen (ed.), *Frauen suchen ihre Geschichte*, pp. 221–49.

problems apparently generated by economic development: the situation of the labouring classes; housing shortages and the break-up of the family; alcoholism and prostitution. For the bourgeois women's movement, the 'pathology of the Modern' was more than a function of scarcity and the problematic of distribution; it was, more significantly, an intellectual and spiritual disorder whose symptoms could be summed up as mechanisation, objectification and the obliteration of the soul and the individual. Modern technology and industry seemed to be the incarnation of masculine principles, a rational system which dominated and exploited the vitality of nature, ignoring and subjugating all individuality and diversity to uniform, mechanical laws of production. Women were like foreign bodies in this object world of machines and bureaucracies; the 'miserable impersonality' of economic life, cast as it was in a masculine mould, was no place for 'natural' feminine interests and sensitivity. What choice did women have? They could either as proletarian women accept the order of things and find work in a factory, or stay as middle-class ladies nestled in their bourgeois surroundings and never venture into the world outside. The example of female factory labour, however, was enough to show how misguided and counter-productive it was for women to accept the situation by striving for formal equality with men. As Helene Lange put it: 'These women represent the bankruptcy of human rights and of a programme which does not proceed beyond emancipation.' To demand equal rights to work, education, sexuality, etc., would not be enough, for if women enjoyed rights which were essentially male-oriented they would be subject to the 'worst type of slavery'. Emancipation was not to be confused with conformity to male standards. Rather, 'the fact that the sexes are different' explained why they could not be part of the 'great cultural systems' in the same way, because 'purely masculine creations' had to be perfected by feminine and motherly values and ideas.[42]

Sober reflection underlay this anti-modernist ideal of a culture that would accommodate the specific nature both of masculinity and of femininity. Women whose fathers and husbands had for two generations been constructing the modern world felt excluded from the gigantic processes of economic and social upheaval, and marginalised to the status of observers. They had been regulated to the role of fulfilling family and representative duties, yet also saw their

---

42. H. Lange, *Die Frauenbewegung in ihren modernen Problemen*, (first published 1907), reprinted Munich 1980, pp. 44ff; Lange, 'Das Endziel der Frauenbewegung (1904)', in Lange, *Kampfzeitem*, vol. I, Berlin 1928, pp. 294–307.

familial labours losing prestige – despite the laudatory tones of soap-box orators – while men's work was earning greater public acknowledgement. Their reaction to this situation was extremely ambivalent. On the one hand they felt they should 'adapt to modern social conditions' (Lange); on the other they criticised the same conditions as 'miserable', masculine and inhuman through and through, and demanded 'motherly policies' that would humanise both family and society at large, and thus place both on a more stable footing.[43] The women of the bourgeois movement were not alone in voicing this kind of social criticism; the German educated middle classes, exposed to the combined abrasive effects of the growth in industrial and technical materialism and the rise of the equally materialistic labour movement, and 'displaced' in the evolving order, also had reason to be discontent. The longing for unity and meaning was reflected in the various 'alternative movements': the youth movement, the 'back to nature' movement and artistic styles such as the *Jugendstil* which emerged around the turn of the century, as well as in extremely nationalistic and imperialistic calls for a *Weltpolitik* that would allow German culture, backed up by the industrial might of the fatherland, to fulfil its mission.[44]

While the educated bourgeoisie mourned the fact that people such as technicians, engineers, chemists and industrialists were now acquiring the status and influence they themselves had once enjoyed, hearts in the women's movement lay with pre-modern, pre-industrial days when society had granted them incomparably more influence and recognition. Although the positive impact of technical and commercial developments on housework was welcome, for now women ceased to be 'nothing more than a factor of labour' (Lange), women could scarcely take advantage of any new-found freedom because men had a firm grip over culture, science, economy and politics. There were two parallel paths leading out of this dilemma. Firstly women's work for the family needed to command higher ideological status; their contribution to the 'physical and mental well-being of the future generation' and to 'the good health

43. Lange, *Die Frauenbewegung*, pp. 30, 154ff.
44. On these 'alternative movements' see U. Linse, 'Die Jugendkulturbewegung', in K. Vondung (ed.), *Das wilhelminische Bildungsbürgertum: Zur Sozialgeschichte seiner Ideen*, Göttingen 1976, pp. 119–37; J. Frécot, 'Die Lebensreformbewegung', in ibid., pp. 138–52; U. Linse (ed.), *Zurück, o Mensch, zur Mutter Erde: Landkommunen in Deutschland 1890–1933*, Munich 1983; D. Sternberger, *Über Jugendstil*, Frankfurt 1977; P. Hampe, 'Sozialökonomische und psychische Hintergründe der bildungsbürgerlichen Imperialbegeisterung', in Vondung (ed.), *Das wilhelminische*, pp. 67–79; T. Koebner et al. (eds), *'Mit uns zieht die neue Zeit': Der Mythos Jugend*, Frankfurt 1985.

of society' (1905 Programme of the General German Women's Association) had to be given its due. To this end, the movement set up women's classes at higher girls' schools, ran educational courses at women's social schools (*Soziale Frauenschulen*), and set about enlightening working-class women – activities which sought to make more systematic and scientific tasks such as housekeeping, child-rearing and health care. Secondly women who wanted to be, or had to be, gainfully employed required maximum support from the state: effective labour and maternity protection for proletarian women, and greater job opportunities in the education and welfare sectors for middle-class women. If, in addition, equal political participation was instituted in the form of universal suffrage and access to public offices, not only would a solution, or at least a partial solution, be found to the various class-related versions of the 'woman question' – the conflict between 'family interests and production interests' (Lange) – but the impact of 'motherly policies' in general would also set the ball rolling for the reforms that society needed.

This was the position formulated by Helene Lange (1848–1930), Gertrud Bäumer (1873–1954), Alice Salomon (1872–1948) and Marianne Weber (1870–1950), and one shared by the vast majority of bourgeois women's associations. Disagreements occurred over tactics rather than overall aims. For example, the campaign by the Women's Association for Reform, established in 1888, for the right of women to university education was more strident and uncompromising by comparison with other groups; the programme of the Union of Progressive Women's Associations (*Verband fortschrittlicher Frauenvereine*), formed in 1899, included the demand for women's suffrage at a time when that of the Federation of German Women's Associations (BDF) did not, because of the views of some of its member associations. Since the aim of the BDF was to provide a large enough umbrella to accommodate the range of its members' class, party and religious allegiances, it only represented views acceptable to a majority – with the result that it moved further and further to the right when joined by the conservative German Colonial Women's Federation (*Deutschkolonialer Frauenbund*), German Evangelical Women's Federation (*Deutsch-Evangelischer Frauenbund*) and National Union of German Housewives' Associations (*Reichsverband Deutscher Hausfrauenvereine*).

The BDF's leaders, however, certainly did not have conservative political leanings. In fact, they placed themselves left of centre on the bourgeois party spectrum.[45] But to maintain the cohesion of the movement, and be able to show the outside world that all (bourgeois) women were united, they put a check on more radical groupings, or even banned them from joining. This happened in the case of the Federation for the Protection of Mothers (*Bund für Mutterschutz*), founded in 1905 – the demands in their manifesto for sexual freedom, for marriage that required neither the recognition of the registry office[46] nor the blessing of the church, and for material security for single mothers, were diametrically opposed to the ideas most of the BDF women had about morality and the family.[47]

45. Gertrud Bäumer, Chair of the BDF from 1910 to 1919, worked closely with Friedrich Naumann and his National-Social Association (*Nationalsozialer Verein*); in 1911 she became a member of the executive committee of the newly formed Progressive People's Party (*Fortschrittliche Volkspartei*), and in 1919 she joined the German Democratic Party (*Deutsche Demokratische Partei* – DDP). Marianne Weber chaired the BDF in 1919–20, and was also in the DDP.

46. After the Reich Law of the Status of Persons was passed in 1875, all marriages in Imperial Germany had to take place at a registry office. A church service afterwards was optional.

47. B. Greven-Aschoff, *Die bürgerliche Frauenbewegung in Deutschland 1894–1933*, Göttingen 1981, pp. 66ff.; Evans, *Feminist Movement*, pp. 115ff.

11
Bourgeois Sexuality, Prostitution and Marriage

To most middle-class women, the 'new ethic' of a Helene Stöcker, who co-habited with a man to whom she was not married, or the 'free love' of an Ellen Key or Franziska von Reventlov, were the height of immorality: flagrant violation of the written and unwritten laws of virtuous womanhood. To say openly that women as well as men had sexual desires and wished to fulfil them, inside or outside marriage, was to break irreversibly with the 'genteel' society which kept such libertarian tendencies at arm's length. Admittedly, bourgeois society was not so prudish and anti-sexual as is sometimes claimed. Sexuality was the subject of heated scientific and political controversies, not only in medical journals: it was anything but taboo.[1] However, it is precisely this remarkable loquaciousness, together with the sheer magnitude of the debate, which suggest that sexuality in the 'bourgeois age' was not without its problems. The breathless endeavours to observe, analyse and classify human sex life seem, rather, like attempts to use 'rational' scientific method to fathom and tame a disconcerting and incomprehensible source of anxiety.

It is no wonder that a society which placed so much emphasis on labour, self-discipline and control of emotions should also seek to regulate human sexuality and harness it to other social norms. From the eighteenth century on there was discussion about why the 'sex drive' needed to be curbed and its uglier manifestations suppressed. Mainly doctors, but theologians and educationalists too, felt called upon to define 'healthy' normality and to diagnose, isolate and cure 'unhealthy' behaviour, and the bourgeois public gleaned such information from medical guides and texts on marriage and upbringing. This literature has never been evaluated, but a cursory examination is sufficient to show that scholarly opinions on the matter were

1. See M. Foucault, *The History of Sexuality*, vol. I, *An Introduction*, trans. R. Hurley, London 1979, pp. 17ff.

diverse and contradictory.

Female sexuality was an especially controversial topic. Entire generations of medical practitioners were occupied with the question of whether women were sexually as excitable as men, though no agreement was ever reached. In the early nineteenth century, some concluded that conception was only possible if a woman was aroused during intercourse, while others thought the exact opposite was true; later on, the widely held belief that the female sexual drive was far weaker than the male was by no means accepted by all. In 1907 Iwan Bloch, a Berlin specialist for skin and venereal diseases, reported that he had 'questioned a large number of educated women on the theory that women are sexually less responsive than men. *Without exception*, they declared the theory to be wrong; many even opined that such responsiveness is greater and more enduring in women.' In Bloch's view, if it really was the case that 40 per cent of all women suffered from sexual anaesthesia and 'lack of appetite', as many of his colleagues suggested, then an explanation was to be found, not in constitutional or genetic factors, but in their husbands' lack of erotic imagination.[2] By contrast doctors such as Richard von Krafft-Ebing and Otto Adler insisted that women were fundamentally less interested in sexual intercourse than men, valuing intellectual compatibility and tender care more than sexual satisfaction and passion. The task of education was to nurture and reinforce such natural leanings, otherwise the whole world would turn into a brothel, ousting marriage and the family.[3] In 1908, just four years after Adler had published his observations on 'the lack of sexual feeling in women', Freud's writings on 'civilised sexual morality' and its significance for 'modern nervous illness' were published. Freud disagreed with Adler and Krafft-Ebing: female frigidity, though common, was neither normal nor desirable, but the harmful consequence of a strict upbringing. Since young girls were forced to repress their sexuality, the reaction of many women to their 'marital duties' was resistance and coldness, and they sought refuge in neuroses and fits of hysteria.[4]

Freud's theory found a chink in the armour of bourgeois sexual

---

2. I. Bloch, *Das Sexualleben unserer Zeit in seinen Beziehungen zur modernen Kultur*, Berlin 1907, pp. 88ff., 478ff.

3. See P. Gay, *The Bourgeois Experience – Victoria to Freud: Education of the Senses*, New York 1984, pp. 154ff.

4. S. Freud, 'Civilized Sexual Morality and Modern Nervous Illness' (1908), in *The Standard Edition of the Complete Psychological Works of Sigmund Freud*, translated under the general editorship of J. Strachey, London, 1953–74, vol. IX, pp. 179ff.

morality. On the one hand, sexuality was recognised as a basic human need: religious marital advice underlined the need for 'bodily pleasure' without which a marriage could not work; medical books recommended that couples should 'keep healthy' by having regular sexual intercourse – between two and four times a week – and predicted (fifty years before Freud) that abstaining women would be prone to 'anaemia, hysteria, disorders of temperament and genital diseases'.[5] On the other hand, what married couples were allowed and, in the interests of health and reproduction, even encouraged to do, was utterly condemned before and outside marriage. The taboo was particularly strict for middle-class women. While they were not allowed to lose their virginity before their wedding night, it was perfectly acceptable for middle-class men to 'sow their wild oats' with prostitutes and in casual relationships with girls from the lower classes. Feminine honour was nothing if not class-related, as Siebert, a medical practitioner who advocated more enlightened sexual morality, was forced to admit around 1900:

If a man pinches a general's daughter on the cheek . . . it is considered coarse; yet should he do the same to a café waitress it is nothing more than harmless fun. Indeed, there are a considerable number of young women whose social milieu is so indifferent to aspersions that may be publicly cast upon their reputations that the pleasure to be had is heavily justified.[6]

Gentlemen students and civil servants could frequently visit such women with impunity, while the young ladies of the bourgeoisie had to protect their chastity. Most would enter into marriage largely ignorant and unprepared, and look back on their wedding night as a nasty shock. Lily Braun's mother, who had married a Prussian officer in 1863, often told her daughter that 'but for the shame she would have felt towards her parents, she would have dearly loved to run away during the first week with her husband. Only gradually did she realise that her husband was no criminal, and her fate not an abnormal one'.[7] Marcella Boveri, a member of the first generation

---

5. O. Funcke, *Vademekum für junge und alte Eheleute*, Altenburg 1908, p. 111; C. E. Bock, *Das Buch vom gesunden und kranken Menschen*, Leipzig 1859, pp. 620–1; for a similar work see H. Klencke, *Hauslexikon der Gesundheitslehre für Leib und Seele: Ein Familienbuch*, Leipzig 1865, pp. 97–9, and Klencke, *Das Weib als Gattin: Lehrbuch über die physischen, seelischen und sittlichen Pflichten, Rechte und Gesundheitsregeln der deutschen Frau im Eheleben zur Begründung der leiblichen und sittlichen Wohlfahrt ihrer selbst und ihrer Familie. Eine Körper- und Seelendiätetik des Weibes in der Liebe und Ehe*, Leipzig 1889, esp. pp. 185ff. This book, first published in 1872, was reprinted ten times in seventeen years, and was one of the most influential and popular medical guides.
6. F. Siebert, *Sexuelle Moral und sexuelle Hygiene*, Frankfurt 1901, pp. 80–1.
7. L. Braun, *Memoiren einer Sozialistin: Lehrjahre*, Munich 1909, pp. 13–14. See

of academic women in America and the wife of a German professor, taught her daughter Margret, born in 1900, that 'women tolerate sexual intercourse merely to have children'. When Margret, at the age of twenty, asked her what 'prostitute' meant, the answer she received was: 'Prostitutes are fallen girls, for sale, who do it for money – who even enjoy it.'[8]

If a middle-class woman also 'enjoyed it', and openly said so, she could easily be regarded as 'bawdy'. This happened to Emma Inhoffen, the wife of a Bonn manufacturer who filed for divorce in 1900. One of his complaints was his wife telling the nanny that 'the most important thing in marriage is sexual satisfaction. It's like making love with an old man' – here she was referring to the plaintiff – 'unless things change, our marriage will end altogether in that respect'.[9] A woman like Marcella Boveri, who saw sexuality as a necessary evil, was much more respected in public than an Emma Inhoffen, who expressed a positive interest in sex. Even women who were not frigid and did indulge in 'bodily pleasures' with their husbands, were better advised not to shout it from the rooftops. A virtuous woman kept her lust under control, and expected her husband to follow suit. He could give free rein to his fantasies and desires with prostitutes and lower-class women; but he should behave in a civilised manner towards his wife.

It is impossible to know how strictly people actually observed the bourgeois code of sexual morality. There is also little evidence of how women dealt with their sexuality. The range of possible individual behaviour was broad and certainly not restricted to the one type of frigid, asexual married woman, as is sometimes assumed.[10] Irrespective of their experiences in the conjugal bed, middle-class women presented themselves to the outside world as disinterested in sex, and looked down on women who transgressed the mores of bourgeois sexual behaviour. Many were involved in what were

---

also Funcke, *Vademekum*, p. 65: 'Tears fill the eyes of thousands of mothers when they read letters from their daughters on honeymoon, which make reference to this difficult yet indescribably important moment.'

8. M. Boveri, *Verzweigungen: Eine Autobiographie*, ed. U. Johnson, Munich 1982, p. 141.

9. Düsseldorf Civic Archives, Landgericht Bonn, 2/427: 'Scheidungsprozeß Inhoffen gegen Inhoffen, Klageschrift von 9.2.1900'.

10. See Gay, *The Bourgeois Experience*, who offers examples intended to counterbalance this distorted image. By contrast, E. Shorter draws highly general and inaccurate conclusions in describing sexuality in both the eighteenth and nineteenth centuries as brutal and extremely unsatisfying for women: *A History of Women's Bodies*, Harmondsworth 1984, pp. 10ff.

known as Moral Associations (*Sittlichkeits Vereinen*), which from the 1880s onwards campaigned against prostitution.[11] The evangelical moral movement condemned prostitution as a crime, and accused the government, which controlled prostitutes through brothels and compulsory medical examinations, of complicity. Following the approach taken in Britain, a more liberal position was adopted by 'abolitionist' women's associations which sought to combat prostitution by abolishing the state licensing schemes that existed in Germany. They had first appeared around the turn of the century, and railed against society's double standards: prostitutes were criminalised, while their male customers were let off scot-free. They rejected the notion of state control, and called on the authorities to adopt positive social policies which would save women from brothels and the streets, to which they were led usually by financial desperation.

While the 'abolitionists' were more sympathetic to the fact that prostitutes often found themselves caught in a trap, they also shared the ideal of the moral movement which held that both men and women should control their sexual urges and express them in marriage alone. For Wilhelmine society, including the women's movement, pre- and extra-marital sex was an absolute taboo that few dared to question. Even for most of the supporters of the bourgeois women's movement, it was wholly unacceptable for the Federation for the Protection of Mothers to demand that a stop be put to the social, economic and legal victimisation of single mothers, that no differentiation be made between legitimate and illegitimate offspring, that women and men should be granted the right to pre-marital sex, and that free love be seen as a positive alternative to conventional marriage.

This Federation's views on the law were also too radical for most members of the Federation of German Women's Associations, who found it particularly difficult to countenance the demand for easier divorce, since they felt this would encourage individual 'egoism' and the break-up of the family. But there was no disagreement over the call for sexual equality in family law. As early as 1876, the General German Women's Association had petitioned the Reichstag to grant women full and independent legal status, institute legal provision for the separation of property, and restrict patriarchal rights. These requests were submitted again in 1888, when the

---

11. Ulrich, *Bordelle*, pp. 136ff.; Greven-Aschoff, *Die bürgerliche Frauenbewegung*, pp. 79–80.

national government was preparing the first draft of a new German Civil Code (*Bürgerliches Gesetzbuch*). But it was not until eight years later – just before the legislation was finally passed – that the BDF organised action intended to appeal to the hearts of the public. They decried the masculine bias of the proposed laws, and campaigned for greater women's rights with all the vigour and rhetoric they could muster. The movement was particularly disturbed by the fact that the new legislation did nothing to alter the privileged position that the Prussian Civil Code had given the man vis-a-vis his family: now as before he had the right to make all the decisions affecting the family; he had the last word on educational matters; he was his children's legal guardian; he was responsible for disposing of any wealth his wife brought into or inherited during the marriage.[12]

By comparison with previous legislation, however, the new Civil Code did advance one important step, in granting full legal status to married women. Henceforth they were entitled to conclude contracts and initiate legal proceedings, even though an extraordinary right of dismissal meant the husband could restrict his wife's business activities. Nevertheless, the money that a married woman earned was now rightfully hers, whereas before it had automatically belonged to her husband. Despite these concessions the new Civil Code was a long way from applying the principle of equality across the board; the continuity of patriarchal prerogatives was particularly noticeable in family law. In the Reichstag, apart from one or two exceptions, only Social Democrats and a few left-wing Liberals fought for sexual equality. Conservatives, the Catholic *Zentrum* and the National Liberals all voted against the Left's motions.[13]

Since the women's movement won little sympathy among the bourgeois parties for its position on the law, and was also uneasy about accepting help from the Social Democrats, it tended to keep to the sidelines, though a mass demonstration was organised in Berlin in 1896. Proper protest was not made until the parliamentary legislative procedure was almost completed. Fear of being infected by the politics of the 'party of disruption' prevented united action with the Left, and although some bourgeois politicians were understanding of, if not wholly behind, the movement's cause, they

12. On the rules of the Civil Code on the family, see Hubbard, *Familiengeschichte*, pp. 49ff.
13. Evans, *Feminist Movement*, pp. 15–16, although he misunderstands part of the Civil Code: compared with the Prussian Civil Code, the new law did *not* make the separation of property more difficult, but allowed it, even though not in every case. Gerhard, *Verhältnisse*, pp. 166–7 and 186–7, is more accurate.

would never have dreamed of relinquishing their own legal privileges lock, stock and barrel. The General Section of the new Civil Code, exuding liberal-mindedness and the spirit of the age, defined women as independent subjects before the law. The Special Section on Family Law, however, created a network of provisions which consolidated the prevailing male-bias of legislation and protected the institution of the family from emancipatory forces that might break structures down. The women's movement found it difficult to make headway against this dual strategy, particularly since its scope for action was limited, not only by external resistance, but by internal differences too. Most middle-class women preferred tentative policies which left room for compromise, and shied away from more direct forms of struggle. They felt they had already made a personal stand against convention and their family's expectations by joining the movement, and were at pains to ensure they did not cement their position as outsiders by radical behaviour which would send waves of panic rippling through their social milieu. But this is not the only factor that should be considered: the women also hoped that they could increase their grass-roots support and thus be in a better position to push through demands which, though careful and moderate, might appear strident and rebellious.

Despite such defensive tactics, the largest and most powerful women's organisation in Imperial Germany kept its distance from the BDF. The Patriotic Women's Association (*Vaterländischer Frauenverein*), founded at the instigation of the royal Prussian household in 1866 and with half a million members in 1913, could not but remain hostile to even the moderate aims of the BDF. Furthermore, it was not interested in issues that specifically related to women: it placed itself solely in the service and care of wounded soldiers and needy civilians. The recognition the 'patriots' earned from the highest authority was sufficient incentive and compensation – their thoughts were a long way from 'special' and emancipatory interests of women.[14]

---

14. See I. Riemann: 'Die Rolle der Frauenvereine in der Sozialpolitik: Vaterländischer Frauenverein und gemäßigter Flügel der Frauenbewegung zwischen 1865 und 1918', in I. Kickbusch and B. Riedmüller (eds), *Die armen Frauen: Frauen und Sozialpolitik*, Frankfurt 1984, pp. 201–24. The historical details in it are, however, vague, or even incorrect. On the Baden Women's Association, which combined welfare work in schemes initiated by the authorities with an interest in the women's movement, and thus felt allied to both the Union of Patriotic Women's Associations and the early bourgeois women's movement, see Bussemer, *Frauenemanzipation*, pp. 165ff.

12

The Social Democratic Women's Movement

For quite different reasons Social Democratic associations of women workers kept their distance from the bourgeois women's movement, which had shown an increasingly marked tendency to regard working women and wives solely as objects of social policy and welfare and not, as Louise Otto had envisaged in 1848, as subjects representing their own independent interests. When formulating their problems and forms of protest, proletarian women had begun to model themselves increasingly on the trade union and other political organisations of male workers. This became evident in the 1880s, when associations of women workers came into being first in Berlin and then in many other towns and, either directly or with the support of middle-class women (Gertrud Guilleaume-Schack and Emma Ihrer among them), highlighted the question of wages and even considered strikes as a means of satisfying higher wage demands.[1] The Anti-Socialist laws in force between 1878 and 1890, which made punishable offences of Social Democratic 'activities against the public interest' and which used the police to deal with any kind of organisation which supported such activities 'in a way which threatened public order, especially harmony between the classes of the population', spelled a swift end to these women's associations: they were banned and their committee members fined and imprisoned. Even the Prussian Law on Associations of 1850 could be invoked in order to dissolve such bodies: as long as it could be proved that they were politically active, pursued political goals or cultivated contacts with political parties, Section 8 came into force, which prohibited women as well as apprentices and young

---

1. *Das Sozialistengesetz 1878–1890*, Berlin 1980, pp. 211–15; Twellmann, *Textband*, vol. I, pp. 166ff.; H. Niggemann, *Emanzipation zwischen Sozialismus und Feminismus: Die sozialdemokratische Frauenbewegung im Kaiserreich*, Wuppertal 1981, pp. 51ff.; R. J. Evans, *Sozialdemokratie und Frauenemanzipation im deutschen Kaiserreich*, Berlin 1979, pp. 56ff. For an English version of parts of this book see Evans, *Comrades and Sisters: Feminism, Socialism and Pacifism in Europe 1870–1945*, Brighton 1987.

people from attending political gatherings and belonging to political organisations. Up until the Reich Law on Associations of 1908, Section 8 remained valid and was an enormous hindrance especially to the Social Democrats in their party political work regarding women.

While trade unions, freed from the repression of the Anti-Socialist laws, were able from the 1890s onwards to admit women members and increase their recruitment and campaigning work among the female work force, the more narrowly political organisations of the labour movement had therefore to continue adjusting to restrictions imposed by legislation on assembly. Admittedly, the Socialist Workers Party (SPD), in existence since 1875, had not at first appeared very interested in women supporters. The initiative came, rather, from proletarian women themselves, who pursued closer contact with and support from the Social Democrats. Starting in 1889 they established informal women's campaigning committees which convened meetings and sent delegates to Social Democratic party conferences. In addition they founded the trade and general associations for working women which concerned themselves above all with the political and cultural further education of women, carrying on the tradition of the workers' educational organisations of the fifties and sixties.[2] In 1893 there were in the German Reich at least thirty-three local associations of proletarian women with over 3,000 members.[3] These were almost all dissolved by the police, despite their decidedly non-political character, but were later re-established, so that in 1907 ninety-four educational organisations existed with over 10,000 members.[4] As in organisations initiated in the sixties by the bourgeois women's movement, regular meetings were held, along with lectures and discussions about literature, the upbringing of children, religion, prostitution, divorce, and the pursuit of 'stimulating social intercourse'. Even after 1908, when women were admitted to the party as members with 'equal rights', women's events continued. Just as female SPD activists were, according to the articles of association, to dedicate themselves chiefly to 'women's campaigning', so the rank-and-file members were authorised by party conference to 'hold at local level their own meetings to promote their theoretical and practical education'.[5]

2. S. Richebächer, *Uns fehlt nur eine Kleinigkeit: Deutsche proletarische Frauenbewegung 1890–1914*, Frankfurt 1982, pp. 181ff.; Niggemann, Emanzipation, pp. 61ff.
3. From Evans, *Sozialdemokratie*, pp. 332–3.
4. Niggemann, *Emanzipation*, p. 64.
5. SPD Party Conference Decisions of 1908 and 1909, quoted in ibid., pp. 71–2.

Apart from the newspaper *Die Gleicheit* ('Equality'), first published in 1891 with an initial circulation of 2,000 and edited by Clara Zetkin, the most important educative and campaign publication was August Bebel's book *Die Frau und der Sozialismus* (Woman under Socialism), which first appeared in 1879 and was already into its fiftieth edition by 1909. It paved the way to the Social Democratic movement for many working-class women, and also for women from the lower and middle ranges of the bourgeoisie. As Bebel explained to his readers both male and female, a woman in capitalist society was doubly disadvantaged. On the one hand she suffered from 'economic and social dependence upon man', and on the other from 'the economic dependence that woman in general, the working woman in particular, finds herself in, along with working man'. A successful battle for professional, legal and political equality could indeed mitigate but never completely eradicate this double disadvantage. A solution to the 'woman question' was possible only if 'the existing state and social order were radically transformed'. Not until the 'social question' had been completely resolved and the economic and social system dismantled could 'sex slavery' finally be abolished.

Succinct analysis and socialist visions of the future were not all Bebel's book had to offer; it also detailed concrete directives for action and showed ways in which proletarian women in particular could shake off their burden. First, they should join with the bourgeois women's movement in the fight for equality for all women in modern life. Second, the proletarian women's movement should fight 'hand in hand with the male portion of the working class' for measures which would 'protect the working woman from physical and moral degeneration, and which promise to secure to her the vitality and fitness necessary for motherhood and for the education of children'. Finally, proletarian women had to enter the common proletarian class struggle and fight for 'the establishment of such conditions as may make possible the real economic and spiritual independence of both sexes, by means of social institutions that afford to all a full share in the enjoyment of all the conquests of civilization made by mankind'.[6] Class-conscious proletarian women and wives logically found their political home in Social Democracy, the only party, as Bebel frequently emphasised, to have learnt from the eighteenth-century debate on human rights. In fact,

6. A. Bebel, *Woman under Socialism* (first published 1879), translated from the 33rd German edition by D. de Leon, New York 1904; 1974 impression, pp. 4–5.

at its founding congress in Gotha in 1875 the Socialist Workers' Party had demanded the right to vote for *all* citizens. The Erfurt Programme of 1891 was even more precise, stipulating that suffrage should be extended to all state citizens 'regardless of their sex'. Moreover it explicitly demanded the 'abolition of all laws which place women at a disadvantage to men in public and civil law'. At the time this was a spectacular advance – no other party in the Reich before 1918 raised such radically egalitarian demands.

Nevertheless, the SPD was not always of one mind, and there were decided opponents to sexual equality. Above all it was, some argued, in the interests of the proletarian family to keep women out of the factories. In 1905 Edmund Fischer, for example, wrote in the *Sozialistische Monatshefte* that the aim of the socialist movement must be to return women to the family. Here lay their 'natural occupation', namely 'the care and upbringing of young children, the embellishment and stabilisation of family life'.[7] While this 'doctrine of nature' provoked strong opposition, especially amongst female party activists, it was difficult to ignore the fact that many social democratic families observed ways which the party took to task. Precisely those better-paid skilled workers who formed the core of the organised labour movement had no desire to see their wives seeking work outside the home. As the Social Democrat Oda Olberg noted in 1905, 'Many party members think like Fischer; most of them feel the way he does.'[8] Even Bebel, who had called on women to 'break out of the narrow circle of domesticity and play their full part in public life and humanity's cultural activities', left no room for doubt that in the socialist society of the future there would be a clear role distinction between the sexes, in which men would shoulder responsibility for the 'defence of the realm' and women the 'care of hearth and home'. He was never able to acknowledge the emancipatory function of work as unequivocally as Clara Zetkin, the first woman leader of the proletarian women's movement.

Zetkin, the daughter of a family of village schoolteachers and herself a trained teacher, had joined the ranks of German Social Democracy at the beginning of the 1880s. At the International Workers' Congress in Paris in 1889 she delivered a speech that was to become famous; entitled 'The Liberation of Women', it immediately became the manifesto of the proletarian women's movement. In it, Zetkin spoke out categorically against any and every prohibi-

---

7. E. Fischer, 'Die Frauenfrage' (1905), in W. Zepler (ed.), *Sozialismus und Frauenfrage*, Berlin 1919, pp. 18–31.
8. Quoted in Niggemann, *Emanzipation*, p. 47.

tion on or limitation to gainful female employment, because it was precisely work outside the family which gave proletarian women economic independence. Women's economic self-sufficiency was, according to Zetkin, the necessary condition for their social and political equality. 'Full emancipation', however – and here Bebel and Zetkin were in complete agreement – could be achieved only through socialism, and for this reason women should join the SPD. Nevertheless Clara Zetkin did not underestimate how hard such co-operation would be in practice: 'Without the support of men, often even contrary to their wishes, women have gathered beneath the flag of socialism.'[9] Just as women in the Party were, for instance, completely ignored in the nomination of delegates to Party conferences, so male Social Democrats at first opposed the recruitment and mobilisation of female members. They did not even want to see their own wives and daughters in the Party; often they forbade them 'to go to meetings, asserting that they should only look after the household, darn stockings, and suchlike'.[10] This negative attitude, still prevalent in the 1890s, did however gradually wane, since by the beginning of the twentieth century the majority of female SPD members being recruited were the wives of male Social Democrats. Their daughters were active mainly in socialist working-class youth organisations, joining the Party at the minimum age of eighteen.[11]

The Social Democrats increasingly provided opportunities for women as well as men within the organisation, with a combination of political education, social functions and welfare work. These opportunities were exploited largely by non-employed women: far more than half of all female SPD members did not seek paid work outside the home. In Hamburg only a quarter of SPD women worked as factory hands, servants and office staff, while the rest were housewives who could more easily find time for attending meetings, demonstrations and women's afternoons. Employed women, on the other hand, had more than enough to do combining jobs with the daily responsibilities of household and family. After a wearing day at the factory their second working day began: food had to be cooked, the house cleaned, groceries and children taken care of. 'Work-free' Sundays were reserved for the weekly wash and

9. C. Zetkin, 'Für die Befreiung der Frau', in *Arbeiterbewegung und Frauenemanzipation 1889–1933*, Frankfurt 1973, pp. 7–12.
10. Quoted in Evans, *Sozialdemokratie*, p. 88.
11. K. Hagemann and B. Söllner, 'Denn der Mann hat gesagt, Es genügt, wenn ich in der Partei bin', in J. Berlin (ed.), *Das andere Hamburg*, Cologne 1981, pp. 235–62.

urgent sewing and mending. There was no time for political or trade union involvement. Neither were single women nearly so free in the disposal of their 'free' time as their male colleagues. Their leisure was mostly taken up with housework, while men spent theirs at the pub, on the football pitch or at political meetings.[12]

The social composition of the female SPD membership – barely 10 per cent of the total membership in 1909 (see Table 6, p. 332) – also shaped the policies of the Social Democratic women's movement. Initially, it had constituted a movement of female workers and had defined the gainful employment of women as the most important condition for female emancipation; but at the turn of the century it began increasingly to take into account the needs of its housewife clientele. In 1904, *Die Gleichheit* started publishing a housewives' and children's supplement, thus taking into account the family bias of the readership. Social Democratic local and trade union magazines began to include 'women's pages', with sewing patterns, fashion tips and advice on household management and childcare. The *Gewerkschaftliche Frauenzeitung* (Trade Union Women's Paper), which appeared in 1916, and *Frauenwelt* (Women's World), which replaced the *Gleichheit* in 1924, sported romantic fiction, articles about 'Negro women's cosmetics', and fashion illustrations. Women leaders in the Party and the trade unions did indeed try to resist women's political work being restricted to matters of specific female interest and the squeezing out of general political themes. In spite of this, a *de facto* division of labour did very rapidly establish itself. As well as campaigning for female suffrage, after 1900 the Social Democratic women's movement concentrated on an area to which women, as the 1911 Communal Programme of the Prussian SPD noted, were 'particularly suited': welfare.

Ever since the SPD had been active in local politics and had won seats in town councils, particularly in southern Germany, it had become more concerned with tackling actual, practical problems. The socialist revolution, which would rid the world of all its social evils overnight, had slipped beyond the horizon, and it seemed

12. See the contemporary texts in K. Saul et al. (eds), *Arbeiterfamilien im Kaiserreich*, Königstein 1982, pp. 196ff., and the impressive reports of the experiences of women factory workers in the Weimar Republic, *Mein Arbeitstag – mein Wochenende: 150 Berichte von Textilarbeiterinnen*, compiled and edited by the Deutscher Textilarbeiter-Verband, Berlin 1930; extracts can be found in F. G. Kürbisch and R. Klucsarits (eds), *Arbeiterinnen kämpfen um ihr Recht*, Wuppertal 1981, pp. 108–18. See also M. Ellerkamp and B. Jungmann, 'Unendliche Arbeit: Frauen in der "Jutespinnerei und -weberei Bremen", 1888–1914', in Hausen (ed.), *Frauen suchen*, pp. 128–43.

more sensible to take pragmatic action than to wait for the New Beginning. The Social Democratic women's movement took this line too; indeed they believed that the local level was by far the best place for constructive measures that would help proletarian women and families. Klara Weyl, who did welfare work for infants and the poor in Berlin, recommended education policy, the health service, inspection of housing and food standards, welfare for the sick and unemployed, care for orphans and infants, and campaigning for kindergartens and crèches, as areas where her comrades could play a useful role. Here they could 'at least to some degree keep the widespread misery of working people in check and so contribute to the spiritual and physical rebirth of the working class'.[13] These were also areas where women, just like their bourgeois 'sisters', could establish and maintain some independence. They did not have to compete against men and accept defeat, as in the battle for greater political participation and influence. The highly practical nature of social work gave women the feeling that they really were making progress. It is clear that at root, people-oriented services were related to the domestic experiences and interests of Social Democratic women – in any case less alien than the kind of political agitation directed mainly at women factory workers. Both they and their 'clients' profited from the value their life-experiences had for direct woman-to-woman help and social welfare for sick and destitute women and families. They were on their own ground, chipping away slowly but effectively at the misery which was the everyday life of too many working-class people.

Even before the First World War, the Social Democratic women's movement was deeply involved in the welfare of mothers and children. It organised trips and walking holidays for working-class children, and created committees for child protection. The numerous pamphlets published on raising a family emphasised the political significance of a sound notion of motherhood: women could, if they wanted, hugely influence the development of their offspring, which would in the long term have a decisive impact on the success of the labour movement. In this light, the social democratic family acquired the status of a cell of Social Democracy, with the mother its nucleus.

Meanwhile women factory workers, once the main and favourite addressees of the proletarian women's movement, were being relegated to second place in recruitment work, even though female

13. K. Weyl, *Die Frau und die Gemeindepolitik*, Berlin 1912, p. 5.

Social Democrats continued to campaign in leaflets, pamphlets and petitions for shorter working hours, equal pay and better health standards. From 1896 onwards legal protection for factory women was one of the movement's central and undisputed demands. Seven years earlier, Clara Zetkin had still strongly repudiated the notion of protection specifically for women, arguing that the equality of men and women should be the guiding principle of socialist policy. But in the 1890s she changed her mind. The argument that special provisions for women would worsen their chances on the labour market compared with 'unprotected' men was not enough to offset the fact that proletarian women bore the triple burden of wage labour, housework and motherhood, and thus needed far greater safeguards than their male counterparts. In particular, women who were pregnant or had just given birth should – not least in the interest of their children – be entitled to time off work, otherwise their health would suffer excessively. Though legislation of 1891 stipulated a six-week break from employment after birth, the shaky financial position of many women forced them to contravene the law. Moreover, existing and subsequent regulations applied to factory women only: servant girls, outworkers and farms labourers had no right whatsoever to the maximum ten-hour working day, work-free Sundays and nights, or (from 1908 onwards) to eight week's holiday during pregnancy.

Little by little, the Social Democratic women's movement moved away from its original theory of emancipation when it realised that women, with their generally lower levels of formal qualification, had to endure a particularly oppressive working life: unhealthy conditions, low pay, long hours, monotonous jobs accompanied by increasing pressure and stress as the pace of work grew faster and faster. Soap-box politics still welcomed female participation in the labour force as a means of broadening horizons and 'political education'. In practical party work, however, the women of the SPD followed the bourgeois women's movement and subscribed to the thesis that motherhood could and should be women's most important social calling. The ideological transfiguration of housewife and mother – in themselves not exactly easy roles – undoubtedly aroused the sympathy of most working-class women, who preferred family life and work, an existence more clearly oriented to meeting personal needs, to the external control they were subject to in a job. For working-class women and girls, 'a job' meant ultimately unskilled, dirty, badly paid and physically wearing work, whose value for character-building was rightly questioned. Employment in mills and paper factories was hardly commensurate with 'self-fulfilment'; its value could be measured in no other terms but the size of the pay packet. It is not surprising that most women were happy to forego the freedom to earn money as soon as their husbands' income was high enough to support the family. It seemed infinitely more sensible to spend one's days as a housewife and mother than to work in an alienating factory.

In both theory and practice, there was common ground between women in the bourgeois and Social Democratic movements: their esteem for motherhood and motherliness as 'natural feminine vocations', and their welfare activities. Nevertheless, they perceived each other as 'enemy sisters' (Bebel). The BDF did not invite any Social Democrats to their founding congress in 1894, partly because they did not wish to lose the goodwill of the police and the authorities, partly out of respect for affiliated conservative associations.[14] A motion proposed by the Union of Progressive Women's Associations, advocating co-operation with socialist groups, was decisively rejected. Social Democrat women also kept well clear of bourgeois 'legalist campaigners for women's rights' (*Frauenrechtlerinnen*), accusing them of half-heartedness and reformism. They adhered to the principle that 'the root cause of the thousand-year-old inferior social position of the female sex lies, not in any "legislation that men passed", but in property relations determined by economic conditions', as Clara Zetkin had put it in 1891.[15] Women would not achieve true emancipation unless property was reorganised on a socialist basis. Thus both the SPD and BDF women shunned official contact, and even overt co-operation. In 1900 the first Social Democratic women's conference left to the discretion of the individual comrades whether they 'occasionally or temporarily work alongside legalists and other bourgeois elements', and recommended they use 'taste and tactical sense' to decide the best solution in a given situation.[16]

While at the local level women from both movements at times came together in concerted action, the leadership remained convinced that social democracy and the bourgeoisie were fighting on different territories for different aims. In the debate over the German Civil Code, which was promulgated in 1896 and came into force in 1900, SPD women stayed very much on the sidelines,

14. Bäumer gives this reason in *Handbuch*, vol. I, pp. 132ff.
15. Quoted in Richebächer, *Uns fehlt*, pp. 180–1.
16. Quoted in Niggemann, *Emanzipation*, p. 87.

whereas the BDF was firmly (though belatedly) committed to formal legal equality for women. The journal *Die Gleichheit* did support most of the middle-class women's legislative demands, but also reminded its readers of fundamental class differences, of which the body of laws governing relations between servants and masters, the *Gesindeordnung*, was a good example. While Social Democrats fought tenaciously for its abolition, the BDF resolutions did not even mention it. The bourgeois movement strongly objected to even a trade union organisation for servants, as well as to the introduction of the eight-hour day for domestic staff. For this reason, Lily Braun, a member of the bourgeois movement until she joined the SPD in 1896, claimed that the 'bourgeois class character of the women's movement' was most obvious in the servant question:

As long as the proletarian women's movement was active outside their own four walls, it could count on the support particularly of women who were not of the entrepreneurial class, and who thus felt they had nothing to fear from the movement's demands. The servant question, however, touched on a nerve in their own domain, in their own homes; it demanded sacrifices of them and, with few exceptions, transformed goodwill into rejection, often even into a hatred which made outcasts of all those who sympathised with the servants' campaign.[17]

Despite some overlap on issues of political and legal equality, the class divide was therefore the crucial axis as far as both movements were concerned. Social Democratic women were particularly averse to being embraced by the middle classes in the name of 'common sisterhood' (Zetkin). Their programme did not call for the dethroning of male domination and the proper involvement of 'the feminine element' in society, politics and culture; its prime concern was the liberation of proletarian women from capitalist economic oppression. Yet behind the revolutionary rhetoric of leading Party activists, there emerged from the turn of the century signs of a pragmatic trend towards reformist social policy, which in the First World War provided a link with the welfare activities of middle-class women.

17. L. Braun, *Die Frauenfrage* (first published 1901), Berlin 1979, pp. 474–5.

III
The Discovery of the 'Modern Woman' 1914–1933

13

The First World War
The Father of Women's Emancipation?

The First World War is often regarded as a catalyst in the modernisation of Germany. It is felt to have speeded up the process by which economic life and the structure of state and society evolved in the direction of a modern, democratically constituted, West European-type polity, and to have prompted such pioneering innovations as co-operation in industrial relations, and growth in the power of parliament and political parties. Developments, it is said, accelerated even further with the 1918 revolution, which would have been inconceivable had the war not brought about the bankruptcy of the authoritarian, monarchical state and its aristocratic representatives. Women also are said to have benefited from the modernising effects of the war: they were increasingly incorporated into the labour market, and their work given public recognition and praise;[1] above all, middle-class women had proved their civic maturity and social responsibility. The question is: did the war in fact make a major contribution to emancipation?

On 1 August 1914 men were not alone in applauding the announcement by Kaiser Wilhelm II that Germany was declaring war on Russia; women also cheered enthusiastically and were part of the 'deluge of patriotic feeling'[2] that seized hold of a large section of the population. The belief that Germans had been compelled to mount a campaign of defence against Tsarism was mixed with undertones of jingoism and imperialism which heralded the war as a god-given instrument for expanding the power of the German Reich at the expense of the envious British and French. Women of the educated bourgeoisie proved most susceptible to stories woven by press and propaganda concerning the encirclement of Germany by jealous neighbours and the need to strike for liberation in the name of

1. See U. von Gersdorff, *Frauen im Kriegsdienst 1914–1945*, Stuttgart 1969, p. 77; S. Bajohr, *Die Hälfte der Fabrik*, Marburg 1984, p. 101.
2. M. Bernays, 'Frauenfragen in der Kriegszeit', in *Die Frauenfrage: Zentralblatt des Bundes Deutscher Frauenvereine*, 16 December 1914, p. 137.

national culture and grandeur. The leaders of the bourgeois women's movement surpassed themselves in emphatic declarations of loyalty and unconditional devotion and sacrifice. Gertrud Bäumer, chair of the BDF from 1910, wrote in a political pamphlet in 1914: 'Whatever they may bring, whatever they take, these times represent the solemn peak of the lives of our generation', and she expressed regret for all those who had died too soon to witness 'the great day of their people'.[3] The bourgeois women's movement did not cease to stress how vital the experience of August 1914 had been, of 'becoming a people', of 'becoming one': 'Germany spoke, felt and wanted through us, our own souls became one with the souls of the people.'[4] These fantasies of amalgamation reflected the longing for *Volksgemeinschaft*[5], the desire for harmony and an end to all differences. Having more or less consistently defended specific feminine interests for over fifty years, the women's movement was now keen to cast off 'the constraints of separatism and particularist aims' and to be absorbed by this 'great and momentous drawing together of all national energies into a powerful common will', as Gertrud Bäumer's appeal to German women in 1914 phrased it. In her autobiography she describes in retrospect the 'tremendous feeling of release we felt from the force of an authority so different from the materialistic and mechanical order of the nineteenth century. Not a system which weighed achievement against reward, risk against profit, commitment against gain, but one of life and death, blood and power, commitment in its purest form and at any price.'[6]

It seemed, moreover, that under such a system women would no longer be measured by the masculine yardstick, but could assert themselves, using their own unique talents and capabilities, and take part in the project which overrode questions of gender and class – war. The sense of national upheaval and calling gave women too a sense of national identity: although the political system of Imperial Germany failed to allow them to co-determine the course of events, they nevertheless felt, as Marie Bernays of the Federation of German Women's Associations expressed it, like 'citizens with obligations towards the general public'.

For most people, however, everyday life took priority: their own

3. G. Bäumer, *Der Krieg und die Frau*, Stuttgart 1914, p. 7.
4. M.-E. Lüders, *Das unbekannte Heer: Frauen kämpfen für Deutschland 1914–1918*, Berlin 1936, p. 3; Bäumer, *Krieg*, pp. 6–7.
5. Since the racial connotations are not readily conveyed in English the German word *Volksgemeinschaft*, literally 'folk community' is used throughout.
6. G. Bäumer, *Lebensweg durch eine Zeitenwende*, Tübingen 1933, pp. 269–70, 280.

homes and private lives seemed more important than obligations to the community. During the first days of August 1914, middle-class women rushed out on shopping sprees to stock up in preparation for the food shortages that were to come. In view of massive price rises, local authorities and women's associations appealed to the patriotism of housewives, urging them to stop panic-buying and continue as normal. Householders were encouraged to think twice before laying off their servants, and to 'try and ensure that staff are at least adequately fed', even if paying them proved more difficult.[7] Despite such appeals, many bourgeois families, uncertain about their financial future, drew tight their purse strings and bade farewell to their servants. Charwomen paid by the hour were taken on instead to help with the more laborious jobs. This placed a considerable extra burden on housewives, for now they not only had all the tasks their maids used to do; in addition they spent countless hours fighting the war from their own kitchens: serious problems arose for private households when the consumer goods market, which had provided most urban homes with food and durable goods, fell into disarray, and basic products were in scarce supply and rationed. People had to queue for hours for the few foodstuffs that could be bought on the free market or, after 1915, acquired with coupons. As quality continued to deteriorate it took great culinary inventiveness to make a meal out of the meagre supplies that were available. Women, particularly in the middle classes, began to produce as much of their own food as they could, so as not to be dependent on the market; provisions were stored wherever space could be made; wartime cookery books on substitute ingredients and budget recipes were highly popular; and women flocked to lectures and courses on how to bottle and preserve.

Even in wealthier families who could afford to keep their servants the range of tasks facing housewives grew and grew. As the war dragged on and supplies worsened, more and more time and organisational skill were needed to procure even the smallest quantities of fuel and provisions. Katia Mann describes how she cycled round Munich for whole days to 'get hold of a few things here and there' or find suppliers who sold butter, eggs or coal at inflated black-market prices.[8] Clothing, fabrics and shoes were also hard to come by, so old, tattered articles of clothing and footwear had to be patched up or converted into something else.

7. Appeal by the Elberfeld Women's Associations, 6 August 1914, in the Wuppertal Civic Archives, S XIII 32.
8. K. Mann, *Meine ungeschriebenen Memoiren*, Frankfurt 1983, pp. 38–9.

Urban working-class women suffered much more than the middle classes as a result of wartime shortages. They were too poor to buy foodstuffs in bulk or on the black market; nor did they have enough storage space to stock up on provisions and preserves. Nothing short of Herculean efforts could compensate for poor-quality – at times non-existent – food supplies, and working-class families scarcely had any spare time and energy. The women did show interest in the lectures, courses and demonstrations held everywhere on such themes as efficient housekeeping, substituting fruit purée for butter, eating fish and cheese instead of meat, and using rye flour instead of wheat flour. But more often than not, advice conflicted with the real possibilities, which were determined by constraints, not only of money, but mainly of time. Before 1914 few working-class women had been able to devote themselves exclusively to home and children; during the war years, it became even more usual for families to have to rely on additional income the mother could earn. The call-up of nine million men, half of whom were married, as early as the end of 1915, meant that their families were suddenly faced with managing indefinitely without breadwinners. Wartime supplementary payments to soldiers' families fell a long way short of needs. In Berlin, where the local authorities had doubled the amount paid by the Reich (few authorities were as generous), the family of a skilled worker with four children received only half the husband's pre-war earnings. It was only for families of unskilled workers with nine children or more – and even in those days this was a rarity – that wartime supplements exceeded the father's peacetime income.[9]

Even if the father had not been called up, a family's income was bound to fall sharply. Although industrial wages for men doubled beween 1914 and 1918, they did not keep pace with the rapid increase in the cost of living, which tripled in the same period. Real earnings for male industrial workers went down on average by one third.[10] Many basic foodstuffs were obtainable only on the basis of exchange or at extortionate prices, especially during the last two years of the war, so the cost of living left wages far behind. Even when working-class families were in a position to lower their already frugal living standards by saving on food, clothing and heating, serious shortfalls still remained, and these could only be

9. U. Daniel, 'Funktionalisierung von Frauen und Familien in der Kriegswirtschaft 1914–1918 – Tendenzen und Gegentendenzen', in *Dokumentation 4. Historikerinnentreffen (TU Berlin, März 1983)*, Berlin 1983, pp. 28–58.

10. J. Kocka, *Facing Total War: German Society 1914–1918*, trans. B. Weinberger, Leamington Spa 1984, tables pp. 19–23.

made up if women (and children) went out to work. Many married women who previously had not, or only sporadically, earned money, were obliged to take a regular job, which drastically cut down the time available for their now even more demanding domestic duties.

In the first two years of the war, it was difficult for women to find jobs, especially in sectors of the economy that had traditionally employed a large female labour force: as far as the war economy was concerned, these were peacetime industries, and could thus be largely starved of raw materials and imported goods. The textile, clothing, footwear and tobacco industries all switched to short-time working, or shed huge numbers of employees. After war broke out, unemployment was initially rife even in such important sectors as electronic engineering and the chemical industry, though a rapid rise in military-led demand proceeded to push production steadily upwards, and manufacturers were faced with a labour shortage. Since an ever-larger section of the male workforce was being sent to battle, from 1916 at the latest the military high command and the directors of the war economy began to search for additional labour reserves. The law passed in December 1916 on 'Auxiliary Service for the Fatherland' (*Vaterländischer Hilfsdienst*) was intended to mobilise the remaining male labour force, transfer workers from civil industries to those crucial for military power, and to limit mobility in the free labour market. Labour conscription applied to men only, even though the bourgeois women's movement, along with General Hindenburg, chief at high command, called on the government to include women in the Auxiliary Service law.[11] Women were expected to join in German industry's war effort on a more or less voluntary basis. Early 1917 witnessed the launch of a vigorous campaign encouraging women to take jobs in essential industries, and thus to allow men to go to the front. High wages for unqualified and semi-skilled work, additional payments in kind from factories, and the threat of loss of wartime supplements were incentives that made jobs in industry attractive, particularly for married women. Some enterprises used social facilities, such as factory housing, as bait in an attempt to encourage women to fill vacancies left after their husbands had been conscripted. Central and regional war authorities set up women's employment agencies whose aim was to mobilise female labour for the war economy.

11. See Bajohr, *Die Hälfte*, pp. 108ff., on the unsuccessful efforts to introduce female labour conscription.

By and large, however, the concerted efforts of state and economy bore little fruit. The armaments industry did take on very many women, but this was not a direct result of the post-1916 recruitment campaign. The size of the industry's female labour force had been rising rapidly since early 1915, and continued to do so over the next three years. By 1917, over 700,000 women worked in the engineering, metallurgical, iron and steel, chemical and mining industries – six times more than in 1913. The firm of Krupp, which had employed only 2,000–3,000 women before the war, had 28,000 on the payroll on 1 January 1918.[12] This sort of explosion was limited to only a few sectors, however. Only half as many women worked in textile and clothing manufacture at the end of 1918 compared to the pre-war period. The overall impression is that the number of women in employment did not rise at a disproportionately high rate during the war. Statistics on sickness insurance funds, which covered female blue- and white-collar workers, servants, agricultural workers and day labourers, showed a 16.7 per cent rise in the number of members between 1 June 1914 and 1 July 1918.[13] This did not mark a sudden jump in the course of female employment; it was merely the continuation of a trend that had begun during the late nineteenth century: higher numbers of women were going out to work (though the *percentage* of women in employment remained almost unchanged), and most were opting for a job in industry and the service sector. The last employment census before the war showed that of the almost ten million women in gainful employment in 1907, 20 per cent were in small- and large-scale manufacturing. The size of the female labour force in trade and industry had risen by 60 per cent between 1895 and 1907, and the number of female white-collar workers even more rapidly. In 1895 more than 20,000 women were to be found in the offices of industrial and commercial enterprises; twelve years later the figure was 150,000. It is true that half of the total female labour force still worked in agriculture as maids, labourers or helping on the family farm, but even in the nineteenth century the relative number had already been falling.[14]

The war did not interrupt these developments, for they were rooted in structural economic transformation (and had thus affected the male labour force at a much earlier stage). Firstly, the number of women in employment went up for demographic reasons; and,

12. von Gersdorff, *Frauen im Kriegsdienst*, pp. 218–19.
13. Bajohr, *Die Hälfte*, table 30, p. 119.
14. See the employment statistics in table 8, p. 334.

secondly, women increasingly took jobs in trade and industry. However, the impression most people gained at the time was that the war had caused rapid and fundamental changes in the nature of female employment. They pointed to the rising number of women railway guards; they saw women delivering mail and serving at post office counters; they heard that women were now wielding pneumatic drills, driving steamrollers, manufacturing grenades, installing motorised farm machinery, and, as the war drew to a close, learning to drive army lorries. Women everywhere seemed to be doing jobs which formerly had been men's. The difference between men's work and women's work was no longer clear cut, and women obviously had neither physical nor psychological problems taking the place of men who had been drafted into the army.

In fact, few jobs in services and manufacturing were safe from women. In formerly 'male' industries such as iron and steel, metal-working and mechanical engineering, for example, the female labour force rose from 7 per cent in July 1914 to 23 per cent just two years later; in the electrical industry it leapt over the same period from 24 per cent to 55 per cent.[15] By comparison, all previous growth rates paled into insignificance. Much can be attributed to the exigencies of the war economy, which not only had to replace conscripted men, but required extra labour power to cope with increased output. Expanding wartime industries provided new and better-paid work for women who had been dismissed from previous jobs during the first few months of hostilities. Relatively high wage levels[16] also encouraged women to give up steady jobs and move to new occupations. In the final analysis, it can be said that the war caused the female labour force not to grow more rapidly than it would normally have done, but to relocate. In any case, developments that struck people at the time as significant were quantitatively of little importance, though as indices of qualitative changes they had great bearing on the public mind.

Basic conditions for female industrial employment had also altered. War had only just been declared when legislation on the protection of workers was annulled, with the result that forthwith there was nothing to prevent women from having to work more

---

15. von Gersdorff, *Frauen im Kriegsdienst*, p. 218; See also M.-E. Lüders, 'Die Entwicklung der gewerblichen Frauenarbeit im Kriege', *Schmollers Jahrbuch*, 44, 1920, pp. 241–67, 569–93, esp. table pp. 592–3 (summary of numbers of employed men and women, based mainly on surveys conducted between July 1914 and September 1918).

16. See Kocka, *Facing Total War*, p. 19, on the change in female earnings in war and non-war industries, 1914–18.

than ten hours per day, at night, on Sundays or under ground. However, by 1916 government authorities began to show concern that the unrestricted exploitation of labour was having counterproductive effects. Fearing that women's health would suffer from long working hours, and that unfavourable conditions would deter many from factory employment, the civil and military administration pressed for shorter shifts and curbs on employers whose contribution to social policy left something to be desired. This enormous pressure forced many munitions factories to introduce the eighthour working day for female (and in many cases male) workers. This happened long before the revolution in November 1918 made the eight-hour rule generally applicable.[17]

In order to render its social policy more effective for factory women, the state set up its own agencies whose purpose was to eradicate all obstacles women faced in employment and to take positive action to 'improve employment capabilities and generate enthusiasm for work among all members of the female labour force, with the aim of achieving maximum increases in production'.[18] Female workers, it was claimed, deserved special provision since by contrast with men they had to harmonise their working lives with domestic and family duties. Consequently, consideration had to be given to family situations, and more crèches, day nurseries, mothers' rooms and mothers' advice centres made available to ensure the optimal mobilisation and utilisation of all women in work. It was suspected that in the absence of such compensations married women with young children would move from job to job, or refuse employment geared to manufacturing in favour of outwork, which was more flexible. In fact, married women tended to avoid factory work during the war all the same. In Bavarian war industries in 1917, for instance, just under 29 per cent of the female labour force were married, as compared to exactly one third in the total female industrial labour force in 1907.[19] They obviously preferred to sit at home sewing and knitting for the army; even cleaners and washerwomen found that their occupations conflicted far less with domestic and family demands than regular factory work would have done.

Consequently, even pursuing social welfare policies designed to

---

17. U. Daniel, *Frauenarbeit und Familie in der Kriegswirtschaft*, unpublished manuscript, Bielefeld 1983, pp. 14ff.
18. Work plan for the Female Labour Exchange of 29 January 1917, reprinted in von Gersdorff, *Frauen im Kriegsdienst*, pp. 129–30.
19. Daniel, *Frauenarbeit*, p. 3.

favour women and families, central and regional war offices enjoyed no more than limited success in their endeavours to encourage into the armaments industry more female labour, particularly married women who, it was hoped, would change jobs less frequently. Nonetheless, such initial attempts to organise the workforce marked a significant early stage in the history of welfarism, which began increasingly to address the sphere of social reproduction – family, health, housing – and thus to affect women directly. Social service institutions, such as welfare centres for mothers and infants, had already existed before 1914, but during the war were greatly extended. Extra resources were invested in housing and health care, and maternity benefit was introduced for the wives of conscripted soldiers. Concern for the demographic situation lay at the root of many welfare measures. The statistical authorities had been monitoring the fall in the birth rate since around 1910; but their anxiety reached almost hysterical proportions during the war. Anything which encouraged people to limit the size of the families was prohibited, a strict ban was placed on the sale of contraceptives, and the penalty for abortion made harsher. In numerous towns, voluntary and official bodies campaigned against all forms of birth control, and also put into action policies favouring the family. Priority was given to large families in the allocation of places in holiday camps and spa resorts, after government authorities had repeatedly stated how crucial it was for the survival of the German people that large families should be helped in every possible way. Likewise the German Society for Population Policy (*Deutsche Gesellschaft für Bevölkerungspolitik*), founded in 1915, recommended positive measures to counteract the decline in fertility, centring its attention on the protection of mothers and female workers, as well as on the care of infants and women in childbed. According to one of the Society's leaflets, only in this way could 'the political and economic power of the Reich be guaranteed to exist in the future', and 'the onslaught of our enemies from the West, the South and East be victoriously driven back'.[20]

A further effect of the war was to consolidate and accelerate trends in social policy which had begun before 1914, and indeed continued after 1918. The addressees and beneficiaries were predominantly women, who, if they belonged to the lower classes, badly needed welfare and supplementary income as a result of their growing workloads. Middle-class women also profited from the

20. Wuppertal Civic Archives, R IX, II.

extension of the welfare state, though in a quite different way. They comprised that 'women's relief force' (Lüders) that formed the link between needy women and official agencies, ensuring on a woman-to-woman basis that the authorities' programmes and measures actually were applied to their 'clients'. General Groener, chief of the central War Office, expressly ordered that as a matter of principle women were to occupy positions of responsibility in official welfare agencies and consultative bodies on women's issues. He believed that the successful organisation and mobilisation of the industrial female labour force was possible only if women were involved at official level. Consequently Marie-Elisabeth Lüders, a doctor of political science and a leading member of the BDF, was put in charge of women's employment exchanges. In January 1918 some 2,000 women were employed in the various agencies with responsibility for women.[21] In addition, by October 1918 approximately 900 factory welfare assistants were employed – before the war there had only been twenty. These were women whose task it was to look after female employees' work conditions, diet and any family problems, such as childcare.[22]

The range of voluntary, direct social work activities performed by middle-class women was, by comparison, far wider. Countless local women's associations – which had been engaged in community welfare long before the war – stepped up their assistance for war refugees, women workers and children. They organised soup-kitchens and supplies of clothing, set up shoe-repair workshops, made jam and preserved fruit for needy families, arranged stays in the country for working-class children who needed holidays, and visited women who worked in the munitions industry, arranging help with the housework and children where necessary.[23] Immediately after the outbreak of war, almost all women's associations, guilds and leagues joined to form a central organisation intended to co-ordinate and guide all the diverse welfare activities. As early as 1 August 1914 Gertrud Bäumer had impressed upon the Prussian Ministry of the Interior that middle-class women were prepared to

21. von Gersdorff, *Frauen im Kriegsdienst*, p. 25. On how these consultative bodies operated A. Seidel, *Frauenarbeit im Ersten Weltkrieg als Problem der staatlichen Sozialpolitik: Dargestellt am Beispiel Bayerns*, Frankfurt 1979, pp. 130ff.
22. Lüders, *Heer*, p. 188. See also the complaint submitted to the authorities by the Secretariat for Women Workers of the General Commission of German Trade Unions, concerning the protection of women workers, to be found in von Gersdorff, *Frauen im Kriegsdient*, pp. 134–5.
23. See, for example, the account by Elly Heuss-Knapp who organised a 'women's home service' in Heilbronn: *Bürgerin zweier Welten*, Tübingen 1961, pp. 146ff.

place themselves at the disposal of the fatherland as 'fighters on the home front'; eight days later saw the birth, with the willing approval of the authorities, of the National Women's Service (*Nationaler Frauendienst* – NFD), to which not only the BDF but also religious and patriotic associations belonged. The NFD worked in close co-operation with local authorities and welfare institutions to alleviate social problems caused or exacerbated by the war, and to ease the burden of those fighting at the front. But this was not all: mobilisation of the mind also came into its own. The NFD organised lectures on 'The German Fleet', or on the consequences of defeat for the workforce, and distributed leaflets on 'the imperative of unbending determination and the justification of our faith and confidence in victory'.[24]

This kind of commitment was different not only in terms of scope and intensity from the voluntary good works that middle-class women had performed either individually or through organisations from the early nineteenth century. What was more important was the heightened status of voluntary social work: no longer was it merely philanthropic charity in the interest of social harmony, but activity esteemed by the public and state alike as a valid, professional contribution to the nation's exercise of its free will. Welfare action by women of the middle classes, planned and organised in line with the strategy being pursued by the War Office, was a novelty in the history of military conflicts, and came to be regarded as a wartime social duty 'necessary both for Germany's ultimate victory . . . and for our success in combat in enemy territory' (Bernays). In the same way as every last drop of energy was somehow being extracted from economic and human resources to meet the colossal demand for soldiers and instruments of destruction, women – as labourers, mothers, housewives and workers in industry and welfare – now joined in the massive process of mobilisation which guaranteed the military its back-up. Marie-Elisabeth Lüders succinctly spelled out the connection between male active service at the front and female welfare service at home: 'Every element in the private lives of women became concerned with the war; of no less import than all other matters related to defensives and offensives. Army reserves passed through infants' homes; the transport of munitions depended on day-nurseries and crèches; air attacks were launched from homes for women workers; heavy barrage

---

24. *Bericht 1915–1917*, published by the Barmen branch of the NFD, pp. 52ff. ('Campaigning and Education').

prepared by welfare agencies and factory welfare assistants.'[25]

Many women involved in the National Women's Service enjoyed the public recognition that they received for their untiring patriotic efforts. They were 'raised above the humdrum of everyday life'; they were told how crucial their work was for the fatherland, and were given a voice in local government and welfare administration. The leaders of the women's movement, for their part, ceaselessly reminded everyone that women were proving themselves, and stressed the fact that, without the organisational co-ordination and training of the women's movement, German women would never have been 'armed for war' so quickly, smoothly and efficiently.[26] At the same time, the BDF could boast that for the duration of hostilities it had suspended its campaigning on specifically female issues, and for the sake of the national interest had unconditionally committed itself to a civic truce between the sexes. It did, however, expect loyalty to bring recompense and reward. After the Imperial government, under pressure from parliamentary forces, in 1917 declared its intention of replacing the three-tier Prussian franchise with equal, direct and universal suffrage, the BDF published a petition demanding that full suffrage be extended to women also, and stressing that they had long since earned this concession. Furthermore, the BDF maintained, positions in central and local government administration should be open to women. While it would have been absurd to claim that all women who had taken up paid employment during the war should be allowed to keep their jobs, qualified posts in areas of social work and welfare needed to be retained, and occupied by specially trained female staff. This was another way in which the bourgeois women's movement hoped to come closer to its aim of humanising society through 'organised motherliness'.

In pinning hopes on the future, the movement did not forget the reality of the war, which dragged on much longer than had been expected. Right up to the bitter end the BDF exhorted Germans to stand their ground. It rejected the Allied offer of a cease-fire in November 1918, giving notice that German women would 'put all their energies into defending to the last' rather than accept the conditions of armistice.[27] During the war the BDF had railed against the efforts of pacifist women to bring about peace. In 1915,

25. Lüders, *Heer*, p. 180.
26. G. Bäumer, *Die deutsche Frau in der sozialen Kriegsfürsorge*, Gotha 1916, pp. 2ff.
27. See von Gersdorff, *Frauen im Kriegsdienst*, pp. 271–2.

for instance, it spurned an invitation to attend an international peace congress in the Hague with the argument that it would be 'incompatible with our national feeling and the national obligations of the German women's movement'.[28]

Pacifism was not writ large in this movement. Even international feelers put out before the war, and meetings and co-operation with women's organisations from other countries, did not alter the fact that in 1914 the sole guiding star of political activity was the interest of the German nation. Very few women resisted the general euphoria of war and actively fought for international understanding and the immediate cessation of hostilities. Members of the German Peace Society (*Deutsche Friedensgesellschaft*), founded in 1892 and with 10,000 supporters by 1914, or of more radical women's organisations – Union for Female Suffrage (*Verband für Frauenstimmrecht*), Federation for the Protection of Mothers (*Bund für Mutterschutz*) – took part in actions, congresses and demonstrations. Great personal hardship and the most severe police repression failed to prevent some from founding a Women's Committee for Lasting Peace (*Frauenausschuß für dauernden Frieden*), which by 1917 had representatives in twenty-nine cities. But its appeals for peace without annexation and reparation had as much impact as the Hague congress. Lida Gustava Heymann, founder of the Union for Female Suffrage and an active pacifist, wrote in her memoirs of the isolation of pacifist women and of how the official women's movement, above all Gertrud Bäumer, scorned their efforts as incompatible with the aims of the BDF.[29]

Social Democratic women were more sympathetic to the pacifists. In March 1915, one month before the Hague conference, Clara Zetkin had called socialist women from eight countries to Bern, where they issued a manifesto protesting against war and advocating social revolution. One hundred thousand copies of the document were distributed illegally in Germany. Whereas middle-class pacifists applauded this action unequivocally, both the government and the leadership of the SPD were hostile. The police used every possible means – including arrest – to prevent distribution of the manifesto, and the Party executive kept its distance from the gathering in Bern,[30] forbidding Party members to obtain the mani-

---

28. Quoted in Greven-Aschoff, *Die bürgerliche Frauenbewegung*, p. 155.
29. L. G. Heymann and A. Augspurg, *Erlebtes – Erschautes: Deutsche Frauen kämpfen für Freiheit, Recht und Frieden 1850–1940*, ed. M. Twellmann, Meisenheim 1977, pp. 121ff.
30. Evans, *Sozialdemokratie*, pp. 277ff.

festo. After the German government had undertaken to respond to Russian mobilisation like with like, declaring, in addition, that it would be no more tolerant towards 'the enemy within', the Social Democratic movement also threw its weight behind Germany's war. Self-preservation and the desire to be involved were the driving forces behind the SPD's parliamentary party when it voted on 4 August 1914 in favour of granting war credits. Similar motives prompted the free trade unions to agree to a truce with the state and with private employers. The hope, cherished before hostilities broke out, that international solidarity among working men and women would impede the war of the ruling classes was dashed: faced with a *fait accompli*, people remained loyal to their own countries and were uncompromisingly vigilant against opposition from within their own ranks.

The Social Democratic women's movement had also harboured the belief that internationalism was the best defence against the conflict that for years had been threatening to envelop Europe. From 1907 to 1910 international socialist women's conferences debated ways in which women could help prevent war, and noted the prophylactic effect of a strictly anti-militaristic upbringing. Many towns witnessed women demonstrating for peace as late as April 1914. But when the conflict suddenly broke out, neither Social Democratic men nor female Party functionaries could come up with strategies for collective opposition. Clara Zetkin's appeal in the SPD women's press for mass protest was so ambiguous as to provide no guidelines for effective action. She warned that if the 'hangman of Russian Tsarism' was allowed to extend his power, it would mean 'the most appalling slavery for all peoples'; yet she did not see any reason to expect emancipation from the 'reactionary' Habsburg dynasty either.[31] Such ambiguity was characteristic of most official and unofficial statements by Party women. There was, additionally, the feeling that one was completely at the mercy of events, incapable of independent action. 'The war was there,' wrote Luise Zietz, the only woman on the SPD executive, a year after the war had started, 'credits had been approved; all matters in which women had had neither say nor influence of any note.'[32]

Women Social Democrats reacted variously to their sense of impotence. Some, like Lily Braun, painted a heroic picture of the

31. C. Zetkin, 'Proletarische Frauen, seid bereit', in G. Brinker-Gabler (ed.), *Frauen gegen den Krieg*, Frankfurt 1980, pp. 144–7.
32. L. Zietz, *Die sozialdemokratischen Frauen und der Krieg*, Berlin 1915, p. 2.

war, justifying it in nationalistic and jingoistic terms. Henriette
Fürth put the case more moderately in 1917:

We abhor war now as we have done in the past . . . but we nevertheless give
our sanction to the battle that has been forced upon us . . . and are
prepared . . . to sacrifice all we posses, our body and soul, until the very
last drop of blood has been split, so that ours will be a victory, a final
victory bringing a peace in which Germany will bring to all the blessings of
a civilisation and culture worthy of mankind.[33]

Luise Zietz, who in the Party executive had opposed the approval
of war credits, was more reserved and pragmatic in thought and deed.
While she followed leadership directives and urged Social Democratic women to help in community social service, child welfare and
care for the sick and women in childbed, she carefully avoided any
kind of military romanticism, refusing to indulge in outbursts of
hatred. Instead she appealed to all socialist women to show international solidarity. It was not until 1917, when she resigned from the
SPD and joined the newly formed Independent Social Democratic
Party (*Unabhängige Sozialdemokratische Partei Deutschlands –
USPD*), that she went on open offensive against the government's
war policy. Clara Zetkin, editor-in-chief of *Die Gleichheit*, had
been opposed totally to the war from the very beginning. After 1916
she gained increasing support from among her fellow socialists:
now that Germany had adopted an offensive war strategy, it was no
longer possible to hold that Tsarist despotism had forced the Reich
to defend itself.

It is difficult to estimate the size of the various factions in the
women's movement, which after 1917 split in organisational terms
too, with some switching to the USPD, others still to the Communist Party (KPD). Even though the most prominent figures left the
SPD, the vast majority stayed.[34] They carried on as they had begun
in August 1914 in the National Women's Service (NFD), co-
operating closely with their middle-class counterparts. While the
latter in the NFD had been primarily concerned to justify their
claim that they had a responsible and valid role to play, the onus for
Social Democrats had been to alleviate the oppressive situation in
which their clients – working-class women – found themselves. This
desire to help had prompted deep involvement in community

33. H. Fürth, *Die deutschen Frauen im Kriege*, Tübingen 1917, p. 59.
34. In 1919 the 'Majority Social Democrats' (MSPD) had 206,354 women members (Thönnessen, *The Emancipation of Women*, p. 114), the USPD about 70,000
(*USPD-Protokoll über die Verhandlungen des ausserordentlichen Parteitages vom 2.
bis 6. März 1919 in Berlin*, Berlin n.d., p. 50).

welfare; when the war made conditions even harsher, social work became the focal point of Social Democratic women's activities. Local SPD women's groups informed their members about state and local authority support schemes, distributed presents to the children of needy families, and advised soldiers' wives on their statutory maintenance and benefit entitlements. Bourgeois and socialist women's associations worked side by side in local NFD centres: political and ideological differences seemed irrelevant in day-to-day welfare and advice work.

Social Democrats now also found their efforts being respected and appreciated by the authorities – this was twice as significant for them as for middle-class women. Just as leading Party functionaries managed to escape from their political ghetto and rose to become serious partners in talks with the government, the rank-and-file dealt with local authorities and sat on various boards and commissions. Not only could these positions of influence be exploited to the benefit of the working classes; they also had the effect of furthering the political integration of Social Democracy, binding it to national causes and interests that transcended class divisions. It is therefore no coincidence that resistance to the war and the refusal to be loyal expressed in demonstrations, hunger revolts and strikes, came from those working-class men and women who belonged to neither organisations nor bore institutional responsibility.

Even as war broke out, nationalist fervour was far from unrestrained among working-class women. From the point of view of the bourgeois women's movement, there was a 'threatening degree of unrest among proletarian women in these very first days', and there were complaints of their lack of 'spiritual' preparedness and their 'deep mistrust of the state and of militarism'.[35] As news of the number of dead and wounded came in place of the rapid victory that had been promised, and as the supply situation grew progressively worse at home, these were the women who turned to more vociferous forms of protest. At the end of 1915 the first food riots occurred in cities: council offices were stormed and food shops looted. The women's wrath was vented on the incompetent and inadequate rationing schemes of both government and local authorities, and also on shopkeepers who were increasingly selling their wares under the counter and at exorbitant prices. There was no mistaking the similarity here with the bread riots of pre-industrial times, which

35. Bäumer, *Lebensweg*, p. 273; see also Heymann and Augspurg, *Erlebtes – Erschautes*, p. 125.

166

had almost entirely disappeared from the urban scene when production had risen, transport systems expanded, real wages increased, and a greater range of imports had become available. Now the war had brought back scarcity. The struggle to find bread, potatoes and butter was an exclusively female one: faced with high prices, food shortages and the responsibility of giving their families enough to eat, women again turned to traditional forms of protest.

Women also caused a stir during the First World War by joining in strikes (which as modern forms of conflict related to wage labour tended to be dominated by men). They played a major role as strikers and organisers in the walk-outs of April 1917, in which some 200,000 people in Berlin alone – mainly those employed in munitions factories – took part; and most importantly in the million-strong strike actions of early 1918.[36] Whereas the April strikers came out for 'Bread, Peace and Freedom', in the January strike the demands were more overtly political: immediate peace without annexations, electoral reform in Prussia, and comprehensive democratisation of the state; better food supplies had become secondary issues by 1918.

SPD Party and trade union functionaries – and the women's movement – tended to be swept along by the tide of action-hungry masses: they neither agitated, nor provoked.[37] Even left-wingers such as Clara Zetkin and Luise Zietz, who had openly opposed the war, had no influence over grass-roots opposition, since they were either in prison or prohibited from speaking in public. Hence the discord and dissatisfaction among working-class women were not transferred into SPD membership figures. In fact, far from gaining new comrades, the SPD actually lost 60 per cent of its female members between 1914 and 1918.[38] Only with the success of the revolution were women once more prepared to join organisations, and this greatly benefited the bodies of the socialist labour movement.

36. W. Albrecht et al., 'Frauenfrage und deutsche Sozialdemokratie vom Ende des 19. Jahrhunderts bis zum Beginn der zwanziger Jahre', *Archiv für Sozialgeschichte*, 19, 1979, pp. 459–510, esp. pp. 503ff.; R. Wurms, 'Krieg dem Kriege' – 'Dienst am Vaterland': Frauenbewegung im Ersten Weltkrieg', in F. Hervé (ed.), *Geschichte der deutschen Frauenbewegung*, Cologne 1983, pp. 103ff.; Seidel, *Frauenarbeit*, pp. 220ff.

37. D. Lehnert, *Sozialdemokratie zwischen Protestbewegung und Regierungspartei 1848–1983*, Frankfurt 1983, pp. 117ff.

38. Even more male members were lost (80 per cent), but this was due mainly to military call-up.

14

The Weimar Republic

Politics and Employment

Although women of the working classes, through their specifically female forms of protest and their participation in political strikes, had contributed to the crumbling of Imperial Germany's domestic legitimacy, they were not directly involved in its final collapse, which came about for military reasons. The revolution that broke out in November 1918 was initially a military revolt: it began when Kiel sailors mutinied, and snowballed into an insurrection by the home army. In many towns workers' and soldiers' councils sprang up; most of them, dominated as they were by trade unionists and Social Democrats, aimed for a fundamental democratisation of the state, local government and factories. Apart from a few exceptions, women had neither a seat nor a voice on the councils, even though Clara Zetkin spurred women to greater involvement and demanded of the councils that they pay more attention to women's issues. When the General Congress of Workers' and Soldiers' Councils convened in Berlin in 1918, among 496 delegates there were only two women: Käthe Leu from Danzig, who presented a report on behalf of the Independent Social Democrats (USPD), and Klara Noack from Dresden, representing the SPD. Leu's proposal – 'rigorously to promote women's interests, which in all areas have hitherto been subordinated' – did earn 'thunderous applause', but was submerged in the debate on more 'fundamental' issues such as nationalisation and general elections.[1]

Nevertheless women do seem to have been gripped by the political unrest and fervent activity of the revolutionary months. They took part in political gatherings, joined parties, trade unions and professional associations, and immersed themselves in political life as they saw it. Two thousand women from Hagen, for example, sent a motion to the Berlin Congress calling for the 'speediest convening

1. *Allgemeiner Kongress der Arbeiter- und Soldatenräte Deutschlands: Vom 16. bis 21. Dezember 1918 im Abgeordnetenhause zu Berlin. Stenographische Berichte*, Berlin 1919, reprinted Berlin 1973, esp. pp. 352–3.

of the National Assembly'. Middle-class women in particular, whose reactions to the revolutionary movement ranged from guarded mistrust to outright rejection, were keen to see the apparent chaos of the Councils superseded by a parliamentary order, and lobbied energetically – as did the bourgeois parties – for elections to a constitutional assembly to be held without delay. When polling was fixed for 19 January 1919, hectic electoral campaigning aimed at women began on all sides. One of the first decisions of the Council of Emissaries of the People (*Rat der Volksbeauftragten*) had been to grant women the rights to vote and to stand in elections, and the parties immediately realised the potential gains to be made. Women's committees looked for suitable female candidates, distributed leaflets and made election speeches. The BDF joined with other women's organisations and committees from liberal and conservative parties to form a Committee for the Preparation of Women for the National Assembly (*Ausschuß zur Vorbereitung der Frauen für die Nationalversammlung*) and, like Social Democratic women, set about informing and educating the new female electorate.

The high turn-out among women voters illustrated how successful these campaigns had been at mobilisation, and how greatly the revolution had politicised women. Almost 90 per cent took advantage of the right they had just won, and in none of the elections during the following fourteen years was the female turnout so high. It was clear that political crisis – the collapse of old powers combined with a sense of new freedoms and threats – had been instrumental in thrusting women into the political process. Parties, foreseeing that women would now feel a need to make up for the past, arranged candidate lists to favour women, with the result that forty-nine, or 9.6 per cent of those elected to the Weimar National Assembly were female. More than half of these were Social Democrats, three came from the Independent Social Democrats, and six each from the Catholic Centre and the liberal-bourgeois German Democratic Party (*Deutsche Demokratische Partei*). The German People's Party (*Deutsche Volkspartei*), whose parliamentary grouping also included the right-wing National Liberals, had only one woman deputy and the German National People's Party (*Deutsch-Nationale Volkspartei*), an offshoot of pre-war conservative parties, had three deputies.

At least ten of the sixteen bourgeois women members had their roots in the organised women's movement; the most prominent were Gertrud Bäumer and Marie-Elisabeth Lüders, both from the German Democratic Party. They at last had the chance to put into practice the notion of 'motherly politics' ('mütterliche Politik' – Helene Lange's phrase of 1914): policies that would preserve and stabilise the family. They demanded that 'the state help the family to meet its various obligations: upbringing, health care, feeding its members, etc.'[2] In fact, all the women in the Assembly, irrespective of party affiliations, concentrated on issues directly concerning women and the family – social policy, education and health care.[3] They left alone the classic realms of economic and fiscal policy, which fundamentally set the limits of social policy. This self-imposed restriction – and on the other hand the strategy of exclusion pursued by male decision-making elites – meant that the more comprehensive objective of the bourgeois women's movement to humanise society, the economy and politics with 'the spirit of motherliness', and to bring the 'influence of feminine culture' to bear in all spheres came unstuck in day-to-day parliamentary business.

The movement's potential for political mobilisation had in any case been almost exhausted when the Weimar Constitution recognised sexual equality as a basic right. §109 did allow for some restriction and modification in the interpretation of the law, for it granted the same civil rights and duties to men and women merely in 'principle'; but the women's movement itself was adamant that men and women had interests and needs that were fundamentally different, and that therefore the sexes were to be regarded not as equal in kind, but as equal in value. Hence it would be wrong to conceive of the movement's tenet of equality as a rigid dogma. It referred, rather, to the conditions allowing the free development of the female character. 'The feminine', however, was subject to laws different from those of 'masculine' culture. At the same time, this concept of natural sexual differences underlay a political programme which the movement proceeded to devise: one which both legitimated the continued existence of the movement even though the constitution formally placed the sexes on an equal footing, and rejected the view shared by many men and women that the movement had now reached its goal and could quietly retire. Activists constantly reiterated that they had only just started – it was not a case of merely achieving equal rights for women, but of 'women

2. H. Lange, *Kampfzeiten: Aufsätze und Reden aus vier Jahrzehnten*, vol. II, Berlin 1928, pp. 134ff. ('Das Staatsbürgertum der Frau').
3. For an account of the course pursued by women in the Reichstag, see C. Koonz, 'Conflicting Allegiances: Political Ideology and Women Legislators in Weimar Germany', *Signs: Journal of Women in Culture and Society*, 1, 1976, pp. 663–83.

creating from the world of men a world which bears the mark of *both* sexes'.[4] Since 'masculine culture' found itself in a crisis characterised by de-individualisation, alienation from nature, technification and objectification,[5] there was all the more reason to inject into society feminine values and orientations and so nurture motherly and humane behaviour at all levels.

Such ambitious and sweeping aspirations (which were hardly ever given precise and concrete expression) could remain but dreams in the social, political and economic reality of 1920s Weimar Germany, particularly since most of the practical activities of the bourgeois women's movement were limited to consolidating and building on occupational and professional gains that had already been won. The Social Democratic women's movement was barely discernible as an independent grouping, and concentrated on recruitment drives and social work. The latter was provided with a more solid institutional framework with the establishment in 1919 of the workers' Welfare Association (*Arbeiterwohlfahrt*). The rather conservative line taken by both women's movements earned them rebukes from the more critical youth movement, which charged them with having lost their innovative and creative power. The razor-sharp edge with which they had once cut into male politics was now blunted, rendering them a harmless and predictable factor in the political system.

Parties did continue to woo the female vote and to accept the presence of a few women in elected bodies; but they kept them well away from high-level politics.[6] Male parliamentarians made no secret of their view that important political decisions could not be taken by women, and the bourgeois parties in particular became even more reluctant to give women candidates favourable positions on the lists for elections to the Reichstag, Land and local governments. As a result the number of women deputies fell: whereas 37 women had entered the first Reichstag in 1920, only 27 won seats at

4. H. Lange, 'Steht die Frauenbewegung am Ziel oder am Anfang?' in *Kampfzeiten*, vol. II, p. 256; A. von Zahn-Harnack, *Die arbeitende Frau*, Breslau 1924, pp. 17–18. Women from the SPD also shared this view: with political equality 'we do not relinquish the right to be human beings of a different type, *feminine human beings*. We would not dream of *denying our womanhood* merely because we have entered the political arena to join the struggle for the people's rights' (Marie Juchacz, quoted in A. Schreiber, 'Die Sozialdemokratin als Staatsbürgerin', in A. Blos (ed.), *Die Frauenfrage im Lichte des Sozialismus*, Dresden 1930, p. 113).
5. G. Bäumer, *Die Frau in der Krisis der Kultur*, Berlin 1927.
6. On the role of women in the Weimar parties see R. Bridenthal and C. Koonz, 'Beyond Kinder, Küche, Kirche: Weimar Women in Politics and Work', in B. A. Carroll (ed.), *Liberating Women's History*, Urbana, Ill. 1976, pp. 301–29; Koonz, 'Conflicting Allegiances'.

the election in May 1924; and though they numbered 41 after 1930, they still accounted for only 7 per cent of all parliamentarians. Women were most strongly represented among Social Democratic deputies, between 11 and 14 per cent. By contrast, the figures ranged between 3 and 9 per cent in the bourgeois camp.[7] Even so, the conservative parties had benefited more than others from female suffrage: statistics on how the sexes voted show that after 1919 women clearly tended to cast their vote in favour of the Centre party in particular, though also for the German National People's Party and the German People's Party. The German Democratic Party, the SPD, and even more so the Communists, had enormous difficulties attracting female voters;[8] to such an extent, in fact, that as early as 1919 the left-wing *Rheinische Zeitung* called it the 'irony of world history' that 'Social Democracy won female suffrage to its political disadvantage, while the bourgeois parties, who denied women their political rights, are almost totally indebted to it'.[9] While such claims were on the whole correct, they were far too simplistic, for there were considerable regional variations in female voting habits. In Berlin, for example, more women than men voted SPD in 1928 and 1930, and in the strongholds of the labour movement – Leipzig, Nuremberg and Magdeburg – the SPD was equally popular with men and women. On the other hand, women in the Catholic Rhineland and in Bavaria showed far stronger allegiances to the Centre and the bourgeois-Christian parties defending the old order, and steered well clear of the Left.[10] Where the

7. G. Bremme, *Die politische Rolle der Frau in Deutschland: Eine Untersuchung über den Einfluß der Frauen bei Wahlen und ihre Teilnahme in Partei und Parlament*, Göttingen 1956, table 39, p. 124; Koonz, 'Conflicting Allegiances', table 1, p. 667.

8. In the Reichstag elections of 1929, 59 per cent of the Centre's votes were from women, 56 per cent of the German National People's Party's, and 51 per cent of the German People's Party's; the figures for the German Democratic Party were 47 per cent, the SPD 43 per cent and the Communist Party 37 per cent (Bremme, *Die politische Rolle*, table 24, p. 76). Unlike the SPD and the Independent Social Democrats, the Communists had serious problems finding female members: in 1923 only 32,856, or 11.2 per cent of the total of 294,230, were women (W. T. Angress, *Die Kampfzeit der KPD 1921–23*, Düsseldorf 1973, p. 395, n. 113). On the KPD's policy on women see S. Kontos, *Die Partei kämpft wie ein Mann: Frauenpolitik der KPD in der Weimarer Republik*, Basle 1979.

9. Quoted in D. Lehnert, *Sozialdemokratie und Novemberrevolution*, Frankfurt 1983, p. 272.

10. Bremme, *Die politische Rolle*, table IV, pp. 243ff. (break-down of election results by party and sex); H. L. Boak, 'Women in Weimar Germany: The "Frauenfrage" and the Female Vote', in R. Bessel and E. J. Feuchtwanger (eds), *Social Change and Political Development in Weimar Germany*, London 1981, pp. 155–73; B. Peterson, 'The Politics of Working-Class Women in the Weimar Republic', *Central European History*, 10, 1977, pp. 87–111 (analysis of results of Reichstag election of December 1924).

restructuring of society through industrialisation had not advanced very far; where female employment outside the home was still insignificant and the fabric of society moulded on traditional and religious norms and orientations: in these situations women who were faced with new challenges and threats tended to be more conservative in their voting than men.

In addition, the generally stronger hold that religion had over women led them to side with parties which were confident about their role as the trustees of Christian mores, and which conveniently reiterated their solid foundation in church traditions and structures. The religious women's movement had an important multiplying effect here. The 174 local groups and 200,000 members (in 1926) of the German Evangelical Women's Federation, the political wing of the one-and-a-half million strong Evangelical Women's Union (*Evangelisches Frauenwerk*), which had left the BDF in 1918 over the issue of female suffrage, maintained close contact with the German National People's Party. The Catholic Women's Federation (*Katholischer Frauenbund*), which had 250,000 members in 1928, was a firm ally of the Centre party. The various associations for mothers and young women were even more closely tied to the Catholic church; with 1,660,00 members they were among the largest women's organisations in the Republic. They regarded themselves as auxiliary organisations of the Catholic clergy, and supported them in their attempts, which had the blessing of the Curia, to mould the parish community along the lines of the model Catholic family, see to its spiritual welfare, carry out charitable works, and protect it from the disintegrating tendencies of public life. Anchored firmly in the petty-bourgeois and rural milieu, these associations gave Catholic women broad scope for activities ranging from strictly religious matters (pilgrimages, spiritual exercises) to welfare and social work.[11] The fact that the female Catholic population was mobilised in such an all-embracing and fundamental manner was directly reflected in the electoral successes of the Centre party. It could be much surer of support from its female power base than from men: although Catholics made up one third of the whole electorate, in 1920 only 20 per cent of men voted Centre as opposed to 29 per cent of women. In Cologne, a stronghold of Catholicism, only 27.8 per cent of men voted for the Catholic party, compared

11. D. Kaufmann, 'Vom Vaterland zum Mutterland: Frauen im katholischen Milieu der Weimarer Republik', in Hausen (ed.), *Frauen suchen*, pp. 250–75; Kaufmann, *Katholisches Milieu in Münster 1928–1933: Politische Aktionsformen und geschlechtsspezifische Verhaltensräume*, Düsseldorf 1984, esp. pp. 77ff.

with 44.7 per cent of women.[12]

It is impossible to determine exactly how female party preferences at Republic level changed between 1919 and 1933 since, unfortunately, relevant statistical data is not available. But there is no mistaking the fact that at least in the months following the collapse of Imperial Germany women felt more favourably towards the socialist parties than they had before. Men *and* women were caught by the tangible swing to the left during the last stage of the war, and particularly during the November revolution. There was a boom in the membership of the free trade unions and socialist professional associations, and both the SPD and the Independent SPD benefited. Other bodies on the political spectrum also gained impetus from political mobilisation, though not as much as the organisations that were regarded as bearers of the revolution. Women were now being urged from all sides to become actively involved in politics and public life; they too were swept along by the spirit of upheaval and radicalism. In 1918 66,000 women had belonged to the SPD, but by 1920 the number had risen to 207,000; in just two years the Independent Social Democracts doubled their female membership, to 135,464 by October 1920; in the same period the number of women organised in the socialist trade unions went up from 442,957 to over 1,700,000.[13] This pattern was especially marked in organisations of white-collar workers. The socialist Central Union of Clerical Staff (*Zentralverband der Angestellten*) included 175,204 women in 1919 – four times as many as the previous year. Membership did go up for the Union of Female Retail and Office Staff (*Verband der weiblichen Handels – und Büroangestellten*), affiliated to the federated Christian trade unions, but lagged way behind the growth in left-wing competition.[14] During the 1920s, however, women's enthusiasm for joining organisations declined rapidly, and it was the left-wing bodies which in

12. Bremme, *Die politische Rolle*, table IV, pp. 243, 248.

13. The figures on the SPD and free trade unions are to be found in Thönnessen, *The Emancipation of Women*, p. 144; on the USPD see R. F. Wheeler, 'German Women and the Communist International: The Case of the Independent Social Democrats', *Central European History*, 8, 1975, pp. 113–39, quote at pp. 123, 129–30. The proportion of women in the USPD's membership fell from 23.3 per cent in 1919 to 15.2 per cent in 1920. There is hardly any data on the female membership of other Weimar parties.

14. The number of women in the Central Union of Clerical Employees rose by 296 per cent, compared to 53 per cent in the VWA (see K. Stehr, *Der Zentralverband der Angestellten*, Berlin 1926, pp. 47–8; *Archiv für Frauenarbeit*, 7, 1919, p. 66; K. Müller, 'Der VWA', in *Internationales Handwörterbuch des Gewerkschaftswesens*, Berlin 1932, p. 1859).

turn suffered most. The Central Union of Clerical Staff saw a 60 per cent drop, while membership of the Union of Female Retail and Office Staff fell by only one third. The Christian labour movement lost comparatively fewer women than the socialist General Federation of German Trade Unions (*Allgemeiner Deutscher Gewerkschaftsbund*).[15]

The left-wing shift was thus rather ephemeral among women; men on the whole showed a more enduring penchant for organisation. In 1920, 27.7 per cent of the total membership of the General Federation of German Trade Unions were women; by 1931, this had dropped to 16 per cent. In the Christian unions, female membership fell from 25.5 per cent in 1922, to 16.3 per cent in 1931. High-flown hopes for a change for the better gave way in the difficult years of the Weimar Republic to disappointment at daily economic and political life, for things were much as they had been before the war. Little trace remained of the lofty promises of the revolution. Democratisation and the introduction of the parliamentary system brought nothing more than protracted crises and coalition governments, with Chancellor and Ministers often changing several times a year. Political murders, attempted coups, revolts by the Left and the Right, corruption scandals – these were normal events. On the economic front, there was neither the new beginning that had been heralded, nor any sign of a boom on the horizon. The eight-hour day soon fell by the wayside; the liquid assets of the middle classes were eaten away by the inflation of 1923; savings accounts and government loans became worthless while shares and fixed capital retained or even increased in value. Entrepreneurs, land-owners and speculators made enormous profits while the middle strata of the bourgeoisie lost their securities; working-class women no longer knew how to feed their families in the face of galloping price rises and wages that could not keep pace with inflation. At certain periods production crises and rationing led to high levels of unemployment. By 1926 10 per cent of wage-earners were out of a job, and from 1929 onwards – the start of the worldwide slump – the number of unemployed continued to shoot

15. Between 1920, when female membership peaked, and 1926 (the low point), the free trade unions lost 61 per cent of their women. By contrast, the Christian Trade Unions saw only 57 per cent leave between 1922 and 1926. However, they did have far fewer female (and male) members than the General Federation of German Trade Unions: in 1923 over 1,500,000 women belonged to the free trade unions, compared to the 230,263 in the General Confederation of Christian Trade Unions (Thönnessen, *The Emancipation of Women*, p. 144; M. Schneider, *Die Christlichen Gewerkschaften 1894–1933*, Bonn 1982, table pp. 770–1).

up, until it reached six million in 1932, the highest figure ever officially recorded.

From the point of view of material conditions, however, the Weimar Republic was not simply one endless catastrophe. Much changed for the better particularly as far as local communities were concerned – and this meant people's everyday lives. Housing construction proceeded steadily: between 1920 and 1932 some 2,600,000 new homes were built. Advances in health care were reflected in the rise in the per capita number of doctors and hospital beds; in many towns the authorities set up a community health service which also fulfilled advisory and welfare functions. The leisure industry boomed – cinemas, dance halls, restaurants, cafés and theatres mushroomed in the cities, and the fun-loving public flocked to them. There was migration into the towns: by 1933 over 30 per cent of Germans lived in towns with over 100,000 inhabitants (the figure in 1910 had been 21.3 per cent), with only a third living in the country. The great cities with their avenues, new office buildings and leisure facilities became the quintessence of modern life in Weimar Germany. But they were also like theatres with two stages, each presenting an entirely different spectacle. On the one, a brilliant and vibrant display of the culture of the Golden Twenties – wealth, art, intellectual life and an exuberant *joie de vivre*; on the other, a tragedy of misery, poverty, and rising suicide, crime and abortion rates.

The type of 'new woman' created by Weimar cultural cricitism was represented by an interesting combination of modernity and tradition, of progress and reaction. The external appearance of young women after the war prompted some observers to ring in the 'age of the liberated woman'.[16] Hair in a bob, cigarettes, casual clothes: these were the trademarks of the modern woman, who took the principle of equality in the Weimar Constitution seriously, and played her part at work and in public life with confidence. But besides externalities, women seemed to want to assimilate male mores too, for the lifestyles of the sexes were converging. For instance, women now frequently went out to work and earned their own money. The occupational census of 1925 found that there were over 1,700,000 more women in full-time employment than in 1907. Although the percentage of women gainfully employed had barely

---

16. E. E. Schwabach, *Die Revolutionierung der Frau*, Leipzig 1928, p. 88; on the 'new woman' see also *Frauenalltag und Frauenbewegung im 20. Jahrhundert: Materialsammlung in der Abteilung 20. Jahrhundert im Historischen Museum Frankfurt*, vol. II, Frankfurt 1980, pp. 105–47.

moved – 34.9 per cent in 1907 to 35.6 per cent in 1925[17] – the impression created in the public mind was that women were more clearly a part of 'objective culture' than before the war. Some had admittedly been forced to leave positions they had occupied during the war, to accommodate the floods of men returning to civilian life after demobilisation,[18] but this was only a short-term downward trend. In fact, what may be regarded as the adaptation of female employment profiles to male norms accelerated in the Weimar years. In 1907 two-thirds of employed women were in agriculture and service, but by 1925 the figure was only 55 per cent and by 1933 51 per cent: industry, craft and services were the sectors towards which female labour increasingly tended.

The media and the architects of social policy in Weimar Germany were not interested in the 'traditional' domains of farming and domestic service. Nor did the spotlight of the emancipation debate fall on the female industrial labour force, which represented 18.4 per cent of all women employed in 1925, or on the small band of women graduates, who as teachers, doctors or lawyers had made their way into higher occupational spheres which formerly had been exclusively male haunts. The hotly-disputed prototypes of female emancipation were in fact the young clerical workers: the children of the new age who were variously celebrated or accursed. The modernity of the Weimar system appeared to acquire the shape of secretaries, shorthand typists and shop assistants. The fact that in 1925 there were almost one-and-a-half million female white-collar workers – three times as many as in 1907, which represented a jump from 5 to 12.6 per cent of all women in work – also justified the marked, though not evenly focused, interest in this kind of New Objectivity woman. While some held that the feminisation of white-collar work was the 'beginning of the real emancipation of women',[19] the 'greatest revolution in the social position of women', more critical onlookers highlighted the ambiguity of this superficial 'modernisation': as early as 1932, the psychologist Alice Rühle-Gerstel had no illusions about the impact women in offices and shops would have on emancipation:

17. Calculated from Willms, 'Grundzüge', p. 35. Willms also explains that the deviations from official figures are due to the inclusion in the statistics of women who assisted in their families' businesses.
18. On demobilisation see R. Bessel, '"Eine nicht allzu große Beunruhigung des Arbeitsmarktes": Frauenarbeit und Demobilmachung in Deutschland nach dem Ersten Weltkrieg', *Geschichte und Gesellschaft*, 9, 1983, pp. 211–29.
19. F. Croner, *Soziologie der Angestellten*, Cologne 1962, p. 180 (in the 1920s Croner was an official in the General Free Federation of Clerical Staff (*Allgemeiner Freier Angestelltenbund*).

These jobs are dubious: as semi-pure as the silk in the stockings and skimpy tops worn by shop girls, and as mixed-up as their minds ... Economic situation: proletarian; ideology: bourgeois; type of occupation: male; attitude to work: female. Beaming figures, casting a light that is sparkling and attractive, and yet which highlights their very ambiguities; but in any case figures iridescently confident of their social and spiritual existence.[20]

Theodor Adorno, to whom female white-collar workers seemed 'as independent ... as dependent men', overlooked the fact, however, that characteristic patterns of the sexual division of labour and power had also emerged in this 'modern' occupational sphere; women performed work that was subordinate, less independent, and worse paid than men's. Industry's enormous demand for commercial and business staff, which had taken root in the late nineteenth century, was related to a process which divided standardised and mechanised work functions in a way that was far from gender-neutral: women were given the most routine and simple tasks, particularly the operation of new office machines, while mainly men were employed in qualified positions such as accounting, administration or management of departments. While men saw it as an affront to their dignity if they had to stoop so low as to become typists, women seemed to be blessed with a certain aptitude for the keyboard: digital suppleness acquired through playing the piano proved to be of practical value here.

Discrepancies in the labour market and the difference between male and female white-collar activities correlated with gender-specific patterns of education and training. Men usually completed a commercial apprenticeship, which lasted several years and introduced them to all aspects of a business; women, by contrast, often had to make do with one year at a commercial school where they learned the basics of typing and office organisation. Less favourable training opportunities were not, however, the only obstacle to promotion from positions as clerks, typists, secretaries or sales assistants. Even more highly-qualified women rarely managed to rise above the clerical level, for both employers and male white-collar workers proved disinclined to blur male–female differences. In the final analysis, packing senior positions exclusively with men satisfied the needs of male employees for status and prestige, and furthered industrial peace. Only in times of crisis – the First World

---

20. A. Rühle-Gerstel, *Das Frauenproblem der Gegenwart: Eine psychologische Bilanz*, Leipzig 1932 (reprinted under the title *Die Frau und der Kapitalismus*, Frankfurt, n.d.), pp. 299–301. See also E. Bloch, *Das Prinzip Hoffnung*, vol. II, Frankfurt 1974, p. 687; T. W. Adorno, *Minima Moralia*, Frankfurt 1973, p. 115.

War or the global economic slump – did women have an opportunity to rise into positions of greater responsibility and replace men who were either sent to war or, as happened in the early 1930s, dismissed for financial reasons. In any case, they earned less than their male colleagues. Wage agreements for commercial white-collar workers in Weimar Germany stipulated that pay for women across the board should be 10–25 per cent lower. The reason proffered was that men generally had higher clothing and living expenses than did women, who could knit, sew, darn and cook.[21]

On closer inspection, the fascinating 'new woman' of the urban office culture turned out to be a projection of the men of the time who, either from fear or from an exaggerated sense of progress, painted a distorted picture of female modernity and ignored traditional structures in the world of work. Office employment may well have helped make female paid labour acceptable, even in bourgeois circles. Especially after hyperinflation had struck, the economic situation of many middle-class families made them realise the prudence of having their daughters trained as clerks or secretaries. But there was also no doubt that a woman's occupation functioned merely as a temporary place of safe-keeping before marriage. A married woman was neither to serve behind a counter nor sit in an office; she was to look after her husband, children and home. In this sense, clerical and office work was a typical female occupation: in 1925, almost all women white-collar workers were single, and two-thirds of them under twenty-five.

Despite the colossal political upheavals that followed the collapse of Imperial Germany, male–female roles and related expectations remained remarkably stable in the post-war period. Family and school prepared girls primarily for their future state as housewives and mothers, while boys were still expected to seek their vocation through an occupation. Domestic science was a compulsory subject for girls in the basic *Volksschulen* in Hamburg, Saxony, Hanover, Oldenburg and Westphalia, and in many districts an integral part of the three-year course at vocational schools.[22] Education at higher girls' schools in Weimar Germany also differed from that in higher boys' schools – this was reflected in the separation of the schools

21. U. Frevert, 'Traditionale Weiblichkeit und moderne Interessenorganisation: Frauen im Angestelltenberuf 1918–1933', *Geschichte und Gesellschaft*, 7, 1981, pp. 513–14.

22. On the introduction of domestic science as a subject in *Volksschulen* from the late nineteenth century onwards, see G. Tornieporth, *Studien zur Frauenbildung*, Weinheim 1979, esp. pp. 95–123, 284ff.; M. Breuer, 'Berufliches Bildungswesen', *Jahrbuch für Frauenarbeit*, 1, 1924, pp. 38–55.

themselves. Since their incorporation into the general secondary education system in 1908, higher girls' schools had been able to shake off their status as 'alien' bodies, and raise their social standing. But the principle still defended, and not least by the women's movement, was this: higher girls' schooling must be equal in value, but not in kind, to boys' schooling. The curricula in such girls' schools (*Lyzeum* and *Oberlyzeum*) accordingly placed emphasis on modern languages, the arts and needlework, whereas boys' schools (*Gymnasium, Realgymnasium,* and *Oberrealschule*) tended to offer mathematics and natural sciences or classics, depending on their specialities. In 1926, 29 per cent of girls in the senior grades of Prussian secondary education were fortunate enough to attend a 'women's school' (*Frauenschule*), where instruction centred on specifically female subjects related to housekeeping, bringing up children, needlework and teaching. Most girls finished their 'higher' schooling when they left the tenth grade of a *Lyzeum* grammar school (at the age of fifteen or sixteen), but boys were far more likely to carry on to the *Abitur*. Only 8 per cent of the 176,575 girls attending Prussian secondary schools in 1926 were in the eleventh, twelfth or thirteenth grades, the *Abitur* years, compared with 25 per cent of boys.[23]

Dissimilar educational routes were an expression of the conviction, still widely held in all social strata, that investing extensive time and money in female vocational training was in principle a waste since, in general, marriage saw to women's needs. In bourgeois and petty-bourgeois circles, the son would usually go on to further study, while his sister would often obtain her school certificate (*mittlere Reife*) from a *Lyzeum*, proceed for a short spell to a commercial school, then earn money in a clerical post to help finance her brother's training. The working classes also preferred their sons to learn something useful. In 1925, for example, almost half of the working-class young men in Fürth took a craft apprenticeship, compared with only 15 per cent of the young women. At the same time 38 per cent of the young women, and 19 per cent of the young men, were unskilled factory workers.[24] However, workers who were themselves skilled and earned higher wages were the very people who seemed keen to ensure their daughters moved up the social ladder, and to train them for white-collar jobs. Before the war, the social profile of most clerical staff was distinctly middle-

23. Calculated from Lundgreen, *Sozialgeschichte*, vol. II, tables pp. 80–1, 103–4.
24. J. Nothaas, *Sozialer Auf- und Abstieg im Deutschen Volk*, Munich 1930, Table III.

class; but the enormous rise in demand for female commercial staff in the Weimar years offered many women from the working classes the opportunity to 'rise' to white-collar status. Vocational guidance agencies reported that ever more young girls wished to become clerical workers or shop assistants. For working-class girls the following was especially apt: 'a non-manual occupation is the most respectable, tailoring the most secure and domestic service the most ardous ... All that can be said of unskilled labour is, "it's easy to earn money".'[25] Occupational psychologists and teachers affirmed that shop assistants regarded themselves as a 'cut above' factory workers, who 'did not know how to behave'. In their turn, shop assistants were outranked by clerks and secretaries whose jobs seemed more worthwhile and better remunerated.

For a working-class woman the main attraction of a white-collar job lay in its social attributes. Although a factory worker would often earn more than a sales assistant or clerk, a post in business and commerce was far more prestigious. Even a job in retailing seemed highly desirable, for it opened the door to meeting a better class of customer, and forced women to be smartly dressed and well-spoken and have good manners. One of the most favoured areas was men's clothing, where rich gentlemen would 'buy a beautiful suede hat or a particularly fine pair of leather gloves, and in so doing become acquainted with the shop assistant' – or so young women in vocational training fancied.[26] Such fantasies were a far cry from reality, but the media went out of their way to fire imaginations. For many girls, the cinema had decided their career. At the movies they saw palatial department stores where 'elegant customers crowded around the counter, making charming conversation with the assistant, until one of them whisked her off to a marriage of happiness and luxury'.[27]

In the inter-war years, these manufacturers of dreams, these 'palaces of diversion', these 'sites of the cult of pleasure' (Kracauer) developed into important instruments in the formation of public opinion, pulling in mass audiences every evening: in 1930 six million cinema tickets were sold every week.[28] Although all sections

25. E. Barschak, *Die Schülerin der Berufsschule und ihre Umwelt*, Berlin 1926, p. 6.

26. Essays written by fourteen- to seventeen-year-old females in further training, on their notions and expectations of work as sales assistants, quoted in E. Lau, *Beiträge zur Psychologie der Jugendlichen*, Langensalza 1925, p.35.

27. C. Dreyfuß, *Beruf und Ideologie der Angestellten*, Munich, 1933, p. 153.

28. C. Dreyfuß, 'Zur gesellschaftlichen Lage des Films', *Neue Blätter für den Sozialismus*, 4/2, Potsdam 1933, p. 91.

of society were fascinated by the new medium, low-ranking white-collar workers – shop assistants, typists and telephonists – were among the keenest and most regular cinema-goers.[29] With film-makers mindful of their audience, it was no coincidence that the talkies had latched on to the figure of the successful and attractive secretary, for she provided the ideal subject for films which set out to show ordinary people how they could rise socially. On the screen the typist or shop assistant appeared young, pretty, sexy and elegant. She could climb the social ladder in two ways: she was either extremely competent and married to her typewriter, thus winning the respect and love of her boss for her untiring commitment to the firm; or she made up for a lack of mental dexterity with physical attractiveness. Cinema-goers clearly thought the second more realistic. In 1930 one official of a white-collar organisation became quite piqued when the audience simply laughed at the 'absurdity' of a film entitled *As Poor as a Church Mouse*, in which the boss led his secretary up th aisle in recognition of her professional skills.[30]

Magazines and newspapers as well as films took up the idea of the new type of white-collar employee. The typist joined the leg-swinging Tiller Girl as the most popular object of satire and media gossip. Cosmetic firms targeted their advertising at women in offices and department stores, adding a layer of prospective upward mobility to their make-up. Even the literature of the day turned its hand to this most promising figure. The numerous pulp novels aimed at female white-collar workers were clearly different from the novels about office juniors and commercial assistants meant for men. While individual competence and honesty were the major factors in the latter, women's novels portrayed secretaries and shop assistants solely as the objects of men's desires, who could achieve the social success they longed for only with the help of fate, luck and coquetry. Normal working life hardly ever appeared in such depictions; if it did, it was swamped by sentimental odes to typing and shop work. The often oppressive family situation of these young women was as rare a theme as the physical and mental pressures of typing, the generally meagre salary, or the chilblains that food shop assistants had to endure. The majority of these putatively self-determining creatures lived with their parents, not least for financial reasons. According to the Union of Female Retail

29. S. Kracauer, 'Die kleinen Ladenmädchen gehen ins Kino' and 'Film 1928', in Kracauer, *Das Ornament der Masse*, Frankfurt 1977, pp. 279–317.
30. Bode, 'Der Beruf der Stenotypistin', *Jahrbuch der Frauenarbeit*, 6, 1930, p. 62.

and Office Staff, almost half of its members under twenty-five earned a maximum 100 Reichmarks per month which, after deductions of national insurance, placed them well below the poverty line in the Weimar Republic of about 100 Reichmarks.[31]

Only a minority could afford to rent a flat or furnished room of their own. It may have been cheap to live with one's parents, but a daughter would be expected to help with domestic chores in her already scant spare time. For 75 per cent of female assistants in retailing the eight-hour day remained on paper, and in many areas small shops also opened on Sundays. It was not only in blue-collar families that daughters would finish work, and then be faced with two hours of housework, while 'fathers and sons thought it the most natural thing in the world to be served by a girl who had returned home from work exhausted'.[32] Young women rarely had a room to themselves where they could seek privacy; one in two of all assistants in food shops, most of a proletarian background, did not even have their own bed.[33]

It should therefore come as no surprise that even the apparently privileged girls in white-collar work longed to marry, give up their job and at last be their 'own master', as one seventeen-year-old shop assistant put it. Their dreams and fantasies may well have focused on the fine gentlemen presented to them in films and novels, but in practice a work colleague with a background similar to their own was more accessible. In 1925 almost every second woman employed in Bavarian industry as a clerk or secretary married a man in a white-collar job; a good third of shop assistants married a man from their own place of work, one quarter managed to rise to the position of wife of a self-employed man, and 40 per cent married 'below their station'.[34] As was to be expected, most left employment for married life, devoting themselves to their families, except if their husband was a shopkeeper: in this case, they stayed behind the counter, unremunerated for their labours, and with the official status of 'assisting relative'.

Women in white-collar jobs married to blue-collar workers were also likely to continue in employment. In 1925, 22 per cent of this

---

31. F. Glaß and D. Kische, *Die wirtschaftlichen und sozialen Verhältnisse der berufstätigen Frauen: Erhebung 1928/29*, Berlin 1930, pp. 21ff., 53.
32. L. Franzen-Hellersberg, *Die jugendliche Arbeiterin: Ihre Arbeitsweise und Lebensform*, Tübingen 1932, p. 47.
33. E. Düntzer, *Die gesundheitliche und soziale Lage der erwerbstätigen weiblichen Jugend*, Berlin 1933, Table p. 42.
34. Nothaas, *Sozialer Auf- und Abstieg*, table VII (Occupation and Marriage in Bavaria in 1925).

group were engaged in full-time gainful employment compared with only 10 per cent of the wives of white-collar workers. Every fifth female industrial worker was married.[35] Factory girls shared the desire to have to 'work' only until they wed, but this frequently proved impractical. In many cases the husband's earnings were insufficient, and especially in periods of high unemployment it often fell to the wife alone to feed the family, since lower female wages improved her chances on the labour market. Pay agreements for manual labour stipulated basic gender-related differentials: as a rule women earned between 20 and 40 per cent less for the same work. When compared to pre-war levels, the wage gap had closed only for skilled female workers; in 1933 they were earning 66 per cent of the male wage, as compared with 58 per cent in 1913–14.[36]

Over half of the female labour force in craft and industry was unskilled or semi-skilled. Opportunities for training arose only in sectors where men were not employed. In clothing and textile manufacture, for example, women were trained as skilled seamstresses or tailoresses. Such exclusively female domains began to die out around 1924, when the era of technical rationalisation set in. Areas of employment that had become open to women during the First World War, then closed after demobilisation, were now again employing increasing numbers of females. Women's employment prospects rose particularly in the chemical, metallurgical and electrical engineering industries as a result of the trend for a greater division of labour to be introduced into production processes, more machines and automated production lines to be installed, and skilled workers to be replaced by unskilled and semi-skilled labour. In 1925 around 22 per cent of the workforce in electrical engineering and the chemical industry were female.[37]

Although the employment of women in 'male industries' during the First World War had provoked excitement and unease in the public mind, the topic was manifestly uninteresting for the 1920s. Indignant voices could perhaps be heard among armchair politicians and in trade union circles, complaining that pro-rationalisation

35. A. Niemeyer, *Zur Struktur der Familie*, Berlin 1931, pp. 111, 115. On reasons why married women took factory work, see D. Hansen-Blancke, *Die hauswirt-schaftliche und Mutterschaftsleistung der Fabrikarbeiterin*, Berlin 1932, esp. pp. 36ff.
36. G. Wellner, 'Industriearbeiterinnen in der Weimarer Republik: Arbeitsmarkt, Arbeit und Privatleben 1919–1933', *Geschichte und Gesellschaft*, 7, 1981, pp. 546. On the development of wage differentials in Weimar Germany see D. Petzina et al., *Sozialgeschichtliches Arbeitsbuch*, III, Munich 1978, p. 99. Female unskilled workers earned 71 per cent of male wages in 1913–14, 62 per cent in 1924, and 70 per cent again in 1933.
37. Kuczynski, *Lage der Arbeiterin*, table p. 210.

employers were relying on cheap female labour and shedding qualified male workers. But as long as the expansion of production continued to create new opportunities for men too, the competition for supremacy on the labour market did not become a hot political potato. The long-term male unemployed were alone in perceiving women as threatening competitors and calling for their dismissal. In times of crisis, however, married women were the first to be denied the right to a job. Paid female labour was in no way generally accepted in Weimar Germany; it was encouraged or discouraged, depending on the state of the economy. Both Left and Right were heard to say that a woman's true place was in the home; she should participate in the world of employment only between school and marriage, thus to earn her dowry. The modernity of the Weimar Republic resided in the fact that all social strata had come to take for granted this 'intermediary stage of personal independence' (Bäumer) for women. There was no fundamental questioning of traditional male and female stereotypes. Once a woman had married, and not chosen an independent farmer, restaurant owner or shopkeeper as her husband,[38] she was expected to play a largely prescribed role that excluded the possibility of gainful employment except in dire circumstances.

Family, Sexuality, and Youth

Though roles were rigidly defined, and socialisation and education tailored to gender-specific aims, even a woman's most important place in the Weimar Republic – the family – was not immune to social change. The Weimar Constitution, which would have sexual equality as the family's foundation, did not achieve its democratic ambitions; indeed they were not even translated into legislation, for the patriarchal family law of the German Civil Code was not revised. But demographic and socio-economic forces were at work, affecting the family and giving rise to structural changes that contemporary observers noted with interest. Since the mid-nineteenth century neither conservatives, liberals, socialists nor the clergy had tired of alerting people to the imminent collapse of family life. In the 1920s the alleged crisis of the family still formed the crux of social and cultural debate, and even the bourgeois women's move-

38. In 1925, 52 per cent of women with self-employed husbands were in full-time employment, mostly classed officially as 'assisting relatives' in their husbands' businesses. See Niemeyer, *Zur Struktur*, p. 115.

ment initiated scholarly research into the 'state and disruption of the modern family'.

There were signs everywhere of the decline and demise of the family: sexual promiscuity; rising divorce and abortion rates; falling birth rates at a time of increasing illegitimacy; higher numbers of married women in work. The root-cause of these disturbing tendencies was identified as the 'boundless egoism' of women who were betraying their natural vocation and striving for greater personal freedom and independence. More than ever marriage and the family, those two pillars of society, seemed to be disintegrating because women, whose calling it was to uphold tradition and morals, were aspiring to the individualistic ethic of the modern age and failing to meet their obligations as mothers of the nation.

Demographers and those responsible for population policy expressed particular concern about the tendency for parents to limit family size. In the nineteenth century contraception and family planning had been confined to the narrow stratum of the educated bourgeoisie but by the beginning of the twentieth had begun to be more widely practised by the petty bourgeoisie and the working classes. On a national average, couples who married in the early 1920s had 2.27 children, but marriages entered into between 1925 and 1929 produced as few as 1.98 children.[39] In other words the two-child nuclear family had become the norm in Weimar Germany. The new middle classes of white-collar workers were even heading for the three-person household. The initiative to use contraception seems to have come primarily from women, as is suggested by the interviews the doctor Max Marcuse conducted in 1912 with 100 married working-class women from Berlin and in 1917 with 300 hospitalised soldiers. The majority of husbands relied on their wives who, it appears, were better informed about methods of family planning and who were also personally more interested in cutting down pregnancies.[40]

But even women were not exactly omniscient in such matters; medical science too had no more than limited knowledge about conception and contraception. The works of Knaus and Ogino, gynaecologists from Austria and Japan respectively, on high mid-cycle fertility, for example, did not become available to the public

---

39. Spree, *Health and Social Class*, table 14, p. 204.
40. Extracts from Marcuse's interviews can be found in A. Bergmann, 'Frauen, Männer, Sexualität und Geburtenkontrolle', in Hausen (ed.), *Frauen suchen*, pp. 81–108, esp. pp. 87ff. See also Linse, *Arbeiterschaft*, pp. 224ff.

until the late 1930s.[41] Women frequently used douching, or insisted their partner practised coitus interruptus. Condoms and diaphragms were either unheard of or too expensive, at least for the lower classes; people also found them difficult to use properly. If contraception had failed, abortion was often the only answer. Particularly in times of economic crisis and high unemployment with falling wage levels, the number of abortions rocketed. Estimates put the figure for 1931 at one million.[42] Abortion was still illegal – nothing could alter this, not even the mass movement of women Communists and Social Democrats, feminists and advocates of sexual reform whose campaign to legalise abortion and abolish paragraphs 218 and 219 of the criminal code ran throughout the 1920s and reached its high point in 1931. Under pressure from the SPD, the Reichstag conceded in 1927 that the punishment for abortion would forthwith be 'only' a 'mild' prison sentence, and that mitigating circumstances would be taken into account. The Communists' demand that the relevant paragraphs be simply annulled, and not replaced with more lenient penalties, failed to win the favour of parliament, and the bourgeois and denominational parties were particularly adamant that the law should not be amended. The 1930 papal encyclical *On Christian Marriage* reaffirmed the Catholic position, equating abortion with murder and prohibiting birth control as a crime against God and nature.

There is good reason to doubt whether Catholic women observed such rulings. The birth rate in Catholic communities also fell after the turn of the century, though somewhat more slowly, and it is arguable whether this was due to the only officially sanctioned method of family planning: abstinence. Whatever the case, the doctrine caused Catholic women trying to limit the size of their families to have the most terrible pangs of conscience. And yet birth control not only made life more enjoyable for these 'egoistical' women; it was also in the interest of all members of the family. Fewer children meant fewer financial pressures and allowed the entire family a higher standard of living. Two children could expect to be given more care and attention than four, five or six. More time and money was invested in their upbringing and education, which

41. Knaus's treatise on the 'physiology of human reproduction' (*Physiologie der Zeugung des Menschen*) was published in 1934, and three years later his book on the 'fertile and infertile days in women' (*Die fruchtbaren und unfruchtbaren Tage der Frau*) which was frequently reprinted.

42. A. Grossmann, 'Abortion and Economic Crisis: The 1931 Campaign against Paragraph 218', in R. Bridenthal et al. (eds), *When Biology Became Destiny: Women in Weimar and Nazi Germany*, New York 1984, pp. 6–68, quote at p. 68.

in turn improved job opportunities and the prospect of upward mobility. Advocates of qualitative population policy – these included Social Democrats and members of the women's movement – were not blind to these interconnections. Since they believed that the fate of the German people hung not on its sheer size, but on its positive capabilities, it was far more important for healthy mothers to bring into the world healthy babies who would survive, and grow up in a stable family environment to become strong, biologically sound human beings. The widely-supported eugenic movement that had emerged as early as the late nineteenth century in Germany as well as England, France and the USA became even more popular after the war, and it was by no means only conservative or racist elements who spoke the language of breeding and selection. Some Social Democrats – the prime example was Alfred Grotjahn, medical practitioner and professor of hygiene – subscribed to projects of 'racial hygiene', and deliberated over the substance of social and family policies that would facilitate what were regarded as desirable demographic developments.[43] In 1926 the Prussian Ministry of Welfare established marriage advice centres whose purpose was to examine the racial hygiene of engaged couples and provide them with information on these matters.[44] The Weimar Constitution spoke of 'maintaining the purity' and the 'recuperation' of the family as important government and community tasks.

There were, however, huge differences of opinion over how all this was to be done. Ideas about racial hygiene did not lead automatically to clear-cut, one-dimensional solutions, but to a whole gamut of options. Some advocated euthanasia for handicapped children and compulsory sterilisation for 'unsuitable' mothers, while others lobbied for positive action and extra resources in social policy that would offset the disadvantages faced by some sections of the population. The decline in the birth rate was a particularly controversial issue: various philosophies interpreted it as either a favourable index of the 'rationalisation of sex life' or a national catastrophe. For conservatives and those with strong religious views, the distinction apparently being made by large sections of the public between sexuality and reproduction was evidence that free sexuality was taking hold, and that all moral codes which had

---

43. See M. Janssen-Jurreit, 'Sexualreform und Geburtenrückgang: Über die Zusammenhänge von Bevölkerungspolitik und Frauenbewegung um die Jahrhundertwende', in Kuhn and Schneider (eds), *Frauen*, pp. 56–81.

44. A.-M. Durand-Wever, 'Ehe- und Erziehungsberatung', in A. Schmidt-Beil (ed.), *Die Kultur der Frau*, Berlin 1931, p. 574.

hitherto held human sexual urges in check were disintegrating; but some Liberals, Social Democrats and sections of the women's movement applauded systematic contraception as the first step to establishing a rational and individually satisfying way of life. Sexologists pointed out the psychological importance of sexuality free of inhibitions and angst, and activists in the Federation for the Protection of Mothers stressed the right of every woman to self-determined motherhood and free sexual relations.

Even before the war the Federation for the Protection of Mothers had set up in some towns centres which counselled women (and men) on sexual and marital problems and informed clients about contraception. In the 1920s this idea was adopted and expanded by other institutions. In 1919 the Berlin Institute of Sexology opened a sexual advice centre headed by Dr Max Hodann, and the Berlin civic authorities ran about a dozen marriage guidance centres which from 1930, following pressure from the Social Democrat public health officer Käte Frankenthal, distributed contraceptives. Like many other doctors, Frankenthal found that almost all patients 'sooner or later asked about methods of birth control'.[45] Although legislation on 'sexual offences' was still in force which restricted the public display and sale of contraceptives, information about the various methods and substances available on the market was readily obtainable. Manufacturers of chemical and non-chemical protectives advertised in newspapers and family journals, and sent price lists and catalogues to young married couples. Condoms were on sale in chemists, hairdressers and tobacconists, and hawkers went from door to door trading suitable wares. Such a confusing array of products may well have been the reason why many women sought the advice of a doctor, from whom more seriousness and less commercial pressure could be expected. In some towns sickness insurance funds were also involved in information and advice work. In Hamburg the Federation for the Protection of Mothers was allowed to operate from the offices of the local sickness insurance fund. But on the whole extensive propagation of knowledge on contraception was left to private initiatives, the most active of which were the Association for Sexual Hygiene and Life Reform (*Verein für Sexualhygiene und Lebensreform*) formed in 1923, and the National Union for Birth Control and Sexual Hygiene (*Reichsverband für Geburtenregelung und Sexualhygiene*), formed in 1928.

45. K. Frankenthal, *Der dreifache Fluch: Jüdin, Intellektuelle, Sozialistin. Lebenserinnerungen einer Ärztin in Deutschland und im Exil*, Frankfurt 1981, pp. 115–16.

Originally structured along anarcho-syndicalist lines, these organisations gained broad grass-roots support and also recruited members from other parties and social classes.[46] For example, the Hamburg branch was led by a Social Democrat member of the City Parliament, and was known in the local male vernacular as 'Paula Hennigsen's indecent club'. Like the advice centres in Berlin, the local offices of the National Union did not limit themselves to giving theoretical information; they also distributed contraceptives and offered courses instructing women how to use them correctly.[47]

Frank and public discussion of sexuality, birth control and methods of contraception was completely new and revolutionary, all the more so in view of the background of taboo and prudishness which had prevailed in Imperial Germany and restricted any official discourse on sexuality – which did exist even then – to academic circles and face-to-face consultation between doctors and their middle-class patients. There was an enormous need for 'enlightenment', debunking and bringing matters into the open: lectures on sex education and family planning were packed, and information leaflets and pamphlets on sex and marriage sold very quickly. Van de Veldes' *Die vollkommene Ehe* (The Perfect Marriage), first published in 1926, was enjoying its forty-third reprint by 1932; and his *Die Erotik in der Ehe* (Eroticism in Marriage), which appeared in 1928, was reprinted eleven times in three years.[48] Hodann's *Bub und Mädel: Gespräche unter Kameraden über die Geschlechterfrage* (Boy and Girl: Friends Talk about Sex), written specifically for working-class youths, was also highly successful. The popularity of the natural sciences encouraged sexuality to be seen as a natural and essential component of every human being. To repress and suppress it was to invite serious psychological and physical disorders and pathologies. Psychoanalysis played a major role in naturalising and

---

46. In 1932, 150,000 people belonged to the various sexual reform organisations. See A. Grossmann, "'Satisfaction is Domestic Happiness'": Mass Working-Class Sex Reform Organizations in the Weimar Republic', in M. N. Dobrowski and I. Wallimann (eds), *Towards the Holocaust: The Social and Economic Collapse of the Weimar Republic*, Westport 1983, pp. 265–93.

47. *Vorwärts – und nicht vergessen: Arbeiterkultur in Hamburg um 1930*, published by the Projektgruppe Arbeiterkultur Hamburg, Hamburg 1982, pp. 149–50. See also K. von Soden, 'Auf dem Weg zur "neuen Sexualmoral"-Die Sexualberatungsstellen der Weimarer Republik', in J. Geyer-Kordesch and A. Kuhn (eds), *Frauenkörper, Medizin, Sexualität*, Düsseldorf 1986, pp. 237–62.

48. The seventh edition of Van de Veldes' monograph of 1928 *Die Abneigung in der Ehe* (Aversion in Marriage) was published in 1929, and a pamphlet entitled *Die Fruchtbarkeit in der Ehe und ihre wunschgemäße Beeinflussung* (Marital Fertility and How to Influence It) was reprinted four times the year it was published (1929).

demystifying sexual life and making it 'natural', although psycho-analytic theories, particularly those on infantile sexuality, often met with rejection. In some circles, above all among young people, it was actually respectable to chat freely about sexuality: to such an extent, in fact, that even progressive thinkers such as Käte Frankenthal ('Sexual matters never presented any problems. From my student days, when I had fully grown up, I made scope for this side of life of my own free will, for it was after all determined by nature') censured the fashionable garrulity with which sexual matters were 'not only openly discussed' but 'treated in such a comprehensive and detailed manner that Germans abroad were noticed for it'.[49]

By contrast with women such as Helene Stöcker, an activist in the Federation for the Protection of Mothers and an advocate of free love, who welcomed the emancipation of sexuality and stressed the liberating effect it could have on women in particular, it seems that many felt overburdened by the pressures for an uninhibited, plea-surable and imaginative sex life.[50] For generations women had been regarded as, and encouraged to be, shy and virtuous beings whose purpose was to put a civilising brake on the rampant passion of male desire. The movement for sexual reform condemned these ideas as outmoded and unscientific, and granted to women the same sexual interests as men. Women too, they said, had a right to orgasm and sexual satisfaction; female frigidity, so frequently observed and complained of, was by no means an innate characteristic, but evidence of male inadequacies. Men would have to learn how to understand, and to take seriously, women's sexuality; all the infor-mation could be gleaned from marital guides. This was the only way to reach the goal of a 'full and perfect marriage', which included a satisfying sex life for both partners.

If the new gospel of the liberated equality of sexuality required men to adopt new modes of behaviour and thought, it dismissed in even more radical and uncompromising tones the myths and codes that had previously been at the heart of female upbringing. As a result the salvation that sexual reform promised to bring could not fail to meet with more scepticism and resistance from women even though they apparently stood to gain a paradise of rich emotional intensity. And yet sex reformers were not content with dethroning old norms and value systems; they laid down new orientations and expectations which in some respects outdid the old rules in their

49. Frankenthal, *Der dreifache Fluch*, pp. 110, 114.
50. Examples are given in Kaufmann, *Milieu*, pp. 83–4.

rigidity and inflexibility. By focusing attention on a *sexually* satisfying and harmonious marriage, and drawing up as well as publi-
cising detailed quasi-scientific instructions, they created a new norm
of rationalised and perfectly planned sexuality which was anything
but simple to execute. Many women obviously regarded such
instructions as an affront, particularly since standards were based
exclusively on the prototype of male sexual bahaviour culminating
in penetration, while all other forms of sexual desire were disquali-
fied as secondary and inadequate.[51] Modern sexuality was founded
on the notion of a woman who ran her household according to the
principles of rational economic management, raised her children in
line with the recommendations of educationalists, was an open and
adaptable sexual partner for her husband, and, if necessary, could
hold her own, as it were, at work. A harmonious sex life, facilitated
by expert scientific guidance and therapy, was both the condition
and crowning point of this modern existence. It guaranteed a
biologically healthy balance of emotions and hormones, without
which it would be impossible to satisfy all other requirements, and
rewarded individual effort and achievement with absolute happiness.

By elaborating their wider objectives, sex reformers answered the
common criticism that they would subject men and women, but
particularly women, to the absolute mercy of their desires and
undermine all the rules and institutions of society that were founded
upon the channelling and control of sexual desire. They claimed it
would be to the advantage not only of the individual, but above all
of the family, for sexuality to be set free of its present bonds and
defined anew. The underlying aim of Weimar's medical practitioners,
social workers, Socialists, Communists and the women's movement, all of whom advocated liberalisation of the sexual code, was
to transform family life into a generally desirable and more attractive mode of existence, and to increase its erotic content.[52] In a world
of such rapid and radical change, marriage also required fundamental modernisation. With more and more couples deciding to have
fewer children, the institutional purpose of marriage was being
modified: other needs were gaining in importance. Since, moreover,
in principle women now also had access to the labour market and
the opportunity to earn their own living, marriage was losing its

51. A. Grossmann, 'The New Woman and the Rationalization of Sexuality in
Weimar Germany', in A. Snitow et al. (eds), *Powers of Desire: The Politics of
Sexuality*, New York 1983, pp. 153–71.
52. Ibid., pp. 155ff.

basis of economic necessity and demanding a less materially-oriented foundation. Consequently educating marriage partners in sexual matters was a means of avoiding the social and economic break-up which was manifesting itself in a sharp rise in the divorce rate – 21 divorces per 1,000 marriages in 1901–5 and 62 by 1921–5. In other words, more liberated sex meant the stabilisation of one of modern society's indispensable institutions.

The sexual reform movement, which tended to be located on the left of the political spectrum, had also identified the 'crisis of the family' as a very serious problem facing the Weimar Republic. To be more precise, it was primarily a 'crisis of the woman', for she seemed to be either consciously evading the challenges laid down before her, or threatening to buckle under the great accumulation of the various burdens she was expected to carry. What was lacking above all was 'motherliness', that great, inexhaustible gift of feminine love and devotion, unrewarded yet infinitely valuable to both the family and society as a whole. In 1929 a 'desperate call' could be heard in a Catholic newspaper for a mother for the 'dying fatherland': 'But she is nowhere to be found. We may see a few women wearing men's hairstyles; we may discover women Olympic champions; and we may hear a young woman cooing for her desires to be fulfilled; yet nowhere do we find a mother.'[53] Catholics were not alone in thinking that women were increasingly taking their cue from male domains and patterns of behaviour, and thereby forgetting their own essential vocation; the demise of motherliness was also bewailed in bourgeois circles. Even the Left was looking for mothers, though Social Democrats and Communists were keen to point out that women did not usually desert their innate motherly duties for reasons of selfishness, hedonism or emancipation, but because of economic necessity.

In fact, mothers really did suffer inordinately in the difficult economic climate of Weimar Germany. They were responsible for keeping the family alive and ensuring it had sufficient food and clothing. If the family's income was reduced, the husband unemployed and unemployment benefit cut, it fell to the mother even more than in 'normal' times to drum up money to cover the family's bare necessities. In 1925, a peak in the economic cycle, almost 29 per cent of all married women had a full-time job; though a complete statistical picture is not available, it can be assumed that the global slump forced even more married women and mothers to take up

53. Quoted in Kaufmann, *Milieu*, p. 221, n. 30.

paid employment. Yet the female labour force was also a victim of the severe unemployment crisis, and had to accept considerably lower unemployment benefit than men. Such conditions called for a premium on frugality, thrift and hard work, and placed an extreme physical load on women. At the very time when mothers' and wives' emotional strength was most needed to keep the family on an even keel, the arduousness of daily life left no room for an excess of feelings: 'motherliness' was spent entirely on the management of scarcity.

Even in less strife-torn periods, and in social strata that were not so exposed to economic crisis, mothers in Weimar Germany did not have an easy life. Conditions did improve in new post-war housing, where running water, gas and electricity were standard facilities. Domestic appliances such as washing machines, electric irons, gas cookers and vacuum cleaners gradually found their way into middle-class homes, while manuals and exhibitions on scientific household management informed housewives on how to save time and energy in the home. The rationalisation of trade and industry ran parallel with the discovery of the home as a workplace which like any other had an optimal organisation. Standardised model homes and kitchens, such as those designed by the Weimar Bauhaus or the *Deutscher Werkbund*, brought efficiency to the forefront of attention, though it was often easier to design such projects than successfully put them into practice. Likewise a penchant for organisational planning and the maximisation of efficiency slowly caught on in private homes. Within one year there were thirty print-runs of Erna Meyer's *Neuer Haushalt* (New Household), published in 1926; attendance at exhibitions such as the 'New Kitchen' in Berlin in 1929 broke all records; and scores of women's and family journals sang the praises of the modern housewife who wielded a whole battery of domestic appliances in her practical and luxurious home, where she contentedly and apparently without effort fulfilled her social reproductive duties with dexterity and diligence.[54] Modernity did not stop at the front door: it also caused fire-side revolutions.

There is probably only a secondary connection between the fact that middle-class housewives, emulating as closely as possible the model of the modern housewife imported from the USA, placed such unquestioning faith in the vision of the future that domestic technology promised, and the fascination that the technicisation and

54. Though it is cursory and more interested in the USA, see S. Giedion, *Mechanization Takes Command. A Contribution to Anonymous History*, New York 1948, especially the section on the mechanization of the household.

mechanisation of all life processes had for Weimar Germans, irrespective of their political allegiances. The middle-class housewife was not willing to pay any price to enter into modernity – her main concern was to save on housework that had previously been done by servants. Immediately after the war, maids – or, as they were now called, 'domestic employees' or 'domestic assistants' – had been in short supply. Efforts by local employment offices to channel into domestic service female factory workers made redundant in the course of demobilisation failed to fill the gap.[55] Increasingly unwilling to accept the limitations placed on personal freedom by domestic service, even after the restrictive law governing relations between servants and masters had been lifted, young women preferred to earn their living in factories or, better still, in offices or department stores. After hyperinflation had decimated the value of liquid assets and credit bills, many families in the middle classes, whose wealth had born the brunt of the monetary crisis, could not afford domestic help. Consequently domestic chores were redistributed to wives and daughters. Faced with this situation, women could and indeed did take advantage of the availability of domestic appliances, and adopted the tenets of industrial Taylorism in organising their work.

A simultaneous – and not inconsiderable – effect of the emergence of scientific and rationalistic domestic management, however, was more exacting standards of levels of comfort and hygiene. In the age of the washing machine and vacuum cleaner, spotless homes, fresh laundry and immaculate clothing moved into the realm of possibility. American research has shown that in the inter-war years middle-class housewives used domestic technology mainly to increase the amount of washing and cleaning they undertook, and to declare war on infectious germs. Time saved on cooking was spent on shopping in a more organised manner, and purchasing foodstuffs of higher nutritional value. In addition more time and emotional energy were invested in childcare.[56] In other words, technical aids by no means

---

55. I. Wittmann, 'Echte Weiblichkeit ist ein Dienen' – Die Hausgehilfin in der Weimarer Republik und im Nationalsozialismus', in *Mutterkreuz und Arbeitsbuch: Zur Geschichte der Frauen in der Weimarer Republik und im Nationalsozialismus*, published by Frauengruppe Faschismusforschung, Frankfurt 1981, pp. 15–48, esp. pp. 29ff; Bessel, 'Beunruhigung des Arbeitsmarktes'.

56. See R. Schwartz Cowan, 'A Case Study of Technological and Social Change: The Washing Machine and the Working Wife', in M. S. Hartmann and L. Banner (eds), *Clio's Consciousness Raised: New Perspectives on the History of Women*, New York 1974, pp. 245–53; T. McBride, *The Domestic Revolution: The Modernization of Household Services in England and France, 1820–1920*, London 1976. No account on the impact of the mechanisation of the German household exists to date.

lightened the load for mothers and housewives; it merely increased the range of their activities. Domestic mechanisation did not further the emancipation of women, at least for the first 'modern' generations. It did not release them from housework and enable them to pursue other interests, but rather bound them more closely to the family, whose comfort and living standards benefited directly.

A thanksgiving was held annually, on the second Sunday in May, to celebrate such female sacrifice. Inspired by the Americans, from 1922 onwards florists and voluntary organisations concerned with demographic developments (they were later joined by Protestant and Catholic associations) pressed for the introduction in Germany of a Mothers' Day. By 1930 at the latest, the 'Day of Honour for German Mothers' had established itself as a general public and family holiday.[57] Children presented their mothers with bunches of flowers, set the breakfast table and recited poetry, and the entire nation made fine speeches in honour of its mothers.

But things went no further. Demands for state support schemes for working mothers and large families never proceeded beyond the planning stage owing to shortages of public funds. However, religious, community and socialist/communist welfare organisations were concerned for mothers: they collected money and arranged convalescent holidays for needy women; more importantly, they ran courses and set up advice centres instructing women in housekeeping and childcare and making them aware of their responsibility for their family's health and well-being.

Ideological blinkers were intended to fix women's sights firmly on their 'natural duties' and to keep attractive alternative conceptions of the world out of view. Those preoccupied with Weimar's social and demographic developments noted with concern that women were relishing even the limited independence their own jobs and money afforded, and formulating ideas that were scarcely compatible with the image of the dedicated mother ever willing to make sacrifices. More highly qualified women and graduates in particular expressed a strong desire not to abandon a professional position, which they had reached only through long and expensive education, simply because they had taken their marriage vows; they wanted to combine matrimony, motherhood and a profession.

57. On the history of Mothers' Day in Germany see the highly stimulating work by K. Hausen, 'Mothers, Sons, and the Sale of Symbols and Goods: The "German Mothers' Day" 1923–33', in H. Medick and D. Sabean (eds), *Interest and Emotion: Essays in the Study of Family and Kinship*, Cambridge 1984, pp. 371–413. The English Mothering Sunday is of earlier and different origins.

After it was decreed at national level in 1908 that women could be admitted to university, the number of female students had spiralled. In the winter term of 1931–2 there were 20,000 (16 per cent of all students) in higher academic education. Women were increasingly tending to regard study not as a fashionable way of passing time, but as preparation for professional life. Occupational statistics show that in 1925 just under 7,000 female graduates were gainfully employed; by 1933, 12,468 women had jobs that required degree-level education. Most of them were teachers in senior schools and doctors, though women chemists, university lecturers, lawyers and judges could also be found.[58] Faced with male competition women generally had to fight hard for such privileges, and required qualifications far exceeding the average to be even considered for a post.[59]

The situation was especially difficult for married women who took the Weimar constitutional clause on sexual equality at face value and claimed for themselves the right to a job *and* a family, a right which was granted to men as a matter of course. Endless debates over female *Doppelverdiener*, 'dual-income earners', the title given to married women in gainful employment, demonstrated, however, how flimsy the law was in reality. Irrespective of their actual economic and family situation, these were the first women to be dismissed from work during demobilisation after the First World War. Cuts made in the civil service in 1923 hit primarily married female civil servants who were felt to be already provided for. Conservative and right-wing campaigners against dual incomes were particularly vociferous as the world economic crisis began to make its mark. A married working woman, they insisted, should make way for an unemployed paterfamilias, thereby easing the labour market situation and strengthening the family. That it was equally valid to classify men with working wives as *Doppelverdiener* dawned on very few people. The Reich government put the nail in the coffin in 1932 with the Law on the Legal Position of Female Public Servants, under which the civil service was legally

58. A. Schlüter, 'Wissenschaft für die Frauen? – Frauen für die Wissenschaft! Zur Geschichte der ersten Generationen von Frauen in der Wissenschaft', in Brehmer et al., *Frauen in der Geschichte*, vol. IV, pp. 244–61, table p. 248.
59. M. Kater, 'Krisis des Frauenstudiums in der Weimarer Republik', *Vierteljahrschrift für Sozial- und Wirtschaftsgeschichte*, 59, 1972, pp. 207–55; in 1925 only 54 out of a total of 14,000 lawyers, and in the summer of 1930 only 4.2 per cent of doctors, were women (pp. 217–18). See also I. Schmidt-Harzbach, 'Frauen, Bildung und Universität', in H.-W. Prahl and I. Schmidt-Harzbach, *Die Universität: Eine Kultur- und Sozialgeschichte*, Munich 1981, pp. 175–213, quote at p. 196.

bound to dismiss married female employees.[60] The effect the law had on the labour market – which was in any case negligible – was less important than its ideological significance as an indication to women that their participation in the labour force was tolerated and welcomed only insofar as they had not yet found a breadwinner in the shape of a husband. As soon as they married their place was in the family which badly needed their motherly presence.

Such views were shared by men and women alike. According to trade union official Gertrud Hanna, single women were 'even more than men committed opponents of married women who went out to work'.[61] Since the war had claimed the lives of two million German soldiers, many women's marriage prospects had been dashed, and thousands upon thousands of widows left to fend for themselves and their children. Unmarried mothers – in the 1920s some 150,000 illegitimate children were born annually – also had to work to earn a living; in times of a surplus of labour, they regarded married women as unwelcome competition. While trade union bodies insisted that only very few married women actually chose to work, since most were forced to because their husbands were either unemployed or earned too little, their justificatory tones were extremely defensive in character. The women's movement was conspicuous by its silence on the matter, and the BDF decided for patriotic reasons not to protest against Chancellor Brüning's legislation on dual incomes. Hardly any women's associations had the courage to brand the discriminatory law as anti-constitutional.

Instead, there was almost unanimous acceptance of women's responsibility for the *Volksgemeinschaft*, where individuals did not assert their 'selfish' interests, and the common weal was the yardstick for one's role and duties. Conservatives, Catholics, *Völkisch* Nationalists and Liberals all subscribed to a concept of the state in which the individual was not an autonomous being, but part of a whole which ascribed a function to each person. The very divisiveness that characterised Weimar politics helped the notion of *Volksgemeinschaft*, which had had positive connotations even before 1914, to retain its utopian and panacean ring. Nationalists and right-wing Christians were not the only ones to adopt the phrase; there was also a broad political consensus in the women's movement that a community (*Gemeinschaft*), nestling upon a harmoni-

60. C. Hahn, 'Der öffentliche Dienst und die Frauen – Beamtinnen in der Weimarer Republik', in *Mutterkreuz und Arbeitsbuch*, pp. 49–78.
61. G. Hanna, 'Die Frauen in den Gewerkschaften', Die Arbeit, 11, no. 5, 1928, pp. 693–703, at p. 697.

ous, intertwined underlay of state and social fabric, was far preferable to a society (*Gesellschaft*) rife with conflicts of interest and class struggle, and that women above all could expect only good from a *Volksgemeinschaft*. *Gesellschaft*, it was said, revolved around the dominance of individuals working in competition for personal ambition. Women's status was marginal, since their worth was measured in terms of 'their husbands' position'. By contrast, a *Volksgemeinschaft* valued 'a woman's own achievements, whether these be in the domestic or another sphere'.[62]

Housewives in particular avidly cherished hopes of the new order. For too long their personal worth and labours had been undervalued and ignored in the social distribution of prestige. It is no coincidence that housewives' associations were among the first and most willing to embrace the national socialist variant of the *Volksgemeinschaft*. In the Weimar Republic they had campaigned for greater public recognition for the 'profession' of housewife, and had in fact managed to bring the interest of middle-class housewives as consumers and employers to the attention of numerous government and local authority commissions. Two national bodies, the National Union of German Housewives' Associations (*Reichsverband Deutscher Hausfrauenvereine* – RDH), formed in 1915, and the National Union of Rural Housewives' Associations (*Reichsverband Landwirtschaftlicher Hausfrauenvereine* – RLHV), formed one year earlier, proved to be exceedingly effective pressure groups. In times of hardship they were even able to provide financial support for members who were hit by inflation or redundancy.[63] The two bodies belonged to the BDF until 1931 and 1932 respectively; with a combined membership of 200,000 in 1928 they were the most powerful organisations in the bourgeois women's movement. They were also the most right-wing, and leading figures in the RDH used their position deliberately to combat any liberal and democratic leanings the BDF showed, and to open the movement to the rising tide of nationalism and racism.

The BDF was more than a forum for party political clashes; it was also a battleground for competing views on the aims of the women's movement. The large housewives' organisations placed emphasis on

62. C. Mleinek, 'Die Wertung der Frauenarbeit', *Archiv für Frauenarbeit*, 9, 1921, p. 77.
63. R. Bridenthal, '"Professional" Housewives: Stepsisters of the Women's Movement', in Bridenthal et al. (eds) *When Biology Became Destiny*, pp. 153–73; Bridenthal, 'Class Struggle around the Hearth: Women and Domestic Service in the Weimar Republic', in Dobrowski and Wallimann (eds), *Towards the Holocaust*, pp. 243–64.

women's familial roles, and celebrated the profession of housewife as the only acceptable feminine way of life and as a major contribution to the wealth of the nation, while workers' organisations of similar party political persuasions insisted that women had the right to work, and stressed the positive significance of occupational life for feminine 'character-building' and the 'furthering of the commonweal'.[64] Ultimately even the most ardent supporters of female participation in the labour force shared the conviction that women should go out to work only for a maximum of ten years in the period between youth and marriage/motherhood. Even the Union of Female Retail and Office Staff, one of the more active and aggressive bodies, insisted that training and a job in commerce or business was a sensible way of preparing for one's real vocation as housewife and mother. In Weimar Germany both the Federation of German Women's Associations and the Social Democratic women's movement firmly believed that motherhood was a woman's 'supreme calling', 'her most important civil duty', and one which, like paid work, had to be 'recognised and valued in economic terms'.[65]

Although women were agreed, irrespective of party political differences and class barriers, that family labours were preferable to any other kind, there was in most cases a lack of unanimity over the day-to-day politics of specific women's issues. Women Social Democrats and Communists fought for the abolition of § 218, while the BDF and church-based organisations could not regard abortion as anything but a criminal offence, though they were willing to accept less severe punishments; Socialist and Liberal women called in 1918 for the law governing relations between servants and masters to be replaced by free bargaining in domestic service, while housewives' associations rejected wage agreements and legislation protecting domestic employees; female trade unionists demanded better and more extensive legal protection for women workers, while supporters of 'open door' policies made a case for reducing the number of specifically female legal stipulations which, they claimed, underpinned the disadvantages women faced on the labour market; some women academics pressed for the freedom to combine work and family, while others joined the campaign against female 'dual income earners'. The process of political polarisation made no excep-

64. K. Müller, *Frauenberuf und Frauenverband*, Berlin n.d. (1924), p. 6.
65. A. von Zahn-Harnack, *Die Frauenbewegung*, Berlin 1928, p. 76; L. Schroeder, 'Die proletarische Frau als Hausfrau und Mutter', in Blos (ed), *Frauenfrage im Licht des Sozialismus*, pp. 148–81; M. Juchacz, 'Die berufstätige Frau', in *Frauenarbeit*, Berlin 1929, pp. 31–5.

tions for women, and the idea of a women's party or electoral list, which was a subject of lively debate in 1919 and 1924, was hardly realistic in view of manifest political disagreement. With women being drawn more heavily into political life as voters and members of trade unions, parties and other organisations, fundamental political differences and class antagonisms became more significant, and overshadowed any common ground shared on specifically female issues. The BDF found it increasingly difficult to integrate its various factions, and it was precisely the larger member organisations who gradually broke away.[66] Problems were compounded by its inability to interest the younger generation in its aims. One searched in vain for women in their twenties, and even those in their thirties were hard to find.[67] The existence of a women's movement seemed irrelevant to many young women who had grown up under the constitutional clause on sexual equality. If they showed any interest at all in joining an organisation, then they opted for mixed groups, sports clubs or cultural associations, and followed the modern fashion of removing, or at least reducing, the barriers between male and female domains.

In 1944 Stefan Zweig reflected: 'In no other area of public life has there been such total transformation within one generation as in relations between the sexes.'[68] With respect to Weimar Germany, however, this observation was true only for *young* people. Although the validity of traditional roles had not disappeared entirely, youthful interpretations of them were freer. In the years between school and marriage – in 1920–4 the average woman married at 25.4, the average man at 28 – young women lived through an 'interim of personal freedom' (G. Bäumer): they were usually employed,[69] earned their own money, joined professional bodies, sports and youth clubs,[70] and took advantage of the growing entertainment

66. Greven-Aschoff, *Die bürgerliche Frauenbewegung*, pp. 111, 122ff., 181ff.
67. von Zahn-Harnack, *Die Frauenbewegung*, pp. 17–18; C. Kirkpatrick, *Nazi Germany: Its Women and Family Life*, Indianapolis 1938, pp. 56–7. On the youth movement's criticism of the women's movement see H. W. Puckett, *Germany's Women Go Forward*, New York 1930, p. 310.
68. S. Zweig, *Die Welt von gestern: Erinnerungen eines Europäers (1944)*, Frankfurt 1949, p. 84. Further quotations on pp. 89–90.
69. In 1925 77.4 per cent of all eighteen- to twenty-year-old women and 67 per cent of all twenty- to twenty-five-year-olds were gainfully employed: Niemeyer, *Zur Struktur*, p. 108.
70. Statistics compiled by the Prussian Ministry for National Welfare in 1928 showed that 34.1 per cent of Prussian girls and 57.9 per cent of Prussian boys belonged to a youth or sports club. See M. Klaus, *Mädchen im Dritten Reich: Der Bund Deutscher Mädel (BDM)*, Cologne 1983, p. 161. According to E. Düntzer, a vocational school medical doctor, in the early 1930s 12 per cent of all female vocational school students were members of a sporting association, and 20 per cent

and leisure culture, where one's sex seemed to be largely irrelevant. The 'modernising' changes of Weimar Germany benefited young women most of all. The cult of youth in the 1920s, the adoration of youthful fitness and dynamism, had removed sexual differences into the background. The young couple now stood centre stage, as Zweig wrote in his memoirs: 'both tall and slim, clean-shaven and short-haired: their friendship even extended to outward appearances.' Young women played tennis, cycled, learned to swim and did gymnastics at sports clubs. In 1929 almost 400,000 women belonged to the German Gymnastic Association (*Deutsche Turnerschaft*), a further 240,000 to the National Union of Women's Gymnastics (*Reichsverband für Frauenturnen*), and various keep-fit clubs counted over two million female members. Research conducted by sports organisations found that young women in particular preferred 'rational forms of sporting activity with a specific objective' – athletics, swimming and competitive events – and found exercises deemed to be feminine and graceful dull by comparison.[71] The unisex trend found its way into fashion too. Whereas before the First World War clothing design had emphasised the polarity of the sexes 'to the point of embarrassing provocation', as Zweig put it, it now borrowed from the standards of men's attire which focused on comfort and practicality.

It is difficult to assess the true impact of the proper German youth movement, which can be traced back to the turn of the century, on relations between the sexes. Although the *Wandervogel* ramblers' associations originally only catered for boys, mixed groups soon emerged, with boys and girls going off hiking together. Just under one third of the 3,600,000 staying overnight in German youth hostels in 1929 were female.[72] The experience of participating independently in leisure activities was enormously significant for the self-confidence of girls and young women, many of whom may have felt their involvement in a youth group to be an act of partial emancipation from parental influence and the strict familial observance of stereotyped sex roles. However, the majority of youth organisations knew nothing of the comradely rapprochement of the sexes about which some women enthused. The large church-based associations organised boys and girls separately, and groups in the

---

of a youth organisation: Düntzer, *Die gesundheitliche und soziale Lage*, pp. 36ff.
71. E. von Lölhöffel, 'Die Frau im Sport', in Schmidt-Beil (ed.), *Die Kultur der Frau*, pp. 449–53.
72. L. Riegger, 'Die Frau in der Jugendbewegung', in ibid., pp. 237–45.

free youth (*bündisch*) movement usually had separate girls' sections. Even in the Socialist Labour Youth (*Sozialistische Arbeiterjugend*), which counted 20,000 young women and 36,000 young men at the end of the 1920s, the women met for special 'girls evenings', despite the official policy of co-education.[73] Although sexual divisions had been eradicated in formal terms, specifically female domains emerged afresh, not least because of the dominant presence of men and their decision-making power.

It cannot be denied that to some degree the barriers between male and female domains became more fluid in the Weimar years, and that young women in particular were given the occasional chance to reap the benefits of what had been exclusively male occupations, social movements and leisure-time activities. However, the gender-related limits of social, economic and political action had remained largely unchanged. To be sure, women now had greater employment opportunities: they could become judges, lawyers, doctors and university professors; they had the right to vote and be elected; concepts of morality became more liberal, and sexual stereotyping eroded, especially among young people. Yet the Republic was a long way from ensuring for women rights, positions of power and influence and rewards equal to those enjoyed by men. To the same degree, the reaction of the women's movement to the partial integration and modenisation which the Weimar system offered was confused and contradictory. On the one hand it upheld the constitutional guarantee of full equality in political, family, occupational and moral affairs; on the other it insisted that the sexes were essentially different, and that women had a particular feminine cultural mission to fulfil. There was no doubt whatsoever that family duties were of prime importance. A synthesis of work and family was inconceivable without extra burdens, and the idea that men might undertake some of the childcare and housekeeping tasks was alien to bourgeois and socialist minds alike. The movement had no answer to the question of how the 'new woman' could resolve the conflict between modern occupational demands and traditional family ties. Instead, it offered women another role: that of dutiful, selfless, conciliatory members of an idealised *Volksgemeinschaft*, whether this be cast in left- or right-wing mould. For many in the bourgeois women's movement, the political constitution of this

---

73. Ibid., p. 242; see also M. Musial, *Jugendbewegung und Emanzipation der Frau: Ein Beitrag zur Rolle der weiblichen Jugend in der Jugendbewegung bis 1933*, dissertation, Essen 1982, pp. 168ff., 193ff., and M. Naujoks, *Mädchen in der Arbeiterjugendbewegung*, Hamburg 1984.

'folk community' was of secondary importance. As Gertrud Bäumer wrote in 1933: 'In the final analysis, the composition of the state – whether parliamentary, democratic or fascist – which will address the contemporary issue of the position and purpose of women, is a matter of the utmost insignificance . . . The fundamental demand will remain the same . . . to allow the cultural influence of women to realise its full potential and act as a free and effective social force.'[74]

74. Quoted in Greven-Aschoff, *Die bürgerliche Frauenbewegung*, p. 187.

IV
Between Tradition and Modernity: Women in the Third Reich

15

National Renewal and the Woman Question

Blond, pig-tailed girls throwing flowers to the great men of the Third Reich; slim teenagers at Nazi Party rallies displaying fitness, agility and the harmoniousness of physical culture; beaming mothers holding out their strapping children for the Führer to see – the pictures captured on newsreels suggest enthusiastic support for the National Socialist regime and its representatives. Hitler himself considered women to be among his most faithful followers, explaining his success by claiming that the new Germany had much to offer to women: 'In my state, the mother is the most important citizen.' But his words were directed to German, Aryan, healthy and politically loyal mothers; for women who failed to meet these requirements, Hitler's *Frauenparadis* meant public humiliation, enforced sterilisation, torture, removal to concentration camps, murder.

Even in the early stages of Nazism foreign observers had expressed doubts about the supposed benevolence of National Socialist policies towards women. Before 1933 left-wing liberal and socialist women in Germany had repeatedly warned that victory for the National Socialists would mean a reversal of the first tentative steps taken towards sexual equality. Indeed Nazi ideology had never made a secret of the fact that it was completely at odds with the aims and achievements of women's emancipation. The political and legal reforms of the Weimar Republic were to be rescinded, and a stop put to the convergence that had been taking place between male and female spheres. 'Emancipate women from women's emancipation,' declared Alfred Rosenberg, editor-in-chief of the *Völkischer Beobachter* (National Observer) in *Der Mythus des 20. Jahrhunderts* (The Myth of the Twentieth Century) (1930). And Hitler stated in 1934: 'the term "women's emancipation" is invented by Jewish intellectuals, and its meaning is imbued with the same spirit'. The post-war women's movement was accused of having incited women to rise against men and of preaching 'unrestrained individualism'.

Women had competed with men for political power, jobs and money, and had in the process neglected their true maternal duties. They had gladly been seduced by the depraved culture of the cities, by the 'glittering carrion of a rotting age', yet their real freedom had not been advanced. Nothing but an organic, national and harmonious *völkisch* state could allow them to be 'true' women again, who in their 'small world' would lay the foundations for the 'great world' of men. By caring for family, home and the German ('Aryan') race, they would rediscover their genuine vocation and be content to leave politics, community life and the world of employment to men.[1] As Josef Goebbels, Minister for Public Enlightenment and Propaganda, said in 1933: 'A woman's first and most fitting place is in the family, and the most glorious duty she can fulfil is to present her people and her country with a child.' Defending the National Socialist position of excluding women from the business of politics and not selecting female parliamentary representatives, Goebbels proceeded to point out that 'things pertaining to men must be left to men: these include politics and the ability of a nation to defend itself'. The mark of a genuine völkisch state was that it re-established the proper and 'natural' sexual division of labour and assigned clearly distinct domains to men and women, putting an end once and for all to any public disregard of the feminine 'mission'.[2]

These were not particularly original arguments; they were, rather, reminiscent of the ideas to which conservative and religious women in the Weimar Republic had subscribed. Housewives' associations, the Evangelical Women's Federation and Catholic organisations had been sharply critical of post-war society's modernising tendencies, and argued for retaining strict segregation of male and female jobs, interests and needs. Yearnings for a *Volksgemeinschaft* in which men and women, notwithstanding their separate domains, would be equally respected were not novel either. The weight of these traditions meant that even the BDF's self-image was not

---

1. Extracts from Rosenberg's book can be found in A. Kuhn and V. Rothe, *Frauen im deutschen Faschismus*, vol. I, Düsseldorf 1982, pp. 58ff. For writings translated into English, see also *Alfred Rosenberg: Selected Writings*, edited and introduced by R. Pois, London 1970. Hitler's speech to the women's auxiliary of the Nazi Party is contained in M. Domarus (ed.), *Hitler: Reden und Proklamationen 1932–1945*, Munich 1965, vol. I/I, pp. 449–52. For a full account of Nazi women policy and the situation of women in the Third Reich, see C. Koonz, *Mothers in the Fatherland*, London 1987.
2. Quoted in M. Schmidt and G. Dietz (eds), *Frauen unterm Hakenkreuz*, Munich 1985, p. 58, and in R. Wiggershaus, *Frauen unterm Nationalsozialismus*, Wuppertal 1984, pp. 15–16.

immune to them. Particularly during the later years of the Weimar Republic, there was a growth in the number of policy statements by leading bourgeois women and female politicians who enthused about a 'new bonding between women and the state' and derived from the notion of motherhood's 'cosmic force' a concept of 'responsible, *feminine* citizenship' that went far beyond mere participation in the political process. Seen from this angle, the limited, though real, opportunities women had had for participation in the Weimar system appeared irrelevant and peripheral. What was important was the internal reconstruction of a degenerate society – a task in which women would be involved primarily through the 'order and meaningfulness of marriage and motherhood'.[3]

While they expressed their agreement with national 'renewal' the bourgeois women's movement, and their liberal representatives in particular, constantly found themselves being accused of defending individual interests and pursuing policies confined to the narrow issue of women and the law. German Nationalist circles saw the BDF merely as a loyal party mouthpiece and exploitative beneficiary of the Weimar 'system', upon which ever fiercer criticism was being heaped. The women's organisations close to the German National People's Party – the German Evangelical Women's Federation, the housewives' and the country women's associations, the League of Queen Louise (*Bund Königin Luise*) – regarded themselves as part of the anti-Weimar opposition forces and as the vanguard of a new *Volksgemeinschaft* in which women could once again define themselves exclusively as housewives and mothers, and not be forced to compete with men for scarce jobs and political influence. The life history of Guida Diehl illustrates the fluidity of the boundaries between these notions and National Socialist ideology. Born in 1868, she was the daughter of a Protestant teacher and his wife, and she trained as a social worker. In 1914 she founded the New Land Movement (*Neulandbewegung*), an unmistakably anti-semitic association of conservative and patriotic women. She joined the German National People's Party in 1918 but left in 1930, along with the majority of her New Land Movement supporters, to join the NSDAP. Guida Diehl exhibited German Christianity, nationalism and anti-semitism combined with a strongly anti-modernist conception of women: she held that gainful employment outside the home and female suffrage were unfeminine and alien to a National

---

3. G. Bäumer, *Die Frau und der Staat*, Berlin 1932, reprinted in Kuhn and Rothe, *Frauen im deutschen Faschismus*, vol. I, pp. 34ff.

Socialist state.[4]

The spectrum of right-wing opinion on 'women in the New Germany' was, however, broad, and not all those in favour of the *Volksgemeinschaft* shared Diehl's convictions. There were some women who upheld the equality of male and female elites and who wished to see talented women among the nation's legal, political, theological and military leaders. They rejected 'petty-bourgeois' notions of womanhood, and condemned those who tended 'yet again to deify for Germans reverence of motherhood and sentimental conceptions of the feminine, both of which are not Nordic but oriental in origin'. Basing their ideas on the figure of the archetypal Germanic woman and on Romantic ideas of a harmonious, fully-rounded personality, a group of Nazi and German Nationalist women developed a new concept of gender relations, very different from the precept, prevalent among male Nazis and the bourgeois women's movement alike, that the sexes had separate domains and responsibilities. The *Denkschrift deutscher Frauen an Adolf Hitler* (Memorandum by German Women to Adolf Hitler), published in 1933, advocated a 'social order of dual yet unitary (*zweieinig*), total human beings' whose principles would include both co-education and female involvement in leadership. Membership of a common race, not sexual division, would be the structuring principle of the new society they desired.[5]

These confident calls for participation and involvement, which so clearly esteemed the achievements of the 'old' women's movement, met with outright rejection in the National Socialist camp. Since its formation in 1919 the Nazi Party had conceived of itself as a purely male body that excluded women from leading positions; moreover, it wasted little time on the 'woman question' either within or outside the Party. While enormous energy went into the organisation of men, female Party members were largely left to their own devices. Nazi propaganda ignored the whole subject almost entirely: apart from a few quotes from Hitler, Rosenberg and Goebbels on the woman as mother and guarantor of racial unity, there were barely any official Party pronouncements. Consequently

---

4. See C. Koonz, 'The Competition for a Women's Lebensraum, 1928–1934', in Bridenthal et al. (eds), *When Biology Became Destiny*, pp. 199–236, esp. pp. 214–15; C. Wittrock, *Weiblichkeitsmythen: Das Frauenbild im Faschismus und seine Vorläufer in der Frauenbewegung der 20er Jahre*, Frankfurt 1983, pp. 115ff.; Kuhn and Rothe, *Frauen im deutschen Faschismus*, vol. I, pp. 64f.
5. S. Rogge-Börner, *Denkschrift an den Kanzler*, reprinted in Kuhn and Rothe, *Frauen im deutschen Faschismus*, vol. I, pp. 71–4; see also Wittrock, *Weiblichkeitsmythen*, pp. 169ff.

Nazi women sought to fill the gap on their own. The 1920s witnessed an astounding amount of activity, which in terms of both organisation and ideology was largely independent. In addition to an array of local initiatives, central bodies emerged, such as the German Women's Order of the Red Swastika (*Deutscher Frauenorden Rotes Hakenkreuz*) (1923) and the German Women's Battle League (*Deutscher Frauen-Kampfbund*) (1926).[6] In accordance with a Nazi Party leadership directive issued in 1931, these groups were dissolved and reformed into a single women's organisation known as the *NS-Frauenschaft*. Its programme represented a curious mixture of beliefs: though Nazi women had no desire to turn back the clock of history, welcoming 'the education and social integration of all women to the benefit of the nation', as they put it, they simultaneously held marriage, family and motherhood to be 'the most obvious way to serve the whole people'.[7]

At the time, similar things were being said by the BDF: in other words, the Nazi manifesto on women's issues was not as innovative as many of the younger Party faithful may have wished. Many younger women joined the NSDAP (the average age of women joining the Party between 1925 and 1932 was thirty-five, considerably lower than in other parties)[8], and they perceived National Socialism as a revolutionary movement that ought unequivocally and radically to dissociate itself from other political groups and tendencies. Lydia Gottschewski, who joined the Nazis in 1929 at the age of twenty-three, was the archetype of such women. They wanted nothing to do with the 'old' women's movement, which was written off as bourgeois, liberal, internationalist and pacifist. They worked in National Socialist girls' organisations – Gottschewski was appointed leader of the League of German Girls (*Bund Deutscher Mädel*, BDM) in 1932 – for the creation of a new, Nazi femininity that cut all spiritual and political ties with the Weimar system and all it represented. So far as they were concerned, the 'post-revolutionary woman, with dyed hair, and painted lips and eyebrows'[9] was a figure of the past. German women no longer followed the dictates of French fashion but discovered their own 'Nordic' style: no make-up, plaits, and plain womanly clothing.

---

6. J. Stephenson offers a detailed account of these organisations in *The Nazi Organisation of Women*, London 1981, pp. 23ff.
7. Kuhn and Rothe, *Frauen im deutschen Faschismus*, vol. I, pp. 66–7.
8. M. H. Kater, 'Generationskonflikt als Entwicklungsfaktor in der NS-Bewegung vor 1933', *Geschichte und Gesellschaft*, 11, 1985, p. 235.
9. H. Krüger, *Die Sendung der jungen Generation (1933)*, reprinted in Kuhn and Rothe, *Frauen im deutschen Faschismus*, vol. I, pp. 29–30.

After Hitler seized power in 1933 the revolutionary sub-culture of what the Nazis idealised as their *Kampfzeit*, or 'days of struggle', was transformed into a mass culture whose codes the whole nation was bound to observe. Undesirable 'elements', incapable of being integrated, were stigmatised and discriminated against, while those willing to conform underwent *Gleichschaltung*, or enforced uniformity. Communist and Social Democratic organisations were prohibited and broken up, thousands of their members were imprisoned and murdered. The bourgeois parties dissolved themselves in the summer of 1933 after the NSDAP had made it plain that they were unwilling to tolerate any competing political forces. Bourgeois women's organisations received a pressing invitation to make a declaration of loyalty to Hitler and to join a single body of German women, under Nazi leadership. Jewish members were to be expelled forthwith, and National Socialist women appointed as leaders. Conservative and *völkisch* associations such as the German Evangelical Women's Federation, the associations of housewives and of countrywomen, the Women's Federation of the German Colonial Society, or the monarchist League of Queen Louise, willingly accepted this appeal-cum-ultimatum. As integral elements in the 'national opposition' they had been closely co-operating with the National Socialists from at least 1930 onwards, and while many German Nationalist women rejected certain populist elements of Nazi policy they tended to agree in matters of *Weltanschauung*.

The BDF was less enthusiastic about *Gleichschaltung*, although it also took a positive stance towards the new regime and cherished some hopes of it. Mainly for formal reasons (the BDF statutes forbade amalgamation with other organisations), in May 1933 the executive committee announced the dissolution of the Federation, thus closing the final chapter in the story of an independent German women's movement. The majority of bourgeois women's associations appear to have offered little resistance to assimilation by the apparatus of the National Socialist state. They would, of course, have preferred to retain organisational autonomy, but ultimately had few objections to Germany's new course – at least no objections that were strong enough to warrant active resistance. The bourgeoisie was amenable to the ideological leitmotifs of Nazism – nationalism, German Christianity, anti-Marxism, anti-semitism – even if the terror used to dispatch 'enemies of the Reich' injured the bourgeois sense of taste and style. The middle classes believed that time would gradually expunge such vulgarity, and that their active involvement would help to stave off Nazism's more plebeian elements.

The 'enemies of the Reich', meanwhile, saw things from a different angle. By summer 1933 at the very latest, when political parties had been banned, the trade unions smashed and the press nazified, Communists, Social Democrats and pacifists had given up all hope of a swift end to what had initially been perceived as the 'masquerade' of Nazism. Many officials had already emigrated, others had been arrested, still others killed. The social network of associations – the elixir of life for left-wing mass movements – had been almost entirely destroyed or placed under Nazi control. Before 1933 nobody could have imagined that the 'national revolution' would be so thoroughgoing and omnipresent. Even Social Democrats had not thought the new incumbents of power capable of the tidal wave of repression and terror that was unleashed once Hitler had seized power. As late as March 1933 trade unions had offered the Führer their loyalty, and joined in the May Day celebrations that were orchestrated that year by the government under the title of 'Day of National Labour'. Yet the following day the SA and the SS occupied all trade union buildings, requisitioned funds and property, and dispatched union leaders to concentration camps. The Communists too, the preferred targets of Nazi terror, having been misled by their disastrous theory of social fascism and designating the SPD as their main opponent, had underestimated the danger until the very last.

For these reasons, the presumed solidarity in action of the anti-fascist groups, which had so often been invoked during the months preceding the Nazi seizure of power, hardly ever came to fruition. Socialist and Communist women also observed their parties' decisions not to join together with other organisations; separate leaflets and separate demonstrations warned of the dangers of the 'Third Reich' of National Socialism. Women were unable to influence their parties' political stance, firstly because neither the SPD nor the Communists had an autonomous women's movement independent of party directives, and secondly because female members constituted a minority and were largely occupied with 'non-political' welfare work. All the same, leaflets and election posters issued at the time do show that the Left took seriously the promises of Nazi ideology. 'Women! To Support National Socialism is to Betray Yourselves', read one SPD newspaper in 1931, while the Communists quoted from prominent Nazi leaders: 'They want to make you into willing breeding machines. They want you to become men's servants and maids.'[10] But warnings went unheeded, and this per-

10. Examples of election posters and appeals by left-wing parties in Hamburg can

213

plexed progressive forces. Having been – at least on a formal level – the most forthright defenders of the Weimar constitutional clause on sexual equality, having paved the way to the law on female suffrage and had a comparatively large number of women delegates elected to parliament, the left-wing parties found it difficult to fathom how women could not only find acceptable but even vote for a party that so decisively rejected such rights and refused as a matter of principle to have female representatives.

In fact the NSDAP managed increasingly to mobilise female support and votes during the last years of the Weimar Republic. Though the male vote for the Nazis in Reichstag elections was always higher than the female, the difference did narrow, and was even reversed in a few (Protestant) areas. In Cologne, a Catholic city, 15.5 per cent of women and 19.8 per cent of men voted NSDAP in 1930; by November 1932 the figures were 19.2 per cent and 21.8 per cent respectively, and by March 1933 there was only one percentage point difference.[11] On average throughout the Reich the Nazis then gained almost 44 per cent of all votes cast, 11 per cent more than four months earlier. If we add the 8 per cent of votes for the German National People's Party, we can say that the 'legal revolutionaries' represented the political will of a narrow majority of the population – including the women.

To understand why women helped to power a party that was so patently opposed to emancipation, it is not enough to refer merely to lack of political experience, the power of political seduction, or naivety. Women voted not only as women but as members of social classes, strata, and religious groups, as individuals in work or married women with unemployed husbands. Their political interests and choices were not determined solely by specifically female issues but were as varied as those of men. Their voting decisions were affected as much by the economic crisis and unemployment as by national slogans and images of 'the enemy within', concepts only very indirectly related to their personal experiences and expectations. They did not necessarily see simply a party that intended to

---

be found in *Arbeiterkultur 1930*, esp. pp. 160ff.; see Kuhn and Rothe, *Frauen im deutschen Faschismus*, vol. I, pp. 29–30, for sources on the anti-fascism of the proletarian women's movement.

11. Bremme, *Die politische Rolle*, table p. 74. In Bavaria in 1933, 36.2 per cent of men and 34.4 per cent of women voted for the Nazis (Boak, 'Women in Weimar Germany', p. 170). These data refute the thesis that women were particularly swayed by the National Socialists. See A. Tröger, 'Die Dolchstoßlegende der Linken: "Frauen haben Hitler an die Macht gebracht"', *Frauen und Wissenschaft*, Berlin 1977, pp. 324–55.

abolish female suffrage and expel women from the world of politics; they also saw a party that was committed to creating jobs and restoring the nation's 'honour'. Whatever individual motivation for voting may have been, the Nazis' election campaign and self-portrayal set little store by propaganda aimed specifically at women. Indeed there is much to suggest that the National Socialists paid far less attention to this area than their opponents claimed. Only sharp counter-propaganda from the Left forced the Nazis publicly to elaborate their ideas about the future role of women. This was particularly the case after they lost the presidential elections in March 1932; Hindenburg had received almost 20 per cent more votes than Hitler, most of these from women, and the NSDAP deemed it expedient to revise its position and neutralise attacks from left-wing and liberal parties. Hitler issued the instruction that women should henceforth be addressed as 'men's comrades in sex and labour', no longer as servants and maids, as Gottfried Feder, a Nazi stalwart from the outset, had put it in a snappy and much-quoted slogan. Nevertheless, this was not to abandon hierarchies: 'Men organise life; women are their support and implement their decisions.'[12]

The semantic innovation soothed the unease that active female Nazis had felt at the Party's official image of women. But it is arguable whether it had much impact on the female electorate. Even proceeding from the rather dubious assumption that the decisive factors in female voting preferences were electioneering statements on women's issues, it does not follow that parties such as the SPD, the Communists or the German Democratic Party could have won the entire female vote by declaring themselves in favour of the political woman, (formal) sexual equality, and a relaxation in the segregation of the sexes in education and culture. In fact the major beneficiaries of female suffrage were parties such as the German National People's Party or the Centre Party, which defended the concept of polarised gender roles; and this was particularly true of the National Socialists. This apparent paradox becomes penetrable if we consider in a sober fashion women's historical experiences of 'emancipation' in the Weimar Republic. Despite new political rights, and the accessibility of more jobs in the white-collar sector, life for most women had not become any easier. Instead the yawning gap between normative constitutional commitments and the

12. A diary entry by Goebbels, reprinted in Kuhn and Rothe, *Frauen im deutschen Faschismus*, vol. I, p. 60.

discrimination of everyday life had given rise to new sources of discontent and uncertainty, with the result that there emerged a longing for stable orientations and certainties. Since in almost every case women had known little but setbacks and disappointment in the 'male' domains of work and politics, it was not surprising that they clung all the more tenaciously to 'female' spheres and turned to family life for shelter from the social and psychological pressures of the 'modern world'. For this reason, there was a great deal of sympathy for the message of *völkisch* and conservative forces, who wished to stabilise and protect the 'small world' of women. The most convincing arguments were put forward by the National Socialists, who fully appreciated the importance of the family as an instrument of population policy, and never missed an opportunity to praise the feats German women performed for their families, their race and their people. Many women may have expected the Nazi government genuinely to improve their situation, to put an end to the see-saw policies which, depending on the general economic climate, sent women off to work, or kept them at home – or both.

16
National Socialist Policy on Women
The Labour Market, Population and the Family

The radical rhetoric of National Socialist Party officials may have fuelled such hopes, but their post-1933 practices spoke a different tongue. Although Nazi leaders did try as far as possible to put their concept of strict gender-specific segregation and division of labour into practice, the exigencies of the situation almost always ran counter to their intentions. It was only in the military and the narrow sphere of political representation that they managed to retain purely male preserves. Women were entitled to join the Party (from 1933 to 1937 they made up between 4 and 5 per cent of the membership, with the number increasing rapidly thereafter),[1] but they were largely barred from offices and positions of power in the party state. However, they were able, as either honorary or paid officials, to exercise power at the grassroots level of National Socialism's mass movements: the National Socialist women's organisation (the *Frauenschaft*), the German Women's Enterprise (*Deutsches Frauenwerk*), the League of German Girls, the German Labour Front (*Deutsche Arbeitsfront*), and the National Socialist People's Welfare (*Nationalsozialistische Volkswohlfahrt*). But they were powerless to influence political directives issued by the upper echelons of the Fascist state.

Though at the level of political organisation the Nazis were consistent both ideologically and in practice, policy was constantly shifting where the female labour force was concerned. During the world economic slump the NSDAP had been among the most vociferous critics of women 'dual-income earners'. Promises to keep married women out of the labour market had also been prominent in their election propaganda. Even unmarried women

---

1. M. H. Kater, 'Frauen in der NS-Bewegung', *Vierteljahrshefte für Zeitgeschichte*, 31, 1983, pp. 206–7.

should, if possible, not compete with men for jobs but engage in occupations 'compatible with their nature' and earn their living in domestic service, agriculture or social work. Statutory reductions in insurance contributions for 'domestic assistants' were intended to make that work more attractive, and income tax relief for employers was supposed to increase demand for domestic staff. These deliberate attempts to direct the labour market enjoyed only limited success, if they were meant to reverse general employment trends. The 'Domestic Service' column of the 1939 Employment Census registered 250,000 more women than in 1933;[2] in other words the decline in absolute numbers, which had been in evidence in 1925, had been halted and even reversed. But the percentage of domestic staff in the total female labour force continued to fall, to 10.1 per cent in 1939 compared with 10.9 per cent six year previously. By contrast the proportion of female public officials, blue- and white-collar workers in services, trade and industry had risen over the same period from 37.2 to 39.6 per cent, from a total of 4,300,000 to 5,900,000. The overall percentage of women in work had grown too, from 34.4 per cent in 1933 to 36.7 per cent in 1939. Notwithstanding all the appeals and entreaties of propaganda, women were taking up paid employment in increasing numbers, and ever more frequently they opted for jobs outside agriculture and domestic service.

The National Socialists had no greater success in their endeavours to drive married women from the labour market. By 1939, 6,200,000 working women were married, 2 million more than in 1933. Most of them were classified for statistical purposes as 'assisting relatives' and as 'genuine labour comrades' (*wirkliche Arbeitsgenossinnen*) in their husbands' and fathers' agricultural, manufacturing and commercial enterprises. But there had also been a clear growth both in the absolute number and in the proportion of married women in non-family employment – women whose job security depended on the market (and who thus 'took men's jobs away', as the critics of female 'dual-income earners' put it) – from 1,300,000 in 1933 to 2,300,000 in 1939. In 1939, at least 35 out of every 100 married women between the ages of fourteen and sixty-five were having to combine home and family duties with full-time employment. As far as they were concerned, the propagandists' promises that they wanted to and could be simply mothers and housewives

2. These and the following statistics have been calculated from A. Willms, *Die Entwicklung der Frauenerwerbstätigkeit im Deutschen Reich*, Nuremberg 1980, tables pp. 67, 77, 99, 100, 104.

were but empty words. Employers could not afford to dispense with cheap labour, and at a time when real wages were rising very slowly families could not survive without the mother's earnings. Moreover economic revival did not follow immediately after the Nazis came to power: in 1935, 10.3 per cent of the workforce were still unemployed, and many women continued to be their family's main breadwinner. In view of this combination of interests, the frequently vicious methods used by local SA troops to force employers to dismiss their female workforce had as little prospect of success as the government's half-hearted propaganda campaigns.[3]

Less leniency was shown in cases where the state, the Länder or the local authorities were the employers. New legislation allowed married women civil servants to be dismissed, discriminatory wage structures were prescribed, and senior positions as well as prospects of promotion closed to women. In education women teachers were removed from positions of management, transferred from higher girls' schools to the lower echelons of the school system, and the ratio between male and female junior teachers was set at 4:1. After 1936 women were not allowed to become judges, public prosecutors or lawyers, and women doctors had enormous difficulty finding hospital training places or posts in medical care administered through health insurance schemes. Government restrictions also suited the wishes of male academics, whose reaction to high levels of unemployment in the world of higher learning was to call for a ban on female competition. Yet in 1933 there were no more than 12,500 women among Germany's 300,000 professional academics, and in the civil service women were seriously underrepresented, making up only 8.7 per cent of the total. On the other hand the number of female students rose rapidly: in the winter of 1931–2, 20,000 women, i.e. 16 per cent of all students, were undergoing university education. In order to pre-empt a surplus on the graduate labour market, and to make it plain that there were limits to how many women one wished to see in privileged professional occupations, Reichsminister Frick introduced discriminatory entry requirements as early as 1933, stipulating that women were to account for only 10 per cent of the annual intake of 15,000 students.[4] Although this ceiling was abolished two years later, the number of female students fell continuously: in summer 1939 there

3. D. Winkler, *Frauenarbeit im 'Dritten Reich'*, Hamburg 1977, pp. 42ff.
4. In 1933 16.7 per cent of all first-year students were women; see I. Weyrather, 'Numerus Clausus für Frauen – Studentinnen im Nationalsozialismus', in *Mutterkreuz*, pp. 131–62.

were 66 per cent fewer (and 50 per cent fewer male students) than in 1933.[5]

When it became apparent around 1938, if not sooner, that the colossal programme of military and economic build-up required more scientific and academic personnel than the falling numbers of students would provide, women were once again encouraged to study, especially in the humanities and medicine. Later, during the war, all the reservations the National Socialists had about women studying were abandoned in the face of the simple need to replace male students and academics who had been sent to the army, and to maintain teaching and research levels in universities. By the winter of 1943–4, 27,442 women were studying again – 61.3 per cent of all students, more than ever before. Despite the intentions of Nazi officials to reduce the female presence in supposedly male occupations, the exigencies of economic boom and military-industrial expansionism carried things in quite the opposite direction.[6]

National Socialist policy on education and training proved to be equally short-sighted and half-hearted. Weimar's educational administrators had constantly aimed to narrow gender-specific qualitative differences and inequalities in senior education; by contrast, the basic assumption of Nazi educational planners was that boys and girls should undergo quite distinct forms of schooling. 'In the education of the girl the final goal always to be kept in mind is that she is one day to be a mother,' wrote Hitler in *Mein Kampf*.[7] All directives issued during the Third Reich concerning primary and secondary education revolved around this definition: all subjects were to guide girls towards their specifically female role in the National Socialist *Volksgemeinschaft*. Domestic science, needlework, childcare, health education and 'racial biology' were compulsory for all girls.[8] In order to proceed to the senior grades of secondary schools, they had to pass an examination in domestic science and prove that holding the *Abitur* did not mean they were incapable of fulfilling their proper vocation as housewives and mothers.

5. See the statistics in Petzina et al, *Arbeitsbuch*, vol. III, p. 169.
6. J. Stephenson, *Women in Nazi Society*, New York 1975, ch. 8 ('Progress, Prejudice and Purge in the Professions') and ch. 9 ('Coordination and Consolidation in the Professions').
7. A. Hitler, *Mein Kampf*, trans. J. Murphy, London n.d., p. 360.
8. On school curricula see G. Tidl, *Die Frau im Nationalsozialismus*, Vienna 1984, pp. 47–53; B. Kather, 'Mädchenerziehung – Müttererziehung?', in Schmidt and Dietz (eds), *Frauen unterm Hakenkreuz*, pp. 22ff.; S. Conradt and K. Heckmann-Janz, '... *du heiratest ja doch!*' *80 Jahre Schulgeschichte von Frauen*, Frankfurt 1985, pp. 133ff.; M. Lück, *Die Frau im Männerstaat*, Frankfurt 1979, pp. 53ff.

When the Nazis came to power they were initially content to inherit the Weimar educational system, and to introduce no more than minor modifications. But after 1937 educational reforms went much deeper. The high school (*Oberschule*) became almost the sole option for girls who wished to go on after basic schooling, replacing the *Lyzeum* and *Oberlyzeum* which in 1931 77 per cent of all girls in higher schooling had attended. By comparison with boys' schools they offered little in the way of natural sciences and mathematics, and even language instruction was limited. Most high school curricula did not have Latin, which was a must for almost all scientific subjects at university. Instead, more scope was given to 'disciplines of feminine creativity' (*Fächer des Frauenschaffens*). After the tenth grade, girls could choose broadly between two-year courses in languages or domestic science, which led to the *Abitur* certificate. In 1940, 15,014 girls had opted for languages, and 11,362 for home economics, though judging by propaganda the latter was clearly the first choice for National Socialism.[9] The homecraft route, popularly known as 'A-level custard-making' (*Puddingabitur*), did not lead automatically to a university entrance qualification. The high school leaver, trained in caring, bringing up children, domestic science and social welfare, could not enrol as an undergraduate until she passed additional examinations in history, mathematics, physics and two foreign languages. But here too a shortage of academics and the effects of war forced political principles to be recast in a more pragmatic mould. After Easter 1941 these additional examinations were dropped and both types of *Abitur* counted as university entrance qualifications.[10]

Similar contradictions between Nazi ideology and practice were to be found in the attitudes of central and Land education ministries to co-education. Although Weimar education policy had, under pressure from religious and conservative forces, adopted the principle that separate schooling for boys and girls was both necessary and desirable, lack of finance in the late 1920s had meant that co-education, which the Social Democrats advocated, became more common. For example in Thuringia in 1933 more girls went to boys' schools than to girls' schools, though in Germany as a whole in 1931 girls made up no more than 6.3 per cent of pupils at higher boys' schools. The Nazis often declared that the principle of mixed schooling was diametrically opposed to their concepts of education;

9. Lundgreen, *Sozialgeschichte der deutschen Schule*, vol. II, p. 81.
10. Stephenson, *Women in Nazi Society*, p. 127.

and yet no amount of appeals from the Minister for Science and National Education, that under no circumstances should girls be admitted to boys' schools, could alter the fact that the percentage of girls who went to boys' schools continued to rise, although at a slower rate than between 1926 and 1931.[11]

The manifest tensions between ideological assertions and actual policies in all matters of female labour and education were multiplied considerably when the campaigns for military conquest, launched from 1939 onwards, demanded maximum economic output while at the same time conscripting ever greater sections of the male workforce to the front. There was more scope than in the First World War for filling vacancies with workers from occupied countries: more than seven million foreigners, including almost one-and-a-half million women, were living and working in Germany in 1944. They were prisoners of war, deported civilians, and 'guest workers' recruited with varying degrees of force (more violence was used in the east than in northern and Mediterranean countries). They were set to work mainly in agriculture and industry. In 1944 foreigners, above all Russians and Poles, made up at least 22 per cent of the labour force in the agricultural sector and 29 per cent in industry. In the Krupp company the workforce was 35 per cent non-German as early as 1943.[12] Although some shortfalls could be made up in this way, labour was still scarce, particularly in the expanding white-collar sector, which suffered a shortage of suitable German-speaking labour.

Administrative, military and economic authorities had realised even before the war that a major solution to this kind of problem would be found in the maximum mobilisation of female labour. Not least, the experience of 1914–18 had shown how much the outcome of war was linked to the planned and co-ordinated employment of women in production and administration. After 1936 government officials and agencies began to give thought to ways of efficiently exploiting the potential female labour force.[13] As war broke out, calls came from all sides to make service compulsory for all German women aged between fourteen and sixty. One of the most vocifer-

---

11. Ibid., pp. 117, 125.
12. I. Schupetta, 'Jeder das Ihre – Frauenerwerbstätigkeit und Einsatz von Fremdarbeitern/-arbeiterinnen im Zweiten Weltkrieg', in *Mutterkreuz*, pp. 292–317; U. Herbert, 'Apartheid nebenan: Erinnerungen an die Fremdarbeiter im Ruhrgebiet', in L. Niethammer (ed.), *'Die Jahre weiß man nicht, wo man die heute hinsetzen soll': Faschismuserfahrungen im Ruhrgebiet*, Berlin 1983, pp. 233–66, esp. p. 263.
13. Winkler, *Frauenarbeit*, pp. 82ff.

ous protagonists of this was Hermann Göring, in charge of building the economy, and chairman of the Reich Defence Council. His decrees of spring 1939 established a legal framework for a general call-up of all women fit for work, but essentially these remained on paper when war started and were applied to only a limited degree in the ensuing years. Although senior Party functionaries constantly drew attention to the fact that a million-strong reserve army of women was ready for action, and was absolutely necessary for the war effort in the armaments industry, administration and agriculture, the top Party leadership, most importantly Hitler himself, was opposed to taking such steps. Total mobilisation was disfavoured for ideological and demographic reasons, as well as from the point of view of strategic power, with the result that for a long time the top leadership was against even a limited degree of compulsory labour.

It was not until 1943, with the declaration of 'total war', that all women between seventeen and forty-five (and later on fifty) were obliged to report to the authorities, who established their fitness and suitability for work. Yet even this regulation made so many exceptions and, in accordance with instructions from on high, was often so loosely applied, that by the end of the year only half a million women had been mobilised.[14] In the 'best circles' the regulation met with disdain, and many women in the middle classes managed to avoid directed labour by string-pulling or by taking what simply appeared to be jobs. As discontent about such inequality acquired ever more menacing and public forms among women of the lower and lower-middle classes, Nazi officials and the security forces started to warn of 'instinctual class struggle' in the proletariat and of the dangers facing 'social peace'. Nevertheless the extremely hesitant and discriminatory fashion in which the rules were applied was not modified: as Sauckel, who was in charge of labour direction, put it in May 1942: 'you don't render anything less distasteful by making it absolutely valid and inflicting it on everyone'.[15]

The wives and daughters of industrialists, army officers, professionals and senior public officials were not alone in resisting the state's exhortations that they should work in offices and munitions factories for the Final Victory; women from the working and

14. Ibid., p. 134ff.
15. Quoted in Bajohr, *Die Hälfte*, p. 274; see also L. J. Rupp, 'Klassenzugehörigkeit und Arbeitseinsatz der Frauen im Dritten Reich', *Soziale Welt*, 31, 1980, pp. 191–205, and D. Winkler, 'Frauenarbeit versus Frauenideologie: Probleme der weiblichen Erwerbstätigkeit in Deutschland 1930–1945', *Archiv für Sozialgeschichte*, 17, 1977, pp. 99–126.

lower-middle classes also sought ways of evading their duties. Many soldiers' wives gave up badly paid jobs because their earnings were subtracted from their wartime benefit payments, which completely cancelled out the material incentive to go out to work. Even a new ruling announced in May 1940, to the effect that two-thirds of the net wage were to be ignored in the calculation of state benefits, made little difference, and widespread antipathy persisted in spite of official complaints. As housework became more arduous as a result of shortages and the rationing of foods and consumer goods, so women, particularly those with children, felt the pressures of full-time employment more sharply. Numerous Nazi institutions, such as the German Labour Front, the National Socialist People's Welfare and the *Frauenschaft*, did turn their attention to the welfare of working women; legislation on the protection of female employees had improved constantly from 1933 onwards; 1942 saw the promulgation of a new law – which went considerably further than the previous version of 1927 – on the protection of mothers, henceforth also giving to blue- and white-collar workers in agriculture and domestic service the luxury of six weeks' maternity leave either side of the birth of their children; in addition, maternity benefit was now being paid at the normal wage level. But the war made all such legal protection, which was exemplary in international terms, inapplicable in most cases. In the armaments industry in particular, and in agriculture and government administration after 1939, many regulations on employee protection had been eased, or even entirely abolished, and the working week, fixed at forty-eight hours before 1939, had continuously been extended. Although some enterprises reacted to the adverse consequences of these developments – falls in productivity, illness, protests from the female workforce – by re-introducing the eight-hour day, after 1943 such consideration was no longer necessary.[16]

Another way of encouraging company workforces to increase their efforts and of attracting badly-needed female workers would have been to pay women higher wages. As early as 1933 the German Labour Front had made a case for equal pay for equal work, but they failed to convince either the Labour Ministry or individual entrepreneurs. Skilled female workers in the Third Reich earned one third, and unskilled workers 30 per cent, less than their male counterparts; wage agreements set salaries for female white-collar workers at 10–20 per cent lower.[17] This problem was exacerbated

16. Winkler, *Frauenarbeit*, pp. 66ff., 154ff.
17. Ibid., p. 74; Petzina et al., *Arbeitsbuch*, vol. III, p. 99.

during the war, when many women were transferred to jobs in other industries where they performed the work of men who had been sent on active service. Female indignation at unfair and unjustifiable wage differentials grew ever fiercer.

It was only in the public services that their protests were successful. In October 1939 the Labour Ministry ordered that women who were performing 'men's jobs' in their capacities as train guards, bus and tram conductors or electricity meter readers would henceforth also be paid 'men's wages'. In the private sector, which was subject to state wage policies, an average 25 per cent pay differential should be the maximum allowed. But under certain rigidly defined conditions female workers on piece-rates in the munitions industry could after 1940 be given pay parity with their male colleagues. Indeed, some manufacturers did so, in the hope of retaining indispensable staff or recruiting new members to the workforce. Female white-collar workers benefited particularly from their strong market position, and often managed to make their way up into the more senior positions and higher wage brackets – always in the knowledge, however, that when the war was over they would have to relinquish their posts to men and be content once again with relatively badly paid jobs in the typing pool.[18] Female blue-collar workers had much less opportunity to improve their standing, and the overall inequality of men's and women's wages changed little.[19]

The industrial and political elite proved to be much more sympathetic where non-monetary benefits were concerned. Improvements in this area cost less, and also promoted social and political integration. Day nurseries and crèches in factories were given enormous support by the German Labour Front, the National Socialist People's Welfare and local authorities alike. The Women's Department of the Labour Front deployed its 10,000 officials and almost 50,000 factory representatives to campaign for a better working atmosphere, and ran training courses in domestic science.[20] Large enterprises appointed social workers who were responsible for dealing with the personal and family problems of women factory workers, and who advised them on 'all aspects of life'.[21]

18. M. Schmidt, 'Krieg der Männer – Chance der Frauen? Der Einzug von Frauen in die Büros der Thyssen AG', in Niethammer (ed.), 'Die Jahre', pp. 133–62.
19. Winkler, *Frauenarbeit*, pp. 126ff., 164ff.
20. Stephenson, *Women in Nazi Society*, pp. 95–6.
21. C. Sachse, 'Hausarbeit im Betrieb: Betriebliche Sozialarbeit unter dem Nationalsozialismus', in Sachse et al., *Angst, Belohnung, Zucht und Ordnung: Herrschaftsmechanismen im Nationalsozialismus*, Opladen 1982, pp. 209–74, quote at p. 254.

Members of the *Frauenschaft* and the National Socialist League of Women Students worked unpaid for periods of three to six weeks so that women factory workers with large families could take an extra paid holiday.[22] All these activities centred primarily around working wives and mothers: the authorities wished to help them combine professional and family duties without too much hardship. However, neither welfare programmes nor lessons in running a household were sufficient to ease the impossible load that working women in particular had to bear during the war, or to obviate the concomitant threats to health and political morality.

The Nazi elite was too concerned about the population's loyalty and staying power to make gainful employment outside the home compulsory for married women across the board. Desperate fear of a political 'stab in the back', of a breakdown of legitimacy, of November 1918 all over again: these were what prevented Hitler from agreeing to Armaments Minister Speer's demands for comprehensive obligatory service for women.[23] A country such as Britain, resting upon a stable democratic order, could with impunity introduce compulsory service for all women in 1941; but Nazi leaders had to be more wary of the volatility of the masses. Consequently they appealed to the willingness of the women of the nation to make sacrifices, and called on their good will to bolster the *Volksgemeinschaft*; but they eschewed obligatory labour. The impact was unimpressive: the number of women in gainful employment rose only marginally during the war, and even fell by 500,000 before 1941. In September 1944 it was 14,900,000 compared to 14,600,000 in May 1939.[24] If we consider that in the first six years of the Third Reich the size of the female workforce had in any case gone up by 2,300,000, it becomes even clearer that the level of post-1939 stagnation deviated sharply from both the labour market patterns before 1939 and the Nazis' intentions to extract a maximum from all available labour reserves. The 1939 population and occupation census recorded almost one million single women and 5,400,000 married women without children who were of working age but did not work; but this potential was not tapped. The only army available for manoeuvres constituted women already in employment. Increased demand for labour in the armaments industries

---

22. Tidl, *Die Frau im Nationalsozialismus*, p. 113. It is estimated that 18,920 women undertook 'factory relief' in 1940.
23. T. W. Mason, *Sozialpolitik im Dritten Reich: Arbeiterklasse und Volksgemeinschaft*, Opladen 1977, esp. p. 31.
24. Winkler, *Frauenarbeit*, table p. 201.

was met, apart from using foreign workers, by structural shifts in the working population, as had been the case in the First World War: women employed in textiles were transferred to chemicals and metallurgy, those in domestic service and agriculture took factory jobs, and the administrative and services sectors, which were growing at an enormous rate, found most of their recruits among young women who had just started working.

The various Labour Service organisations, that were greatly expanded during the war, were also relatively unsuccessful at mobilising extra labour power. Voluntary Labour Service (*Freiwilliger Arbeitsdienst*) had existed in Germany since 1931, its aim being to reduce the excessively high level of unemployment by employing young men and women on community projects. The National Socialists took over this scheme, along with many others, and extended it. From 1934 onwards all girl school-leavers who wished to go to university had first to serve their nation for six months as a 'maid of labour' (*Arbeitsmaid*). They would help out for several hours per day in large families, in day nurseries or on farms. In the afternoons they would return to the camps in which they were accommodated, to receive political instruction. In June 1938, 24,652 young women were engaged in Reich Labour Service, compared with almost 300,000 men. Although legislation of 1935 had decreed that labour service was binding for all young Germans, in practice it was in the first instance applied only to young men. Not until September 1939, three days after German troops marched into Poland, did the Reich Labour Leader receive the directive 'to enlist for the fulfilment of Reich Labour Service duties single girls between the ages of seventeen and twenty-five who are not in paid employment, not in full-time education or undergoing vocational training and who are not indispensable to the running of a family agricultural business'.[25] Throughout the period, 'maids of labour' were predominantly employed in agriculture, a sector suffering from severe labour shortages as a result of conscription and the drift of workers to the towns. After the summer of 1941, Labour Service was extended by another six-month period, this time in munitions factories, military administration, government bureaucracy and hospitals. In introducing this measure the regime was reacting to protests from the armed forces and industry, which were opposed to what they regarded as the irrational and counter-productive

25. Quoted in L. Kleiber, '"Wo ihr seid, da soll die Sonne scheinen!" Der Frauenarbeitsdienst am Ende der Weimarer Republik und im Nationalsozialismus', in *Mutterkreuz*, pp. 188–214, this passage p. 212.

policy of removing thousands of young women from the labour market for months at a time, and called for a more effectively organised deployment of labour resources. But even compulsory wartime labour failed to satisfy their demands, largely because of the high and rapid turnover of young women. Such drawbacks were rectified in 1944, when the time limits to the length of service were lifted. However, victory was no more likely to be won in this way than it was through the assignment of girls to anti-aircraft units.[26]

The Reich Labour Service is yet another example of the contradiction between ideal aims and real possibilities for action in National Socialist policy on women. It had initially been conceived as a method of easing the hopelessly high labour surplus during the global economic slump; but after 1936, when full employment had been reached and there was even the prospect of a labour shortage, it had completely lost its original *raison d'être*. While Hierl, the Reich Labour Leader, had with Hitler's backing adhered rigidly to the notion that the six-month period of service was to serve a primarily political and educational purpose, and to 'bring up the youth of the German *Volksgemeinschaft* in the spirit of National Socialism, and to teach them true respect for manual labour',[27] other power elites saw this as a rather secondary, even irrelevant mission. As far as the armed forces and the munitions industries were concerned, the main point was to use women to fill as many as possible of the crucial wartime positions in manufacturing and administration that had been vacated by men called up to fight. Agriculture could recruit foreign workers, and as for the ideological schooling of young women, the bonding of their souls to the soil and heritage of Germany would have to wait until the war was over.

The so-called Year of Duty (*Pflichtjahr*), introduced in 1938 by Göring, also failed to impress industrial circles. It declared that all single women under twenty-five who wished to work in the textile, clothing or tobacco industries or to apply for a white-collar job in the public or private sector would first have to work one year in domestic service or in agriculture. This attempt directly to control occupational choices did have some positive impact in the short term: women farmers and large families in particular benefited from

26. On the history of Labour Service, see S. Bajohr, 'Weiblicher Arbeitsdienst im "Dritten Reich": Ein Konflikt zwischen Ideologie und Ökonomie', *Vierteljahrshefte für Zeitgeschichte*, 28, 1980, pp. 331–57, and J. Stephenson, 'Women's Labor Service in Nazi Germany', *Central European History*, 15, 1982, pp. 241–65.
27. Quoted in Kleiber, '"Wo ihr seid, da soll die Sonne scheinen!"', p. 211.

the extra hands, and, in purely quantitative terms, the agricultural scheme was sizeable: in 1939, 217,000 girls were serving their Year of Duty, and as many as 335,972 by 1940.[28] In the long term, however, the overall structure of the labour market continued to change of its own accord; the government managed to induce only temporary fluctuations. In addition the industrial sectors affected by these policies complained that whole age groups of girl school-leavers were not available for employment, and bemoaned the fact that pro-agricultural measures generated setbacks and delays in the rest of the war economy. Despite this, neither Reich Labour Service nor the Year of Duty was abolished; even the declaration of 'total war' would not persuade the party-state leadership to recognise the primacy of industry and subordinate all other economic and ideological aims to it.

It is debatable whether this approach was as irrational as some historians claim.[29] In terms of a policy of agricultural autarchy, it seems far from unreasonable occasionally to send young women to work on farms; the hesitancy shown by the Nazis in conscripting all able-bodied women without young children for wartime service may have run counter to the interests of the armaments industry, but it had a positive impact on the domestic balance of power and on the population's attitude to the system as a whole. Even if it is true that war and the conquering and colonisation of new *Lebensraum* formed the *raison d'état* of National Socialism, that all spheres of policy were subordinated to this ultimate aim, there were also recurring and awkward conflicts between means and ends in the matter of how best to co-ordinate various policies in the short and medium term. Even plans projected beyond the war, on the ideological, social and economic shape of a 'Great German Reich', sometimes collided with the available options for immediate, necessary action, giving rise to what appear to be 'irrational' decisions.

It seems, then, that the mobilisation, direction and control of female labour resources as dictated by the economic climate represents only one of many competing elements in the Nazi regime's attitude towards women. Great emphasis was placed on population and family policy, which in the early years of the Third Reich had been relatively simple to dovetail with employment policy. For example, the explicit aim of loans for married couples, introduced in 1933 with the Law on the Prevention of Unemployment, was to

28. Winkler, *Frauenarbeit*, pp. 58, 90.
29. Winkler, Bajohr, Stephenson and Rupp, for example.

woo married women off the labour market. Young married couples were entitled to a single interest-free loan of up to 1,000 Reichmarks (the average annual income of a wage-earner was 1,520 Reichmarks in 1933) on condition that the wife gave up her job when she married and undertook not to take up paid employment for the duration of the loan period, as long as the husband had a regular income. This money, which was paid out in the form of shopping coupons, was meant to facilitate marriage and the establishment of a home, and to create alternative, unpaid work for young working women. At the same time it acted as an incentive to couples to produce as many children as quickly as possible, since with each child the debt decreased by a quarter, with the result that with the birth of a fourth child a couple had 'paid off' their debt.

An indication of how seriously the regime took this aspect of population and family policy is the fact that even during the period of full employment the loan scheme continued to operate, even though its function for the labour market (i.e. making jobs available to unemployed men) had now itself become redundant. In fact after 1937 working women who wanted to marry were not obliged to leave their jobs in order for their husbands to be entitled to a loan. The creation of families and stimulation of the birth rate were given even greater priority in the ensuing years. The government levied high taxes on childless couples, while large families were offered tax advantages. In addition various forms of financial assistance existed for families with several children: after 1936 the families of blue- and white-collar workers earning less than 185 Reichsmarks per month received 10 marks per month for the fifth and every subsequent child; two years later child benefit was given for the third and fourth children too. This costly state benefit package, from which at least 2,500,000 children and their parents profited in 1938, was financed out of unemployment benefit funds, which were buoyant thanks to the salutary effects on the economy of military build-up.[30]

Plans for offering more generous support to large families had been tabled in central and local government since the First World War, if not before. Weimar Germany had also witnessed lively debate about pro-birth family policy and material incentives to increase numbers of children. Fears of 'the death of the nation' were not, after all, invented by National Socialists, but dated from around the turn of the century (in Germany and elsewhere) when

---

30. T. Mason, 'Women in Germany 1925–1940: Family, Welfare and Work', *History Workshop*, 1, 1976, pp. 74–113; 2, 1976, pp. 5–32, quote at pp. 95ff.

the birth rate began to decline steadily. In 1899 there had been 35.6 live births per thousand head of population, but there were only 27.5 by 1913. Minor fluctuations (attributable to the war) produced a short-term revival, but the downward trend accelerated in the Weimar Republic, reaching its nadir during the economic slump: 15.1 births per thousand head of population in 1932. The annual growth rate of the population had been 1.57 per cent in 1902; now it was a mere 0.43 per cent.[31] The logic of national power politics dictates that near-zero population growth would arouse the worst kind of fears among politicians of any country; but for German National Socialism, bent on extending *Lebensraum* through imperialism, it represented a massive threat to the very crux of the system. In view of a rapid decline in fertility, the argument that the flourishing of the German people was being hemmed in by its eastern borders was ultimately unconvincing. Both the colonisation of Eastern Europe and the military subjugation of neighbouring states in the north and east required a 'master race' that was strong in both quality and quantity; neither needed a dystrophic 'national corpus' (*Volkskörper*) that also appeared to be suffering from hereditary diseases, social aliens and miscegenation.

It should therefore come as no surprise that the National Socialists, in contrast to previous governments, not only adopted a concerned tone when discussing population problems, but also wasted no time after seizing power in introducing a series of measures intended to stop, and reverse, the dangerous decline. The arsenal of weapons wielded by politicians responsible for these affairs included more than just the carrot of financial incentives to stimulate the birth rate; the stick was used too: new legislation included the re-introduction of §§219 and 220 of the Criminal Code. Having been annulled in 1926 as a result of pressure from the SPD, in their new form the laws made provision for a more vigilant clamp-down on, and harsher punishments for, abortion. At the same time local government and privately-run sexual advice centres were closed, and contraceptives made more difficult to obtain.[32] Henceforth women were to be unable either to prevent or to terminate pregnancies, and the distinction between sexuality and reproduction was blurred in the interest of population growth.

It may never be possible to establish for certain whether the rise in

---

31. Hohorst et al., *Arbeitsbuch*, pp. 29–30; Petzina et al, *Arbeitsbuch*, vol. III, p. 32.
32. Mason, 'Women in Germany', p. 102; Stephenson, *Women in Nazi Society*, pp. 61ff.

fertility that occurred between 1934 and 1939 – the rate had reached 1924 levels again by 1939, at 20.4 births per thousand head of population – can be attributed to material inducements or to the fact that child-bearing was governmentally ordained, so to speak. There is even some evidence to suggest that it would have occurred without the influence of Nazi policy. The average number of children per marriage did not rise: in fact even though the total number of births was higher in 1933–8 than it had been in the preceding five-year period, all the efforts of the authorities to break the mould of the two-child family failed. Couples who married in 1920 produced on average 2.3 children; but the figures for 1930 and 1940 fell to 2.2 and 1.8 respectively. The average size of households and families continued to decrease in the years of the Third Reich: the average household of 1933 contained 3.6 people, but only 3.27 in 1939.[33] It is clear that neither the prohibition of abortion nor child benefit or loan schemes deterred married couples from limiting their offspring. The main reason why the birth rate went up was that more people were getting married. In 1932 there were 7.9 marriages per thousand head of population and 11.2 by 1934; although the level did not remain as high, until 1939 the number of marriages was 20 per cent above the mean for 1923–32. While the adverse economic climate of the latter years of the Weimar Republic had tended to make the prospect of settling down unattractive, the Nazis' rosy promises that better times were round the corner, plus real falls in unemployment, seem to have been conducive to marriage. The marriage loan scheme may also have prompted couples to make their love affairs legal. Further evidence supporting the thesis that marriage was extremely fashionable among young Germans of the Third Reich is the fact that the number of illegitimate children born in the period 1936–9 was extraordinarily low (7.7 per cent of all births compared with 12.2 per cent in 1926–30). More marriages meant more children, even though the size of the nuclear family did not increase. Few women took full advantage of state maternity benefits, and most seem to have been content with two children.

The Nazis spared no expense in encouraging citizens to excel themselves at reproduction; their vigorous campaign demonstrated enormous imagination. Apart from financial and material perks for large families, carefully staged propaganda ensured that women never lost sight of their most important civic duty. Mother's Day,

---

33. Hubbard, *Familiengeschichte*, pp. 101, 125; *Gesellschaftliche Daten 1982*, p. 19.

which the Third Reich had inherited from the Weimar Republic, was celebrated as a national holiday; especially productive mothers were honoured in public, politicians made speeches, and presents were handed out. On Mother's Day in 1939 the state awarded some three million women the Cross of Honour of the German Mother, a medal for outstanding feats of child-bearing: bronze for four or five children, silver for six or seven, and gold for eight or more. Members of the Nazi youth organisations were obliged formally to greet bearers of these medals, which further emphasized their political significance. National Socialism needed children for its ambitious plans to conquer Europe, and leading politicians constantly reminded women that every baby they brought into the world represented a 'battle fought for the survival or death of the nation'.[34]

The regime was not content to let matters rest with fine words. The National Socialist cult of the mother was locked into a whole network of welfare provision through which the state hoped to make motherhood easier, attune it to the needs of the day, and ultimately control it. In celebration of Mother's Day in 1934, the Reich Mothers' Service (*Reichsmütterdienst*) was established. This was a joint project of the National Socialist *Frauenschaft* and the *Frauenwerk* (the umbrella organisations for women's associations still operating), and the National Socialist People's Welfare, and followed on from initiatives that local authority and voluntary bodies had taken in the Weimar years. The Reich Mothers' Service ran training courses for mothers, and organised trips and holidays for women and their children. By 1936 there were already 150 such schools training women in their vocation as mothers and housewives. Twelve two-hour lessons covered how to run a household in a businesslike and efficient manner, design a comfortable home, care properly for infants and bring up children in a responsible manner.[35] They were certainly in demand: by March 1939 more than 1,700,000 women had attended the 100,000 courses being run throughout the country, and by 1944 the number had risen to five million.[36] In addition, mothers' advice centres had been established, replacing the marriage and sexual advice centres that had been closed in 1933. They offered advice and information on urgent

---

34. Hitler in a speech to the National Socialist *Frauenschaft* in 1934, reprinted in Domarus (ed.), *Hitler*, p. 451.
35. Hausen, 'Mothers, Sons, and the Sale of Symbols and Goods', p. 397; S. Dammer, 'Kinder, Küche, Kriegsarbeit: Die Schulung der Frauen durch die NS-Frauenschaft', in *Mutterkreuz*, pp. 215–45, here pp. 234ff.
36. Stephenson, *Nazi Organisation*, p. 165; Dammer, 'Kinder, Küche, Kriegsarbeit', p. 237, provides detailed statistics.

matters relating to child care, and also provided material aid, mainly in the form of children's clothing, beds and food. Official statistics indicate that 25,000 advice centres were operational in 1938, and their services called upon by ten million women.[37] Courses on household management run by the *Frauenwerk* were also very popular. By 1938, 1,800,000 women had been instructed in the art of making the most of available clothes, preserving home-grown fruit and vegetables, and giving their family healthy food at minimal cost (though by no means with minimal effort).[38]

As a result of such measures motherhood and the work of housewives were 'professionalised' in an unprecedented manner. Greater recognition was accorded to the contribution that women in the home made to the *Volksgemeinschaft*: in other words, the demands of the middle-class housewives' associations of Weimar Germany had largely been satisfied. In fact it was middle-class women who derived the greatest benefit from this 'professionalisation'. They ran the courses, attended mainly by young factory and office workers, guiding them in how to be 'proper' mothers and housekeepers, while in their own homes a servant girl would tidy up, do the cleaning and prepare meals. Despite the acute shortage of labour it did not occur to the Nazis until late 1944 to do away with such luxury. The women of the bourgeoisie also managed quite successfully to steer clear of the authorities' attempts to enlist the services of all for the common good. They could afford to give up a few hours here and there for the *Frauenwerk* or the *Frauenschaft*, but it was the women of the working and lower-middle classes who, increasingly, had to combine paid employment with their family duties, and were therefore less and less able to be domestic 'professionals'. During the war it was above all these women who had to bear the painful consequences of Nazi policy: clothing and food shortages, longer working hours, bombed-out homes, sons and husbands killed or wounded at the front.

Women who failed to fulfil the racial, social and political requirements of the Nazi pedigree had discovered the savage side of German Fascism at a much earlier stage. They enjoyed neither maternity nor child benefits, nor holidays; their children were not welcomed, or even tolerated, by the regime. Marriage loans were granted only to couples whose offspring would be free of social and biological flaws. Accordingly all applicants underwent a medical

37. Stephenson, *Women in Nazi Society*, p. 45.
38. Stephenson, *Nazi Organisation*, pp. 165–6; Tidl, *Die Frau im Nationalsozialismus*, pp. 136ff.

examination, both to look for hereditary disease and to establish whether social norms had been contravened even by the couple's family relations.[39] It is impossible to say with any certainty whether the fact that relatively few couples applied for a loan – in 1935 only a quarter of those who married[40] – was due to fear of a possibly embarrassing investigation into their backgrounds, or to a preference for the wives to keep their jobs and manage without the extra money. In any case, in October 1935 a regulation was introduced obliging anybody intending to marry to undergo a medical examination. Registrars could not allow marriage if the couple were not in possession of a health certificate. One month earlier the Nuremberg Law on the Protection of German Blood and German Honour had forbidden marriage between Jews and 'citizens of German and racially-related blood'. Now 'good Germans' could not consider black people or gypsies as potential spouses either. Transgression of this law meant imprisonment.

The National Socialists were thorough and systematic in the pursuit of their ideological aim to take the German people back to the state of 'racial purity' they held to have existed in the deep Germanic past. A policy of selection and elimination, conducted in a sober and calculated fashion, was intended to drive members of 'inferior' races from the 'corpus of the nation' (*Volkskörper*), and to breed a pure 'master race' from the remainder. The term 'race' had not only biological but also a combination of social and medical connotations. In the most strident traditions of social medicine and public health, prostitution, alcoholism, criminality and long-term dependency on welfare benefits were all regarded as potentially hereditary symptoms of disorders that were all the more threatening in view of the tendency for those who carried these diseases – and who were hence deemed 'unfit for community life' (*gemeinschaftsunfähig*) – to have more children and thus reproduce much more quickly than 'racially worthy' members of the population. The same was applied to those who suffered from physical and mental disability: like the 'social outcasts' they were also to be denied the right to have children. Racist and eugenic ideas such as these were by no means original or unique to Germany; the crucial

39. G. Bock, 'Frauen und ihre Arbeit im Nationalsozialismus', in Kuhn and Schneider, *Frauen*, pp. 113–49, quote at p. 131.
40. Stephenson, *Women in Nazi Society*, p. 46. The rejection rate was a very low 3 per cent. See G. Bock, 'Racism and Sexism in Nazi Germany: Compulsory Sterilization and the State', in Bridenthal et al. (eds) *When Biology Became Destiny*, pp. 271–96, quote at p. 285. See also Bock, *Zwangssterilisation im Nationalsozialismus*, Opladen, 1986.

point is that the Nazis were not content merely to continue a debate: they wanted action. As early as July 1933 they passed a Law on the Prevention of Hereditary Diseases in Children, which made provision for the compulsory sterilisation of men and women suffering from mental deficiency, schizophrenia, epilepsy, deafness, blindness and hereditary physical disabilities. By 1939, 320,000 men and women had been forcibly sterilised, three-quarters of these for mental deficiency or schizophrenia.[41] In 1935 it was ruled that abortion was also permitted for eugenic reasons: the Fascist regime showed little compunction in conveniently abandoning its pro-birth stance in order to protect the German people from 'inferior material'. After 1938 Jewish women were allowed to terminate a pregnancy on demand, for the Nazis valued their children as little as they did the offspring of gypsies, mixed marriages and women labourers from the occupied lands to the East. The policy of selection and elimination culminated in the establishment of concentration and extermination camps. Here women whose qualities failed to match the Nazis' exacting demands were first of all forcibly subjected to gynaecological experiments, and then, if they had survived this torture, starved or murdered.[42]

Consequently German Jewish women, gypsies and prostitutes experienced as few of the benefits of National Socialist veneration and support of motherhood as did Polish and Russian women. The Nazi regime had little respect for their families either, while the racially 'superior' Aryan family enjoyed the special protection of the state. There can be no doubt that the purpose of family policy in the Third Reich lay primarily in its intended effects on population development. This was made particularly clear in 1938, with the passing of legislation which standardised and updated law on marriage and divorce. The most important amendment to the divorce law, which had not been altered since 1900, was nothing short of revolutionary. The new §55 ruled that no reasons had to be given for a marriage to be terminated if the couple had been separated for three years or more. The principle of irretrievable breakdown was not entirely new: late eighteenth-century Prussian law had also recognised it. In both cases, its introduction was prompted by

---

41. Bock, 'Racism', pp. 279–80.
42. S. Milton, 'Women and the Holocaust', in Bridenthal et al. (eds), *When Biology Became Destiny*, pp. 297–333; H. Elling, *Frauen im deutschen Widerstand 1933–1945*, Frankfurt 1981, esp. pp. 23ff.; Schmidt and Dietz (eds), *Frauen unterm Hakenkreuz*, pp. 126ff.; S. Jacobeit and L. Thomas-Heinrich, *Kreuzweg Ravensbrück*, Leipzig 1987.

concern for population development. The Nazis hoped it would make divorce and re-marriage easier, and in all probability push up the birth rate. It also facilitated divorce in cases where Jews and Gentiles had married before the Nuremberg decrees were passed.

The liberalisation of the divorce law (for which the women's movement had fought in vain in the 1920s) led directly to a rise in the divorce rate, with every fifth divorce granted on the basis of § 55.[43] Unlike Weimar conservatism, which regarded a high divorce rate as evidence of a widespread crisis of the family, the National Socialists saw it as the opportunity for new families to be created: in other words, as a good thing for national development. A family was worth protecting and keeping only inasmuch as it produced healthy, racially 'superior' children raised in the spirit of National Socialism. If it no longer, or only unsatisfactorily, fulfilled this function, then its existence was no longer justified, and it could be dissolved by request of the couple, or by direct order of the state. Children from politically suspect families were taken away from their parents and brought up in homes run by the regime – a fate also shared by 'Aryan' children of Polish parents.

There was even talk of departing from all existing norms of family life in an attempt to speed up the production of perfect 'human material'. Many Nazi leaders believed monogamy to be a hindrance to population growth, and advocated political and material support for single mothers. In 1935 Heinrich Himmler, the Reichsführer SS, established the *Lebensborn* movement (literally, 'fountain of life'), whose statutory task was to 'further the number of children in SS families, protect and administer to all mothers of good blood, and care for needy mothers and children of good blood'. There were fourteen *Lebensborn* homes, providing ante- and post-natal care for the wives of impecunious SS men. They also cared for single women expecting the children of members of the SS, or indeed of any soldiers of the Wehrmacht; these women were given the opportunity of having their babies discreetly and then giving them away for adoption. Approximately half of the 12,000 births registered in *Lebensborn* homes between 1935 and 1945 were illegitimate.[44] Heavy war losses made it even more essential to encourage illegitimate motherhood, in order to offset the inevitable falls in the number of marriages and births. In an open letter of 1939 to an

43. Stephenson, *Women in Nazi Society*, p. 43. On the debate over divorce law in the Weimar Republic, see C. Jellinek (ed.), *Frauen unter deutschem Recht*, Mannheim 1928, pp. 33–9; Blasius, *Ehescheidung*, pp. 155ff.

44. Schmidt and Dietz (eds), *Frauen unterm Hakenkreuz*, p. 93.

unmarried mother whose husband-to-be had been killed in action, Rudolf Hess, Hitler's official representative, urged her to 'put aside worries that may be justified in normal times' for the duration of the war. Hitler and Himmler even went so far as to moot the possibility of changing the 'satanic' marriage laws which existed, to give every German man two wives and hence push up general levels of fertility.[45]

Throughout the Third Reich, however, marriage laws remained in force, and public morality continued to observe monogamy and condemn single mothers and illegitimate children. The discrimination against single mothers in the German Civil Code was not amended either, and their social status improved only marginally. In 1937 the Minister of Justice decreed that single women could henceforth choose whether they were addressed as *Frau* or *Fräulein*, and in 1939 that single mothers could no longer be automatically dismissed from the civil service.[46] As in the case of divorce law, in their policies towards unmarried women the Nazis exceeded – at least in some respects – the demands that radical women's organisations had been making for several years in an effort to end the stigma that single mothers and illegitimate children had to endure. However, their motives were entirely unrelated. The ultimate criterion for the Nazis was the total number of children who were 'fit for breeding', 'racially pure' and 'Aryan'; as with all aspects of their family policy, the tentative steps they took to make extra-marital motherhood socially acceptable were intended to increase output by improving production conditions.

In the National Socialist state the family took a back seat, while for Conservatives, Liberals, Catholics, Protestants, Social Democrats and Communists alike, it was a central social institution. Even though it was irreplaceable in the long term as the site of security and care for coming generations, and despite the soothing assurances of Nazi politicians, the familial influence on the intellectual and social development of children was minimised as much as possible. Children belonged to their mothers (and fathers) only while they were still very young – and even then training courses and advice for mothers ensured that the state's interests were not neglected. Political leverage over children increased once they started school. Even in the general school system, boys and girls were exposed to the ideology of National Socialism, for teachers

45. Kuhn and Rothe, *Frauen im deutschen Faschismus*, vol. II, pp. 116; Schmidt and Dietz (eds), *Frauen unterm Hakenkreuz*, p. 76.
46. Stephenson, *Women in Nazi Society*, p. 65.

238

were under strict instruction to educate their pupils in the spirit of the *Volksgemeinschaft* and to develop their racial awareness. Apart from schools, the most important agencies were the newly-formed youth organisations whose goal it was to create a body of youth that was devoted, malleable and willing to make sacrifices for the sake of the nation. The highest authority binding upon young people was not their parents but the Führer: his orders carried more weight than any parental bidding, and if there happened to be conflict between the wishes of the Führer and the wishes of the parents, then the child, with the backing of the youth organisation, had to obey Hitler. Extreme examples of children who denounced their parents as politically unreliable suggest that the Nazi programme of education did bear fruit. If a family tried to resist the state's claim to absolute power, then it forfeited its right to exist and was replaced by public institutions of upbringing and education. In this sense the National Socialist state earns the label of 'modern' that some historians and sociologists have attributed to it.[47] For beyond the backward-looking rhetoric there lay a political strategy of retaining only those links with the past that were in tune with the system's aims.

47. See in particular H. Schelsky, *Wandlungen der deutschen Familie in der Gegenwart*, Stuttgart 1960, esp. pp. 306–7, 336; R. Dahrendorf, *Society and Democracy in Germany*, London 1968, pp. 402–3.

17

Resistance and Mass Loyalty
Women on Both Sides

If we compare Nazism's ideological attitudes towards women with the regime's actual policies, the contradictions are obvious. Although a woman's place was supposed to be with the family, mothers continued to work in all sectors of the economy. Single women were by no means limited to 'womanly' occupations either. Motherhood – eulogised and venerated as the life-long vocation of every German woman – was reduced to a short period between giving birth and sending children to school. Beyond that, a mother had her job; but the influence she was able to wield over her children was vastly curtailed. National Socialist propaganda had promised largely to exclude women from public life, and to return them to the private domain; but the state apparatus simultaneously encroached upon the family sphere, leaving neither women nor children unaffected. As millions of women were embraced by Nazi mass organisations and hundreds of thousands were appointed to positions of minor leadership, foreign observers never ceased to be amazed at the extent to which these supposedly 'private' German women were being politically mobilised. Some observers are of the opinion that, notwithstanding numerous verbal assurances to the contrary, the emancipation of women made 'great leaps forward'[1] during the Third Reich and particularly during the war, while others are more cautious, declaring that some women in selected female spheres experienced no more than 'substitute emancipation'.[2]

In fact not a single woman managed to rise to the decision-making centres of the party state. In this respect the Third Reich was no different to the parliamentary systems that preceded and followed it. Its novelty lay, rather, in the fact that the National Socialist elite publicly boasted its exclusive and aggressive male

1. S. Haffner, *The Meaning of Hitler*, trans. E. Osers, London 1979, p. 36.
2. Mason, 'Women in Germany' p. 101.

character, while democratically constituted institutions tend not to portray themselves in terms of gender. Nor was the segregation and hierarchical arrangement of male and female spheres of influence a feature of Nazism alone, for in the Weimar Republic female politicians and Party members had been concerned with – indeed were only allowed to be concerned with – issues relating to female experience. National Socialism took up this paradigm of distinct domains of political responsibilities, but by comparison with other movements its ideologues had far less trouble openly defending it. Indeed, it went further: in attempting to integrate into the political system the whole of society, or in this case the *Volksgemeinschaft*, and not only its male half, and to envelop all in organisational structures which generated loyalty, National Socialism created a plethora of public offices that allowed women to participate in the exercise of state power. Hundreds of thousands, even millions, of women worked as honorary and paid officials in the mass organisations of the *Frauenschaft*, the National Socialist People's Welfare, the German Labour Front, the League of German Girls and so forth. Their brief was to do the bidding of their Party superiors and advise, educate, guide and organise their female clientele, deterring them from certain occupations while encouraging them in others. There is no doubt that the regime consciously offered women this opportunity to become involved in precisely circumscribed areas of activity in lieu of true equality. From the women's point of view, however, it meant involvement in public life and recognition to a far greater degree than ever before.

One of these women was Melita Maschmann. As a full-time official she enjoyed a meteoric, though by no means unusual, rise to the top. Having joined the BDM (the League of German Girls) at the age of fifteen in 1933, she was soon promoted to the position of BDM Press and Propaganda Officer, and was also the leader of a Reich Labour Service camp for young women. The inhabitants of the village where the camp was situated accepted her as a 'representative of the National Socialist leadership', and entrusted important community tasks to her. Although she was not in a position to impose sanctions on behaviour, her very office was sufficient to secure her obedience and effective authority.[3] In her capacity as BDM Press Officer she had a further share of power, and was able to issue instructions to male subordinates.

3. M. Maschmann, *Fazit: Mein Weg in der Hitler-Jugend*, Munich 1983, esp. pp. 116ff.

There were many Melita Maschmanns in the Third Reich, though not all of them climbed so high up the official ladder. Nazi mass organisations were structured on a strictly vertical basis, with a myriad of departments and divisions arranged hierarchically. Hence the existence of numerous positions of leadership. The *Frauenschaft*, for example, included 223,024 unit, 59,802 cell, 22,593 local, 725 district and 32 Gau (region) level leaders. Over one million of the approximately 3,300,000 women in the *Frauenschaft* and *Frauenwerk* in 1939 held some official position.[4] In the *Frauenschaft* they were responsible for the ideological and political development of members, collected membership dues, distributed propaganda and headed the organisation's weekly evening meetings. In the *Frauenwerk* they concentrated on their clientele's domestic and mothering skills, helped set up training centres for mothers and, in the tradition of bourgeois women's associations, ran welfare schemes. Activists, most of whom came from the (petty) bourgeoisie, invited women to attend courses on sewing, cooking and infant care, organised housewives' afternoons and cookery demonstrations, worked in neighbourhood care, visited the sick in hospital, sent presents to children whose fathers had been killed in action, and ran what was known 'Operation Patchwork' (*Flickbeutelaktionen*), in which women from the *Frauenwerk* mended clothes for large working-class families.[5] Although most of these functions were honorary and unremunerated, for the women involved they meant public recognition, a rise in political status, and the chance to exercise power, none of which should be underestimated.

Membership of the League of German Girls was also an opportunity for participation and promotion. Like other Party bodies, it comprised an impressive number of subdivisions with corresponding positions of intermediate leadership. About ten girls formed a *Mädelschaft* or team, which was under the command of a team leader. Four teams made a *Schar*, or company, four companies a group, between three and five groups a ring, between four and six rings an *Untergau*, while twenty *Untergaue* comprised an *Obergau*. The thirty-five *Obergaue* were subordinate to the overall Leader of the Reich Youth (*Reichsjugendführer*). Bearing in mind that the League of German Girls had 600,000 members by the end of 1933, it is easy to estimate the number of girls who were able to act as leaders

---

4. Dammer, 'Kinder, Küche, Kriegsarbeit', p. 224.
5. See Tidl, *Die Frau im Nationalsozialismus*, pp. 106ff., on the range of activities in which the *Frauenschaft* and the *Frauenwerk* were involved.

at the various levels.[6] In accordance with the principle of putting 'youth in charge of youth', special training courses and conferences taught girls how to hold positions of responsibility, even when they were still quite young. They had little influence over superiors, and the *Reichsjugendführer*, as well as the chief officials of the various specialist departments, were always male; but for their subordinates – the girls they were in charge of, and these girls' parents – they were figures of state authority, and hence had some personal power. In their role as miniature Führers they were enmeshed in a meticulously designed system both of duties and responsibilities, and of rights and privileges, which the Nazi regime employed to make its *Volksgemeinschaft* loyal and disciplined.

Even 'ordinary' members of Nazi mass organisations were part of this elaborate construction that made all previous attempts to administer society on such a large scale pale into insignificance. The leader of the German Labour Front, Robert Ley, sketched out the underlying scheme in this way: 'We start when a child is three years old. As soon as he even starts to think, he's given a little flag to wave. Then comes school, the Hitler Youth, the SA, and military service. But when all that is over, we don't let go of anyone. The Labour Front takes hold of them again, and keeps hold until they go to their grave, whether they like it or not.'[7] Ley may have had boys in mind when he said this, but in practice the regimented beguilement applied to girls and women too. At the age of ten they entered the Hitler Youth, spending the first four years in the Young Girls (*Jungmädel*) section, the next four with the BDM proper, and then (after 1938 at least) they moved on to another BDM body, 'Faith and Beauty' (*Glaube und Schönheit*). At twenty-one they transferred either to the *Frauenschaft* or to the *Frauenwerk*. Along the way they had six months of labour service or, depending on their intended occupation, the Year of Duty in the domestic or agricultural sector. They were under the constant supervision of the Führer, whose watchful eye, though distant and indirect, bound them to faithful and selfless devotion towards the *Volk*.

In 1939 a regulation was introduced requiring every German girl of 'Aryan' blood to be part of the 'State Youth'. As members of an alien race Jewish girls were excluded. But even before this date more than half of all young people belonged to the Hitlerian youth

---

6. Klaus, *BDM*, p. 89. In the Hitler Youth as a whole there were 403,000 male and female leaders in 1935, and as many as 720,000 three years later (ibid., pp. 89, 93).
7. Quoted in ibid., p. 139.

organisation; even in 1936, 60 per cent of all those between ten and eighteen belonged, although the percentage was initially much lower among girls than boys. In 1932 girls accounted for a quarter of the total membership, and it was six years before the difference had been eroded.[8] Although membership was voluntary, schools and Nazi institutions put a great deal of pressure on the young to join up. Often places on training courses could be procured only with the aid of a Hitler Youth membership card, and from 1935 onwards applications for posts in the civil service were successful only if the candidate had been active in the movement. In most cases, however, such incentives were unnecessary: children and teenagers seemed interested enough in Nazi organisations without having to be prompted. For many the opportunity of being involved in a youth group was most appealing: you could get away from your parents for a while, meet people of your own age and 'do a bit of living'.

Unlike anything that had preceded it, National Socialism understood perfectly how to institutionalise youth as a particular social role, and to mould its form and content. Thirteen-year-old *Jungmädel* and *Pimpfe*, the girls and boys in the Hitlerian organisations for young teenagers, did not feel like children; but at the same time they were not adults either. By giving young people their own organisations, codes of behaviour, uniform, obligations and responsibilities, the Nazi regime managed to lend this transitional phase of personal development a tangible, precisely defined shape. The opportunities the Hitler Youth offered must have seemed particularly attractive to girls, who, in comparison to boys, were much more closely tied to the family. A youth group provided at least temporary escape from the restrictions and duties that typified female socialisation; the chance to shake off the bonds of omnipresent maternal authority for a few hours represented a slice of personal freedom not be scorned, even if this freedom had its limits within a BDM group. For being commanded by a 'leader' who was only slightly older than oneself was something fundamentally different from having to do housework or darn socks while mother looked on. Any team leader with a modicum of imagination had no trouble turning her girls into enthusiastic BDM members, particularly since youth groups offered exciting leisure activities such as camping,

---

8. D. Reese, 'Bund Deutscher Mädel – Zur Geschichte der weiblichen deutschen Jugend im Dritten Reich', in *Mutterkreuz*, pp. 163–87, quote at p. 174; Kater, 'Frauen in der NS-Bewegung', p. 221.

bicycle rides, hiking trips with overnight stays in youth hostels, and sport. In much the same way as their brothers, girls went off on tours, engaged in organised outdoor activities and entered sports competitions. Hardly any groups ever mentioned 'settling down in a cosy home'; less attention was paid to Hitler's dictum that one day all girls would be mothers than to the sections of *Mein Kampf* in which he stressed the necessity of 'physical fitness' through sport and competition for women as well as men.

Although the educational concepts applied to the girls of the BDM and to the boys in the Hitler Youth were not noticeably different, great emphasis was placed upon the organisational separation of the sexes. When girls held their evening events in their hostels, or went off camping at the weekends, there were, naturally, no males present. It was only on official occasions that the BDM and the Hitler Youth appeared together. This structural principle was yet a further expression of the fundamental National Socialist political and pedagogical tenet that women and men belonged to separate domains, and that any tendencies which might ignore or transcend gender barriers were to be stamped out. However, because efforts to 'equalise' the sexes in Weimar Germany had made little impact, the institutional re-enshrinement of sexual segregation appeared less revolutionary than might at first seem to be the case. Most young people took such segregation for granted, particularly since it added to their own group's homogeneity and camaraderie.

To the ears of most girls (and boys) in youth organisations, words such as comradeship, and the idea of being together with people of their own age, must have had a magic ring. In her autobiographical novel *A Model Childhood*, Christa Wolf describes how ten-year-old Nelly found her first evening with the *Jungmädel*, and how on the way home it was fun

to become familiar with a new word by repeating it to herself: 'comradeship' meant the promise of a loftier kind of life . . . far removed also from the white figure in the store smock who was standing outside waiting for Nelly: her mother had probably been waiting for a long time. Where had she been this late? She should wipe her feet well, she had probably walked through every puddle in town. What had she been doing? Singing? You can sing at home just as well. Not a word about 'comradeship' . . . Where Micky [the team leader] sang and played and marched with them and taught them games, there was something her mother couldn't give her, something she didn't want to miss.[9]

9. C. Wolf, *A Model Childhood*, trans. U. Malinero and H. Rappolt, London 1983, pp. 189–90. Renate Finckh, a jeweller's daughter, also recalls the 'wonderful

If the mother's reaction to the time, energy and emotion her daughter invested in the BDM was marked by distrust, scepticism and jealousy, it would merely spur the girl on to even greater commitment, as a way of expressing her need finally to cut the umbilical ties and to start leading her own life. Melita Maschmann speaks of the same kind of generation gap. She wanted to distance herself from her authoritarian, elitist and conservative mother, so in 1933 she joined the BDM, secretly, and against the will of her parents whose sympathies lay with the German Nationalists.

Christa Wolf's parents kept a grocery store, whereas Melita Maschmann came from a middle-class family who had a chauffeur and several servants. The 'young lady' was fascinated by the National Socialist idea of a classless, organic national community, threw off the class values she had acquired from her family, and joined her comrades from the working class and lower middle class in the League of German Girls, to 'help build a *Volksgemeinschaft* in which people would live together as one family'.[10] She refused to join the youth group of the League of Queen Louise, which existed until 1934, because there she would find only the 'arrogant, superficial and boring' girls from backgrounds similar to her own. The members of the League looked down on the young Nazi girls, whose social origins and general demeanour seemed far too 'common' (even though their political ideals were almost identical).[11] In other words, things that appealed to some were objectionable to others. Many girls threw themselves into the sporting and girl guide-type activities that the Hitler Youth offered, and enjoyed the adventure of trekking through the countryside, sitting round campfires, and taking part in competitions. Others were put off precisely by the unfeminine conduct encouraged in the *Jungmädel* and BDM. Older girls tended to have less time for the ethos of paramilitary service, with its uniforms and compulsory labour. Neither were they all absolutely thrilled by the idea of becoming 'fully trained' for their future roles as housewives and mothers, which was the womanly vocation recommended by the BDM leadership from

---

feeling of "us"' in the Hitler Youth. She found in it her 'emotional home, a safe and secure refuge, and not long after I joined [the BDM], where I was given status'; R. Finckh in conversation with H. Mundzeck in C. Schüddekopf (ed.), *Der alltägliche Faschismus: Frauen im Dritten Reich*, Berlin 1982, pp. 69–79, quote at p. 71. See also R. Finckh, *Mit uns zieht die neue Zeit*, Baden-Baden 1979, and the accounts by girls and young women of their experiences under Fascism in H. Thurnwald, *Gegenwartsprobleme Berliner Familien*, Berlin 1948, pp. 152–68.

10. Maschmann, *Fazit*, p. 21.
11. Koonz, 'Competition', p. 212.

1936 onwards, not least because of increasing antipathy towards the encouragement of masculinity in female youth.[12] Sixteen- and seventeen-year-olds were not very keen on all-girls folk dancing either: they would have preferred to be listening to American jazz and dancing with young men. For them the BDM represented yet another one of those unpleasant obligatory organisations. The pressure to conform mounted even further after 1939: as the specifically youth-oriented, and hence more palatable, activities of the girls' groups were curtailed, compulsory service and the deployment of 'voluntary' labour became more common. The state harnessed the priceless labour power of its youth wherever it could: to pick vegetables and collect money for winter relief schemes, distribute ration cards, work the land and gather the harvest, answer the telephone in government offices, or help the armed forces spot enemy aircraft.[13]

Despite the intensified pressure, open resistance to compulsory service in the Hitler Youth after 1939 was sporadic and infrequent. Most girls were fairly happy to take part, and many were promoted to the position of 'Leader'. Some, however, did try to avoid recruitment, and a number joined opposition groups, such as the mainly middle-class 'Swing' gangs in northern Germany which rejected the system's codes of behaviour, or the proletarian 'Edelweiss Pirates', who actively fought the regime. The church also was to some extent a breeding ground for protest. Autonomous Catholic youth groups emerged, for example (official Catholic organisations had been dissolved in 1937); some in the Protestant Confessional Church attacked the religious 'heresies' of German Christians, thereby gradually distancing themselves politically from the National Socialist regime. Though they tended to work behind the scenes, women played an important role here,[14] as they did in the organised resistance of the illegal workers' movement. After left-wing bodies had been broken up, and the more prominent members had either emigrated or been arrested, it was frequently up to women to maintain existing contacts and establish new groups. Working in front organisations and local neighbourhoods, they tried to keep underground activity alive, smuggling leaflets in prams, hiding wanted men in their homes, supporting the families of those who

---

12. Klaus, *BDM*, pp. 93ff.
13. Reese, 'Bund Deutscher Mädel', pp. 174ff.
14. W. See and R. Weckerling, *Frauen im Kirchenkampf: Beispiele aus der Bekennenden Kirche Berlin-Brandenburg 1933–1945*, Berlin 1984; G. Szepansky, *Frauen leisten Widerstand: 1933–1945*, Frankfurt 1983, pp. 57ff., 107ff., 276ff.

had been interned or murdered. This everyday form of resistance, which was always dangerous, may not have been so stunning as the organised actions of the Red Chapel, the White Rose or the conspirators of 20 July 1944, but it corresponded to women's more limited opportunities for mounting much more than logistical and welfare back-up.[15]

Despite the many taps the resistance managed to deliver to the regime's heels, and irrespective of its more spectacular actions, which were punished with Draconian severity, the Nazi leadership's fears of a stab in the back akin to that of 1918 were unfounded. The mainly female home front stood firm: though acts of sabotage became more frequent, there was no sign of the mass strikes that had occurred in the First World War; though dissatisfaction with difficult working and living conditions became more pronounced, food riots and hunger protests did not break out. It was not only the terror, the network of police spies and informants and the constant look-out for 'subversive' and 'treacherous' statements that kept the population submissive until the bitter end; the inspirational force of the *Volksgemeinschaft*, the national community standing by its Führer through thick and thin, continued to shine bright, fading little even in the shadow of evacuations, air raids and rising casualty lists. Direct, mass protest could never have developed: the organisational and ideological embrace of National Socialism was far too firm and all-encompassing, particularly for women. Even if most of the twelve million women in the numerous Nazi organisations of 1939 were not themselves ardent National Socialists, twelve years of being educated and bombarded with propaganda by the *Volksgemeinschaft* cannot have left individual consciousness and collective memory unmarked. In addition the impact of welfare measures – marriage loans, child benefit, holidays for mothers, better protection of mothers – reinforced popular loyalty.[16] Thanks to the German Labour Front's programme of 'Energy through Joy' (*Kraft durch Freude* – KDF), many families from the lower classes had been able to go on holiday for the first

15. This is a major reason why resistance by women is often overlooked. For recently published works which look at this question using a systematic and biographical approach, see Kuhn and Rothe, *Frauen im deutschen Faschismus*, vol. II, pp. 143ff.; Elling, *Frauen im deutschen Widerstand*; Szepansky, *Frauen leisten Widerstand: 1933–1945*; G. Schefer, 'Wo Unterdrückung ist, da ist auch Widerstand – Frauen gegen Faschismus und Krieg', in *Mutterkreuz*, pp. 273–291; Jacobeit and Thoms-Heinrich, *Kreuzweg Ravensbrück*.

16. See the oral history interviews by A.-K. Einfeldt, 'Auskommen – Durchkommen – Weiterkommen', in Niethammer (ed.), '*Die Jahre weiss man nicht*', pp. 267–96.

time ever: in 1938 alone, 10,300,000 people had a vacation, while 54,600,000 took part in sport and leisure activities organised by KDF.[17] Moreover, we simply have to remember that compulsory service for women was only gradually enforced (and even then never fully), and that every effort was made to maintain adequate food supplies, to realise that the political elite was at great pains to keep up the spirits of the female home front, especially during the war.

The suppression and crushing of any radical political alternative was certain to render all the more effective a policy that wielded both the incentive of welfare benefits and social palliatives and the deterrent of denunciation and execution. By contrast with the situation in 1914–18, there were no organisations, parties or associations in Germany which could have ignited and mobilised any latent forces of resistance. The Catholic and Protestant churches might have filled the gap, but they were either too deeply integrated into the system, or had been muzzled by terror.[18] In exterminating its opponents, National Socialism demonstrated a degree of efficiency that at the time was matched only by Stalinism.

The system was little worried by whether these opponents were men or women. Once women had been branded as 'enemies of the Reich', neither pregnancy nor motherhood could save them from arrest or murder. Even when choosing its torturers the Nazi regime did not create a strict sexual division of labour. Between 1942 and 1945 some 3,500 women were trained as SS guards in the women's concentration camp at Ravensbrück and assigned to the women's sections of other camps.[19] Many had volunteered in answer to newspaper advertisements which promised high wages, good conditions and chances of promotion. They acted no differently from their male colleagues, torturing and abusing women prisoners, crushing babies against walls, and killing children while their mothers were forced to look on. They selected suitable women for work and for medical experiments, and sent the rest to the gas

17. Mason, *Sozialpolitik*, p. 185; H. Spode, 'Arbeiterurlaub im Dritten Reich', in Sachse et al., *Angst*, pp. 275–328.

18. Hardly any information on the role of religious women's organisations that continued to exist, for example, through affiliation to the German Women's Enterprise is available which could be fruitfully used for academic research. For an outline of the Evangelical Women's Enterprise (*Evangelisches Frauenwerk*) see G. von Norden, 'Frauenbild und Widerstand: Zur Situation des evangelischen Frauenwerkes im "Dritten Reich"', in G. von Norden and F. Mybes, *Evangelische Frauen im Dritten Reich*, Düsseldorf 1979, pp. 7–29, and J.-C. Kaiser, *Frauen in der Kirche*, Düsseldorf 1985, pp. 163ff; Koonz, *Mothers in the Fatherland*, ch. 7.

19. Schmidt and Dietz, *Frauen unterm Hakenkreuz*, p. 138.

chambers. Only hairstyle and clothing differentiated them from the men of the SS.

The sexual differences so greatly emphasised by National Socialist ideology were blurred both by 'unity in death' and 'unity in suffering'; in surveying the scenes of destroyed cities too, the eye could no longer make out the 'natural' inequalities. Ursula von Kardorff, a journalist in Berlin, noted in her diary in 1944:

The creature dressed in trousers, putting out incendiary bombs like a fireman; hacking a way into caved-in cellars with a pickaxe; perched on a rooftop in a steel helmet, keeping firewatch; dragging furniture out of burning rooms; estimating the damage done by anti-aircraft fire and air raids as well as any trained artilleryman; this sexless, brave, competent being: is it really still a woman? Does it still need protecting? Women have stopped fainting and having migraines; they are no longer moody, nor are they creatures of luxury: now they are beasts of burden.[20]

These beasts of burden had little in common with the National Socialist woman portrayed in the speeches and writings of the more prominent Party officials. The system had fallen far short of its declared aim to offer women 'the chance once again to fulfil their true duty and mission: motherhood and the family' (Goebbels in 1933). Long before the war had even started, policy had in practice begun to deviate from ideology: the percentage of married women and mothers in the workforce had never been as high as it was in 1939, and very few women had been persuaded by pro-natal propaganda to have more than two children.

Viewed against the background of Weimar Germany, National Socialism does not appear to be a 'regression' into dark and distant days of discrimination against women; it was, rather, a highly ambiguous period in history which witnessed a unique confluence of 'modernist' and 'traditionalist' tendencies. In a few areas, such as voting rights, access to the upper echelons of the civil service, and family planning, the fruits of hard fought battles were destroyed; in many areas (most notably with respect to the labour market), the Nazi state represented but a smooth continuation of existing structures and processes, together with all their unfavourable aspects (lower wages and less upward mobility). By contrast, where youth policy, divorce laws and social organisations were concerned, the Third Reich offered women novel opportunities for participation and recognition in public life, and, indeed, many women benefited in an unprecedented fashion from such socio-political innovation.

20. U. von Kardorff, *Berliner Aufzeichnungen 1942–1945*, Munich 1982, p. 127.

Obviously such opportunities were not designed to aid emancipation; within the logic of the system, they were meant to make women malleable and accommodating, further the regime's domestic stability, and reinforce population policy. Yet in this respect National Socialism was not fundamentally different from the polities that preceded and succeeded it; neither did its vile intentions detract from the actual effect of the opportunities it created. For these reasons recent works on Nazism, notwithstanding their authors' understandable abhorrence of the regime's barbarism, fail to provide a convincing account when they describe the period in terms of 'degradation' with 'disastrous consequences . . . for women's campaign for emancipation', or as 'regression into an existence marked by humiliation and deprivation of rights'.[21] This kind of interpretation not only tends to exaggerate the gains made by the women's movement, and to paint too rosy a picture of sexual equality in the Weimar Republic; it is also misleading in that it calls political ideology social reality. The contention here is not that the National Socialist regime did not adopt a posture that was as anti-modern as it was anti-feminist. But it should not be forgotten that the actual outcome of policy was sometimes different, and often diametrically opposed, to its intended effects. Moreover an approach which holds that Nazism exercised absolute tutelage and deprived citizens of their rights, tempts us to regard women as nothing but victims of an omnipotent, totalitarian polity which excluded them, and as the helpless prey of a chauvinist, elitist band of male rulers. The logical conclusion from this argument is that if women allowed themselves to be 'mastered' by an instrument of repression for a whole twelve years, they must have been pitifully stupid, naive and cowardly. The immense ability of the regime to mobilise the population, and the relative rarity of deliberate acts of political resistance, however,

---

21. Wiggershaus, *Frauen unterm Nationalsozialismus*, p. 5; R. Thalmann, *Frausein im Dritten Reich*, Munich 1984, introduction. See also Koonz, 'Competition'; Schmidt and Dietz, *Frauen unterm Hakenkreuz*; Tidl, *Die Frau im Nationalsozialismus*. The thesis that National Socialism applied a constant and long-term brake on the emancipation of women is also untenable if Germany is compared with other countries. Female participation in the labour force developed similarly in countries with other systems of government, while in social policy (protection of mothers and child benefit), Germany was way ahead of its neighbours. French women were not given the vote until 1945, and neither in France nor in Britain, where female suffrage was introduced in 1918 and 1928, did female involvement in politics advance any more quickly than in Germany. Many states in the USA had legislation on sterilisation that was similar to that of the Nazis; Mother's Day has been a national holiday in France since 1920; and both France and the USSR meted out Draconian punishments for abortion and bestowed money and public honour upon women who were particularly fertile.

suggest that women who satisfied the political, racial and social requirements – and the vast majority did – did not perceive the Third Reich as a women's hell. Much of what it introduced was doubtless appealing, the rest one learned to accept, and, in a state which also denied many political rights to most men, the lack of opportunity for involvement in decision-making cannot have been particularly worrying.

V
Opportunities and Limitations in the New Republic 1945–1988

18

A Fearful Peace
Hunger Replaces Bombing in Post-War Germany

On 8 May 1945, when Hitler's successor, Dönitz, announced the unconditional surrender of the Third Reich, few Germans felt that they had been liberated from a barbaric, inhuman, criminal regime. It was left to the surviving victims of National Socialist rule, to the millions of conscripted labourers, prisoners of war, concentration camp inmates, and others who had suffered racial or political persecution, to experience the day as one of salvation and liberation. The mass of 'good' Germans were not celebrating: on the contrary, they perceived the surrender as a defeat and a humiliation. The whole of Germany was occupied by Allied troops, who did not exactly handle the population with kid gloves. 'They talk of re-educating us for freedom and democracy and poke their noses into everyone's business', wrote Ursula von Kardorff, herself certainly no supporter of National Socialism, of her experiences in the American Zone. 'You feel as though you were sitting in the class-room and continually having your knuckles rapped, and even the best behaved student will eventually react to such treatment with wilful stubbornness.'[1] Few Germans were able or willing to face the fact that they had for twelve years supported, or at least tolerated, a regime that was guilty of countless crimes against humanity. In April 1945 an American intelligence officer reported that 'the German people completely lack any sense of their defeat and its implications . . . Even those Germans who recognise the "collective guilt of the German nation" seldom number themselves among the guilty'.[2] Bourgeois circles, industrialists and higher officials were particularly reluctant to recognise the break with the previous

1. von Kardorff, *Berliner Aufzeichnungen*, p. 270.
2. U. Bosdorf and L. Niethammer (eds), *Zwischen Befreiung und Besatzung: Analysen des US-Geheimdienstes über Positionen und Strukturen deutscher Politik 1945*, Wuppertal 1977, p. 38.

order: their motto was 'continuity and preservation' and they hoped for the support of the Western powers in their efforts to rebuild the economy and the administration on the basis of time-honoured patterns of ownership and authority.[3]

Those outside the ranks of the bourgeoisie, most of whom had been left with nothing to preserve, were less concerned with continuity and more interested in political change. In many cities middle-class residential districts had been spared the bombing, while in working- and lower-middle-class quarters there was often not a stone left standing. Millions of people had lost not only their homes but all their household possessions, and by the end of the war had nothing but the clothes on their backs. Having experienced total loss, they were better prepared to distance themselves from National Socialism and to hazard a new beginning without political compromises. Anti-capitalist feeling was widespread and the call for denazification and democratisation found a ready response. Many districts formed their own anti-fascist committees where former trade unionists, Social Democrats and Communists came together with representatives of church organisations to seek solutions to the pressing problems posed by the desire for self-government and political reorientation, and to the need to recruit new administrative personnel.[4] The first priority was to provide food and shelter for the population: in view of the catastrophic living conditions in most cities all other considerations took second place.

About a quarter of all dwellings had been destroyed by the effects of war: in the cities it may have been as many as half or more. To add to this, the flight, deportation or resettlement of more than ten million Germans from the Eastern Territories, which now belonged to Poland or Russia, as well as from Czechoslovakia, Rumania, Poland itself and Hungary, led to an unimaginable housing shortage. In 1946 there were fourteen million households and eight million available dwellings.[5] Citizens whose homes were intact or only slightly damaged had to make rooms available to refugees or to families who had become homeless, with the result that tensions and arguments among the people increased as each day passed. Fuel was in short supply, and during the cold winters that followed the war

3. Ibid., document 11, esp. pp. 145–55.
4. L. Niethammer et al. (eds), *Arbeiterinitiative 1945: Antifaschistische Ausschüsse und Reorganisation der Arbeiterbewegung in Deutschland*, Wuppertal 1977.
5. C. Kleßmann, *Die doppelte Staatsgründung: Deutsche Geschichte 1945–55*, Göttingen 1982, pp. 39ff., 52; J. Kocka, '1945: Neubeginn oder Restauration?' in C. Stern and H. A. Winkler (eds), *Wendepunkte deutscher Geschichte 1848–1945*, Frankfurt 1979, pp. 143–4.

there were many deaths from hypothermia, especially among the elderly. Even more critical was the food situation. Although control and rationing of food supplies had come into force as early as 1935, Germans had adequate food supplies even during the war years – at the expense of people in occupied territories and in concentration and forced labour camps. In contrast to the First World War, hunger began only after hostilities had ended. 'During the war,' recalled a Berlin woman, 'we were bombed, but had assurance of getting food supplies; when the war ended there were no more bombing raids but there was also nothing to eat.'[6] Officially every citizen had a right to a grocery ration which was graded according to profession or occupation, and which could be purchased by means of ration cards in the shops and stores. In Berlin white-collar workers were allowed a daily consumption of 400 grams of bread, 40 g. meat, 10 g. fat, 20 g. sugar, 40 g. assorted foodstuffs (oatmeal, ground rice, etc.) and 400 g. potatoes, while manual workers, especially those engaged in heavy labour, received more of everything. The levels were much lower for 'non-employed family members' such as housewives, children and pensioners; only potatoes were available to all in the same quantity.[7] In the British Zone the calorific value of daily rations distributed in April 1946 averaged 1146; those living in the French Zone were worse off still, while those in the American Zone did somewhat better.[8] But even these minimal levels often had to be reduced, because the loss of farmland in the Eastern Territories, poor harvests and transport difficulties meant that foodstuffs simply were not available in sufficient quantities. The winter of 1946–7 in particular brought the food shortage to crisis proportions, and in many cities this led to hunger marches and strikes.

This situation of acute shortage was especially hard on women. Traditionally, after all, it was up to them to keep the family adequately fed and clothed and to maintain a warm, clean and comfortable home. It had been difficult enough to live up to these expectations during the war; the end of the war brought, instead of an immediate improvement, a whole host of additional and seemingly intractable difficulties. Only very rarely could women count on any help from men, for nearly four million men had died in

6. Quoted in S. Meyer and E. Schulze, *Wie wir das alles geschafft haben: Alleinstehende Frauen berichten über ihr Leben nach 1945*, Munich 1984, p. 92.
7. Ibid., p. 91.
8. A.-E. Freier, 'Frauenfragen sind Lebensfragen' in A.-E. Freier and A. Kuhn (eds), *Frauen in der Geschichte*, vol. v, Düsseldorf 1984, pp. 18–50, quote at p. 28.

battle, and in 1945 11,700,000 were prisoners of war. It was to be ten years or more before the last German troops came home. Thus millions of women had to fend for themselves and their children without the aid of a male 'provider' and head of household. For them, the end of the Third Reich heralded no new beginning, no *'Stunde Null'* ('zero hour'), but rather a continuation of their toil under straitened circumstances. In the first weeks and months following the occupation they also came to know defeat and the 'right of the victor nations' in a particularly harsh and literal way when it was acted out on their own bodies: in the Russian and French Zones, rape was frequent.[9] In the Western Zones the borderline between rape and prostitution was often a fluid one: many American and British soldiers paid for their pleasures in cigarettes, chocolate and bread. Both young girls and married women had liaisons with members of the occupying forces, and the women's families, who gained materially from these contacts, generally turned a blind eye. Children were overjoyed at the gifts these strangers brought, and 'a ten year old boy, on hearing of such things from other children, wished with all his heart for an "Englishman" for his mother so that she need not go hungry any longer'.[10]

But most women had to get by without an 'Englishman' or an 'American'. They queued at food shops and government offices, exchanged items of value they had salvaged for butter and eggs on the black market, organised foraging expeditions and persuaded farmers' wives to part with a few potatoes or some bacon in exchange for clothing or household items that had been well preserved. The men's war was over, but the women's battle for bread and coal continued, growing ever more bitter and desperate as provisions and supplies became scarcer. In Cologne at the end of 1945 only one in eight children attained the normal weight for their age, and by the middle of 1946 the average weight of adult males in the American Zone was reckoned at about eight stones (112 lb.).[11]

9. See accounts and descriptions in A. Kuhn and D. Schubert, 'Frauen in der Nachkriegszeit und im Wirtschaftswunder 1945–1960', in *Frauenalltag und Frauenbewegung im 20. Jahrhundert*, vol. IV., Frankfurt 1980, pp. 9–10; von Kardorff, *Berliner Aufzeichnungen*, pp. 297–8; Meyer and Schulze, *Wie wir das alles geschafft haben*, pp. 63ff.; Bordorf and Niethammer, *Zwischen Befreiung und Besatzung*, p. 73.

10. Thurnwald, *Gegenwartsprobleme Berliner Familien*, pp. 197, 146–7. See also L. Niethammer, 'Privat-Wirtschaft', in Niethammer (ed.), *'Hinterher merkt man, daß es richtig war, daß es schiefgegangen ist': Nachkriegserfahrungen im Ruhrgebiet*, Berlin 1983, pp. 17–105, esp. pp. 22ff.

11. Kocka, '1945: Neubeginn oder Restauration?', p. 144.

But malnutrition, emaciation and exhaustion were diagnosed not only among men and children, especially since the military authorities, who established daily ration quotas for the German population, were of the opinion that non-employed women could make do with a minimal calorie intake. The idea that housework done with little or no nourishment could cause as much stress and strain as work in a rolling-mill or a machine shop never occurred to these male officers and bureaucrats. Doctors and social workers pointed out that housewives were particularly prone to chronic exhaustion and that this could only be alleviated by better nourishment. Instead, however, many women were doing without a part of their own ration and giving it to their husbands and children.[12] A study of 498 families living in Berlin in the years 1946/47 came to the following conclusion: 'The burden of day-to-day work carried out by most women has become not only more complex and difficult, but is also increasing disproportionately to the scant opportunity they have to recover their strength through eating and sleeping.'[13] To ensure survival from one day to the next, women had to do an enormous amount of work, using the maximum available time and energy. After they had queued for hours to obtain the allotted rations – and in this they were by no means always successful – they had to begin an intensive process of food preparation. A great deal of ingenuity and imagination went into the daily task of conjuring up an edible meal out of ground rice, pearl barley and potatoes. Women who lived on the land or who could call a small allotment their own were considerably better off. They could grow potatoes, fruit and vegetables and trade the surplus for other foodstuffs and necessities. But town-dwellers' balconies also were turned over to vegetable gardening and keeping small livestock. Many communities provided families with garden space or with allotments in order to help them provide for themselves. The authorities called upon people to gather mushrooms and nuts as supplementary and substitute provisions; in 1946 in the Rhine-Palatinate alone three million kilogrammes of beech nuts were collected, yielding 700,000 litres of oil.[14]

These tasks were seen as extensions of housework and were undertaken almost entirely by women (and children), who tried to

---

12. See contemporary accounts and documents in D. Schubert, *Frauen in der deutschen Nachkriegszeit*, vol. I: *Frauenarbeit 1945–1949*, Düsseldorf 1984, pp. 164ff.
13. Thurnwald, *Gegenwartsprobleme Berliner Familien*, p. 86.
14. Freier, *Frauenfragen sind Lebensfragen*, pp. 40, 49.

fill the gaps in provision by a Herculean effort of self-exploitation. But for this, a substantial proportion of the population of Germany would have starved to death. Women's work went even further than the provision and preparation of food. Clothes had to be washed and mended, no easy task in view of the shortage of soap and thread. Women's magazines published tips on how to get clothes clean, in the absence of soap, by using ivy leaves, chestnuts, potato peelings and ox-gall. Rips and holes in clothes and stockings could be invisibly mended with human hair. The motto was 'old into new'; discarded suits and military greatcoats were turned into women's and children's clothes.[15] Since economic reconstruction was a lengthy and halting process, and the production of raw materials and capital goods took precedence, many household items for daily use were simply not available, and women had to make do with labour-intensive substitutes. But even after the currency reform of 1948, when the long-awaited consumer goods were offered in shop windows for sale to those with 'hard' German marks, most families could not afford very many of the new luxuries and had to continue with their regime of thrift.

The Allied military governments encouraged and indeed expected the people to help themselves, because initially their policy was to solve the problems of the occupied country with a minimum of outside aid. To ensure that Germany would be able to finance its own reconstruction, as well as war reparations to former 'enemy states', with a minimum of delay, priority had to be given to stepping up industrial production – indeed, 80–90 per cent of the most vital productive plant in the Western Zones was undamaged. This required a workforce, and the foreign prisoners of war and conscripted labourers who had made up 29 per cent of all workers in 1944 were no longer available. As early as the summer of 1945 the Allied Control Council gave orders that every man between the ages of fourteen and sixty-five, and every woman between the ages of fifteen and fifty who had no children or dependent relatives to care for, was to register at the appropriate employment office where he or she could be called up for compulsory service if required. This was aimed primarily at former National Socialists and their families, but even unemployed men and women who were not politically compromised were required to perform heavy labour for a minimal wage, clearing away mountains of rubble and repairing damaged houses, factories and roads. In Berlin alone in the summer of 1945

15. Schubert, *Frauen in der deutschen Nachkriegszeit*, pp. 196ff.

some 40–60,000 *Trümmerfrauen* – women whose job was to clear away the rubble – were at work.

Many women were also employed in the building trade and in industry, at least as long as a male workforce was not available. The rigid barrier between men's and women's work had been lifted during the war, and this was allowed to continue, especially since the traditional 'women's industries' – textiles, clothing and food production – were operating only on a limited scale. Women continued to work in male occupations, but the vast majority were in semi-skilled and unskilled positions. It was expected that the German troops and prisoners of war would soon be home, and, in addition, there was a rapidly growing potential labour force in the form of refugees and deportees, with the result that few businesses took the trouble to help their 'temporary' female employees to obtain better qualifications. From 1947 onward they were progressively squeezed out of their workplaces to make room for the men who were returning home.[16]

Although more than six million women in the British and American Zones were in paid employment in 1947, the proportion of women in work stood at 28.3 per cent, which was considerably lower than before the war (in 1939 it had been 35.2 per cent).[17] For many women paid work held no attraction, because prior to currency reform there was little or nothing to buy with their wages. In 1947 a pound of butter cost 230 marks under the counter; this was approximately equal to a month's salary for a skilled worker in the British Zone. In any case the black market would recognise only barter, or cigarette currency, so workers began demanding part of their wages in goods, whose exchange value was far greater than the purchasing power of money.[18] A woman who in 1945 had taken a job with AEG in Berlin to feed herself and her three children said on looking back: 'Nowadays I say to myself, careful management and foraging would have been a lot more use to me and my children than all that business of going out to work . . . My friend told me how she used to go out, at that time, and all about what she brought back, potatoes and all sorts, and how she traded this and that.'[19]

16. Ibid., p. 76.
17. W. Abelshauser, *Wirtschaft in Westdeutschland 1945–1948*, Stuttgart 1975, p. 109. Since the proportion of men in employment had also dropped (from 67.7 per cent in 1939 to 61.2 per cent in 1947), the number of women as a proportion of the total workforce had remained more or less the same (35 per cent in 1939, 35.7 per cent in 1947).
18. Kleßmann, *Die doppelte Staatsgründung*, pp. 49–50.
19. Quoted in Meyer and Schulze, *Wie wir das alles geschafft haben*, p. 99.

Working women simply did not have the time to stand for hours outside shops, or to resort to those other means of getting food and household necessities, the black market and the foraging expeditions. Mothers with small children in particular preferred these alternative methods of subsistence, which gave them a better chance of survival in a time of goods shortages and inflationary money supply. Refugee women, who had for the most part been resettled in rural areas, went into service with farmers for payment in kind, or else paid their rent with housework and farm labour. Added to this there were millions of women and children from the cities who had been evacuated to the countryside, where they too were able to survive the early post-war years.[20]

Many families had been torn apart by forced resettlement, and men returning from the war were often unable to find their families. In 1946 the Red Cross and similar organisations were handling nearly ten million search requests: mothers seeking their husbands and children, children their parents, soldiers their families. But even when families were reunited all was not necessarily sweetness and light. Men who had survived war, prison camp and internment were not unmarked by their experiences. Even those who came away without visible wounds were scarred; many were exhausted and emotionally crippled after years of senseless fighting and killing. 'Perhaps,' mused Ursula von Kardorff in August 1945, 'the hardest task for women in this war is the one they are only now facing: to furnish the understanding, the emotional balance, the rebuilding of confidence, the encouragement needed now by so many totally beaten and desperate men.'[21] All too often attempts to reconstruct former relationships failed. The experiences of the individuals concerned were too disparate, in many cases impossible to communicate; their demands and expectations were too contrary, the time they had spent apart too long. It was not always possible to bridge these gaps at a time when the outward circumstances of day-to-day living were already so difficult. Often the men, whose self-esteem had plummeted in the wake of military defeat, could not get their bearings in post-1945 civilian society, and could not cope with the changes in social relations and expected behaviour. Women complained of the inability or unwillingness of their husbands to adapt, as in this reader's letter to the women's magazine *Constanze* (1948):

20. As late as April 1947, statistics in the four occupied Zones showed that more than 3 million evacuees had not yet returned to their place of origin; Kleßmann, *Die doppelte Staatsgründung*, table p. 355.
21. von Kardorff, *Berliner Aufzeichnungen*, p. 279.

My husband came back after nearly five years in a prison camp. For the first three or four weeks we were very happy. But now it's one row after another. The reason: he orders me about and is never satisfied. I've changed so much, he says, I'm not a proper wife any more. I was twenty-three when we married. Now I'm thirty-one. For six of those eight years I've been on my own, and I've had to get by as best I could. Now that he's back he really should be giving me some help. But he insists on my looking after the entire household (we have two lovely children) while he sits in the corner, reads the paper, complains and gives orders. Haven't these men had enough of giving orders yet? He says he's entitled to a comfortable home. But to my way of thinking he's not 'entitled' to anything. How will we ever get things back to rights again?[22]

All too often things could not be got 'back to rights', as is amply demonstrated by the high divorce statistics of the post-war years. In 1939 there were 8.9 divorces per ten thousand of the population: the figure went up to 11.2 in 1946 and 18.8 in 1948.[23] A good many marriages, hastily contracted during the war, did not survive the burdens and privations of peace. Women had no wish to place themselves once more under orders, when for years they had managed on their own; men could not or would not accustom themselves to their wives' increased self-possession and autonomy. Added to all this was the alienation of the children, who not infrequently perceived the father as an unwelcome intruder. Mother was, and remained, the centre of the family, since it was her work and her talent for management that ensured the family's well-being.[24] Father's claim to leadership was not accepted, and this only served to bring out latent feelings of inferiority and to further weaken the confidence of many returning soldiers.

These tensions and conflicts brought new life to the old debate about the continuing 'crisis of the family'. Sociologists, pointing to the high divorce rate, the growing number of extra-marital relationships and the changes in moral standards, diagnosed widespread 'social dissolution'. Many women whose husbands had been killed and who received the state widow's pension – the 1950 census counted 3.3 million widows, nearly twice as many as in 1939[25] – did not want to remarry, preferring a form of cohabitation known as *Onkelehe* – 'uncle marriage'. In this way they kept their pension

22. Reprinted in Kuhn and Schubert, 'Frauen in der Nachkriegszeit', p. 21. See also G. Baumert, *Deutsche Familien nach dem Kriege*, Darmstadt 1954, pp. 132–3.
23. Kleßmann, *Die doppelte Staatsgründung*, p. 57.
24. Thurnwald, *Gegenwartsprobleme Berliner Familien*, pp. 97, 198–9.
25. According to Schelsky, *Wandlungen*, there were 2.5 million widows and orphans who had to be cared for in the Federal Republic in 1951.

rights and their financial independence, and public opinion had no choice but at least to tolerate this unorthodox behaviour.[26] Some millions of women had to give up the idea of marriage altogether, because whole cohorts of marriageable men did not return from the war. At the war's end there were 7,300,000 more women than men living in Germany, and the female 'surplus' was greatest among those between twenty and forty years of age. In 1946, in the three Western Zones, there were 100 men aged twenty to thirty for every 167 women in that age group, and for those aged thirty to forty the ratio was 100 to 151.[27] Of replies to a questionnaire published by the women's magazine *Constanze* in 1948/49, 61 per cent believed that these 'surplus' women had a right to a 'free' sexual relationship, 10 per cent had no opinion and 29 per cent held that 'free love' was immoral.[28]

26. Baumert, *Deutsche Familien nach dem Kriege*, p. 65. Of 100 people interviewed in Darmstadt in 1950, 41 found cohabitation acceptable (pp. 176–7).
27. Ibid., table p. 15.
28. Quoted in Kuhn and Schubert, 'Frauen in der Nachkriegszeit', p. 56.

19

Family or Career?
Women's Dilemma in the Land of the
Economic Miracle

During the immediate post-war years observers felt that relationships within the family were under stress and gender relations
disordered; by the onset of the fifties, however, the major talking
point was the concept of *Fluchtburg Familie*, i.e. the family as the
castle, a place of refuge from the outside world. In 1953 the
newspaper *Frankfurter Illustrierte* called this 'retreat into the smallest social circle' a 'sign of the times' and declared, briefly and
succinctly: 'Much of our society has collapsed in the last decades,
but the family has held together.'[1] A well-known study conducted
in 1955 by the sociologist Helmut Schelsky gave learned confirmation of this judgement. On the basis of profiles of 167 families
compiled by students in Hamburg in 1949 and 1950, Schelsky came
to the conclusion that the events of the war and the post-war years
had indeed constituted an 'exceptional danger to the family', but
that in the end this threat had revived powerful regenerative and
stabilising forces which served to strengthen family ties. In the
midst of a society characterised by disorganisation and fragmenta-
tion the family had shown itself to be 'society's last bastion, the
ultimate place of safety', a lifeline and a ray of hope for the rootless
individual and at the same time 'the last stable structure remaining
in this society'.[2] Not only women but men too directed all their
energy and attention towards the family, and it was here that they
sought emotional and social support. On the one hand this tended
increasingly to encapsulate and isolate families so that they looked
upon the political and cultural activity of the outside world with
disinterest. Women on the other hand gained in authority and
profited from a more positive valuation of 'their' preserve. The

1. Reprinted in ibid., p. 69.
2. Schelsky, *Wandlungen*, pp. 63, 87ff.

conditions that obtained during and after the war, according to Schelsky and other writers, had led to the acceptance of a new concept of marriage as a partnership or comradeship in which the couple were fundamentally equal. In a 1951 survey entitled *Leitbilder gegenwärtigen deutschen Familienlebens* (Models for Contemporary German Family Life), over two thirds of the couples questioned were in favour of such a partnership; marriages in which the husband took a leading role and this was accepted by the wife were in the minority with only 14 per cent.[3] But other surveys showed that the tenacity of patriarchal ideas varied according to the social stratum under investigation: the dominance of the husband was considerably more evident among the farming population than among the educated middle classes or in working-class and white-collar families.[4]

But while partnership and comradeship may have been the dominant principles of family life in the post-war period, it was by no means true that the women and men of the fifties had similar perspectives on how their lives might progress, or that they had equal power of decision and freedom of action. On the contrary, Schelsky identified a noticeable trend towards 'restoring the old familial order and way of life' in which men took care of the financial support of the family while women saw to running the household and bringing up the children. After the immense effort and strain of surviving the forties, it appeared that women longed to throw off the burden, and they seemed pleased to accept the offer of a 'normal' role as housewife and mother, as presented to them by churches, academics, voluntary organisations and politicians. Women's magazines, which during the late forties had placed so much emphasis on the independence of the wartime and post-war generation of women, began in the fifties to extol the housewife, who, content with looking after husband and children, left political and social involvement to her spouse.[5] Women who could not marry because of the shortage of men following the war, and who had to work for their own living, were seen as pitiable creatures whose lives would remain ever unfulfilled. Single, widowed and divorced women were increasingly seen as surplus and 'marginal', while the

3. G. Wurzbacher, *Leitbilder gegenwärtigen deutschen Familienlebens*, Dortmund 1951, pp. 88ff.
4. Ibid, p. 159–60.
5. Kuhn and Schubert, 'Frauen in der Nachkriegszeit', pp. 39ff.; see also A. Seeler, 'Ehe, Familie und andere Lebensformen in den Nachkriegsjahren im Spiegel der Frauenzeitschriften', in Freier and Kuhn, *Frauen in der Geschichte*, vol. v., pp. 90–121.

complete family of father, mother and (two to three) children became once more the unassailable social norm.[6] The prevailing economic situation also lent support to the restoration of traditional family structure and role definition. In the early fifties, when unemployment figures averaged 1.5 million annually, the idea of giving jobs to married women frequently met with objections. Even in 1955 by the sociologist Helmut Schelsky gave learned confirmation of this judgement. On the basis of profiles of 167 families compiled by students in Hamburg in 1949 and 1950, Schelsky came conference of the German Federation of Trade Unions in 1955 a female speaker reported that it was common practice in the Ruhr for women who want to get married and who have been working to be dismissed on the day they marry, because the employers think it's enough if the husband is earning'.[7]

Thus various forces and circumstances combined to return the woman to the domestic sphere and to make her role within the family both appealing and unavoidable. Women soon began to respond to these messages: in 1950 only one married women in four went out to work, whereas in 1939 the proportion had been almost one in three. Most women preferred to be able to give all their attention to household and children and to live in harmony with the prevailing social conventions and ideals. Their days were more than filled, if they wanted to keep up with rising expectations as to the quality and comfort of life and new ideas about home décor. Very few households had modern appliances as yet; washing machines and refrigerators were in short supply, as were hot water heaters and central heating.[8] Dirty clothes had still to be washed in large tubs and scrubbed on washboards, and perishable foods bought fresh every day. Although the currency reform of 1948 meant that everything (or nearly everything) was once more available in the shops, clothes and consumer goods were, in practice, beyond reach of the 'ordinary citizen' at first, because wages and salaries were still dragging hopelessly behind inflated prices. Under these circumstances, housework was still a survival skill, and only great thrift, careful planning and home production of foodstuffs and clothing made it possible to stretch a husband's earnings far enough to keep the family.

In 1952 West German economic recovery began to pick up speed as a result of massive injections of American capital. It was not until

---

6. Meyer and Schulze, *Wie wir das alles geschafft haben*, pp. 164ff.
7. Reprinted in Kuhn and Schubert, 'Frauen in der Nachkriegszeit', p. 88.
8. Baumert, *Deutsche Familien nach dem Kriege*, p. 115.

then that improvements could be felt by the mass of people who were dependent on wages and salaries. Now it became possible to save up for new consumer goods such as television sets or household appliances.[9] By 1962, 79 per cent of all private households had a radio, 65 per cent a vacuum cleaner, 52 per cent a refrigerator, 34 per cent a washing machine, and the same percentage a television set. One in four of the citizens of the Federal Republic could afford to go away on holiday. At the same time more money was being spent on more nutritious and expensive foods: people were eating fewer potatoes and less bread, and instead bought citrus and other fresh fruit, meat, eggs and dairy products. The consumption of luxury goods such as beer, wine, coffee, tea and cigarettes also increased enormously during the fifties.[10] This higher standard of living could only partly be afforded out of the single income of the family man. Generally he earned enough to meet the family's basic necessities, but the rising expectations brought by the new consumerism could often only be met if his wife also went out to work. The family more and more became a 'community of wage earners and home builders' (Pfeil). People lived from one acquisition to the next, and advertisers were forever inventing new ways of motivating people to buy more consumer goods. They were helped in this by rapidly changing fashions: the household furnishings and fittings assembled by a young married couple before the First World War were expected to last a lifetime, but the three-piece suite bought in the nineteen-fifties was hopelessly outmoded after ten years and had to be replaced by a newer design.

Rising social aspirations were the major reason why married women failed to take advantage of the increase in prosperity, as sociologists and arbiters of family policies had hoped they would, by withdrawing more completely than ever before from working life outside the home so that they might exist exclusively for their families. On the contrary: the population and occupation census of 1961 showed a clear increase in the proportion of married women in employment: 36.5 per cent, as against 26.4 per cent eleven years previously. One in three working women had children at home. When the sociologist Elisabeth Pfeil interviewed 1,000 working mothers in 1956–7, she found that only 13 per cent went out to work purely from economic necessity, while 49 per cent did so in order to

9. A.-K. Einfeldt, 'Zwischen alten Werten und neuen Chancen: Häusliche Arbeit von Bergarbeiterfrauen in den fünfziger Jahren' in Niethammer (ed.), *Hinterher merkt man*, pp. 149–90, esp. pp. 167ff.
10. *Gesellschaftliche Daten 1982*, pp. 193, 195, 197.

finance household acquisitions or home building projects, or simply to raise their general standard of living.[11] Many of these women had feelings of guilt towards their children, and society did its part to magnify such pangs of conscience. Social scientists, church leaders and politicians observed with anxiety and concern that the sociali- sation function of the family was in danger of being swamped by materialistic preoccupations, and were harshly critical of working wives and mothers who neglected home and children for the sake of pecuniary gain. The term 'latch-key kids' came into currency, and the whole nation pitied the poor little ones who had to sit at home all alone and unsupervised while their mothers worked for a new television set. Seldom did anyone put in a good word 'for the woman who honestly admits that she is working because she wants a stake in this world of consumer goods that is daily forced upon her attention'. After all, why should it be women who were ex- pected to think in non-materialistic terms 'in a society as powerfully ruled by economic considerations as our own'?[12]

In the face of such strong public pressure it is not surprising that young women in the early sixties still expected to arrange their futures according to the old, accepted pattern. In 1964 a survey of 800 twenty-three-year-old men and women in the Hamburg area confirmed that ideas about appropriate gender-role behaviour were still very much the same: women saw their employment as second- ary, and themselves as working for only a short time after marriage. Their partners on the other hand wese expected to be ambitious and success-oriented at work in order to achieve a higher income and greater social prestige for the family. They themselves wanted to stop working when they had their first child, 'without any intention of returning to work or indeed any wish to do so'.[13] In practice only seven out of ten young women gave up work after the birth of their first child; the other 30 per cent could not afford the luxury of being full-time wives and mothers.[14] The discrepancy between desire and reality was also influenced by demographic forces. The age at which people married was constantly decreasing – the average age of

11. E. Pfeil, *Die Berufstätigkeit von Müttern*, Tübingen 1961, p. 79.
12. G. Strecker, 'Wie modern ist die Frau heute?', in *Frauen in Politik und Beruf*, Opladen 1965, pp. 27–36, quote at p. 33. Elisabeth Pfeil also refused to speak of 'materialism' in this context, and attributed to working mothers a 'desire to partici- pate in cultural life' (*Die Berufstätigkeit von Müttern*, p. 111).
13. E. Pfeil et al., *Die 23 jährigen: Eine Generationenuntersuchung am Geburten- jahr 1941*, Tübingen 1968, p. 365.
14. E. Pfeil, 'Nach der Heirat im Beruf?', in *Frauen in Politik und Beruf*, Opladen 1965, pp. 21–7, quote at p. 23.

women marrying for the first time was 25.4 years in 1950 and 22.7 years in 1975, and for men the figure went from 28.1 years down to 25.3 years over the same period. This meant that the period of time following the end of formal education or training, traditionally a time for young people to save money with a view to equipping a household and starting a family, was constantly growing shorter. Often both partners wanted to continue working after marriage, because the double income was needed to pay for essential household items. But the next generation was not slow in arriving – in 1969 half of all first children were born in the first year of marriage, and nearly 37 per cent within the first seven months[15] – and for simple economic reasons many women failed to realise their desire to stop work at this time. For the time being they remained at work and left their babies with grandmothers or other relatives.

The growing number of married women and mothers in the labour force was helped along considerably by the economic expansion of the 1960s. At times of full employment when more workers were urgently needed, both trade unionists and employers welcomed married women as 'colleagues'. The expansion of the service industries created many new jobs, and the number of women employed in offices and in civil service posts increased two and a half times between 1950 and 1980. White-collar jobs had accounted for only 21.3 per cent of all women in employment in 1950, in 1980 for 55.9 per cent. The overall percentage of women at work rose by a fifth over the same period: in 1950, 44.4 per cent of all women between the ages of sixteen and sixty-five were employed, while in 1980 the figure was 52.9 per cent.[16] The increase in employment among married women was still greater: from 26.4 per cent in 1950 to 48.3 per cent in 1980.[17] More and more women remained at their

15. *Zweiter Familienbericht*, published by Bundesminister für Jugend, Familie und Gesundheit, Bonn 1975, table p. 152.
16. The decrease in the overall proportion of women at work at this time (from 33.4 per cent in 1961 to 30 per cent in 1970) is largely due to changes in the age profile of the West German population. In 1950 only 14.6 per cent of all women were over sixty years old, while in 1970 this age group constituted 22.1 per cent and in 1979 23.2 per cent of the female population. At the same time, the number of women over sixty in employment decreased rapidly: in 1950, 15.8 per cent of married women in this age group were employed, but by 1970 this proportion had dropped to 6.4 per cent and in 1980 it was only 0.8 per cent. See Willms, 'Grundzüge', p. 53.
17. Willms, 'Grundzüge', p. 35. The proportion of married women in employment rose in all age groups: among those aged twenty to twenty-nine from 27.4 per cent in 1950 to 57.8 per cent in 1980, among those from thirty to thirty-nine from 26 per cent to 51 per cent, and among those from forty to forty-nine from 25.4 per cent to 36.7 per cent (ibid, p. 53).

chosen occupation through all the phases of the female 'life-span', so that the three-phase model of women's employment propounded in 1956 by Alva Myrdal and Viola Klein can today only be applied with reservations. Myrdal and Klein proceeded from the assumption that women would withdraw from the labour market when they married, and return to work after fifteen to twenty years, when their children had grown up and become independent.[18] But figures taken from a supplementary survey to a mini-census in 1974 showed that one woman in three remained at work without interruption, while 30 per cent had returned to work after an absence of several years and a further 37 per cent had elected to stay at home for good.[19] Because rapid structural changes in the economy make it increasingly difficult for older women to return to their former occupation or indeed to find a job at all, more and more women are now trying to reconcile career with family life. Young women of the 1980s no longer start from the premise that they will spend their lives as housewives and mothers, as their predecessors expected to do in the sixties. Instead they look forward to a lifetime in employment, to be interrupted only briefly while their children are small. As soon as the children can go to a day nursery, these mothers hope to get their jobs back, where possible on a part-time basis.[20]

The infrastructural conditions for a career of this sort have improved considerably over the last few decades: In 1960 day nursery places were available only for one out of every three children between the ages of three and six, while in 1981 four children in five were able to attend nursery.[21] However, since almost all such establishments are open only in the morning, many mothers must seek part-time work so that they can care for their children themselves in the afternoons. In 1984 21 per cent of all employed women were at work for less than forty hours per week.[22] Once seen as the ideal way for women to work outside the home, a way of reconciling family and career without difficulty, part-time work has come under increasing criticism in the last few years. Most part-time jobs demand few qualifications (cleaning jobs for example); they are generally poorly paid and offer little in the

18. A. Myrdal and V. Klein, *Women's Two Roles: Home and Work*, London 1968, pp. 26ff.
19. *Frauen und Bildung*, published by Bundesministerium für Bildung und Wissenschaft, Bonn 1977, p. 28.
20. G. Seidenspinner et al. (eds), *Mädchen 1982*, Hamburg 1982.
21. *Frauen in der Bundesrepublik Deutschland*, published by Bundesminister für Jugend, Familie und Gesundheit, Bonn 1984, p. 33.
22. Calculated from *Die Zeit*, 31 May 1985, table p. 24.

way of job security, worker rights or welfare benefits. In areas where qualifications are required, part-time workers have little chance of promotion and are the first to be dismissed, because they are not considered to be committed fully to their work. Despite these serious disadvantages, part-time jobs are very much in demand among married women,[23] because unlike full-time employment they offer women a chance to earn money and keep in contact with the outside world, even during periods when housework and family duties mount up.

Married women's reasons for continuing at or returning to work have changed radically over the last thirty years. In her surveys of 1957–8 and 1964, Elisabeth Pfeil gained the impression that her subjects were increasingly likely to have 'psychological' reasons for going out to work, although economic considerations were clearly still the primary motivation.[24] A survey of 1973 suggested that the reasons given by women with children for going out to work depended to some extent on their husbands' income, but also on their own occupational standing. Four out of five women whose husbands earned more than 2,000 marks per month said that job satisfaction and the social opportunities that work offered (human contact, financial independence, involvement in the professional world) were for them the decisive factors. For these women financial considerations such as raising the level of family income, major household acquisitions and a sense of financial security in their day-to-day lives tended to face into the background. But the lower the husband's income, the greater the importance attached to purely financial reasons and the less the emphasis placed on the social aspects of women's employment.[25] All the same, research conducted in 1981 indicated that even women doing piecework, who had to look after home and children as well as working in a factory, did not regard their work solely as a means of earning money, but also valued the social contact and personal recognition it brought. Although they were under constant pressure from doing more than one job and had hardly any free time to call their own, these women did not want to give up working, because 'just having the one life with the family isn't enough'.[26]

23. The availability of part-time jobs in Germany lags far behind the demand: in 1982 there were 228,164 women in search of such jobs and 9,082 vacancies; *Probleme der Frau in unserer Gesellschaft*, published in Deutscher Bundestag, Bonn 1984, tables pp. 36, 40.
24. Pfeil, *Berufstätigkeit von Müttern*, pp. 76ff.: Pfeil, Die 23 jährigen, pp. 364–5.
25. *Zweiter Familienbericht*, table p. 159.
26. R. Becker-Schmidt et al., *Nicht wir haben die Minuten, die Minuten haben*

The role of the woman who is 'only a housewife', who ever since her marriage has spent her life looking after her home and family, has since become 'problematic', as sociologist Helge Pross put it in 1975: 'Whenever employed and non-employed women are together, the latter tend to go on the defensive.'[27] In a survey conducted in 1975 and entitled *Die Wirklichkeit der Hausfrau* (The Reality of being a Housewife), Helge Pross found that the majority of these women, who were spending sixty hours a week cleaning, washing dishes, shopping, cooking, washing and mending clothes and ironing them, playing with the children and supervising their homework, were basically content with their lives; yet there was a growing sense that the role of housewife was not enough. Full-time housewives valued the flexibility of their working day and thought that they had more freedom to spend their time as they chose than women who went out to work, but nevertheless they were critical of their own social and economic dependence and felt that they were 'standing in their husbands' shadow'. Young women especially missed the contact they had had with colleagues outside the home and the money they had earned for themselves, and were not comfortable with the monotony and isolation of life within the family. Most striking in this context were the doubts about the 'meaning of life' harboured by younger middle-class women who had been happy at work. They had the experience of being valued as individuals on the basis of their own achievements and abilities, and of being relatively free to decide for themselves and do what they wanted. The life of a housewife and mother, on the other hand, meant subsuming one's own individuality in the service of others (husband and children). This diffuse discontent with 'existing for others'[28] may well have played a considerable role in the decision of half of Helge Pross's respondents to have opted for employment, had they had the choice all over again.[29]

Since the 1970s German women have progressively tended to

uns, Bonn 1982, p. 11; Becker-Schmidt et al., *Eines ist zuwenig – beides ist zuviel: Erfahrungen von Arbeiterfrauen zwischen Familie und Fabrik*, Bonn 1984.

27. H. Pross, *Die Wirklichkeit der Hausfrau. Die erste repräsentative Untersuchung über nichterwerbstätige Ehefrauen. Wie leben sie? Wie denken sie? Wie sehen sie sich selbst?* Reinbek 1975, p. 13.

28. See E. Beck-Gernsheim, 'Vom "Dasein Für andere" zum Anspruch auf ein Stück "eigenes Leben": Individualisierungsprozesse im weiblichen Lebenszusammenhang', *Soziale Welt*, 34, 1983, pp. 307–40; also studies by S. Kontos and K. Walser, . . . *weil nur zählt, was Geld einbright: Probleme der Hausfrauenarbeit*, Gelnhausen 1979; and I. Ostner and B. Pieper, *Arbeitsbereich Familie*, Frankfurt 1980.

29. Pross, *Die Wirklichkeit der Hausfrau*, p. 249.

seek out alternatives to their traditional role of exclusive domesticity, and have been increasingly assertive in their demands for individual space and new opportunities. This owes a good deal to the improved educational opportunities enjoyed by ever greater numbers of women and the correspondingly higher expectations they have come to nurture. In 1960 only a quarter of fourteen-year-old girls went on to secondary modern (*Realschule*) or grammar (*Gymnasium*) school education, but the expansion of the education system helped to double this proportion in less than twenty years. At the same time the discrepancies between boys' and girls' education began to close; in 1960, 13.4 per cent of seventeen-year old boys went to grammar school as against only 8.7 per cent of girls of the same age, while by 1979 the percentages were 20 and 20.8 respectively.[30] Until well into the 1970s parents made different plans for their daughters' education from those they made for their sons', based on the principle that girls would eventually get married and become their husbands' responsibility, so that investment in their education would pay no dividends. Insofar as education beyond the basic levels was considered, girls went to the less academically oriented *Realschule*. Female educational requirements appeared to be more than met with a *mittlere Reife* (GSCE equivalent), and this was also shown by the fact that girls who went to grammar school were far more likely to leave after the tenth grade (normally at sixteen) than their male counterparts. Even in 1975, when girls made up 48.4 per cent of the grammar school population, they comprised only 39 per cent of those who left with the higher school certificate and university entrace qualification, the *Abitur*.

Since fewer girls than boys were sitting for the *Abitur*, women were likewise under-represented at the universities. But here too they gained something from the expansion of tertiary education: in 1960 only 4.4 per cent of all nineteen- to twenty-one-year-old women became students, while twenty years later 16 per cent did so. At the same time men saw their lead over women considerably reduced: the proportion of female students went from 23.9 per cent in 1960 to 36.7 per cent in 1980.[31] In fact, however, women were far more likely than men to go to teacher training establishments (*Pädagogische Hochschule*), where they were trained only for primary and non-academic secondary school teaching. In the winter

30. *Grund- und Strukturdaten 1981/82*, published by Bundesminister für Bildung und Wissenschaft, Bonn 1981, p. 37.
31. Ibid., pp. 106ff.

term of 1960–1, 27.4 per cent of all female students were registered at a non-university teacher training school, as against only 5.9 per cent of male students, and ten years later this disproportion had hardly changed. Divergent preferences were also in evidence at the universities, where women generally did not choose to study the same subjects as men. In the technological, applied science and engineering faculties women made up barely 4 per cent of students even in the winter term of 1982/83; in physics, chemistry and computer studies they came to just over 20 per cent. On the other hand they were over-represented in the humanities subjects such as German or English, and also in education and psychology. It was only in the medical faculties of universities that the proportion of women, 38.8 per cent, was approximately equal to the proportion of women among students generally.[32]

By deciding to study subjects less favoured by men, women were choosing at the same time to follow different professions. The 'old' women's movement had given its seal of approval to teaching, medicine and childrearing as appropriate activities for women, and women in the Federal Republic continued to show a preference for these. But even within those relatively narrow professional fields there were further gender-specific preferences. Thus in 1974, 45 per cent of paediatricians were women, but only 4.5 per cent of all surgeons, 15.1 per cent of gynaecologists and 17 per cent of dentists.[33] Women teachers were mostly to be found in elementary and non-grammar education, and a study commissioned by the German Ministry of Education in 1981 reached the following conclusion: 'Despite a fundamental feminisation of the teaching profession, the division into male and female areas of responsibility has remained intact.'[34] Promotion evidently also 'befits' men more than women: out of approximately 24,000 heads of school in 1975, only 3,000 were women (that is, 12.8 per cent), although women comprised 53.3 per cent of school staff. In the school inspectorates the air was even more rarified as far as women were concerned: in

32. Calculated according to *Bildung im Zahlenspiegel 1984*, published by Statistisches Bundesamt, Stuttgart 1984, table p. 98.
33. *Frauen und Bildung*, published by Bundesministerium für Bildung und Wissenschaft, Bonn 1977, p. 15.
34. *Bildungs- und Beschäftigungssystem 4: Zur Situation von Mädchen und Frauen im Bildungswesen*, published by Bundesminister für Bildung und Wissenschaft, Bonn 1981, p. 154. In 1974 72.4 per cent of all primary school teachers were women. In the grammar schools, however, in 1978 only 35.9 per cent of the teachers were women, a figure not much higher than that of 1960. In vocational schools female staff were, and are, under-represented – in 1978 only 32.7 per cent, as against 39.1 per cent in 1960. Ibid., table p. 155.

1975 only 8.8 per cent of school inspectors were women.[35]

Opting for 'woman's work', which generally carries lower prestige, lower earnings and less chance of promotion, was never, and is not today, the privilege of the university-trained woman, but is the dubious prerogative of women at all social and educational levels. In Germany in 1982 37 per cent of all women trainees were concentrated in four occupations: hairdresser, salesgirl, office clerk and doctor's receptionist. In these occupations women made up 90 per cent of the workforce, whereas in the four jobs most favoured by men (car mechanic, electrical fitter, engine fitter, joiner) they were hardly to be found at all, with 1.3 per cent.[36] Figures for 1975 and 1977 show that of assistants to pharmacists, doctors and dentists, 100 per cent were women; likewise 96 per cent of secretaries, 95 per cent of legal assistants and 93 per cent of nurses. Their bosses, on the other hand, were overwhelmingly male: 80 per cent of doctors, 50 per cent of pharmacists and 97 per cent of lawyers were men.[37] Many girls never completed a professional or occupational training, but went straight from school to seek unskilled or semi-skilled jobs. Boys were far more likely to embark on an apprenticeship: in 1960 they made up over 64 per cent of all apprentices and trainees, and in 1979 they still comprised 62 per cent.[38] These figures reflect the continuing differences in work orientation between men and women: because a man's occupation plays a central role in his life, because he expects to spend the greater part of his life pursuing it and because it has enormous bearing on his social status, investing time and money in training is considered an important and sensible precaution. But girls, despite equality of education at school, still hold fast to the social ideal of the housewife and mother and look on their paid occupation as secondary. These attitudes, nurtured by the gender-determined social role models and expectations still reflected in family life, kindergarten, schooling and in the media,[39] are in their turn exploited by employers who count on women to be less willing to become qualified and usually offer them only unskilled or

35. *Frau und Gesellschaft: Zwischenbericht der Enquete-Kommission des Deutschen Bundestages*, Bonn 1977, tables pp. 84–5.
36. Calculated according to *Frauen in der Bundesrepublik Deutschland*, tables pp. 13–14.
37. *Frauen und Bildung*, pp. 25, 44.
38. *Bildungs- und Beschäftigungssytem*, table p. 55.
39. On the teaching of gender roles at school see M. Borris, *Die Benachteiligung der Mädchen in Schulen der Bundesrepublik und Westberlin*, Frankfurt 1972; Conradt and Heckmann-Janz, ' . . . *du heiratest ja doch auch*', pp. 190ff. On sex-role stereotypes in the media, see C. Schmerl, *Das Frauen- und Mädchenbild in den Medien*, Opladen 1984.

semi-skilled positions. A recent study of women workers in the electrical industry showed that companies generally preferred to train women to perform specific tasks, rather than spend time and money helping them to gain qualifications.[40]

For the most part, better-trained female labour is not even desirable, because businesses can profit from the polarisation of the workforce that this hierarchy of qualifications brings about. Men are ten times more likely to have a skilled job than women; women outnumber men in the lowest ranking white-collar jobs by four to one; positions of leadership and power in administration and management are occupied almost without exception by men; the word 'promotion' is rarely uttered when it comes to women.[41] This is certainly not entirely due to a lack of motivation or ability on their part. Cost-benefit calculations, fear of competition and the desire of male employers and colleagues to keep the power in their hands: these must be accounted the most persistent and effective reasons for keeping women at the bottom of the occupational ladder. Just how difficult it is to break down such resistance was demonstrated in recent years by a government-sponsored experiment entitled *Mädchen in Männerberufens* (Men's Jobs for Young Women). Since 1978 a total of 1,200 young women received training in over seventy technical trades, mostly in the fields of metalwork and electronics. Although these female apprentices 'proved themselves' and the number of young women applying for similar apprenticeships increased, this publicly acclaimed success did little to change the attitudes of employers, and in 1984 a Federal Government information pamphlet stated: 'In general, girls are less likely to be taken on by industrial concerns in a permanent capacity.'[42]

The fact that the hierarchy of qualifications and job status does discriminate by gender is once again reflected in levels of income. In 1981 the average gross weekly earnings of women employed full-time in industry were 31.2 per cent below those of male workers, and women in white-collar jobs in trade and industry were generally earning 35.4 per cent less than their male counterparts. In the 1950s the earnings differential was even greater: statistics from the years 1950 and 1957 show that female industrial workers earned 45.7 per cent less and female white-collar workers 43.7 per cent less

40. This survey was carried out by Iris Bednarz-Braun of the Deutsches Jugendinstitut in Munich. See *Frankfurter Rundschau*, 11 April 1985, p. 13.
41. I. Peikert, 'Frauen auf dem Arbeitsmarkt', *Leviathan*, 4, 1976, pp. 494–516, esp. pp. 497ff.
42. *Frauen in der Bundesrepublik Deutschland*, p. 14.

than male colleagues. But since 1978 the wage and salary gap has not diminished significantly; indeed movement towards pay parity for women and men, already very slow, has completely ground to a halt.[43] In most cases gender-determined differences in wage and salary levels can be attributed to the fact that women and men are allotted different job categories: since men are clearly over-represented in the higher-status categories, it follows that their incomes are correspondingly higher. But even within a given job and pay category, conspicuous discrepancies have been identified.[44] Even where men carried out the same work as women, they were better paid – an injustice for which a number of women workers in the 1970s found redress through the courts.

These women were able to cite the Federal Republic of Germany's Basic Law (*Grundgesetz*), whose Article 3 was a legally binding formulation of the concept of equal rights for men and women. Unlike the Constitution of the Weimar Republic, which gave only civil equality to both sexes, this more recent equal rights legislation was intended to apply to all areas of life. The incorporation of such far-reaching legislation in the text of the Constitution was by no means a matter of course. The Parliamentary Council, whose sixty-five representatives (including four women) had the task of formulating the Constitution, were initially not prepared to establish unconditional legal equality between the sexes. The desire to retain the more restrictive formulation of the Weimar Constitution, and the plea that 'different things should be treated differently', were not confined to the Christian Democrat (CDU) and Free Democrat (FDP) deputies. The SPD members too were at first reluctant to support their party comrade Elisabeth Selbert, who was committed to the struggle for a more fundamental and far-reaching statement of equality. Twice her motion that 'men and women have equal rights' was defeated in committee by the CDU and FDP delegates, and only massive public protests by female trade unionists and women's organisations succeeded in securing its acceptance.[45]

A political activist since before 1933, Elisabeth Selbert had learnt from the experiences of the Weimar Republic. The 1919 constitu-

43. Ibid., table 11, p. 23.
44. In 1980 male industrial workers in the lowest paid category took home 20 per cent more pay than their female colleagues, and male white-collar workers 18.6 per cent more. Calculated according to *Gesellschaftliche Daten 1982*, p. 181.
45. See A. Späth, 'Vielfältige Forderungen nach Gleichberechtigung und "nur" ein Ergebnis: Artikel 3 Absatz 2 GG', in Freier and Kuhn, *Frauen in der Geschichte*, vol. v, pp. 122–67.

tion had emancipated women only in a political sense, leaving their inequality in family and economic matters untouched. The *Grundgesetz* was intended to complete the unfinished work of emancipation. Parliament was mandated to amend any laws that contravened Article 3 and bring them into line with the new legal position. But the Basic Law was to be binding not only upon the state, but also upon the two sides of industry in their wage and salary negotiations. The demand for 'equal pay for equal work,' which had remained ineffectual in the Weimar Republic, now acquired greater political impetus. Wage agreements continued to incorporate special provisions for the lower remuneration of women's work, but in the trade unions, and especially among unionised women, resistance to such an openly discriminatory wages policy was growing. Following a case in which an unskilled woman worker, with the support of her union, took her case through all the available legal channels, the Federal Labour Court in 1955 ruled that henceforward any agreements that paid women less than men for the same work violated the principle of equality of the sexes and was therefore void. At the same time, however, the court suggested that wage levels should be more precisely determined in relation to the job, and that jobs should be graded according to physical difficulty. Insofar as women did less arduous work, they could be paid less, without infringement of the law. So wage agreements began to speak not of 'female wage groups' (*Frauenlohngruppen*), but of 'light wage groups' (*Leichtlohngruppen*): in effect, no change in the discriminatory policy towards women.[46] Employers were well pleased to hear the land's highest legal authority make such pronouncements, since it would spare them a greatly increased wages bill. But the trade unions too were very understanding about it, because higher wages for women might well have delayed the attainment of more important trade union goals such as the implementation of the forty-hour week or the extension of paid holidays.[47] By way of compensation they sought wage increases for the lowest-paid groups. They also attempted to translate into wage negotiation policy some of the more recent findings of occupational health research, which indicated that the stress present in the typical female working environ-

46. G. Krell, 'Gesellschaftliche Arbeitsteilung und Frauenlöhne', in *Frauen als bezahlte und unbezahlte Arbeitskräfte: Beiträge zur Berliner Sommeruniversität für Frauen*, Berlin 1978, pp. 58–68.
47. C. Pinl, 'Viel Trost und wenig Taten – Die Frauenpolitik der Gewerkschaften', in ibid., pp. 282–9; C. Sachse, 'Frauenemanzipation und Gewerkschaften in der BRD', in ibid., pp. 272–81.

ment should be taken as much into account as physical effort in the setting of wage levels. Although they had some success in upgrading women's work – between 1960 and 1980 the wage differential between the lowest paid men and women in industry decreased from 31.2 to 20.6 per cent – endeavours to raise the proportion of women in the higher paid jobs clearly failed. In 1980, 56.3 per cent of the male blue-collar workforce were in the highest paid categories of skilled jobs, as against only 5.4 per cent of women in manual work, a structural inequality which had, if anything, become more pronounced since 1965.[48]

Women's lower income levels and the periodic interruption of their working lives are reflected once again in pensions. In 1980 men who had had white-collar jobs and had paid insurance contributions received an average pension of 1,459 marks per month, while women had to be content with 688 marks; manual workers, if they were male, drew 1,052 marks on average while women received only 377 marks.[49] A woman who has never been in gainful employment receives no pension in her own right, but is 'taken care of' on the basis of her husband's contributions. On his death she receives 60 per cent of his pension – even though the transition from a two-person to a one-person household means an average drop of only 27 per cent in household expenses. With this scale of values governing social insurance it is hardly surprising that a large number of women who are left on their own cannot manage on their pensions and have to rely on further sources of income. Women, especially older women, are well represented among the clients of social security agencies. Every fourth recipient of welfare aid in 1979 was a woman over sixty.[50]

The difference between the average male and the average female life pattern – women primarily bring up children and keep house, men go out to work – can be seen to operate to the disadvantage of women both in the job market and in the social security system. So long as wage and pension levels are based on the fact that women do

48. In 1965 52.8 per cent of men and 5.5 per cent of women belonged in this category; see Peikert, 'Frauen auf dem Arbeitsmarkt', p. 498; *Gesellschaftliche Daten 1982*, p. 181.

49. *Leben in der Bundesrepublik Deutschland: Frauen '80*, published by Bundesminister für Jugend, Familie und Gesundheit, Bonn 1980, p. 34. Even by 1983 the differences of 53 per cent and 64 per cent respectively between men's and women's pensions had not decreased; see *Frauen in der Bundesrepublik Deutschland*, p. 51.

50. *Gesellschaftliche Daten 1982*, p. 298. See also S. Koeppinghoff, 'Endstation Sozialhilfe: Defizite der Einkommenssicherung von Frauen im Alter' in I. Kickbusch and B. Riedmüller (eds), *Die armen Frauen: Frauen und Sozialpolitik*, Frankfurt 1984, pp. 252–65.

the vital work of familial and social reproduction without pay or social insurance, very little can be done to alter the highly resistant structures that underlie sexual inequality. Legislation alone does not have sufficient power to bring about these changes; compensatory political intervention in the social system and the labour market is required. Only action of this kind can give the support necessary to make the demand for equal rights a reality in the family and at work, and to anchor it in the relevant social institutions. The second paragraph of Article 3 of the *Grundgesetz* is a rare example of legislation that is ahead of the social reality of its time.

The fact that equal rights for men and women came to be included at all in the constitution of 1949 may be attributed to the experiences of war time and the post-war years, a period when women had to do without men and when their independence was daily demonstrated. As gender roles 'normalised' in the fifties, the political will and spirit that had sought to bring day-to-day practice into line with the law began to falter. Although the founding 'mothers' and 'fathers' of the Federal constitution had charged the legislative bodies with amending of all laws that ran counter to the equal rights principle within four years, neither parliament nor the government felt called upon to hurry themselves to meet this deadline. In theory, on 1 April 1953 all legal regulations that discriminated against women in favour of men became invalid, and this included those paragraphs in the Civil Code of 1900 which gave to the husband alone the right of decision over 'all questions concerning common married life' (§1354) and gave precedence to the father's opinion in any controversy concerning the upbringing of his children (§1634). For the next five years judges had to give rulings in disputes between married couples without the help of any detailed legal guidelines and solely on the basis of the equal rights clause. Finally, on 1 July 1958, the so-called Equal Rights Law came into force, abolishing certain male prerogatives: §1354 was dropped completely; §1356 upheld the basic right of married women to take up paid employment; §1363 established joint ownership of property as the norm; and §1364 gave each partner the right of disposal over his or her own individual wealth (the 1900 Civil Code had entitled the husband to administer and derive benefit from his wife's wealth). But parliament and the government were unwilling to relinquish the father's prerogative in disputes over the upbringing of children, or his legal status as representative of the family. Only after the intervention of the Federal Constitutional Court, which declared in 1959 that these privileges were unconstitutional, were the newly formulated §§1628 and 1629 dropped from the Civil Code.[51]

The concept of the 'housewife's marriage' (*Hausfrauenehe*), however, grounded as it was in the old German Civil Code, remained unaffected by the legislative tinkering of 1958 – the idea of a 'natural functional division' between the sexes was still unchallenged. §§1356 and 1360 laid down that women 'contribute as a rule by their running of the household' to the family upkeep. They were only to be permitted to seek paid employment if 'this can be reconciled with their responsibilities to the marriage and to the family'. For the 4,500,000 married women who held jobs in 1961 these regulations meant that their own double burden of family and paid work had the official sanction of the lawgivers, while their husbands had no corresponding formal responsibility for the household or for childrearing. The family name too was still the legal province of the husband, according to the Civil Code: 'The surname of the family is the husband's surname.' Women themselves might be permitted to keep their maiden names, but children always had the father's surname. By imposing these limitations the CDU/FDP coalition government were to a large extent able to impose on the nation their own concepts of marriage and family law; SPD proposals to liberalise women's rights in respect of surnames, divorce and financial independence failed to find the sympathy of Parliament.

The first Christian Democratic governments adopted a programme of traditional family legislation and family policy that was very successful in re-establishing the classical model of the bourgeois family as 'the natural origin and source of state order' (Würmeling). From 1953 onwards there was a Ministry of Family Affairs, under the direction of Franz-Josef Würmeling, who instituted an eight-point programme designed to help large families. Using measures reminiscent of the Third Reich – child allowances, tax concessions, reduced rates for family rail travel, convalescent holidays for mothers – he sought to ease their economic situation and create incentives for bringing more children into the world. In contrast to their National Socialist predecessors, however, the makers of family policy in the Federal Republic were not particularly aiming for better population figures: in view of the enormous rise in the birth rate after 1945 this was in any case not necessary. Between 1950 and 1960 the population of the Federal Republic increased by 6 million, or 12 per cent, an increase attributable in approximately

---

51. Soergel-Siebert, *Kommentar zum Bürgerlichen Gesetzbuch*, vol. V: *Familienrecht*, Stuttgart 1971.

equal proportion to the birth rate and to immigration. Before the Berlin Wall was built in 1961 some 3,300,000 people from the GDR and East Berlin alone came to live in the Federal Republic; in addition there were nearly another half million emigrants from Eastern Europe. In the sixties, when the East German refugees stopped coming and it became necessary to recruit workers from other countries, the number of births rose appreciably, and remained at over one million per year from 1961 until 1967.[52] Ministers had no need to worry about population growth in the Federal Republic.

Things were different in the German Democratic Republic. The emigration of millions of people, which was not halted until 1961, was a serious headache for the country's leaders. Only optimal employment of all population reserves could mitigate the problems posed by the absence of an adequate workforce and set in motion the long-awaited economic resurgence. The GDR therefore had a considerable interest in encouraging both single and married women to go out to work, and quickly went about improving their qualifications and training. In order to dovetail employment and population policies, the social infrastructure as it affected mothers was considerably extended: by 1977 crèche places were available for 58 per cent of all children up to the age of three, and kindergarten places for 88 per cent of three- to six-year-olds (in the Federal Republic the figures were 1.5 per cent and 75 per cent respectively).[53] Maternity leave was extended to six months, and since 1972 women who go out to work have had the right to a whole year of (unpaid) 'baby leave' with job guaranteed and insurance contributions maintained. Since 1976 this 'holiday' has even been a paid one for second and subsequent children. The success of these policies in the labour market is obvious: in 1978, 87 per cent of all women of working age were gainfully employed, and half the workforce was female (in the Federal Republic the figures were 52.4 per cent and 38 per cent respectively).

This type of 'total' intervention in the lives of women by a 'totalitarian' regime was greeted in the Federal Republic of the early fifties and sixties with mistrust and massive opposition. Giving married women and mothers incentives to go out to work was, in

52. The reasons for this increase are plain: for one thing, the children of the baby boom years of 1934 to 1941 were beginning to start their own families; for another, the decreasing age of marriage served to condense the number of births over time.

53. R. Wiggershaus, *Geschichte der Frauen und der Frauenbewegung in der Bundesrepublik Deutschland und in der Deutschen Demokratischen Republik nach 1945*, Wuppertal 1979, p. 165; *Leben in der Bundesrepublik Deutschland: Frauen '80*, p. 24.

the eyes of West German arbiters of family and social policy, tantamount to deliberately destabilising the family. It is true that the Christian Democratic government also brought into effect certain measures designed to ease the situation of working mothers: from 1952 onwards women could leave work for the last six weeks of a pregnancy and first eight weeks after the birth, with full pay. But the notion of deliberately encouraging paid employment as an individual or social goal for women was quite alien to the policy pursued in the Federal Republic. Indeed, as long as there was an excess of male labour, it was not expedient. Instead, politicians and academics extolled the 'natural' mother-role and criticised married couples who decided against having children or who were moved by financial considerations to have no more than one child.[54]

By contrast, the three-child family, with mother concentrating her energies on bringing up the next generation while father earned the family's living, was regarded as morally and socially 'healthy'. A limited amount of statutory financial support was offered, together with welfare and housing assistance, the intention being to protect women against economic pressures that might otherwise compel them to go out to work. A glance at the statistics, however, shows that this entire arsenal of measures and the financial resources commandeered to put them into effect were simply not sufficient to stop the increase in the numbers of married women in paid employment. Even official philippics against hedonism, consumerism and the unwillingness of parents to make sacrifices failed to have much impact: not the three-child but the two-child family became the norm, and remained so. At the same time the proportion of childless or one-child marriages decreased considerably during the 1950s and 60s,[55] probably largely on account of the improved economic prospects for most families.

In terms, however, of the social acceptability and observance of the principles of 1950s' family policy, whose predominantly religious foundations were enshrined in marriage and family law, the Christian Democrats were more successful; indeed, so much, that the underlying philosophy remained essentially undisturbed until well into the 1970s. Even though Würmeling was not to succeed

54. See D. Haensch, *Repressive Familienpolitik*, Reinbek 1969, esp. pp. 74ff.; K. Jurczyk, *Frauenarbeit und Frauenrolle: Zum Zusammenhang von Familienpolitik und Frauenerwerbstätigkeit in Deutschland 1918–1975*, Frankfurt 1978, pp. 89ff.
55. 23.9 per cent of marriages solemnised in 1951 had no children after twenty years, and 18.6 per cent had only one child, while the figures from 1961 were 17 per cent and 15.5 per cent respectively; Hubbard, *Familiengeschichte*, p. 101.

with his intention of abolishing civil marriage – which was after all a hard-won concession of 1875 – the dissolution of a marriage was at any rate to be made much more difficult and to be judged entirely according to 'ethical' criteria. The greatest 'immorality' was considered to be the National Socialist marriage law of 1938, which allowed divorce to take place without apportioning blame to either partner following three years' separation. It is true that according to this law a non-consenting partner could lodge an objection, provided the instigator of the divorce was wholly or mostly to blame for the breakdown of the marriage. But the Supreme Court of the Third Reich had very seldom allowed such objections, especially in the case of young married couples, who might be expected to marry again and produce children. In 1946 the clause establishing irretrievable marital breakdown as the criterion for divorce, together with the non-consenting partner's right of objection, was incorporated into the new marriage legislation decreed by the Allied Control Council.

In the 1950s the Federal Supreme Court issued a series of highly restrictive rulings, based on the religious concept of the indissolubility of marriage. The objection of one partner to a proposed divorce was almost always given precedence and the plaintiff was then punished for his or her moral lapse by the forcible maintenance of the failed marriage. This practice was very much in accord with the government's family policy. In 1961 the Bundestag passed an amendment to the impugned principle of marital breakdown, which laid down these Supreme Court decisions in statutory form and upheld the actions of the 'guilty party' as the sole criterion for divorce.[56] The Federal Government saw this 'reform' as being of great benefit to women,[57] because it protected the rights of wives who would not consent to a divorce. But the premise that women who had been betrayed and abandoned by their husbands would in most cases wish to hold on to the broken bond lacked any factual foundation. Although men were actually three or four times more likely to be the 'guilty party' in divorce cases, the fact that women brought more than twice as many divorce proceedings demonstrates

56. W. Zeidler, 'Zeitgeist und Rechtsprechung', in Zeidler et al. (eds), *Festschrift H. J. Faller*, Munich 1984, pp. 145–64.
57. As late as 1980 a compilation by the SPD Minister for the Family, Huber, consisting of important laws and statutory measures from 1949 onwards that were relevant to women, contained the words 'August 1961: Family law amendment comes into force: improved protection of the rights of wives whose husbands sue for divorce on grounds of marriage breakdown'; *Leben in der Bundesrepublik: Frauen '80*, p. 43.

that they had far less of an interest in continuing the beleaguered relationship than did their husbands.[58] The reformulation of the principle of irretrievable breakdown and the tightening up of the divorce law were therefore entirely for the benefit of the 'rigorous moralising' (Zeidler) of conservative judges and politicians.

In the late 1960s, however, Parliament, government and the judiciary embarked collectively upon a process of re-thinking, especially as it became obvious that the rising divorce rate was not about to be halted by harking back to traditional rules of moral conduct. In the years 1961–5 there were 103 divorces for every 1,000 marriages; in 1971–5 the figure rose to 231. The new divorce law passed by the social-liberal coalition in 1977 included the right to a divorce without blame, and established breakdown of the marriage as the overriding factor in granting divorces. On the question of surnames, too, a liberal approach prevailed: after 1976 a couple could choose the wife's maiden name as family surname. Reforms of marriage and family law did away with the gender-based division of labour according to which women were responsible for the household and men were supposed to be gainfully employed. The ideal from now on was to be a partnership of equals, in which both partners took decisions together and determined their spheres of activity as they saw fit.

58. See statistics in Hubbard, *Familiengeschichte*, p. 92.

20

The Politicisation of Private Life
From the Women's Committees to the New Women's Movement

In rewriting the laws that governed marriage and the family, parliament and government had to take account of the 'new concept of the roles of men and women', as the government's major report on the family, the second of its kind, phrased it in 1975. Greater participation by girls in education, and the growing trend towards the employment of women irrespective of age and marital status, had progressively undermined the traditional idea of a 'natural functional division'. In a survey carried out in 1964, 75 per cent of the men and 72 per cent of the women questioned held the opinion that a women's place was in the home, but eleven years later 'only' 42 per cent of the men and 35 per cent of the women thought this.[1] Of course, women were paying a high price for greater freedom of choice and action, since few men were as eager to share housework and child care as they were to share the earning of a living. A survey conducted in Baden-Württemberg in 1983 showed that only 20 per cent of women with full-time jobs had husbands who helped at home. A 1982 study of married women factory workers reached a similar conclusion, but noted that the willingness of men to help with housework was 'considerably greater' than it had been in the previous generation.[2]

The convergence of sex roles showed itself in striking and conspicuous ways in the youth culture of the late 1960s and 1970s. In the rock-and-roll era of the fifties sexual stereotyping had continued uninterrupted: Teds and Rockers emphasised their masculinity with leather jackets, motorcycles and an overtly aggressive stance, but expected their 'birds' to behave in a clinging, feminine manner and to wear petticoats and high heels. By contrast, the hippies and

1. *Frauen und Bildung*, p. 20–1.
2. *Frauen in der Bundesrepublik Deutschland*, p. 92; Becker-Schmidt et al., *Nicht wir haben die Minuten*, p. 47.

flower children of the late 1960s demonstrated by their mere appearance that they considered the difference between men and women to be far less important. The jeans and T-shirt generation of the seventies minimised the outward differences between the sexes still further. Short, tightly fitting skirts and dresses, and shoes with high heels, were rejected as attributes of an objectified femininity, and for some years such clothing was considered taboo by many girls and young women. Physical sex differences were not to be accentuated and artificially underscored by fashionable clothes and accessories, but rather to be made invisible as far as possible by identical clothing and hairstyles. This radical claim to equality also stood midwife to the 'new' women's movement which began to emerge in 1968 from the anti-authoritarian youth and student movement. This new feminism was to have a powerful influence on the political and cultural climate and on public opinion in the Federal Republic of the 1970s – as it did in many other Western countries.

In 1968 the Berlin Action Council for the Liberation of Women (*Aktionsrat zur Befreiung der Frau*) entered the limelight by setting up children's playgroups as a radical alternative to existing authoritarian child-care facilities, and by bitterly attacking the exploitation of women in the family and in society. In the same year the Frankfurt Women's Council (*Weiberrat*), referring to the comrades of the German Socialist Students' Federation, coined the slogan *'Befreit die sozialistischen Eminenzen von ihren bürgerlichen Schwänzen'*, which might be translated as 'Free the socialist lords from their bourgeois pork swords'.[3] By now, the traditions of the 'old' feminism had entirely disappeared. Even if the young women activists had been aware of them and had wanted to seek out the surviving vestiges of the old movement for continuity's sake, it seems probable that they would have been disappointed. At the time of the Weimar Republic the bourgeois women's movement had already lost much of its political impetus and could no longer mobilise popular support; there were no new ideas to kindle enthusiasm, and the campaign for a 'more feminine culture' had foundered amid parliamentary defensive tactics. The Social Democratic women's movement, a loyal appendage of the SPD, expended its energy on welfare politics, while Communist Party women tried to woo the female industrial proletariat with the slogans of class

3. 'Vom SDS zum Frauenzentrum', *Frauenjahrbuch*, vol. I, Frankfurt 1975, pp. 9–48; U. Linnhoff, *Die neue Frauenbewegung: USA–Europa seit 1968*, Cologne 1974, pp. 38ff.

struggle and got nowhere. After 1945, when the 'new' National Socialist 'women's movement' was clearly in a state of collapse, young women who had been politically committed during the Third Reich retired from public life. They saw themselves as having been betrayed, misled and abused by the older generation, and wanted nothing more to do with politics.[4]

Women who had been actively involved before 1933 in party politics or in charitable organisations had less difficulty in making common ground with the new republic. There were many among them who regarded losing the war as the chance to make a new beginning in politics, and the end of the Third Reich as a symbol of the final bankruptcy of a male-dominated and male-oriented society. Letters to newpapers in 1946 frequently put the proposition that it was now time for women to 'have their turn' at taking over political responsibility. New, unorthodox ideas were aired: there should be a 'single organisation representing the interests of all women, one that recognises no class distinctions', or a 'Federation of Mothers'.[5] In many towns, immediately after surrender, women formed non-party and non-denominational committees to advise and assist local administrative bodies in their work of reconstruction; they also set up advice centres for women, and campaigned for equal rights in politics, in economic matters and in society as a whole.[6] Women were also involved in considerable numbers in the anti-fascist committees that sprang up spontaneously around the country.[7] Here they were mainly concerned with looking after the interests of women whose husbands had been taken prisoner, with the care of returning evacuees and refugees, with the setting up of sewing-rooms and of places where people could seek refuge from the cold. The particular tasks that the committees set themselves made 'political' involvement easier for women. When it came to solving immediate problems of survival, such as how to provide people with food, fuel and living accommodation, women felt personally involved and responsible, and in these areas they had no doubt of their competence.

---

4. See Thurnwald, *Gegenwartsprobleme Berliner Familien*, pp. 148–9; A. Hauser, 'Frauenöffentlichkeit in Stuttgart nach 1945', in Freier and Kuhn, *Frauen in der Geschichte*, vol. V, p. 60. At the women's conferences that took place in 1947 and 1948 the attendance was almost entirely representative of the forty- to sixty-year-olds. See Kuhn and Schubert, 'Frauen in der Nachkriegszeit', pp. 150ff.
5. Kuhn and Schubert, 'Frauen in der Nachkriegszeit', pp. 27, 35.
6. Ibid., pp. 25ff.; Hauser, 'Frauenöffentlichkeit', pp. 70ff.
7. In Stuttgart in the autumn of 1954, for example, one in four of the members of the work committees was female. See Hauser, 'Frauenöffentlichkeit', p. 68.

But most women were so completely taken up with ensuring the day-to-day survival of their families that they had no time for political work. According to the estimates of the American military government in Bavaria in 1948 only 8 or 9 per cent of all women were active in political parties, trade unions, women's organisations or church welfare groups.[8] A further inhibiting factor was the rapid return to more traditional forms of political organisation. In the Soviet Zone political parties were permitted from June 1945 onwards, and in the Western Zones some two or three months later. But with the exception of the newly-formed anti-fascist committees, women kept their distance from party politics. Conflicts of principle between different political philosophies, differences of interest between regions or Zones, political differences between the occupying powers – these had in their view little to do with the pressing problems of human beings suffering from hunger, homelessness and fuel shortages. A survey conducted in the American Zone at the beginning of April 1946 found that only 16 per cent of women – as compared to 35 per cent of men – considered a new political direction to be of significance in the reconstruction of Germany.[9] Women were not interested in party politics, but rather in concrete and constructive measures to improve immediate living conditions. As political groupings and institutions began to turn towards 'higher' objectives and to tread the well-worn paths of ideology and competition for office, women withdrew more and more from public participation in politics.

But the women's committees, too, were short-lived. The initial hope that women could be organised and mobilised without regard to differences of class, party or religious faith proved unrealistic within the political framework of reconstruction. Women's committees rapidly broke up over irreconcilable divergences of interest, or else continued to exist only as organisational shells. In 1947, when 204 women from a variety of parties and organisations came together in Bad Boll to hold a conference on the merging of all women's organisations in the Western Zones, women on the Left barely got a word in. At the second meeting in Bad Pyrmont a month later, the Düsseldorf chairwoman of the Women's International League for Peace and Freedom was most insistent in her pleas to women to avoid political trench warfare; 'Men have already taken up their old positions and are bombarding one another with

8. Freier, *Frauenfragen sind Lebensfragen*, p. 46.
9. Ibid, p. 41.

doctrines, but we women want no part of this,'[10] But her appeal had no effect – instead, all the traditional arguments and organisational divisions were revived and perpetuated, the old boundaries redrawn. The attempt to put up a common umbrella over women who had joined different parties and organisations, thus to keep alive the idea of a common body representing women's interests, was doomed to fail from the outset. The German Women's Circle (*Deutscher Frauenring*), founded in 1949, found no favour with the well-supported churchwomen's guilds nor with the housewives' and countrywomen's organisations, and neither was it supported by Social Democratic women or women trade unionists; consequently it soon began to develop a structure and a programme reminiscent of the 1932 Federation of German Women's Associations. The election of Agnes von Zahn-Harnack, the BDF's last president, as one of the active directors of the *Frauenring*, and the group's commitment to 'motherly politics', further symbolised the continuity between the two organisations.

Thus there could be no question of an active, living women's movement during the early years and decades of the Federal Republic, any more than there had been in the Weimar Republic, when the movement had dissolved into isolated organisations and warring factions. Nevertheless, repeated attempts were made to bring about loose co-operation between the various organisations, until in 1969 over a hundred women's groups and organisations with some ten million members between them (as estimated in 1984) came together in the German Womens' Council (*Deutscher Frauenrat*). Every woman trade unionist, every female member of the CDU and the SPD, every woman who was actively involved in a Protestant or Catholic women's guild, was now also a member of the German Women's Council.[11] But despite its numerical strength this organisation never had more than a shadowy political presence. Although officially recognised as the women's lobby in parliaments, it rarely gave evidence at parliamentary committee hearings. Its rules specified that any common demands must be unanimously approved, and the heterogenous nature of the member organisations generally put paid to any such common proceedings. The very existence of a federation of all politically active women was therefore not widely known.

The 'new' women's movement which sprang up during the 1970s

---

10. Reprinted in Kuhn and Schubert, 'Frauen in der Nachkriegszeit', p. 152.
11. Wiggershaus, *Geschichte der Frauen und der Frauenbewegung*, pp. 93ff.

likewise took no notice of the German Women's Council and the 'old' women's movement traditions buried within it. It was not until 1977 that the first meeting took place between traditional women's organisations and autonomous women's groups. Although the autonomous women made every effort to create historical and contemporary parallels between the 'old' and the 'new' movements, the gulf could not be bridged. The distance in age and experience was too great, the goals and the actions contemplated to achieve them too different. The earlier movement had emphasized the supposedly natural difference between the sexes, had indeed taken it as a starting point in formulating its social and political demands. The new feminists, like the old, were not concerned simply with equal rights, but neither were they talking about a 'feminine culture' which was intended to complement the masculine one and thus transform it. Rather, they were convinced that patriarchal society with its particular forms of work and family structure would be unable to function without the unpaid domestic labour of women. Only a wholesale refusal to continue this disregarded, invisible labour, supposedly performed out of love, would at last end the exploitation of women by men and force society to adopt different modes of functioning. All demands of the new women's movement – whether for 'wages for housework' or 'half of all skilled and professional jobs to go to women' – had as their goal the transformation of female labour inside and outside the domestic sphere, and this was not possible without calling into question the whole principle of gender-determined division of labour.[12] It was this radical rejection of housework and the traditional role of women in the family that most clearly distinguished the new movement from its predecessor, which had been concerned with the revaluation of housework as a profession and with stabilising the family as the natural place for all women.[13]

In terms of models and strategies for political action the old and new movements also had little in common. The young feminists

12. The sectarian controversy over whether the battle should be for the remuneration of housework or for greater levels of participation in the non-domestic economy dominated the second Women's Summer University in Berlin in 1977, but it proved impossible to arrive at a recognition of the common ground of both demands, namely that they were both attacks on the gender-based division of labour in family life and in paid employment. See the contribution to the debate by G. Bock, 'Lohn für Hausarbeit – Frauenkämpfe und feministische Strategie', in *Frauen als bezahlte und unbezahlte Arbeitskräfte*, pp. 206–14, and A. Tröger, contribution to panel discussion: 'Die Hälfte aller qualifizierten Arbeitsplätze für Frauen', in ibid., pp. 506–12.

13. Other divergences between the old and new women's movements are described in H. Schenk, *Die feministische Herausforderung*, Munich 1980, pp. 104ff.

accused the establishment women's organisations of harbouring 'parliamentary illusions' and of displaying excessive political modesty;[14] in doing so they clearly revealed their own origins in the extra-parliamentary opposition. But they had, in fact, soon distanced themselves from the student movement and its successor, the 'New Left', taking a position that cut across conventional political and class lines. According to the Berlin Action Council in 1968, the class struggle must be taken 'into marriage as well', because a political and economic revolution alone would not lift the oppression of women or end their incarceration in the private domain. A wealth of personal experience lay behind the resolve of the women activists of 1968 to separate themselves from the male Left, as shown in this account by a former woman student from Berlin:

All the rights and liberties we gained in universities, the countless political actions and especially the much heralded new era of sexual freedom, simply piled a larger load onto our shoulders: now men had even less time or inclination to stay at home and help us with the children and the housework. We typed their speeches, we tried to follow what they said at meetings, we made ourselves look nice as we had always done, we swallowed the Pill every day or put up with abortions. Our exploitation in the home, the satisfaction of their sexual desires – all this was supposed to be just our private problem. We should stop doing things the way we have been. They did the real political work, and they pitied us or made fun of us because we 'weren't that far advanced yet'. Well, now we no longer want to be 'as far advanced' as they are. We don't want to imitate them, we have different objectives.[15]

What these objectives were remained unclear initially. Women with children involved themselves in the alternative playgroup movement and transferred their pursuit of liberation onto the next generation, who were to be brought up in an anti-authoritarian spirit free of gender-role expectations or behavioural taboos so that they might grow into self-aware and enlightened human beings. Other women experimented with alternative lifestyles, hoping that the dissolution of the nuclear family would create free space in which a new, repression-free relationship between the sexes could develop.[16] Women's groups existed only in a few of the larger university cities, such as Frankfurt, Berlin and Munich, where they

14. *Courage*, 2 Nov. 1977, pp. 52ff. See account of this meeting in *Dokumentation der 1. Berliner Frauenkonferenz der traditionellen Frauenverbände und der autonomen Frauengruppen 16.–18.9.1977*, Berlin 1978.
15. *Dokumentation*, p. 38.
16. See *Kommune 2: Versuch der Revolutionierung des bürgerlichen Individuums*, Cologne 1973, esp. pp. 65ff., 129ff.

formed part of the student and political sub-culture. The development of a women's *movement*, which had its own programme of action and its own political goals, and which was not confined to theoretical discussion inside the academic ghetto, was in large measure due to the debate initiated by the social-liberal government around the proposed reform of §218, the law prohibiting abortion. Following the example of the women's movement in France, West German women initiated a campaign to legalise abortion. In June 1971 the magazine *Der Stern* published names and photographs of 374 women together with their appeal: 'We have had abortions! We ask no charity of the lawgivers and we want no piecemeal reforms! We demand the unconditional repeal of §218!' Within six weeks 2,345 women had publicly stated that they had had abortions, and a further 86,100 men and women had made declarations of solidarity.[17]

The abortion issue revived the anger and frustration of many women, and goaded them into public action, just as it had once done in the 1920s and early 1930s. The reason for this was that the abortion law affected women's lives as almost no other law could. The number of illegal abortions in the Federal Republic was estimated at a million per year, and no woman could be certain that she herself would not one day need to resort to an *Engelmacherin* – an 'angel-maker'. By now, contraceptives had become accepted at all levels of society, but until the advent of the contraceptive pill women were totally dependent on their partners' co-operation and sense of responsibility. They alone had to cope with the consequences of a shared sexual experience. The prohibition of abortion touched a particularly raw nerve in the relationship between the sexes: men (husbands, lovers) could beget a child against a woman's wishes, possibly without actually intending to do so, and men (politicians, doctors, judges) could then decide that a woman should bear this unwanted child and take lifelong responsibility for it. Under the slogan *Mein Bauch gehört mir* ('My belly belongs to me') women battled against this objectionable domination. They broke up hearings where male experts, male doctors, clerics and lawyers were debating whether to retain §218 or to liberalise it. In 1971 surveys showed that women were 71 per cent in favour of legal abortion; two years later the figure had risen to 83 per cent.[18]

Public opinion was largely sympathetic and supportive of this

17. A. Schwarzer, *So fing es an! Die neue Frauenbewegung*, Munich 1983, pp. 22ff., 224; Schwarzer, *Frauen gegen den §218*, Frankfurt 1971, p. 151.
18. Schwarzer, *So fing es an*, p. 44.

demand, and the social-liberal government drafted a bill that would allow abortion, paid for by the health insurance schemes, up to the third month of pregnancy – the so-called *Fristenlösung* (time-limited abortion). Despite massive intervention by the Catholic Church, which regarded this as official sanction for the murder of unborn children, the law was passed by the Bundestag in 1974. But an appeal to the Federal Constitutional Court, lodged by the Christian Democratic majority in the Bundesrat and the CDU/CSU coalition party in parliament, resulted in 1975 in the new legislation being declared unconstitutional. In 1976 another law was passed, making abortion legal up to the twelfth (in some cases the twenty-second) week of pregnancy if there were eugenic, medical, criminological (e.g. rape) or social reasons. This did make free, legal abortion more readily available, but women were still forced to run the gauntlet of obligatory counselling sessions and to search for willing doctors, and for many this posed serious problems. In Catholic districts even these restricted rights to abortion remained largely theoretical because doctors and clinics refused to perform the operation.[19]

Despite the fact that it had not attained its goal, the campaign surrounding §218 was a great success for the women's movement as a whole. For the first time in the history of the Federal Republic, women of different ages, occupations and social classes had joined collectively in a movement based on common concerns, showing that women did have a gender-based identity of interest. Action groups had been started in nearly all the larger towns and cities, and these groups carried on beyond the abortion campaign. In 1972 delegates from forty local groups met for the first national women's conference in Frankfurt, which discussed not only §218, but also the situation of women in paid employment and the 'function of the family'. The conference ended with a comprehensive list of demands – including part-time work for men and women, equal pay for equal work, paternity as well as maternity leave of one year, unconditional repeal of §218 – and with an unambiguous commitment to autonomy for women. In order to establish themselves as an 'independent force' and to dismantle the structural foundations of male authority and the mechanisms of male domination, women would have to organise separately from men.[20] According to the Frankfurt Women's Council of 1972, 'after this congress there is

19. Pro Familia Bremen (eds), *Wir wollen nicht mehr nach Holland fahren. Nach der Reform des §218 – Betroffene Frauen ziehen Bilanz*, Reinbek 1978.
20. Schwarzer, *So fing es an*, pp. 28–9, 127.

one thing we can no longer doubt: we have a German women's movement'.[21]

The movement kept itself in the public eye by means of spectacular action: women disrupted beauty contests, bricked up sex shops, sat in at churches and at doctors' conventions, organised §218 tribunals and generally sought to highlight the many forms of male force against women. The women kept a critical distance between themselves and official party and parliamentary politics, preferring to trust to processes of change initiated from grassroots level in both the public and the private domain. Behind the slogans 'Women Together are Strong' and 'The Personal is Political' lay an entirely new understanding of the process of political organisation, and this in itself was for a long time the greatest strength and the greatest attraction of the feminist movement. In many towns women's centres were set up, where women could meet, celebrate, put on exhibitions and plan their participation in co-ordinated actions. From 1973 onwards the West German women's movement began also to embrace the idea of consciousness-raising imported from the United States, and *Quatschgruppen* ('chat groups') were started, especially in university towns. This was where the women's movement had its strongest support: among women students, who were young, well educated, independent-minded, and sensitive to discrimination and oppression. These young women were no longer prepared to have the question of women's place in society treated as a marginal issue. In academic life women felt themselves to be doubly excluded: according to 1977 figures 34.4 per cent of students were women, but only 5.5 per cent of their professors and 13.6 per cent of middle-ranking academics.[22] At the same time the accepted canon of relevant topics for human and social sciences simply did not include women. Massive pressure from women students, and the development of autonomous feminist modes of discussion in women's study groups, at women's conferences and in feminist periodicals, were not least among the forces that changed this situation. From the late 1970s onwards, issues specifically germane to women became part of the accepted curriculum, and even male academics and university policy makers were increasingly prepared to regard sexual inequality as a serious theoretical and practical challenge.

Although the universities were its most stable anchor, the wom-

21. Quoted in *Frauenjahrbuch*, vol. I, p. 41.
22. *Grund- und Strukturdaten 1981/2*, pp. 109, 158.

en's movement did not remain trapped in an ivory tower. Local women's centres organised advice sessions to give information to women about the possibilities and conditions for obtaining abortions; they maintained a record of women's experiences with local gynaecologists; they set up emergency telephone services for women who had been raped, and they publicised issues of concern to women. One of the major issues they took up, one which 'public opinion' had previously always greeted with a deadly silence, was that of everyday violence against women. In 1976 feminists in Berlin opened the first women's refuge, where women who had been battered or maltreated by their husbands could come with their children to find shelter and a new perspective on life, and where the residents themselves were responsible for the day-to-day running of the house. At first, initiatives of this sort stirred up a great deal of anger, and were often represented as feminist campaigns of persecution directed against the stability of the West German family. But today they have come to be considered worthy of support even by the CDU. There are now publicly funded women's refuges in over 100 cities and towns. Some communities are experimenting with a night taxi service, to make it easier for women to participate in the evening cultural life of the city without fear of harassment and rape by men. The establishment of equal opportunities posts, women's units, women's committees and women's representatives on city councils and regional and national government bodies has become almost a matter of course, regardless of which party is in power.

Thanks to its radical critique of patriarchal power structures and privileges and its deliberately provocative stance, the German women's movement succeeded for a time in establishing itself as an 'independent force' in politics. It stimulated public debate, influenced political decisions and gave political legitimacy to women's concerns. Women involved in the trade unions or the political parties also benefited from the existence of such a power base, because in the event of a conflict they could call upon a large number of active, self-aware 'sisters'. Thus the impact of the new women's movement went far beyond its activist base: although the committed membership was essentially limited to a small circle of young women with good educational qualifications – mostly students and (unemployed) academics[23] – the topics it brought to public

---

23. Schwarzer, *So fing es an*, p. 41, estimates the size of the women's movement in 1973–4 at 'between 100 and 200 groups and several thousand activists'. The two most important feminist magazines founded in 1976–7, *Courage* and *Emma*, were selling 60,000 and 100,000 copies respectively in the summer of 1981 (ibid, p. 78).

consciousness succeeded in interesting and involving many more. At the same time the 1970s women's movement had the benefit of a political climate in which reform and social change were encouraged under the heading of 'equal opportunity'. Social morality and political culture were changing; there was a new openness and a readiness to assimilate new ideas, lifestyles and social relations. At many levels of society, people were now examining their own lives and values and responding positively to the demand for an end to repression and discrimination.

The economic crisis of the late 1970s brought with it a neo-conservative backlash; the era of reform was at an end. Conservatism became politically institutionalised once again with the return to power in 1982 of the Christian Democrats. This turn of events radically altered the scope for activity open to the women's movement. There are many indications that German women's opportunities in the field of employment and careers will be considerably reduced over the next several years. The meteoric rise in the numbers of women students appears to have been halted: since 1982 the absolute and relative numbers of young women beginning a course of study have dropped, and in view of drastic cutbacks in staffing it seems likely that in the future female professors and university lecturers will become a greater rarity than ever.[24] In the non-academic labour market women are also falling behind. Of 2.14 million registered unemployed in September 1984, almost a million were women (46.1 per cent), while the percentage of women in the workforce overall came to only 39.5 per cent.[25] In all probability this gap will widen over the next few years. The growing pressure towards rationalisation based on new technologies such as microelectronics is likely to lead to massive redundancies, particularly in the service industries (business, banking, insurance), i.e. those with a high proportion of women workers. Because these women have jobs and skills which are easily rationalised and automated under the new technology (more than 70 per cent of their work can be done by machines) they will be the first to suffer from its negative impact. In those professions likely to benefit most from rationalisation (engineers, technicians, programmers), on the other hand, there are very few women. The Battelle Institute in Frankfurt recently

24. See Memorandum II of the Arbeitskreis der Wissenschaftlerinnen an den Hochschulen von Nordrhein-Westphalen (Working Committee of Women Academics in Universities in North-Rhine-Westphalia): *Privilegiert – und doch diskriminiert*, n.p., n.d. (1985).
25. *Die Zeit*, 22, 1985, p. 26; 23, 1985, p. 24.

conducted an investigation into women's working conditions, comparing the situation in Germany with the more advanced state of technological innovation in the United States, and came to the conclusion 'that women will have little or no opportunity to participate in new technology, because only rarely do they have the training for the new jobs it provides. Because they are victims of both general social prejudice and the current practices of personnel departments, women are rarely given the chance for further or re-training'.[26]

The tendency for average male and female life patterns increasingly to converge, which was very much encouraged in the 1960s and 1970s, seems also to have reversed in the face of current and expected economic developments. The change has been accompanied by a palpable restoration of old-style government policies in respect of women and the family. Where the social-liberal governments of the seventies tried to ease the burden of woman's dual role as wage earner and carer for her family, the Christian Democratic government which took power in 1982 aimed to strengthen the 'gentle might of the family' and sought to restore the appeal of the domestic role for women. The encouragement of a 'new spirit of motherliness' not only dampens pressures on the labour market, but also aids population policy. Since 1972 there have been fewer births than deaths annually in the Federal Republic, and the 1978 birth rate was half that of 1964. At the same time a growing number of marriages remain childless, and the number of single people who decide against marriage and a family is on the increase. Politicians of all hues consider this 'reproductive strike' by women to be a serious threat to future generations, and argue for lasting changes in family policy and taxation. Only in this way, according to the well-known exponent of family law and former president of the Federal Constitutional Court, Zeidler, 'will it once again become easier for young women to take on as a permanent way of life the role of bringing up a family, a role which for many of them has always been the ideal and natural one'.[27] Encouraged and supported by pro-family measures, women are now supposed to quit paid employment, leaving

---

26. C. Krebsbach-Gnath et al., *Frauenbeschäftigung und neue Technologien*, Munich 1983, p. iv. See also the analysis by the 1984 specialist conference of the Arbeitsgemeinschaft Sozialdemokratischer Frauen (ASF) on technological developments in the Federal Republic: *Sozialdemokratischer Informationsdienst 'Frau und Gesellschaft' Dokumente Nr. 23*: 'Neue Technologien – Auswirkungen auf Lebenszusammenhänge von Frauen', Bonn 1984.
27. W. Zeidler, 'Ehe und Familie', in E. Benda et al. (eds), *Handbuch des Verfassungsrechts der Bundesrepublik Deutschland*, Berlin 1983, p. 601.

behind them the double burden and the stressful existence of the career woman, in order to dedicate themselves to raising a family, if possible a large one.

The fact that women do not go out to work purely for economic reasons, but increasingly value their jobs as a means of self-realisation, is conveniently ignored by therapeutic proposals of this sort. Apparently the idea of standing the supposedly natural gender-based division of functions on its head and recommending to men that they make the family their 'permanent way of life' also does not bear thinking about. But the solution that would be most in accord with the equal rights clause of the *Grundgesetz* – namely that men and women might split the work of raising a family as well as that of earning a living – seems also to have been crossed off the list of available options. At present it seems that dividing the gender roles would in any case not find favour in society as a whole. There is too much resistance, especially among men who fear that their sense of worth, which is intimately bound up with their occupation, will be called into question, and their power within the family diminished. When Helge Pross asked 400 men in 1976 what they thought of such role division, only 10 per cent were in favour; 33 per cent were definitely opposed to it, and 55 per cent avoided the issue. The suggestion that a man might take over the role of 'house-husband' met with even greater resistance: just under one fifth agreed, while the others rejected or tried to qualify the proposal.[28] Part-time work is sought almost exclusively by women – in 1984, 93 per cent of part-time workers were female – and the small number of men who have reduced their weekly working hours meet with distrust and suspicion from colleagues and superiors. To work less appears to mean not to regard one's occupation as central to one's life. Not without reason, this is interpreted as an all-out attack on the value system of a bourgeois society ruled by the work ethic, where the occupational system 'is, with respect to the demands placed on the labour force, based to some extent on the existence of "jobs for one-and-a-half people"'.[29] Women are expected to decline the challenges of the world of work, at least for a time, in order to give their attention to housework and motherhood; but such family-oriented behaviour on the part of men generally receives a negative response.

28. H. Pross, *Die Männer: Eine repräsentative Untersuchung über die Selbstbilder von Männern und ihre Bilder von der Frau*, Reinbek 1978, pp. 103ff.
29. E. Beck-Gernsheim, *Der geschlechtsspezifische Arbeitsmarkt: Zur Ideologie und Realität von Frauenberufen*, Frankfurt 1976, p. 173.

At the same time there are attempts at political rethinking which should not be ignored. In North-Rhine-Westphalia, the Land government recently put into effect a whole package of favourable regulations concerning women who work for the local authority, and which 'apply equally to male public servants' – including part-time working and childcare leave.[30] Since 1986 childcare leave (at present limited to twelve months) has been with pay, and it is open to fathers as well as mothers, unlike the maternity leave provision introduced in 1979. Even if the underlying ideological premises, and the chances of such idealistic schemes succeeding, must be regarded with a certain scepticism,[31] it is as well to remember that official initiatives of this sort would have been inconceivable ten or fifteen years ago. In the last decade women's concerns have become primary political considerations which no party can afford to overlook, and this is due not least to the pressure exerted by the new women's movement. For example the CDU, fearing the loss of votes among its female supporters, did not push through the restrictions on abortion rights that the Catholic Church, the medical profession and many male party members wanted. Instead, in 1985, it initiated a Party Women's Congress, where it sought to portray itself as progressive and pro-women. The SPD stresses its historic mission as the vanguard party of women's liberation, while it is at the same time confronted by increasingly radical demands from its women's section for a higher proportion of leadership positions and areas of responsibility to be given to women, and for 'positive discrimination' to be applied. Although increasing numbers of women are active in party politics, they are massively under-represented among office holders. For decades male party officials saw no problem in this; however, since they have found that electoral lists composed entirely of women are very successful in local elections and that female candidates get a clear majority on open lists, all the parties have been trying to counteract the impression that they want women only to swell party funds or provide secretarial back-up.

In view of this greatly increased and probably enduring sensitivity to women's issues at governmental and party-political level, it is the more surprising that the autonomous women's movement

30. *Ministerialblatt für das Land Nordrhein-Westfalen*, 45, 27 June 1985, pp. 858–9.
31. See for example E. Beck-Gernsheim, *Vom Geburtenrückgang zur Neuen Mütterlichkeit? Über private und politische Interessen am Kind*, Frankfurt 1984, esp. pp. 153ff.

appears to have voluntarily withdrawn from public life. Since the late 1970s the movement has retired ever more deeply into a women's subcultural ghetto, and has to a large extent forfeited its power to define political debate. It has become a social 'scene', unable and unwilling to carry women's issues into the political arena or to point the way to new areas of action. Instead of reaping the benefit of increased political interest in women's issues, the movement declines to participate in discussions of issues such as women's unemployment, and falls back on expecting nothing of the 'patriarchal institutions of male society'.[32] The women's movement has always embraced a latent tension between radical demands for social equality and the utopian concept of a better society, one that will function according to principles and rules fundamentally different to those which currently prevail. At present, utopianism tends to prevail, as the slow progress towards realisation of the demand for equality is all but halted by the continuing employment crisis and the new lease of life enjoyed by conservative values. A large segment of the women's movement today tends toward seeking its legitimation and direction in a new concept of the 'feminine being', and in a return to mothering, personal love and mysticism. In the seventies there was much discussion of Shulamith Firestone's manifesto *The Dialectic of Sex*, which spoke not simply of 'the elimination of male privileges*, but of the sex *distinction* itself'.[33] But in the eighties the stress is on a new femininity rooted in motherhood, and on the 'politics of difference'.[34]

This change of perspective cannot produce an argument against the current economic trend of shrinking employment opportunities for women. Rather, it is in harmony with those political interests among employers and social policy makers that seek to push women back into a tailor-made domestic role based on their supposed 'natural breeding and nurturing instinct' (Zeidler) – a fate many women have recently been trying to avoid, and with some success.

32. This was the stated position of the Bielefeld women's conference in November 1983 on the subject of 'The Future of Women's Work'. The programme stated: 'For example, our objective is not to make demands on the state, political parties, trade unions, in short, on the patriarchal institutions of male society, as this has so far achieved nothing for us, just as conventional political activity in the form of party politics achieves nothing for us. It is much more a case of making demands upon ourselves, that is, of mustering the strength that every woman needs in the strategies of survival and tactics of resistance she employs against everyday male oppression . . .' (p. 4a).
33. S. Firestone, *The Dialectic of Sex*, London 1979, p. 19.
34. B. Sichtermann, *Femininity: The Politics of Difference*, Cambridge 1986; G. A. Erler, *Frauenzimmer: Für eine Politik des Unterschieds*, Berlin 1985.

It is questionable whether this state of affairs will be accepted by the mass of women. There are many indications that women are not as ready as they once were to be sweet-talked into the role of either full-time housewife or dual-role worker, all according to prevailing economic conditions. At the same time women at all social levels expect much more in the way of equal employment and career opportunities. Ideas about what is appropriate for women, how they should live and what they may demand, have been changing rapidly in recent years. Once such a process of social and cultural change is under way, it seems to take on a momentum of its own, and despite certain clearly visible contrary trends it appears unlikely that conservatives' attempts to turn back the clock will ever be entirely successful. One cannot imagine that women will submit without protest to social and employment policies that render their participation in working life more difficult, and force them to exchange it for still more unpaid and unacknowledged labour in household and family as well as honorary (and equally unpaid) activity in neighbourhood and welfare schemes. Even the Christian Democrats can no longer count unreservedly on the 'gentle might of the family', and are evidently under considerable pressure to rid themselves of unpopular reactionary elements who block pro-liberation initiatives. In all political parties there is a keener awareness that they must either take seriously the growing desire of women to achieve real equality, or else risk losing the female vote, and with that a good deal of political power. How they propose to resolve the impending conflict between the rising level of self-awareness and expectation among women on the one hand, and the actual chances of realising these expectations on the other, remains to be seen.

Two Hundred Years of
Women's History:
A Critical Appraisal

There is no doubt that the world has changed considerably for women over the past two centuries. Sophie La Roche, for example, born in 1730, would hardly feel at home in the 1980s. She took it for granted that her duties as a spouse, mother and housewife should take precedence over her literary ambitions, that her works should be published anonymously or under Wieland's name, and that the royalties should be spent only with the prior consent of her husband. Today she would encounter women writers who vigorously assert their entitlement to professional careers, independence and active involvement in public life and who run their private lives on the basis of an equal partnership. Women from other social classes – maids, day labourers, farmworkers – would presumably also have enormous problems coming to terms with the forms of employment, family relationships and morality which characterise the lives of modern day bank clerks, factory workers and housewives. Some things would seem familiar and as they should be; others would seem 'topsy-turvy'.

In this final section an attempt will be made to draw together systematically the major effects of change in the lives of women. The question arises as to whether, and if so how, such changes have affected the balance of power between men and women. Has the sexual inequality of nineteenth- and twentieth-century bourgeois society diminished? Have women profited more than men from the economic, legal, social and political developments? Or, despite all the undeniable changes which have taken place, have male–female relations basically remained the same? Are men still the masters?

Work

The growth and structural change in Germany engendered by the process of industrialisation from the 1830s onwards transformed the work of women in a particular way; both their visible, paid work in the outside world and their invisible, unwaged labours in the home and for the family were affected. In purely quantitative terms, there has been little variation in the number of women in gainful employment over the past two centuries. In the period from 1882 to 1980, between 30 and 35 per cent of women worked to earn money (see Table 7, p. 333), and although there are no comparable statistics for before 1882, there is much evidence to suggest that, as a proportion of the total female population, the number of women employed in agriculture, trade and domestic service was neither much higher nor lower.[1] In other words, 'women's work' was not created by

307

industrialisation, as some books, including those given to school-children, would have us believe; nor is it synonymous with factory work, which initially only a few women entered. The vast majority of nineteenth-century women worked either in farming, in domestic service, as casual labourers, or assisting in the family business (see Table 8, p. 334). Much of the evidence suggests that their situation worsened during the course of that century; this was particularly true in the case of smallholders. Wives and children had to compensate for the growing shortage of farmhands. At the same time workloads, especially for women, appear to have increased as a result of agricultural commercialisation and more intensive farming methods. The first machines were designed to ease male labour, while women had to carry on as before; and once mechanised, many jobs hitherto done by women, for example in the creamery and dairy, would be taken over by men.

In the nineteenth and twentieth centuries it became more and more common for women (though less so than for men) to turn away from farming and to seek employment in factories, offices, banks and shops. In the towns, where there was a steady growth in population from the 1840s and a virtual population explosion after the 1880s, and in the surrounding areas, women enjoyed far greater job opportunities than in the country. Whilst it was still customary for wives and unmarried daughters to help in the family business in some branches of craft, trade and commerce, many firms also took on extra young women to work both in the home and in the business. In the second half of the century, moreover, there was a sharp increase in the size of the female factory labour force. Nor should we forget the army of women who washed, sewed and ironed on a casual basis for private families, or who stayed at home spinning, making lace and embroidering, then sold the finished articles to manufacturers, retailers and private customers. Although many of these home-based industries were being destroyed as industrialisation progressed, new types of centralised and decentralised employment opportunities for both men and women were

---

1. Employment statistics for Prussia show that the percentage of women of working age who were actually employed was 29 per cent in 1816, 25.6 per cent in 1846 and 1855, and 31.3 per cent in 1861 (see table 1). The statistics did not, however, record women who were self-employed, or who were incorporated into the family business. Statistics for the German Reich in 1882 included 'relatives assisting in family businesses', and calculated the female employment quota to be 37.5 per cent (Willms, 'Grundzüge; in Müller et al. (eds), *Strukturwandel*, table p. 35); hence we can justifiably say that in real terms female employment had remained at roughly the same level.

springing up. Initially it was almost exclusively young, single women who took factory jobs, with married women preferring to be homeworkers, particularly in the linen, clothing and tobacco industries. However, from the early twentieth century, the ranks of the female factory labour force were progressively swelled by mothers and married women.

Female factory labour was novel in two ways: firstly, women worked outside the home in a commercial environment; secondly they worked alongside men, or so it seemed. Early investigators into female factory labour were perturbed less by the health risks than by the moral dangers they believed would arise from the physical proximity of male and female workers. The traditional separation of gender-specific spheres of activity seemed to have been abolished. Male workers may have perceived things in a similar light when they vehemently objected to the presence of female colleagues. What lay at the bottom of their polemic against such 'dirty competition' was perhaps less a concern about job security, or an attachment to the ideal bourgeois family, than an aversion to a world that seemed to have been turned upside down, where the same spheres, even the same jobs, belonged to men and women alike.

In reality, however, women rarely performed the same work as men. As had been true when the white-collar sector expanded in the late nineteenth century, a clear distinction between men's and women's spheres, between men's and women's jobs, between men's and women's wages, persisted also in the blue-collar industries. For one thing female labour was either absent from, or only marginal to, many sectors: initially it was concentrated in textile manufacturing, and barely present in the food, paper and metallurgical industries. From 1900 onwards the number of women in chemical and electrical engineering plants began to rise. But even in those branches of the economy where the female labour force was relatively well represented, male–female divisions tended to persist. Men were usually entrusted with better-paid managerial and supervisory functions while women were left with lower wages, worse working conditions and monotonous jobs in mass production. This pattern was repeated in the white-collar sector. Here too the feminisation of the office did not mean that men became superfluous; rather, 'men's work was placed on a higher plane', as a 1907 publication of one union of male office and clerical workers put it; 'the minor jobs', in particular the use of new office technology, could now be left to women, while men could get on with the 'more important business'.

In the decades that followed, dualism of the labour market remained a characteristic feature in the development of industry and enterprise. Even today it cannot be said that the same qualitative and quantitive conditions apply to both sexes at work. It is still the case that far fewer women than men complete vocational training; that they tend to opt for 'women's' jobs, which are less secure in times of economic recession, that they are more vulnerable to the vagaries of unemployment; that they are paid less than men; and that they are generally less upwardly mobile. The unfavourable balance sheet is an outcome of the socially maintained rule of inequality which holds that a woman's sex predestines her to a primarily home-based existence, providing unpaid labour for husband and children. Only when she is not called upon to commit herself to family life may she participate fully in the labour market. Since the industrial production process, and its accompanying service sector, function on the principle that a given human labour supply is both infinitely available and infinitely employable, women cannot but be the second choice in the distribution of paid jobs, for the general consensus of our culture dictates that their primary responsibilities lie in the everyday, biological sphere of social reproduction in the family.

From a historical point of view, however, it would be erroneous to claim that sexual inequality in employment persists merely because modernisation has not proceeded far enough; because somehow a brake has been put on social progress; because the untimely remnants of pre-industrial traditions have created obstacles to the equality of opportunity that was anchored in the original bourgeois vision of a non-sexist society of industrious human beings. On the contrary, the distinction between paid employment and family-related labour, the demarcation of a separate field of activity entitled 'housework', are the natural bedfellows of industrialisation, the other side of the coin of socio-economic modernisation. It is, of course, true that in the social milieu of peasants, craftsmen and the lower estates of pre-modern society, responsibility for the household economy and the family offspring also lay with the *Hausmutter*. In this sense the much-evoked notion that a woman's 'traditional' and 'natural' duties are cooking and childcare does have a genuine historical root. But we should also recall that in the eighteenth and nineteenth centuries 'household' referred to much more than it does today: the functions of production and consumption were indivisible, and male and female activities in the 'whole household' were defined according to quite different criteria.

This is not to say the sexes were equal, for both custom and the law recognised the man as head of the domestic community, with the woman firmly subordinate to him. But in her own, precisely defined realm, which was protected from male invasion by cultural norms, she was an authority unto herself. Moreover, it was taken for granted that, notwithstanding social hierarchies, men and women were mutually dependent, not only for bringing up their children but also for making a living and maintaining the household. Bourgeois industrial society destroyed this unquestioned state of affairs by replacing the unity of life and work with separate domains that were clearly distinct in spacial, material and social terms. It established a new sexual division of labour whereby the extra-domestic sphere of work, along with its monetary rewards, was the male preserve, while women were still tied to their old domains.

While the production forms, organisational principles and normative systems of the bourgeois society of labour became established ever more quickly after the mid-nineteenth century, this process brought about a shift, not only in the overall axes, but also in the co-ordinates of female experience. Housework had formerly been a sphere of activity in itself, one of economic and social significance; now it increasingly became a mere subset of gainful employment outside the home. The housewife came to rely on the money her husband earned 'out at work'; without it she was unable to purchase goods that could not be produced at home, or to process semi-finished products. As an unremunerated activity that absorbed the household's earned income, housework henceforth had minimal social status which was not enhanced even when, in the second half of the nineteenth century, society began to insist upon a rise in standards. Women of all classes came under pressure to step up their domestic efforts and administer to their family's needs in a more rational way. They were burdened with more and more responsibility, yet they were not personally provided with the economic means to do the job. Doctors, the clergy, industrialists and politicians all opined that wifely virtues would determine whether a man turned into a drunkard or a reliable worker; that a family's health depended on the domestic skills of the mother; that her care decided whether a baby survived or not; that her educational aptitude and the love and attention she lavished on her children would have a decisive impact on their future careers. The additions to the list of duties she was expected to perform was not offset by the fact that housework was made less strenuous by domestic appliances, which, although they first appeared in the

1920s, did not become widely available until the 1960s.

The paradigm of polarised gender roles, which assigns to women a conditional, contingent and subordinate place in the realm of paid employment, is almost as valid to today as it ever was. Women generally do not call this model into question, except for some highly qualified and ambitious professional women who demand the same opportunities for employment and mobility as men, and a redistribution of familial duties. Since the early part of this century women have had greater access to privileged professions, though at the cost of adopting male perspectives and behavioural patterns almost without modification. To cheer this as an overture to the unstoppable 'civil advancement of women' would be to distort the overall picture in a most irresponsible manner. For although, a few exceptions notwithstanding, there is today no formal legislation barring women from professions, the unabated power of informal mechanisms of exclusion makes it impossible to write the history of female employment as that of a largely successful struggle for equality. At the very time when the privileged few are managing to gain a foothold in politics, education and the economy, unemployment among women is growing disproportionately, and indeed can be expected to be exacerbated by the coming wave of rationalisation in the services sector. The displacement of women from the labour market appears to be outstripping the creation of new jobs and the removal of obstacles to careers. Unlike the first industrial revolution, which compensated for the decline in traditional job opportunities with the expansion of new ones, and unlike the second industrial revolution in the 1920s, when the rationalisation of commerce generated new jobs for women, the third revolution is unlikely to provide alternative sources of employment. What will remain is the 'gentle might of the family'.

Family, Marriage and Children

For two hundred years it has been said that a woman's substantive destiny (Hegel) is found through the family. During this period, however, the significance of family, marriage and children has undergone marked changes. Between 1871 and 1979 in Germany, the percentage of married women compared with the female population as a whole rose from 33 per cent to 47.2 per cent, and the percentage of single women fell from 58.8 per cent to 35.4 per cent. This was, in part, a consequence of the changing age structure of the population; declining birthrates and rising life expectancy constantly pushed up the average age. In addition marriage has become a considerably less complicated matter for young people. Besides the abolition of state-imposed marriage restrictions, better employment opportunities have allowed men and women to save in a relatively short time enough money to get married and settle down. This pattern has been reflected statistically, both in the gradual fall in the average age at which people marry, and in the rise in the proportional number of married women (and men) in the lower and middle age groups – within one century (1871–1970) the percentage of unmarried women among all females between twenty and thirty fell from over 60 per cent to 27 per cent, and from almost 20 per cent to barely 9 per cent in the thirty–forty age range.

The conditions under which women have entered into wedlock have also changed considerably. In nineteenth-century peasant, bourgeois and aristocratic society, it was normal for parents to arrange marriages, often with prime consideration being given to economic prospects. In the twentieth century it has become more and more common for men and women freely to choose to marry without parental orchestration (although this is not to say that economic motives are unimportant). Furthermore partners are more frequently exercising the legal right to dissolve marriage: the divorce rate rose from 1.5 per cent of all couples who married in the period 1881–5 to 23.1 per cent in 1971–5; in the majority of cases, divorce proceedings were initiated by women, and this has become increasingly the case. Ever since marriage has become a normal and freely-chosen mode of life for growing numbers of people, it has apparently also become more susceptible of dissolution. The significance of the divorce option becomes much clearer if we bear in mind the history of the duration of marriage: no more than 36 per cent of all widows and widowers living in Berlin in 1875–6 had been married for longer than twenty years; a century later the figure was approaching 80 per cent.

These figures suffice to suggest that for increasing numbers of women (and men) marriage is a rich life experience that extends over several decades. Coupledom has shifted to centre stage; the rise in life expectancy has meant that relationships have become prolonged and more exclusive, though at the same time partners have become more prone to mutual criticism, estrangement and, if they so desire, separation. As the extent to which couples expect marriage to be founded upon loving devotion, mutual understanding and shared interests has grown, so their expectations have become correspondingly more ambitious and open to disappointment. This ambivalent process of individualisation, by which the 'institutional dignity' that marriage once had has been lost, has been accompanied by a transformation in the functions ascribed to marriage by the outside world. Changes in reproductive behaviour made irrelevant the main purpose of wedlock as defined by the Prussian Civil Code of 1794: 'the procreation and raising of children'. Marriages have been producing smaller families for about a century, and for longer in the middle classes. Couples who married before 1905, and who were still together in 1939, had an average of 4.67 offspring, while those marrying fifteen and twenty years later produced only half as many children. Public officials and white-collar groups were the harbingers of this development, with peasants and blue-collar workers following suit after some twenty years.

In the long term smaller families have considerably eased the workload on women. In the nineteenth century the youngest child was often born after the eldest had flown the nest; nowadays the time devoted almost exclusively to rearing infants has been condensed into less than ten years. However, standards of childcare and education began to rise sharply at the end of the eighteenth century, affecting the working classes by the early twentieth. This, in conjunction with the tendency for childhood and youth to be prolonged, has meant that having fewer children has not automatically eased a mother's burden. Nowadays it is not only infants who need her care and attention; the mother of a schoolchild is also busy with various school matters, such as liaising with teachers on her offspring's progress. In addition she organises the entertainments and leisure activities that seem to be a natural part of childhood, or at least in the status-conscious and upwardly mobile middle and lower-middle classes. Even the vast expansion of day care facilities in the 1970s aimed less at relieving her burden than at enriching the intellectual and physical development of children.

Despite the ambivalent nature of the course of history, there can be no doubt that the modern-day woman is less tied to her children – and hence to her family – than her counterpart of 200, 150 or even 100 years ago. There are now longer periods in her life when she is not committed to her infants' needs for constant attention, when her existence does not have to revolve constantly round her family and home. But what has this meant for the relations between men and women? Is the female life cycle adapting to the male pattern, or do the dissimilarities persist?

In attempting to answer these questions the first thing to remember is that since 1900 it has become increasingly common for

married women with children to go out to work. While the decline
in self-employment, particularly of males in agriculture, has
brought about a drop in the number of women assisting in their
husbands' businesses, jobs in manufacturing and services have at-
tracted ever more married women. Taking women married to a
wage-earning husband as a whole, the percentage of those employed
on the free labour market, i.e. not as 'assisting relatives', has grown
rapidly, from 12.8 per cent in 1950 to 49 per cent in 1979.[2] The
figures reflect the redistribution of female employment opportunities away from family-related to market-related activities, and the
convergence between the proportionate levels of male and female
employment. Moreover, they also mirror the shorter phase when a
woman's energies are invested entirely in giving birth to and caring
for infants. As soon as their children reach school age, many women
return to their jobs, though this often gives rise to great physical and
mental strains. Since as a rule responsibility for all the housework,
as well as for the child's school and other activities, lies with the
mother, women have had to make far more sacrifices than their
husbands in adapting to male employment patterns. The disparity
has not been eased – indeed it has been reinforced – by the growth
in recent years in part-time work for women.

Although by comparison with her predecessors the contemporary female is more at liberty to take up paid employment outside the
home, it should not be forgotten that the improvement is relative:
she still faces great career disadvantages because, essentially, family
ties remain paramount. Evidence to the contrary can only be found
very recently, in the post-materialistic middle classes, where some
women elect both to pursue a life-long career and to organise their
family lives so that domestic duties are divided equally between
partners. More generally, if a woman wants to have children, she is
confronted by the dilemma of choosing between her job and her
family – a choice that men rarely have to make. Even the new set of
'career women' have resorted to the classic arrangement where
grandmother or a paid domestic help does the housework. The costs
of such 'modernisation' are borne by cleaners and child-minders,
who are unable to take a similar path, as well as by the career-
minded women themselves, whose new-found freedom cannot be
bought without emotional stress and money.

2. W. Müller, 'Frauenerwerbstätigkeit im Lebenslauf' in Müller et al. (eds),
Strukturwandel, p. 63.

Education

Education is an area that illustrates clearly the way in which family roles create serious obstacles for women who wish to be successful at work and in public life. For it is above all in education that women have gained enormous ground over the last two centuries; and yet this has barely affected the second-class status they have in other institutions of society. While girls accounted for roughly 50 per cent of pupils in all types of German schools in 1980, from primary right up to grammar schools, in vocational education and training they are considerably under-represented. The discrepancy is even larger in universities, and this is also reflected in young people's educational ambitions: of all sixth formers in 1984 who were asked whether they intended to go on to university, only 9.5 per cent of males said no, compared with 23.8 per cent of females. The advice given to women by Germany's university professors in 1897, to train as medical and legal assistants rather than doctors and lawyers, seems to carry weight even now. In 1975 20 per cent of doctors were female, compared with 93 per cent of nursing staff, while women comprised 3 per cent of lawyers and 75 per cent of assistants in that profession. The numerical equality of the sexes in primary and secondary education is not carried over into vocational and tertiary levels, and hence fails to have any significant impact on the inequality of career opportunities.

Indeed it is in senior schooling that the proportion of females has risen markedly. As early as the nineteenth century most girls were already attending elementary schools. Having been introduced in Prussia in 1763, the compulsory education system was catering for 60 per cent of children in 1816, and by the 1880s was attended by almost all, though boys were slightly better represented. There were far more serious differences at senior levels, which remained male-dominated throughout the century. The various types of higher schools – *Gymnasien, Oberrealschulen, Realgymnasien*, which were academically oriented in varying degrees – were open to boys only, and offered a *Mittlere Reife* or the *Abitur*. For girls the higher girls' school, the *höhere Mädchenschule*, existed, but this did not lead to a qualification suitable for entry into either an occupation or university. Whereas ever since 1834, when the *Abitur* had become the sole entrance requirement for budding undergraduates, *Gymnasien* had been at least indirectly linked to employment, higher girls' schools had to wait until the early twentieth century before they were permitted to award their pupils a qualification that would help them in their careers. From 1896 onwards, girls in Prussia could, having completed higher school, take a *Gymnasium*-type course, and then sit the *Abitur* externally. In 1908, they were included into the normal pre-university and university system throughout the Reich. Girls then gradually began to catch up with boys: in 1921, 20 per cent of senior school pupils were female, and 25 per cent by 1931. But it was only the expansion of the education system in the 1960s and 1970s that managed to create equal educational patterns.

The incorporation of higher girls' schooling into general state education and the qualification and employment system at the beginning of this century was not, however, accompanied by a convergence between the aims of male and female education. It was, rather, the case that until well into the 1950s the education of senior girls was thought to be of equal value, but not identical, to that of senior boys. In the Weimar Republic most boys and girls were taught different curricula in separate schools. The Third Reich widened the gap even more by shifting emphasis to home economics for senior girls, at the cost of other subjects. And despite the declared intention of the Federal Republic not to carry on Nazi traditions, the *F-Abitur*, the 'women's *Abitur*', was still being passed in many girls' schools in the 1960s. Indeed the regional governments took variously long times to introduce co-education in general – equal *and* identical schooling for both sexes at senior levels.

Modern schools regard themselves as non-sexist institutions which apply the same educational principles to girls and boys. Yet, despite this, the hidden curriculum – the subterranean plan setting out some paths for men, and others for women – comes into play when young people leave school, or even before. Insofar as they have any vocational qualification at all, girls choose different careers to boys; normally these jobs are less qualified, lower paid, and have lower status. Even in the professions, which are now by no means an exclusively male preserve, the range of career options for women is narrow, and the prospects for mobility limited. The majority of women who have had academic schooling become teachers or doctors, but rarely rise to the position of head or superintendent.

A similar pattern is found in universities. While the percentage of female students in tertiary education in Germany has risen sharply in the twentieth century – from 6.3 per cent before 1914 to just under 38 per cent in 1983 – extremely few women become lecturers and professors. The most recent signs are that women are being easily discouraged by poor employment prospects. In 1981 17.9 per cent of women between the ages of nineteen and twenty-one went on to further study, but two years later only 16.8 per cent did, even though more had suitable entrance qualifications. By contrast the figures for males in the same period were 23.7 per cent and 25.8 per cent respectively. The tendency of women to retreat is due not to a lack of aptitude or qualifications but to a lack of confidence and to the unabated strength of family-related orientations and patterns of socialisation.

Bodies

When, in the nineteenth century, men pondered on the most elegant and reliable argument they could employ to keep women out of qualified occupations and public life, they were particularly fond of pointing out that women were prone to the cyclical fluctuations and changes in form and function which their bodies underwent. It was quite obvious, they argued, that menstruation, pregnancy, childbirth and lying-in were enough to prevent women from being serious competitors for men's careers and power; their place was at home, in the kitchen and looking after the children. Entire generations of medical practitioners endeavoured to prove that women were more excitable, capricious and sickly than men, and thus to deny them suitability for responsible roles in the labour market and in politics.

These depictions were, of course, gross exaggerations; but they did contain an element of truth. So long as women continued to marry and immediately place their bodies in the services of human reproduction, they were bound to spend tens of years busy with pregnancies, birth and childcare, and be largely excluded from the world outside their own front doors. Pregnancy could be expected every other year, provided couples regularly indulged in 'marital embraces' – and indeed doctors encouraged them to do so, pointing out that their health would benefit. Successive births and abortions led to infirmities and, ultimately, to high mortality rates. In 1928, for every 100,000 live births, 544 mothers died in the process (the figure was 22 in 1979); towards the end of the eighteenth century the mortality rate had been two or even three times as high.

The risks mothers ran did not diminish until family planning was made possible via effective contraception, and pre-natal care and obstetric practices improved. When that happened, pregnancy, childbirth and childbed not only became less hazardous; they were now no longer the determining factors of the female experience. By having only two children, and by reducing childbearing to a few years, women can now be as little dependent on their physical attributes as men. 'Emancipation' of this kind should certainly in theory be conducive to greater female integration into the extra-domestic spheres of employment and public life; but, for reasons we have already discussed, the actual spin-offs have been highly unsatisfactory. The very fact that the female body gives life to and bears new human beings still engenders the argument that women should also take life-long responsibility for raising children and looking after the family household – even though the male anatomy is equally well suited to the task.

In view of lower fertility rates since 1900, it has often been concluded that women have gone on maternity strike, so to speak, in an effort to gain more freedom and opportunities. There is no prospect of the strike being called off, however, for it is widely felt that the one- or two-child family is ideal, and so why do different? At the same time, women prepare for the children they plan in a far more deliberate and meticulous manner than ever before. Pregnancy is not concealed as if it were an embarrassing condition, as was the case until relatively recently; the expectant mother today can easily show herself off with pride, and celebrate the child-to-be. The rediscovery of 'naturalness' has been accompanied by more strident criticism of the way in which bodily processes have been over-rationalised and repressed. There has almost been uproar over the fact that 98 per cent of all births in Germany take place in hospital; home-births and midwives are becoming increasingly popular. This is presumably not only an expression of the sense of unease about excessive technology and alienation from nature, a feeling that has recently become widespread; it also reflects a specifically female longing for a uniquely feminine power – a 'women's room' where they can develop their own strength and productivity free from male interference.

That modern-day women perceive their bodily selves in a far more conscious and positive fashion than did their mothers and grandmothers is only possible because, unlike a century or two ago when the physical human being was still largely an unknown quantity, they are relatively well equipped to control their bodies. Although methods of preventing and terminating pregnancy were not unknown in the eighteenth and nineteenth centuries, they were much more hazardous than modern techniques. Fewer births have reduced the vulnerability of female reproductive organs to disease, and thanks to the progress of medical science the complications of some births are easier to tackle successfully than was the case 50 or 150 years ago. However, the widespread use of contraception was far more responsible than medicine for boosting life (and survival) chances. All social and religious groups had begun to adopt methods of family planning and contraception by the 1920s, if not earlier, even though the Catholic Church still forbids its followers to use any form of mechanical, chemical or hormonal contraception. Since the 1960s the Pill has meant that women no longer have to rely on their partner to prevent unwanted pregnancy, even though at the cost of possible long-term health risks.

The practice of birth control is an indication that women currently regard sexuality not as being inextricably linked to reproduction but as an independent element of human needs and pleasures. Of course, nineteenth-century women did not see sex as a subsidiary function of procreation either, but none of them could be sure that the ultimate joy of 'marital embraces' would not be pregnancy. Only the availability of reliable forms of contraception has allowed women to satisfy their sexual desires with the same carefree passion as men have since time immemorial, and to have pre- and extra-marital relationships without being betrayed by any 'side effects'. While it would have been scandalous in bourgeois and petty-bourgeois families of the nineteenth and early twentieth centuries for a woman to gain sexual experience before marriage, today it is taken for granted that pre-marital sex is part of being a teenager.

Public behaviour of the sexes also reflects the twentieth century liberalisation of sexual conduct and the greater leniency of social rules about bodily boundaries. Around 1900, if a couple wanted to go for a swim on the North German coast, they were obliged to use separate beaches: men had to stay at least 500 metres away from female bathing areas. In sport too, an exclusively male pursuit in the nineteenth century, gender-specific barriers and taboo zones have been eroded. Girls and young women gradually began to take an ever more active part in training, games and competitions. Their involvment was encouraged on a massive scale by the Third Reich's cult of physical fitness. Despite this, imbalances persist even today, as evidenced by the fact that although in the Federal Republic the number of women participating in sport has risen faster than that of men, in 1980 only a third of the members of the German Sports Association (*Deutscher Sportbund*) were female (20.7 per cent in 1960). Moreover, men and women go in for different sports. This is a reflection less of their respective physical make-up than of culturally defined norms of behaviour.

Attitudes to female sexuality illustrate particularly well how converging codes of behaviour have not only had a positive and liberating impact, but have also given rise to new pressures and tensions. Women now enjoy greater freedom, physical independence and scope for self-determination, but new demands are made of their sexual demeanour and appearance; they are expected to be rational beings, and yet at the same time preserve their erotic sensuality; they should be able fully to satisfy all kinds of male desires. Over the last twenty years the norms of physical femininity and female sexuality have become far more demanding, a fact for which the visual media are particularly responsible. The female body is now the preferred vehicle for selling all manner of products and messages, ruthlessly touted as objects of male desires. Simultaneously women are supposed to keep their bodies in much better condition than ever before, and to adorn themselves in line with the latest trends. Numerous women's magazines, whose circulation runs into millions, discuss body care, make-up, perfume and clothing. Ever-changing fashions dictate the depth of the hemline and the height of the heel. And while the designers of women's fashions are predominantly male, men themselves are at most only marginally subjected to such scrutiny. Their 'masculinity' seems not to be questioned, for it is not, at least not to the same extent, artificially created, decorated and emphasised.

A long-term historical perspective should not, however, ignore the fact that men and women have grown more similar in their external appearance. In the 1920s women began to adopt male hairstyles, clothing styles and fashion accessories. An 'emancipated' woman – or an 'unfeminine' (*entfraulicht*) woman, as the 1966 Duden dictionary put it, reflecting the spirit of the age – had her hair in a bob and smoked cigarettes; Marlene Dietrich was not the only one to wear trousers, a tight jacket and a trenchcoat. The contrast between men's and women's clothing, itself largely a product of the nineteenth century, grew less striking in the Weimar years, and finally disappeared with 1970s jeans culture. Since the mid-eighties, however, the pendulum has swung back again, and female fashion is again becoming glamorous and decorative – a tendency that could be interpreted either as depicting a new feminine self-awareness or as compensating for the loss of actual opportunity.

The Law

When, from the late eighteenth century onwards, positive civil law was elaborated, codified and implemented, women found themselves in a somewhat paradoxical situation. On the one hand they were recognised as free, independent subjects before the law; as married women, on the other, they were ruled by a kind of exceptional law only partially overridden by general legal entitlements. In this respect, the German Civil Code (*Bürgerliches Gesetzbuch*), introduced in 1900, was only a slight improvement on previous legislation, which in the case of Prussia was the 1794 Prussian Civil Code (*Allgemeines Landrecht*). While the general section of the German Civil Code granted women full legal capacity and competence, the section on family law stipulated certain restrictions on married women, and was only marginally more liberal than the Prussian Code. Hence, even after 1900 a married man was entitled to annul any contract made by his wife, and forbid her from entering into gainful employment providing he could convince a *Vormundschaftsgericht*, a court dealing with questions of guardianship and jurisdiction in such affairs, that her working would run counter to 'the interests of marriage'. Like the Prussian Code before it, the German Civil Code entrusted all responsibility for marital affairs to the husband: he had the last word in matters relating to the upbringing of children, of whom he was the legal guardian; he had the right to administer and enjoy the wealth his wife brought into the marriage in addition to that accruing to her during the course of their marriage. By contrast, monies the woman herself earned belonged to her alone, but that was all; her husband had the automatic right of disposal over the rest. In the case of divorce law, the German Code was even more regressive than the legislation of 1794. In reducing the number of legitimate reasons for ending marriage, it hit women particularly hard, for they were more likely to petition for divorce than men.

Although Article 109 of the Weimar Constitution of 1919 bestowed 'the same fundamental civil rights and duties' on men and women, and Article 119 defined the 'equality of both sexes' as the foundation of marriage and the family, the patriarchal family law of the German Civil Code remained in force. Article 128, which provided for an end to the special conditions pertaining to female public officials (the 'clause on celibacy'), failed to have effect, because legislation introduced concerning 'dual-income earners' made it possible for married women employed by the Weimar civil service to be dismissed. In 1933 the National Socialists extended these laws, prohibiting outright the employment of married women in central, Land and local government administration. Initially, the legal discrimination of women persisted in the Federal Republic. As a result of pressure from interest groups, a clause on equality was written into the Federal Republic's *Grundgesetz*, which outdid the Weimar Constitution by decreeing male–female equality to be binding in all aspects of the law. After 1949, however, certain pieces of legislation were enacted that explicitly discriminated against women. For example, the 1950 provisional Federal Personnel Law (*Bundespersonalgesetz*) included a clause on celibacy for female public officials; the family law set out in the German Civil Code was still valid in 1953, and was not replaced until 1958 by what was termed the Law on Equality. But married women had to wait until 1977, and the First Law on the Reform of Marriage and Family Law, before a genuine improvement in their legal position came about. The image of the marriage between man and housewife, which was still woven into the fabric of justice in the 1950s, was replaced by the model of marriage based on a partnership that assigned equal responsibilities to men and women for household and childcare. In addition, new legislation on names signalled an end to the male monopoly on family titles.

Women have also benefited from constantly improving legal protection at work. Laws on the protection of mothers have been augmented throughout the twentieth century, and wage and salary differentials between the sexes have gradually narrowed. In 1955 the Federal Labour Court made *Frauenlohngruppen* – special wage-rate groups for female labour – illegal, thus putting a stop to a form of discrimination that was nothing but sexual. And although in subsequent wage agreements these groups, largely comprising women, were redefined as *Leichtlohngruppen* ('light wage groups'), whose wages were lower than those of groups performing comparable work, the Court's ruling did provide a precedent which was successfully invoked in later disputes. In addition, since 1980 there has been statutory provision for the 'equal treatment of men and women at work', making it expressly illegal for women to be disadvantaged in matters of application for employment, promotion and pay.

In conclusion, it can be said that over the last two hundred years the law has been sensitive to women's demands for equality. In some respects, it has proceeded even further than have the material conditions of male–female relations. Following the logic of its own internal political development, the law in recent times is increasingly reaching the stage where new stipulations set down in accordance with the binding principle of equality are such that it is arguable whether they will be able to affect social conditions in any tangible way.

Politics

In the nineteenth century political institutions gradually adopted parliamentary and democratic procedures. Women, however, were almost entirely left out of this process. The spasm of political fervour that was the 1848 revolution gave way to a funereal peace regulated by strict laws on association. After 1850 women in Prussia were forbidden from attending political meetings and joining political parties and organisations. Similar rulings came into force in other German states. When the restrictions were lifted in 1908, at first few political parties showed any serious interest in recruiting women. In fact they did not do so until 1918, when in the wake of the November revolution women had been granted full voting rights. Henceforth, parties put up female candidates: the National Assembly of 1919 included forty-one women, or 9.6 per cent of all deputies. Female presence in parliament was never as strong again until the Bundestag elections in 1983.

Even recently, women were still under-represented in political parties, in Germany. In 1970, they constituted 10 per cent of the CSU membership, 13.6 per cent of the CDU, 15 per cent of the FDP and 17.3 per cent of the SPD (compared with 23 per cent in 1931). Women who do join parties rarely manage to rise into the hierarchy of officials; the size of the female membership is not reflected at executive level. Meanwhile, it has become acceptable for Land governments and the Federal Cabinet to include a 'token woman', who is usually put in charge of education or family policy. As was true of the Weimar Republic, female members of the Bundestag are hard to find on parliamentary committees on economic, financial, budgetary, home or foreign affairs; they are packed into the committees responsible for local government, youth, family, social and health policy, and education and science. The Greens are the only party which offers women the chance to be more fairly represented and attempts to break down gender-related divisions between the various spheres of politics.

There is also recent evidence, however, of organised resistance to male dominance and discrimination against women in the SPD and in the CDU, though in the case of the latter it is somewhat more reserved. The emancipatory offensives launched within parties have been enormously reinforced by the fact that since the 1970s women have become far more politicised. More women than men are joining parties across the spectrum, and they are less content to put up with unimportant functions. They are giving notice that unless they receive equal treatment, if necessary through forms of positive discrimination, they may even go so far as to strike and boycott elections. Almost seventy years after civil emancipation, women are discovering the extent to which their co-operation and collaboration is indispensable for the incumbents of political and government offices, and are increasingly bringing to bear the weight and influence they have as voters and party members to deepen their involvement in politics, work and social life.

There are undeniable signs that women are more vigorously asserting their right to a voice in the affairs of other social institutions and organisations too. Since the beginning of the 1970s trade unions, for instance, have gained more female than male recruits; by comparison with twenty years ago, more women are now standing in elections to works councils – and with tangible success. But since only one in five females in employment is unionised, compared to 43 per cent of males, it is clear that, despite some positive signs, women are still far less inclined to be involved in the representation of their professional interests. There are various reasons why. Firstly, a job does not tend to dominate a woman's life as much as it does a man's, with the result that work-related concerns seem less pressing; secondly, married women in employment are too busy with their domestic and family duties to be active in a union as well. This lack of female enthusiasm for organisations, political parties and unions is, however, only one side of the coin. For their part, trade unions have not exactly welcomed women with open arms: specifically female grievances have not been high on the list of union priorities.

It should not be forgotten, nevertheless, that trade unions were among the first bodies to defend and adhere to the principle that men and women should belong to common organisations. In historical terms, the fact that today almost all associations, political groups and institutions open their doors to both sexes is relatively new. The Free Church communities that emerged in the 1840s took the first tentative steps into new territory by granting women the same rights of speech and participation as men. By contrast the social and political movements of the era of revolution strictly segregated the sexes, with the formation of separate women's associations in towns merely emulating the structure of organisations that had existed before. The early labour movement was less averse to experimentation. The Working Men's Brotherhood of 1848–9 was keen to speak on behalf of women as a matter of principle, and rebuked the decision of the newly-formed Association of Cigar Workers not to allow women members. Right up until the 1890s many professional associations tenaciously upheld their all-male status, so that female blue- and white-collar workers saw fit to create separate associations representing their own particular concerns. Once trade unions had agreed to the principle of joint organisation, however, it did not mean that they automatically took on board the principle of equal status. If women wished to belong to a large body that would wield real, effective power vis-à-vis the rest of society, then they had to pay the price within the union: this ranged from discrimination in the election of delegates to a moratorium on sexual equality in wage agreements. Though very critical of the various mechanisms of internal exclusion, women active in trade unionism and Social Democracy were resolved not to retreat, but pinned their hopes on eroding male prejudices and patriarchal resentment with rational argument.

Women of the bourgeoisie chose a different route in their efforts to put women's issues on the political agenda. As has been seen, they joined a multitude of local and national associations that were formed from the 1860s onwards. In attempting to understand why these women opted for an autonomous form of organisation, it is not enough to say that they were merely reacting to the existence, or creation, of contemporaneous all-male bodies. A more decisive motivation was provided by their urge to find a collective way of representing shared female experiences, expectations and interests. Contemporaries, then, were by no means disturbed by the mutual exclusion of men and women since, after all, the distinction between male and female spheres was part and parcel of the bourgeois conception of the world. The revolutionary thrust came, rather, from the demands women made in public: their demands rocked that very conception of the world. In pressing for better employment and educational opportunities, for equal political and legal status with men, for the chance to play a part in public life, the women's movement punctured the separation of gender-specific domains, blurring the division of labour that lay at the heart of the bourgeois social design. At the same time the bourgeois women's movement itself remained a captive of this polarised way of thinking; it was ultimately a curiously ambivalent and indecisive political force. While insisting that male domains be accessible to (single) women, it was firmly attached to the notion that a woman was by virtue of her nature bound to motherhood and the family. This particular 'women's room' was to be preserved, even assigned higher social status.

At first the pronouncements of the bourgeois women's movement, encapsulated in the motto 'equal in status, not in kind', met with rejection and resentment; in the longer term, however, they proved to be relatively compatible with underlying currents of economic expansion and political participation. From the early twentieth century numerous professional and political male preserves were opened to women too: they could now go to university, have academic careers, vote and stand in elections, work in 'male' industries, and find jobs in business and commerce. Not even the Third Reich could fulfil its declared intentions to reverse the trend. The integration of women into the world of employment pressed on, and the state itself was added to the battery of instruments that loosened familial ties and orientations. At the same time, however, the fundamental differences between male and female lives were left untouched – and in this respect, much of the situation today in the Federal Republic is as it ever was. Almost without exception, women continue to be responsible for housework and childcare, while from childhood onwards the male of the species prepares for its future out at work and in public life. Female participation in the labour force thus rarely acquires the classic dimensions of a vocation or profession. Consequently, the mechanisms of structural sexual inequality rooted in employment, politics, culture and the public sphere are constantly being reinforced. For two hundred years now, these mechanisms have acted like a one-way street, allowing women slowly to move into areas dominated and defined by men, but blocking men's path to the responsibilities, burdens and joys of family life. Only a thorough and systematic redistribution of housework, family duties and employment opportunities will make two-way traffic possible.

Table 1: Female Employment in Prussia 1816–61

	1816	1846	1855	1861
Servants 'for the personal comfort of the master and mistress'	71,855	133,018	152,148	214,472
Maids and servants in agriculture	532,788	558,716	571,168	500,532
in trade & commerce				70,752
Manual workers/day labourers in agriculture	368,537	596,805	647,115	565,705
in trade & industry				450,068
Assistants in small-scale industry	11,439			18,292
Factory workers		57,269	74,872	90,360
Total female employment	984,619	1,345,808	1,445,303	1,910,181
Total female population over 14 years of age	3,390,000	5,260,000	5,640,000	6,100,000
Percentage of female population in employment	29	25.6	25.6	31.3

Source: Jahrbuch für die amtliche Statistik des Preußischen Staats, vol. II, Berlin 1867, pp. 251, 259ff. The figures do not include women employed in their husbands' farms or businesses, or self-employed women.

Table 2: Industrial Female Labour in Prussia in 1875

The 166,422 women workers recorded in a survey of industry were distributed as follows:

	%
Spinning and weaving mills, dying and bleaching plants	53.1
the Tobacco industry	14.3
Sugar processing	7.2
Paper manufacturing	7.0
the Mining, iron and brick industries	6.8
Lace-making, and the crochet, embroidery and knitting industries	3.4
Pottery, china and glass factories	2.8
Other industrial occupations	5.4

Calculated from E. Engel, 'Ergebnisse der Gewerbezählung vom 1.12.1875', *Zeitschrift d. Kgl. Preuß. Stat. Bureaus*, 17, 1877, pp. 259–60.

Table 3: Age and Marital Status of Female Factory Workers in Prussia in 1875

Age	Total %	Single %	Married %
16–18	25.1	99.4	0.6
18–25	43.0	88.6	11.4
Over 25	31.9	44.0	56.0
	100%	77.1%	22.9%

Calculated from A. Thun, 'Beiträge zur Geschichte der Gesetzgebung und Verwaltung zu Gunsten der Fabrikarbeiter in Preußen', *Zeitschrift d. Kgl. Preuß. Stat. Bureaus,* 17, 1877, p. 63.

Table 4: Number of surviving children born to couples married before 1905 and still together in 1939

White-collar workers	3.09
Public officials	3.15
Businessmen	3.84
Artisans	4.41
Industrial workers	4.67
Independent farmers	5.40
Agricultural workers	6.05

Calculated from A. von Castell, 'Forschungsergebnisse zum gruppenspezifischen Wandel generativer Strukturen', in Conze (ed.), *Sozialgeschichte der Familie,* pp. 161–72, esp. p. 167; R. Spree, *Health and Social Class in Imperial Germany,* trans. S. McKinnon-Evans (Material Word Ltd) and J. Halliday, Leamington Spa, 1988, table 14, p. 204.

Table 5: Organisations affiliated to the Federation of German Women's Associations (BDF) in 1913

	Year founded	Membership
General German Women's Association	1865	14,000
General German Association of Women Schoolteachers	1890	32,000
General German Women's Union of Guest-House Owners	1906	350
General German Association of Female Housekeepers	1895	5,000
Baden Union for Women's Advancement	1911	4,500

cont. on page 330

Table 5 cont.

	Year founded	Membership
Trade Organisation of German Nurses	1903	3,500
Federation of Midwives Associations in the Kingdom of Saxony	1909	1,300
German Federation of Women Abstainers	1900	2,100
German-Evangelical Women's Federation	1899	13,650
German Fröbel League	1873	7,000
German Union for the Right of Women to Vote	1904	8,000
German Union for New Women's Clothing and Culture	1907	4,205
German Association for the Prevention of Abuse of Intoxicating Beverages	1883	39,000
German Branch of the International Abolitionist Federation	1904	1,200
Women's Federation of the German Colonial Society	1907	15,000
West German Union for Women's Suffrage	1909	1,200
Women's Union of the Province of Saxony	1908	2,739
Central Union of Bavarian Women's Associations	1909	18,945
Jewish Women's Federation	1904	32,000
Cartel of German Women's Clubs	1910	?
Commercial Union for Women Employees	1889	34,000
District Union of Upper Bavarian Women's Associations	1909	4,000
District Union of Swabian Women's Associations	1909	3,027
Prussian Regional Union of Women Technical Schoolteachers	1895	3,100
Regional Association of Prussian Schoolteachers	1894	4,600
Northern Union of the German-Evangelical Women's Federation	?	1,750
Prussian Regional Association for Women's Suffrage	1907	3,700
Union of Legal Protection for Women	1904	?
Rhineland-Westphalian Women's Union	1901	18,000
Silesian Women's Union	1903	12,000
Silesian Union for Women's Suffrage	1908	800
Senior and Middle Schools' Section of the General German Association of Women		

Table 5 cont.

	Year founded	*Membership*
Schoolteachers	1900	2,400
Union of Graduate and Student Women Teachers	1903	688
Union of German Women Post Office and Telegraph Officials	1912	6,800
Union of Women's Associations in the Duchy of Brunswick	1907	?
Union of Housework	1909	13,500
Union of Progressive Women's Associations	1899	1,500
Union of Central German Women's Associations	1908	3,000
Union of North German Women's Associations	1902	14,300
Union of East Prussian Women's Associations	1911	5,412
Union of Palatine Women's Interest Associations	1900	2,287
Union of West Prussian Women's Associations	1905	3,700
Union of Württemberg Women's Associations	1906	4,600
Union for the Advancement of Women's Housekeeping Skills	1902	12,000
Affiliated Commercial Associations of Women Office Workers	1901	16,000
Association for Women's Education and Studies	1888	4,800

In addition a large number of local associations, with a total membership of 85,475, were directly linked to the Federation of German Women's Associations, so that total membership was almost 470,000 in 1913. It should be noted that some women may have been counted twice in these statistics.

Source: A. Bensheimer, 'Die Organisation des Bundes Deutscher Frauenvereine', in *Jahrbuch der Frauenbewegung 1913*, Leipzig 1913, pp. 12–73.

Table 6: Women in the SPD and Free Trade Unions

	SPD		Trade Unions	
	Female members	*Percentage of total membership*	*Female members*	*Percentage of total membership*
1892			4,355	1.8%
1900			22,844	3.3%
1906	6,460	1.7	118,908	7.1%
1910	82,642	11.5	161,512	8.0%
1913	141,115	14.4	223,676	8.8%

Source: H. Niggemann, *Emanzipation zwischen Sozialismus und Feminismus*, Wuppertal 1981, pp. 77–8.

Table 7: Female Participation in the Labour Market 1882–1980

	1882	1895	1907	1925	1933	1939[1]	1950[2]	1961	1970	1980
Total female population (millions)	23.07	26.36	31.26	32.21	33.53	35.4	27.09	29.77	31.78	32.18
Number of women in employment (millions)	7.79	8.22	9.74	11.48	11.48	12.8	8.48	9.94	9.58	10.48
Percentage of women in employment	33.8	31.2	31.2	35.6	34.2	36.1	31.3	33.4	30.2	32.6
Percentage of women of working age in employment				48.9	48.0	49.8	44.4	48.9	49.6	52.9
Percentage of married women under 60 in employment				29.1	30.1	33.8	26.4	36.5	40.9	48.3

Sources: A. Willms, 'Grundzüge der Entwicklung der Frauenarbeit 1880–1980', in W. Müller et al. (eds), *Strukturwandel der Frauenarbeit 1880–1980*, Flankfurt 1983, p. 35; Willms, *Entwicklung der Frauenerwerbstätigkeit im Deutschen Reich*, Nuremburg 1980, p. 109; D. Petzina et al., *Sozialgeschichtliches Arbeitsbuch*, Munich 1978, vol. III, pp. 22 and 54.
[1] Territory as at 31 December 1937.
[2] Territory of Federal Republic of Germany.

Table 8: The Structure of Female Employment 1882–1980

	1882	1895	1907	1925	1933	1939	1950	1961	1970	1980
	%	%	%	%	%	%	%	%	%	%
A: *Structure of Female Workforce*										
'Assisting Relatives'	40.7	34.1	35.2	36.0	36.1	36.3	32.0	22.1	14.5	7.9
Servants and Domestic Staff	17.9	18.2	16.1	11.4	10.5	10.5	9.0	3.4	1.4	–
Blue-collar										
– Trade and Industry	11.8	17.0	18.3	23.0	22.9	24.8	51.4 }	30.9	34.2 }	31.4 }
– Agriculture	15.5	16.6	14.5	9.2	7.5	6.2		1.1	0.6	
White-collar & Public Officials	1.7	2.6	6.5	12.6	14.8	15.6		29.8	44.4 }	55.9 }
Self-Employed	12.3	11.4	9.2	7.7	8.0	6.4	7.6	7.3	5.0	4.8
B: *Women by Sector as % of Female Workforce*										
Agriculture	61.4	53.5	49.8	43.3	40.5	38.3	35.2	19.7	10.6	7.0
Domestic	18.0	18.2	16.1	11.4	10.5	10.5	9.0	3.4	1.4	–
Craft & Industry	12.8	16.8	19.5	24.8	23.6	25.0	24.8	32.6	35.3	29.6
Services	7.7	11.5	14.6	20.5	25.4	26.1	31.0	44.3	52.8	63.4

Sources: Willms, 'Grundzüge', p. 35; *Statistisches Jahrbuch 1981 für die Bundesrepublik Deutschland*, published by the Statistisches Bundesamt, Stuttgart 1981, p. 95.

Bibliography

H. Arendt, *Rahel Varnhagen: The Life of a Jewish Woman*, New York 1974

A. Bebel, *Woman under Socialism*, New York 1904

H. L. Boak, 'Women in Weimar Germany: The "Frauenfrage" and the Female Vote', in R. Bessel and E. J. Feuchtwanger (eds), *Social Change and Political Development in Weimar Germany*, London 1981, pp. 155–73

R. Bridenthal and C. Koonz, 'Beyond Kinder, Küche, Kirche: Weimar Women in Politics and Work', in B. A. Carroll (ed.), *Liberating Women's History*, Urbana 1976, pp. 301–29

R. Bridenthal, 'Class Struggle around the Hearth: Women and Domestic Service in the Weimar Republic', in M. N. Dobkowski and I. Wallimann (eds), *Towards the Holocaust: The Social and Economic Collapse of the Weimar Republic*, Westport 1983, pp. 243–64

—— et al. (eds), *When Biology Became Destiny: Women in Weimar and Nazi Germany*, New York 1984

J. Carlebach, 'Family Structure and the Position of Jewish Women', in W. E. Mosse et al. (eds), *Revolution and Evolution: 1848 in German-Jewish History*, Tübingen 1981, pp. 157–87

R. J. Evans, *The Feminist Movement in Germany 1894–1933*, London 1976

——, *Comrades and Sisters: Feminism, Socialism and Pacifism in Europe 1870–1945*, Brighton 1987

J. C. Fout (ed.), *German Women in the Nineteenth Century: A Social History*, New York 1984

B. Franzoi, *At the Very Least She Pays the Rent: Women and German Industrialization, 1871–1914*, Westport 1985

P. Gay, *The Bourgeois Experience — Victoria to Freud: Education of the Senses*, New York 1984

——, *The Bourgeois Experience: The Tender Passion*, New York 1986

A. Grossmann, '"The New Woman", the New Family and the Rationalization of Sexuality', Ph.D. dissertation, Rutgers University, 1983

——, '"Satisfaction is Domestic Happiness": Mass Working-Class Sex

Reform Organizations in the Weimar Republic', in M. N. Dobkowski and I. Wallimann (eds), *Towards the Holocaust: The Social and Economic Collapse of the Weimar Republic*, Westport 1983, pp. 265–93

——, 'The New Woman and the Rationalization of Sexuality in Weimar Germany', in A. Snitow et al. (eds), *Powers of Desire: The Politics of Sexuality*, New York 1983, pp. 153–71

A. K. Hackett, 'The Politics of Feminism in Wilhelmine Germany, 1890–1918', Ph.D. Dissertation, Columbia University 1976

——, 'Feminism and Liberalism in Wilhelmine Germany, 1890–1918', in B. A. Carroll (ed.), *Liberating Women's History*, Urbana 1976, pp. 127–36

K. Hausen, 'Family and Role Divisions', in W. R. Lee and R. J. Evans (eds), *The German Family*, London 1981, pp. 51–83

——, 'Mothers, Sons, and the Sale of Symbols and Goods: The "German Mothers' Day" 1923–33', in H. Medick and D. Sabean (eds), *Interest and Emotion: Essays in the Study of Family and Kinship*, Cambridge 1984, pp. 371–413

——, 'Technical Progress and Women's Labour in the Nineteenth Century: The Social History of the Sewing Machine', in G. Iggers (ed.), *The Social History of Politics: Critical Perspectives in West German Historical Writing Since 1945*, Leamington Spa 1985, pp. 259–81

D. Hertz, 'Salonières and Literary Women in Late Eighteenth Century Berlin', *New German Critique*, 5, 1978, pp. 97–108

T. G. von Hippel, *On Improving the Status of Women*, Detroit 1979

R.-E. B. Joeres and M. J. Maynes (eds), *German Women in the 18th and 19th Centuries*, Bloomington 1986

M. A. Kaplan, *The Jewish Feminist Movement in Germany: The Campaign of the Jüdischer Frauenbund 1904–1938*, Westport 1979

——, 'Tradition and Transition: The Acculturation, Assimilation and Integration of Jews in Imperial Germany: A Gender Analysis', *Leo Baeck Institute Yearbook*, 27, 1982, pp. 3–35

——, 'For Love or Money: The Marriage Strategies of Jews in Imperial Germany', *Leo Baeck Institute Yearbook*, 28, 1983, pp. 263–300

C. Koonz, 'Conflicting Allegiances: Political Ideology and Women Legislators in Weimar Germany', *Signs: Journal of Women in Culture and Society*, 1, 1976, pp. 663–83

——, *Mothers in the Fatherland: Women, the Family and Nazi Politics*, New York 1987

N. Luhmann, *Love as Passion: The Codification of Intimacy*, Cambridge 1986

T. Mason, 'Women in Germany 1925–1940: Family, Welfare and Work', *History Workshop*, 1, 1976, pp. 74–113; 2, 1976, pp. 5–32

S. Meyer, 'The Tiresome Work of Conspicuous Leisure: On the Domestic Duties of the Wives of Civil Servants in the German Empire (1871–1918)', in M. J. Boxer and J. H. Quataert (eds), *Connecting*

Spheres, New York 1987, pp. 156–65

J. Pauwels, *Women, Nazis and Universities: Female University Students in the Third Reich, 1933–1945*, Westport 1984

B. Peterson, 'The Politics of Working-Class Women in the Weimar Republic', *Central European History*, 10, 1977, pp. 87–111

R. Pore, *A Conflict of Interest: Women in German Social Democracy, 1919–1933*, Westport 1981

C. M. Prelinger, 'Religious Dissent, Women's Rights and the Hamburger Hochschule für das weibliche Geschlecht in Mid-nineteenth Century Germany', *Church History*, 45, 1976, pp. 42–55

J. Quataert, *Reluctant Feminists in German Social Democracy, 1885–1917*, Princeton 1979

J. Stephenson, *Women in Nazi Society*, New York 1975

——, *The Nazi Organisation of Women*, London 1981

——, 'Women's Labor Service in Nazi Germany', *Central European History*, 15, 1982, pp. 241–65

W. Thönnessen, *The Emancipation of Women: The Rise and Decline of the Women's Movement in German Social Democracy 1863–1933*, London 1970

R. F. Wheeler, 'German Women and the Communist International: The Case of the Independent Social Democrats', *Central European History*, 8, 1975, pp. 113–39

C. Wolf, *A Model Childhood*, London 1983

S. Zucker, 'German Women and the Revolution of 1848: Kathinka Zitz-Halein and the Humania Association', *Central European History*, 13, 1980, pp. 237–54

Index

338

Index

Index